Social Groups
in Action and Interaction

Social Groups
in Action
and Interaction

Charles Stangor

Psychology Press
New York and Hove

Published in 2004 by
Psychology Press
29 West 35th Street
New York, NY 10001
www.psypress.com

Published in Great Britain by
Psychology Press
27 Church Road
Hove, East Sussex
BN3 2FA
www.psypress.co.uk

Please visit www.psypress.com/stangor

10 9 8 7 6 5 4 3 2 1

Library of Congress Cataloging-in-Publication Data
  Stangor, Charles.
    Social groups in action and interaction / by Charles Stangor.
      p. cm.
    Includes bibliographical references and index.
    ISBN 1-84169-406-1 (hbk) – ISBN 1-84169-407-X (pbk.)
  1. Social groups. 2. Social action. 3. Social interaction. I. Title.
    HM716.S73 2003
    305–dc21

                                         2003007279

Contents

About the Author

Charles Stangor is professor of psychology in the social psychology area at the University of Maryland, and has also taught at the University of Tübingen in Germany. He received his B.A. from Beloit College in 1973, and his Ph.D. from New York University in 1986. Dr. Stangor is the recipient of research grants from the National Institute of Mental Health and from the National Science Foundation. He has published 7 books and over 50 research articles and book chapters, and has served as an associate editor of the *European Journal of Social Psychology*. Dr. Stangor's research interests concern the development of stereotypes and prejudice, and their influences upon individuals who are potential targets. Dr. Stangor has also won a distinguished teaching award from the University of Maryland. He is a charter fellow of the *American Psychological Society*, and currently serves as a member of the executive committee of the *Society of Experimental Social Psychology*.

Preface

Social Groups in Action and Interaction is designed to summarize current knowledge about social groups. The book is primarily written from my perspective as a social psychologist, but I have attempted to make it relevant for instructors and students in other domains, including business, communications, education, management, social work, and sociology.

I have attempted to integrate two topics that have traditionally been covered in separate courses—intragroup relations (for instance, conformity, minority influence, group decision making, leadership, and task performance) and intergroup relations (e.g. social categorization, social identity, intergroup conflict, stereotyping, prejudice, and discrimination). In addition, topics that are not unique to either of these two approaches, and yet are important aspects of group relations, such as culture, crowd behavior, social representations, and negotiation, are also covered.

It seems appropriate and, indeed, necessary for students to learn both of these topics together. For one, current models increasingly bridge and connect the two domains. Examples of this bridging include self-categorization, perceived legitimacy, evolutionary psychology, social identity, social impact and dynamic social impact theories, social influence, and conformity. Furthermore, from a practical perspective intergroup relations are becoming more and more relevant to intragroup processes as working groups become increasingly culturally, racially, ethnically, and age diverse.

I have attempted to provide a balance of basic and applied research orientations, and the described research includes descriptive, correlational, experimental, and meta-analytic research methodologies. Chapter 2 contains an introduction to research methods that is useful for understanding the research presented in this book and for interpreting other research reports that might be assigned to the students. Chapter 10 includes practical information for creating effective working groups and considers some common groups (juries, teams, and electronically-communicating groups). Chapter 13 highlights practical methods of improving intergroup attitudes.

The book is designed to serve as a textbook for an undergraduate or graduate course on group behavior. My attempt was to write succinctly and engagingly for undergraduates, but to be thorough enough for graduate students. I regularly teach a graduate course on this topic, and I believe that if my students learn everything in this book, they will have mastered the basics. Of course, there is not enough space to review every wrinkle and research result, and therefore graduate courses should be supplemented with primary source readings and ample classroom discussion.

I believe this book simultaneously serves the needs of even the most demanding instructor while it can be enjoyed by students. I have tried to make it thorough, interesting, integrative, and accessible, and to provide an effective pedagogy. From the instructor's perspective, I think you will find this book will help students enjoy learning about group behavior, understand groups well, and think critically and creatively about group process. From the student perspective, the book is short and succinct, the concepts are easily grasped, and there are many helpful examples. I hope that the book represents the most important concepts—in essence what a student might highlight in a longer book.

I have also included a large bibliography, which should be useful for both students and instructors. Each chapter has several figures or tables that organize findings and convey the results of the central empirical studies described in the chapter. Each chapter ends with a chapter summary, a set of review and discussion questions, and recommended readings.

Supplements to the Text

Additional support for the text is provided in two ways:

CD-Rom containing instructor's resources for use on courses with *Social Groups in Action and Interaction*. Resources include:

- Multiple-choice questions
- Answers to the Review & Discussion questions printed here in the book
- Powerpoint lecture slides containing figures and text from the book
- Classroom activities
- Essay questions

Web site. Please visit www.psypress.com/stangor for additional information and resources to supplement and support the book.

Acknowledgments

I am particulary thankful to my students, whose questions, comments, and complaints taught me how to better conceptualize group behavior, and helped me make the book more useful. My wife, Leslie, supported me as only she can during and after the long hours in front of the word processor. Thanks also to the Department of Psychology at the University of Maryland, to the members of the Society for Personality and Social Psychology, and to the staff at Psychology Press.

I would also like to thank the helpful comments of the manuscript reviewers, especially Richard M. Sorrentino at the University of Western Ontario. They helped shape the book and make it more user-friendly, and they caught some of the most glaring errors.

I am always interested in receiving comments from instructors and students. You can write me at the Department of Psychology, University of Maryland, College Park, MD 20742 or contact me via e-mail: stangor@umd.edu. I hope you find this book useful and enjoyable.

Orrtanna, Pennsylvania
May 2003

Defining the Social Group

Contents at a Glance

*T*he earliest human beings lived a nomadic life, moving regularly from place to place in search of food and hunting and eating together in small groups. Since then, as the number of people on the planet has increased, the life of human beings has also become more complex. People developed new abilities, new skills, and new traditions. We learned to farm and to build shelter. We developed art, culture, and technology, as well as complex systems of government. Nations and races evolved, and the scale of both trade and warfare increased. And these changes continue at an even greater rate today as we continue to develop our world through globalization in communication, trade, and technology.

Although people and their worlds have changed dramatically over the course of our history, one fundamental aspect of human existence remains essentially the same. Just as our primitive ancestors lived together in small social groups, including families, tribes, and clans, people today still spend a great deal of time in social groups. We go to bars and restaurants, we study together in schools, and we work together on production lines and in businesses. We participate in art, music, and sports groups. We form governments, and we turn to chat rooms and user groups on the Internet to communicate with others. It seems that no matter how much our world changes, humans will always remain social creatures. No matter whether it is in families, fraternities, courtrooms, or psychotherapy sessions, we spend a lot of time (and some administrators who sit on a lot of committees would probably say too much time) with others, in groups. Indeed, it is probably not incorrect to say that the human group is the very foundation of human existence—without our interactions with each other, we would simply not be people, and there would be no human culture.

Because people play such an important role in our lives, it is perhaps no surprise that, when we are asked to indicate the things that we value the very most, we frequently mention our relationships with others (Baumeister & Leary, 1995; A. P. Fiske & Haslam, 1996; Kuhn & McPartland, 1954; McGuire, McGuire, Child, & Fujioka, 1978; Reis, 1990). We realize that it is through others—our families, friends, and colleagues—that our own lives are defined. Other people teach us what it means to be human—what we should and shouldn't do, what we should and shouldn't think, and even what we should and shouldn't like and dislike. And we also join and use groups to accomplish more specific goals. We rely on groups, such as courtroom juries and political caucuses, to make important decisions for us. When we work together on a class project, volunteer at a homeless shelter, or serve on a jury in a courtroom trial, we count on others to work with us to get the job done. We develop a trust with the people that we work with, and we expect that they will come through to help us meet our goals.

Although human groups form the basis of human culture and productivity, they also produce some of our most profound disappointments. Our relations with others do not always work out in ways that benefit the group members. Social groups sometimes create the very opposite of what we might hope for, such as when a peaceful demonstration turns into a violent riot, the members of a clique at a high school tease other students until they become violent, or when the members of one ethnic group systematically attempt to destroy each and every member of another group. Groups also cause difficulties when a family becomes dysfunctional and abusive, the members of a cult commit mass suicide, or a gang of young hoodlums beats another child to death. In many cases groups also seem to make very poor decisions, such as when political or military leaders dramatically underestimate the strength of an opponent, putting civilians or soldiers in grave danger. In fact, taking all of the data together, one psychologist once went so far as to comment that "humans would do better without groups!" (Buys, 1978). What Buys probably meant by this comment, I think, was to acknowledge the enormous force of social groups, and to point out the importance of being aware that these forces can have both positive and negative consequences.

The goal of this book is to investigate the human group. We will study how the groups that we belong to influence us and how we influence the other people in the groups we belong to. We will consider both benefits of group membership—for instance, feeling appreciated, loved, cared for, and protected by others that we know and trust—as well as the difficulties that groups create. I hope you will not only be interested in groups for their own sake, but also because you—as a member of many social groups—will learn something about your relationship with others and about yourself by better understanding how groups work.

Studying Groups

Let's begin our investigation by considering some of the most fundamental questions about social groups—what they are, and what characteristics they are likely to have. Then, after reviewing in chapter 2 the scientific methods that are used to study social groups, we will turn in chapter 3 to a fuller consideration of why people join groups and what benefits they might expect to gain from group memberships.

Varieties of Social Groups

As you might well imagine, studying human groups is not an easy task. One problem is that groups come in so many different forms and sizes, and they develop for so many different reasons. Because there are so many types of groups, researchers from many different areas study them (Levine & Moreland, 1998; Moreland, Hogg, & Hains, 1994; Sanna & Parks, 1997; Steiner, 1974; Zander, 1985). Among others, psychologists, sociologists, anthropologists, criminologists, educators, political scientists, social workers, organizational psychologists, and family therapists are all interested in social groups, and researchers in each of these fields have conducted research to learn about group behavior.

Although each of these disciplines has a common interest in studying and understanding groups, most fields tend to focus their research efforts on particular groups and particular topics that are of interest to them. An organizational psychologist, for instance, might study factory workers, looking perhaps at the amount and type of communication among the group members or their reactions to being observed by superiors, with an emphasis on improving group performance. A counselor might study therapy groups, measuring the outcomes of therapy on psychological well-being and the group members' feelings about the effectiveness of the therapy. And a sociologist might be interested in how large social groups perceive their status in a society, perhaps investigating how African Americans, as a large group of individuals with common interests, react to current political events that affect them.

The goal of this book is not to focus on any one particular type of group, but rather to attempt to find basic principles that we can use to understand all social groups. However, because the groups that we are interested in studying range so dramatically in size and purpose, it is convenient for us to divide them into some basic categories, and we will organize our discussion in the chapters to come around these different types. The groups that we will be concerned with are described below, and are summarized in Table 1.1.

TABLE 1.1
Varieties of Social Groups

Group	Definition	Examples
Reference group	A group of individuals that we look up to and identify with because we admire and want to be like those who belong to it	Friends, work colleagues, sports players
Working group	A group consisting of between about 3 and 12 individuals who are actively attempting to meet a specific goal	A jury, a study group
Social category	A large and relatively permanent social group, such as people who share a gender, a religion, a nationality, or a physical disability	Men, women, Europeans, Americans, the elderly
Culture	A large social group made up of individuals who are normally in geographic proximity with each other and who share a common set of beliefs and values, such as language, religion, and family practices	Western, Eastern; African Americans, Asian Americans
Crowd	A large number of individuals who come together in a common place for a common purpose	People shopping in a store, a riot or a mob

Note. This table presents some of the types of social groups that we will be considering in this book as well as some examples of each type.

Reference Groups

Reference groups are perhaps the most important of all groups. A **reference group** is a group of individuals that we look up to and identify with because we admire and want to be like those who belong to it. Important reference groups might include our family, our colleagues or coworkers, the cliques and crowds in our high school or college, or the baseball players on our favorite sports team (Hyman, 1942; Newcomb, 1943; Stouffer, Suchman, DeVinney, Star, & Williams, 1949). In some cases we are already a member of the reference group, and in other cases the reference group might be a group that we do not belong to (such as one that we might look forward to someday joining).

Reference groups are important because their members provide models for us, and these models shape our attitudes, beliefs, and behaviors. A child who starts to swear or an adolescent who starts to smoke have probably been influenced by the "peer pressure" brought by the members of a reference group. The child is not swearing because he likes to so much as because he thinks that others will accept him if he does. On a more positive side, a teenager may develop a passion for lacrosse because she emulates the older members of the high school team, or a scientist may work long hours to make contributions to her field because other scientists have inspired her efforts. We are likely to become prejudiced or tolerant, to declare a major in psychology or architecture, and to prefer jazz to classical music, in part because people we care about support and share these values. In short, because we look up to and care about them, our attitudes, beliefs, and behaviors are determined in large part by the beliefs and values of our reference groups.

Dyads

A **dyad** consists of two individuals who are in a close relationship, such as a strong friendship, a dating relationship, or a marriage. It has been argued that the dyad is a simple group, at least in the sense that there is a strong bond between the individuals (Clark & Reis, 1988; Lickel, Hamilton, Wieczorkowska, Lewis, Sherman, & Uhles, 2000; Thibaut & Kelley, 1959) and many people do define dyads as groups. Although this is not unreasonable, dyads are usually studied separately from larger social groups, and we will not address them in great detail in this book. The reason for this is primarily because in most cases the dyad does not usually produce a "group feeling" on the part of the individuals who comprise it, and as we will see later in this chapter, this feeling is an important part of group behavior. There is a large literature on dyads and romantic relationships, which is available for study if you are interested (see, for instance, Berscheid & Reis, 1998).

Reference Group: A group of individuals that we look up to and identify with because we admire and want to be like those who belong to it.

Dyad: Two individuals who are in a close relationship, as in a strong friendship or a marriage.

Working Groups

One of the types of groups that we will consider most fully is the *working group*. A **working group** comprises between about 3 and 12 individuals who are actively attempting to meet a specific goal. The working group may form for only a short period of time in order to meet a short-term goal, or it may be more permanent. Examples of working groups are juries, decision-making groups in business or other organizations, academic committees, class seminars, group therapy sessions, and sports teams. Working groups usually meet and work in face-to-face settings, but in some cases (such as communication among the soldiers on a battlefield or among the scientists working on a space mission) the group members may be linked electronically.

Social Categories

Unlike working groups, which are small and focused on a specific task, **social categories** are large and relatively permanent social groups, such as people who share a gender, a religion, a nationality, or a physical disability. Social category members are connected, not so much because they have a common goal or task, but rather because they share a common feature that is important to people in the society. The members of a social category normally do not choose to join these groups; membership is usually determined by their physical characteristics, such as their gender, ethnicity, or age. Furthermore, because social categories are so large, the people who belong to them may have no knowledge of or direct contact with each other.

Each person is a member of a number of different social categories, any of which can provide meaning and value for the person. Consider an Asian-American woman, who is also a devout Buddhist and a grandmother. Each of these social category memberships can be important as a source of pride, comfort, and friendship for her. On the other hand, some social categories, such as being overweight, can also result in prejudice and discrimination toward the individual. In fact, the social categories that are the most important, and which have been most fully investigated, are those that form a hierarchical system of status within a culture or society. Some social categories (for instance men and European Americans in the United States) have greater access to resources and higher status than other social categories (for instance women and African Americans). As we will see in chapter 12, these hierarchical relationships frequently lead to conflict between social categories.

Cultures

Another type of very large social group, and one that has profound consequences for human development and activity, is the *culture* (A. P. Fiske,

Working Group: A group consisting of between about 3 and 12 individuals who are actively attempting to meet a specific goal.

Social Categories: A large and relatively permanent social group, such as people who share a gender, a religion, a nationality, or a physical disability.

Kitayama, Markus, & Nisbett, 1998). A **culture** is a large social group made up of individuals who are normally in geographic proximity and who share a common set of beliefs and values, such as language, religion, and family practices. Although cultures can sometimes be associated with a single social category (for instance, we might speak of an African-American culture in the United States), in other cases individuals from many different social categories share the same culture (in the United States, as an example, there is a common "American" culture which is shared, to a large degree, by the members of the many different ethnic groups who live here). Individuals who grow up in the same culture develop common values and opinions, and these differences are exceedingly important for understanding both how people feel about themselves and how they relate to others. As we will see in the chapters to come, although the variation in backgrounds, beliefs, expectations, and behaviors of people from different cultures may be advantageous for diverse working groups, these differences may also potentially produce misunderstandings and conflict.

Crowds

Still another type of social group which is both important, and which has been extensively studied, is the *crowd*. A **crowd** is a temporary collection of a large number of individuals who come together in a common place for a common purpose, such as to see a sporting event or a rock concert or to attend a political rally. As we will see in chapter 11, although crowds are a normal part of everyday life and are not normally destructive, they may in some cases become so when a precipitating event turns the crowd into a violent mob.

Common Themes

As you are hopefully beginning to appreciate, there are many different varieties of social groups. Furthermore, they each have different functions for the people who belong to them, and they exist for different reasons. They also vary dramatically in size, from families and working groups made up of several or a few members to large social categories and cultures made up of millions of people, most of whom do not know each other at all. However, although the fact that there are so many different types of groups to study, and so many different reasons for doing so might lead you to expect that a single approach to studying social groups would not be possible, it is our goal to attempt to do just that. One goal of this book is to search for basic principles that are common to all types of groups, even though the groups that we will be studying are of different sizes, consist of many different sorts of people, and have formed for many different reasons. The task of developing

Culture: A large social group made up of individuals who are normally in geographic proximity with each other and who share a common set of social norms.

Crowd: A temporary collection of a large number of individuals who come together in a common place for a common purpose.

common themes that we can use to understand and predict group behavior will not be easy. And yet such an approach will be exceedingly useful, because it will provide a common language for understanding group behavior that can be used by scientists and other individuals, no matter what type of group they are interested in or what their purpose for studying groups.

Social Science and the Social Group

Because social groups are so ubiquitous, and because they are so important to our existence as humans, they have been studied extensively and we have learned much about them. Let us consider how groups are studied from a scientific perspective.

Studying Groups Scientifically

The formal scientific study of social groups began in the early part of the twentieth century, with the development of the *social sciences*. The **social sciences** are approaches to understanding human behavior that are based, as are the natural sciences such as chemistry and physics, upon careful scientific analysis. Examples of social sciences include such fields as anthropology, criminology, education, management, psychology, and sociology. An important aspect of the social sciences is that their approach to studying human behavior is **empirical**, meaning that the conclusions that are drawn are not based upon speculation, but rather on the systematic collection of data. Many empirical methods have been developed by social scientists, and these developments have produced dramatic advances in our understanding of social groups. Because the research that forms the basis of this book is empirical, it will be important for you to have a good understanding of empirical methods, and we will discuss these techniques in chapter 2.

Levels of Analysis

Although social scientists agree that the groups can and should be studied empirically, they may nevertheless disagree about the appropriate level for such study. This question, which concerns the appropriate *level of analysis* for the study of social groups, is one that has continued to be of concern to social scientists, and one that we will return to frequently. In the study of social groups, the level of analysis question involves either focusing upon groups as groups (the **group-level approach**) or focusing upon the individuals who make up social groups (the **individual-level approach**). Scientists who favor the group-level approach argue that to fully understand groups we must study the group itself. These researchers feel that social groups are entities of

Social Sciences: Approaches to understanding human behavior that are based upon careful scientific analysis.

Empirical: Based upon systematic collection of data.

Group-Level Approach: An approach to studying groups in which the focus is upon the groups themselves rather than on the individuals who make up the groups.

Individual-Level Approach: An approach to studying groups in which the focus is upon the individuals who make up the groups.

their own and cannot be understood merely as a collection of individual group members. Individual-level scientists, on the other hand, feel that it is possible (and indeed preferable) to study groups by focusing research efforts on the people who make up the group.

Group-Level Approaches

Many important social scientists, and particularly Cooley (1909), Mead (1934), Simmel (1955), McDougall (1920), and Durkheim (1938/1982) took the group-level approach to thinking about social groups (see Steiner, 1974, for a review). These scientists felt that it is not possible to understand groups by looking merely at the individuals who form them. They felt, rather, that just as the taste and smell of a chocolate cake is much more than the flour, cocoa, sugar, and other ingredients that make it up, so social groups are much more than just the people who belong to them. According to this approach, social groups (and most importantly cultures) are responsible for the positive characteristics of human beings, including art, literature, science, language, and morality, and these characteristics cannot be reduced to the contributions of individuals alone.

Some influential social scientists, including Gustave Le Bon (1896/1960) and William McDougall (1920), believed that groups could possess a **group mind**, defined as a collection of interacting individual minds. According to McDougall, the group mind represented the individuals "thinking together" as a single group. McDougall felt that the group mind, which reflected the fundamental and shared qualities of the group itself, produced thinking and behaving that was different from what any individual group member could produce. McDougall argued that it was the group mind, rather than any individual mind, that allowed the creation of art and music and other aspects of culture.

Individual-Level Approaches

Other social scientists, and particularly psychologists, have preferred to take the individual-level approach, feeling that it is more appropriate to study groups from the point of view of the individual, focusing on how individual group members perceive and interact with others in the group. These scientists doubted the existence of the group mind as separate from the minds of the individual group members. For instance, one important individual-level scientist, Floyd Allport, argued that there could be no group mind because "There is no nervous system of the crowd." Therefore, he felt that "there is no psychology of groups which is not essentially and entirely a psychology of individuals" (F. H. Allport, 1962, p. 5).

Group Mind: A collection of interacting individual minds.

Comparing the Approaches: Deindividuation

The different approaches taken by group-level and individual-level social scientists can perhaps be best demonstrated in terms of a concrete example. Consider a phenomenon known as **deindividuation** (Festinger, Pepitone, & Newcomb, 1952; Zimbardo, 1969), that occurs when the normal restraints on behavior are loosened, and people behave in an impulsive or deviant manner (Diener, 1980; Reicher, Spears, & Postmes, 1995). Deindividuation frequently produces negative outcomes, such as when a crowd gathered for a peaceful protest becomes so involved in its cause that it becomes violent and begins to riot.

A Group-Level Approach

A scientist working at a group level of analysis would argue that deindividuation is best understood by looking at the group as a whole. For instance, Le Bon (1896/1960) was interested in the behavior of crowds. Le Bon noticed that people often became deindividuated in crowds, and that this deindividuation frequently reduced the normal controls and restraints of society that were initially present. Once the crowd became deindividuated, emotions began to spread through the crowd (he called this *social contagion*), which then led to violent behavior. Thus Le Bon argued that crowds were an example of a case in which a group developed a group mind, which was different from any of the minds of the individuals alone. He felt that once deindividuation occurred, crowds lost their ability to reason, became driven by emotion, and lost the restraints normally posed by society. The outcome was often mass riots and violent behavior.

An Individual-Level Approach

Although Le Bon's analysis might suggest that deindividuation was best understood from a group-level approach, individual-level social scientists have also studied deindividuation (Diener, Fraser, Beaman, & Kelem, 1976; R. D. Johnson & Downing, 1979; Zimbardo, 1969). One approach has been to create deindividuation in the research laboratory and to assess its effects on the behavior of individuals. In one experiment, Philip Zimbardo (1969) had some college students in his lab dress in their own normal clothes, whereas others were asked to wear costumes with hoods that hid their identity. The idea was that putting on the costumes would deindividuate the students. Zimbardo found that the students who wore the costumes used more profane language in their conversations and also (when given a chance to do so as part of a study on learning) delivered more and stronger electrical shocks to

Deindividuation: A state that occurs when the normal restraints on behavior are loosened and people behave in an impulsive or deviant manner.

other students. These findings again seemed to suggest that deindividuation could release individuals from the constraints of society.

Comparing the Two Approaches

You can see that although group-level and individual-level approaches represent very different ways of thinking about and studying an idea such as deindividuation, they are nevertheless each able to effectively provide information about the phenomenon. And this example demonstrates how the same type of behavior can be found in different social groups and can be studied by social scientists using different approaches. Furthermore, we can see that, despite differences in emphasis, both group-level and individual-level approaches provide important, and in this case similar, findings about group behavior. In fact, in many cases the data that are collected to study group behavior can be analyzed at both the individual and the group levels (Kashy & Kenny, 2000; Kenny & la Voie, 1985). We will discuss deindividuation more fully, and consider some other explanations for it, in chapter 11.

The Group Dynamics Approach

Although both the group-level and the individual-level approaches provide effective avenues for studying groups, neither seems complete on its own. The group-level approach suggests that we can well understand groups without taking into consideration the individuals who make them up, whereas the individual-level approach ignores the existence of groups, as groups. As a result, some social scientists became dissatisfied with both approaches, which led them to develop still other ways of thinking about social groups. These approaches can be said to be based upon the principle of **interactionism**, meaning that they assume that social behavior is determined in part by the individual and in part by the relationship between the individual and the group. In this section and the next we will consider two interactionist approaches—the *group dynamics* approach and the *self-categorization* approach.

Kurt Lewin's Contributions

One interactionist approach is known as **group dynamics.** Group dynamics is based on the idea that group behavior is a system of reciprocal interactions between groups and individuals. Group dynamics was developed in large part by the social psychologist Kurt Lewin (1890/1947), who trained many of its proponents at the Research Center for Group Dynamics during the 1930s, 1940s, and 1950s. In 1951, Lewin summarized his belief that both individuals

Interactionism: The assumption that social behavior is determined in part by the individual and in part by the relationship between the individual and the group.

Group Dynamics: An approach to studying social groups, developed by the social psychologist Kurt Lewin, that is based upon the principle of interactionism.

and groups were important in what has now become a well-known equation in the social sciences:

$$Behavior = f \text{ (Person, Environment)}$$

This equation indicates that the behavior of an individual is a function of (that is, depends upon) both their individual (person) characteristics as well as the influence of the other people in their social environment. In Lewin's approach, all behavior involves interactions between groups and individuals, and neither the individual nor the group is real, except in terms of the other. For instance, Lewin would propose that the comments made by a woman attending a group meeting will depend not only on her own beliefs, but also on what she thinks the others believe and how she expects they will react to her opinions. The relationship is dynamic because changes in the group affect the individual, and changes in the individual affect the group. In short, Lewin felt that you cannot understand people without understanding their groups, and at the same time you cannot understand groups without understanding the individuals who belong to them.

Social Perception and Interpretation

One of the most important aspects of Lewin's approach is the importance that he placed on **social perception.** Social perception refers to the process of thinking about others with the goal of understanding and learning about them (S. T. Fiske & Taylor, 1991; Kelley, 1967). You've engaged in social perception if you've ever tried to guess what others are saying or thinking about you, or tried to figure out whether someone likes you or not, without actually asking them, but rather by making inferences on the basis of what they do or say around you. It is the interpretation of social behavior that lies at the heart of Lewin's approach. Lewin understood that it was just as important to study how people perceive the behavior of others, and how they use that behavior to make inferences about those people, as it was to study social behavior itself (Asch, 1952; Festinger, 1954; Heider, 1958; Sherif & Sherif, 1967).

The Influence of Group Dynamics

Social Perception: The process of thinking about others with the goal of understanding and learning about them.

Thanks to Lewin's ideas and insights, the group dynamics approach became one of the most widespread and productive approaches to studying social groups. Other social scientists, including many of his students, were inspired by Lewin's ideas, and subjected them to empirical tests. Much of this work was summarized in an influential book by Cartwright and Zander (1968), which has remained one of the most important books about social groups.

We will base our study of social groups to a large extent upon the group dynamics model, with the goal of using the empirical study of social groups to uncover general principals of group activity. Lewin also believed that it was important to conduct research that has relevance for everyday social groups (rather than only studying groups created in the laboratory), and we will also follow that suggestion.

Self-Categorization Theory

A second interactionist approach to the study of social groups is based on the principle of *self-categorization* (Hogg & McGarty, 1990; J. C. Turner, 1987; J. C. Turner & Oakes, 1989). Like group dynamics, self-categorization also focuses on the process of social perception—the ways in which the individual perceives his or her interaction with other people. However, rather than focusing primarily on the individual's perceptions of the *other* people in the group, self-categorization focuses just as much on how individuals perceive *themselves* as part of the group. **Self-categorization theory** proposes that when we are interacting with other people we may sometimes act as individuals, but at other times we may act more as members of a social group.

To get an idea about how social categorization works, imagine for a moment that two college students, John and Sarah, are talking at a table in the student union at your college or university. At this point we would probably not consider them to be acting as group members, but rather as two individuals. John is expressing his opinions, and Sarah is expressing hers. Imagine however, that as the conversation continues, Sarah brings up an assignment that she is completing for her women's study class. It turns out that John does not think that there should be a women's studies program at the college, and tells Sarah so. He argues that, if there is a women's studies program, then there should be a men's studies program too. Furthermore, he argues that women are getting too many breaks in job hiring and that qualified men are being the targets of discrimination. Sarah feels quite the contrary—arguing that women have been the targets of sexism for many, many years, and even now do not have the same access to high-paying jobs that men do.

According to the principles of self-categorization, John and Sarah have now changed their perceptions of each other. The interaction which began at the individual level (that is, as two individuals conversing) has now turned to the group level, in which John has begun to consider himself as a man, and Sarah to consider herself as a woman. In short, Sarah is now arguing her points not so much for herself as she is as a representative of the social category of women, and John is acting as a representative of one of his group memberships—namely, men.

Self-Categorization Theory: A theory that proposes that when we are interacting with other people we sometimes act as individuals and sometimes as members of a social group.

The Flexibility of Social Categorization

One of the important ideas behind the self-categorization approach is that social perception and social interaction are very flexible. Sometimes people think of their relationships with others at the individual level and sometimes at the group level. Furthermore, which groups are important to us can vary from time to time. In our example, self-categorization might not always have had the outcome of separating John and Sarah into two separate social categories, but might rather have led them to perceive each other as members of the same group. Such a change from individual to group level perceptions might have occurred if a group of students from another college, each wearing the hats and jackets of that school, were to have shown up in the union. The presence of these outsiders might have changed the direction of social categorization entirely, leading both John and Sarah to think of themselves as students at their own college. And this social categorization might have led them to become more aware of the positive characteristics of their college (the excellent basketball team, lovely campus, and intelligent students), in comparison to the characteristics of the other school. In this case, rather than perceiving themselves as members of two different groups (men versus women), John and Sarah might begin to perceive themselves as members of the same social category (students at their college).

In short, the social categorization approach argues that people vary from day to day, and even from moment to moment, in terms of whether we think of ourselves primarily as individuals or primarily as members of a group. And the group memberships that we find most important also vary depending upon how we happen to feel about each group at a given time. If our tennis game is going well, we are happy to categorize ourselves as a tennis player and to enjoy the positive feeling we get from the game. But if we are not playing well or have just lost a big match, we may switch to other self-categorizations—perhaps considering ourself as a student at an outstanding university or as a member of a fantastic sorority.

In-groups and Out-groups

Self-categorization provides an important approach to understanding group behavior because it specifies how individuals are likely to think about themselves and others. According to self-categorization theory, once we categorize ourselves as a group member, we may begin to compare our own group to groups that we do not belong to. In this case we make a comparison between an **in-group** (that is, a group that we belong to) and an **out-group** (a group that we do not belong to). Furthermore self-categorization makes it clear that each individual has many different in-group memberships that can be

In-group: A group to which one belongs.

Out-group: A group to which one does not belong.

compared to many different out-groups. As we will consider more fully in chapters to come, the differentiation between in-groups and out-groups usually occurs such that the in-group is seen more favorably than the out-group, and this basic (and natural) tendency has important implications for group behavior.

You can see that in the self-categorization approach, as in the group dynamics approach, the individual's perception (in this case of both herself and others) is critical. However, whereas the group dynamics approach focuses primarily on how we perceive the groups that we belong to, self-categorization theory focuses on when and how we see ourselves and others as individuals and as group members. Self-categorization theory has provided an important, interactionist, foundation for the study of social groups, and we will discuss it more fully in chapter 5.

Properties of Groups

Although it might seem that we could easily recognize one when we come across it, it is actually not that easy to define what we mean by a social group. This difficulty stems in part from the fact that groups come in so many different sizes and form for so many reasons, but also because different researchers who have tried to define groups have focused on different fundamental properties of groups (Borgatta, Cottrell, & Meyer, 1956; DeLamater, 1974; Mullen & Goethals, 1987; Steiner, 1974). That groups can be understood from so many different perspectives presents a great challenge to those who attempt to define them, but also an opportunity for us to consider some of the important underlying properties of social groups. In this section we will consider some of these properties, as they have been considered by social scientists.

Social Groups versus Social Aggregates

Table 1.2 represents a sample of the many different definitions of the social group that have been proposed by social scientists. Although these definitions show that different scientists have thought somewhat differently about groups, all of the definitions nevertheless contain a basic similarity. Each definition attempts to explain how we know when we have a meaningful social group, rather than a collection of people who, although they might be together in the same place at the same time, are not really a group.

Imagine, for instance, a half a dozen people waiting in checkout line at a supermarket. You would probably agree that this set of individuals should not be considered a social group, because the people are not meaningfully

TABLE 1.2
Some Definitions of the Social Group

In terms of interaction

". . . any number of persons engaged in interaction with one another in a single face-to-face meeting or a series of such meetings. . . ." (Borgatta & Bales, 1953)

"A group is defined by the interaction of its members. If we say that individuals A B C D and E form a group, this will mean that . . . A interacts more with B, C, D and E than he does with M, N, O, P, and Q, . . . whom we choose to consider outsiders or members of other groups." (Homans, 1950, p. 84)

". . . persons who are interacting with one another in such a manner that each person influences and is influenced by each other person." (Shaw, 1981, p. 454)

In terms of interdependence

"A group is a collection of individuals who have relations to one another that make them interdependent to some significant degree." (Cartwright & Zander, 1968, p. 46)

". . . interdependent individuals who influence each other through social interaction." (Forsyth, 1999, p. 5)

"A dynamic whole based on interdependence rather than similarity." (Lewin, 1997, p. 131)

"A group is an aggregation of . . . people who are to some degree in dynamic interrelation with one another." (McGrath, 1984, p. 8)

In terms of structure

"A group is a social unit which consists of a number of individuals who stand in (more or less) definite status and role relationships to one another and which possesses a set of values or norms of its own regulating the behavior of individual members, at least in matters of consequence to the group." (Sherif & Sherif, 1956, p. 144)

"Over time the relations between members should tend to become stabilized, organized and regulated by the development of a system of role and status differentiations and shared social norms and values that prescribe beliefs, attitudes and conduct in matters relevant to the group." (J. C. Turner, 1987, p. 19)

In terms of self-categorization

"A . . . criterion is that the interacting persons define themselves as members." (Merton, 1957, p. 286)

"A group exists when . . . people define themselves as members of it. . . ." (Brown, 2000, p. 3)

In terms of social identity

"A social group can be defined as . . . individuals who share a common social identification of themselves or . . . perceive themselves to be members of the same social category." (Turner, 1982, p. 15)

"A . . . psychological . . . group is . . . one that is psychologically significant for the members." (J. C. Turner, 1987, pp. 1–2) related to each other. A group of people who are in the same location, but who are not meaningfully related to each other, and thus who do not appear to make up a social group is called a **social aggregate.** As other examples, the individuals watching a movie at a theater or those attending a large lecture class might also be considered to be social aggregates.

Of course, a group of individuals who are currently a social aggregate may nevertheless easily turn into a social group if something happens that brings them "together." For instance, if a man in the checkout line of the grocery suddenly collapsed on the floor, it is likely that the others around him would quickly begin to work together to help him. Someone would call an ambulance, another might give CPR, and another might attempt to contact his family. Similarly, if the movie theater were to catch on fire, the aggregate might turn into a group as the individuals attempted to leave the theater. It has been a challenge to characterize what the "something" is that makes a group a group, but it is exactly this characteristic that the definitions in Table 1.2 are trying to capture. As a first pass, we might simply call it something like "groupiness"—the perception (either by the group members themselves or by others) of being part of a group.

Similarity

Perhaps the essential feature of a social group is similarity among the group members. A group can only be a group to the extent that its members have something in common—at a minimum they are similar because they belong to the group! If a collection of people are interested in the same things, share the same opinions and beliefs, or engage in similar behaviors, then it seems they should be considered—by both themselves and others—to be a group. However, if there are a lot of differences among the individuals, particularly in their values, beliefs, and behaviors, then they are not likely to be a very good group. According to this perspective, the similarity among group members is similar to that among objects. Just as Fords, Chevies, and Porsches are all categorized as cars because they share similar features and functions, so people become a social group when they are similar (Lewin, 1948/1951/1997; Campbell, 1958; Heider, 1958).

It is probably no surprise to you that similarity should be considered such an important component of groups. People generally get together to form groups precisely because they are similar—they are all interested in playing bridge, listening to rock and roll, or passing a chemistry test—and groups tend to fall apart because the group members become dissimilar and thus no longer have enough in common to keep them together. In fact, groups in which the members have similar ideas about appropriate group goals and the means of attaining those goals have been found to be happier, more sat-

Social Aggregate: A group of people who are in the same location, but who are not meaningfully related to each other, and thus who do not have entitativity.

isfied, and even more productive in comparison to groups in which the members have different perspectives about the meaning and goals of the group (Bottger & Yetton, 1987; Klimoski & Mohammed, 1994; Larson & Christensen, 1993; Simpson & Harris, 1994).

Similarity and Liking

It turns out that similarity is important to groups because we tend to like people who are similar to us, such as those who share our personality and opinions, and we tend to dislike those who are different from us. Although this may be so obvious that it doesn't even need to be demonstrated, a number of research programs have done so anyhow (Byrne, 1969; Griffitt, 1966). In one important study demonstrating this principle, Theodore Newcomb (1961, 1963, 1965; Newcomb, Koening, Flacks, & Warwick, 1967) studied how new college students developed friendships when they first came to their school. He found that groups of friends developed in large part on the basis of initial similarity in interests and opinions—such as their majors, interests in sports, and political values.

Similarity and Group Perceptions

Although we might agree that groups must have at least some *actual* similarity, as Lewin pointed out, the *perception* of similarity among group members is just as important. Collections of individuals are more likely to be perceived as groups, rather than as individuals, when they are seen to have similar characteristics. People who live in the same neighborhood, who are seated together around a conference table, or who are working together on a task are likely to be seen as similar, for instance in terms of their personality characteristics, and thus are likely to be considered as a group (Arkin & Burger, 1980; Dasgupta, Banaji, & Abelson, 1999; Stotland, Cottrell, & Laing, 1960; Wilder, 1986). And we consider people in terms of their social categories—such as "Europeans," "Asians," and "Africans"—in part because people from these groups share some fundamental physical features.

Because similarity is such an important part of group membership, we may take advantage of these perceptions by emphasizing our similarity to other group members when that turns out to benefit us, but we may prefer to de-emphasize our similarity to others when that similarity is not so flattering. Children who wear the clothes of their crowd or gang are highlighting their similarity to their peers, because they want to be part of and accepted by the group. On the other hand, teenagers who get tattooed may be doing so to demonstrate that they are different from other groups (such as adults) (Jetten, Branscombe, Schmitt, & Spears, 2001).

Interaction and Interdependence

Although similarity is critical, it is not the only factor that creates a group. As can be seen in Table 1.2, other group researchers have argued that groups are groups to the extent that their members have *interaction* with each other, and particularly when this interaction makes them *interdependent*. **Interaction** refers to communication among group members (Homans, 1950; Kretch & Crutchfield, 1958; Lewin, 1948; R. K. Merton, 1957). Although interaction is usually considered to occur primarily in small groups that meet together in a single place, it is not impossible for it to occur among individuals who are at great distances from each other. Individual members of an Internet newsgroup, for instance, might have frequent interactions, and feel as if they are a group, even though they have never met face to face.

Interaction is particularly important when it is accompanied by **interdependence**—the extent to which the group members are mutually dependent upon each other to reach a goal (Cattell, 1951; Homans, 1961; Thibaut & Kelley, 1959). In some cases, and particularly in working groups, interdependence involves the need to work together to successfully accomplish a task. Individuals playing baseball are dependent upon each other to be able to play the game and also to play well. Each individual must do their job in order for the group to function. In other cases, for instance among the members of social categories such as women or Jews, interdependence refers to the perception by the group members of being united toward reaching a broader goal, such as improving their social status or changing the negative beliefs that others hold about the group (Gurin & Townsend, 1986). When group members are interdependent, they report liking each other more, tend to cooperate and communicate with each other to a greater extent, and may be more productive (Deutsch, 1949a, b).

As we will discuss more fully in chapter 3, interdependence among group members can include more than just working together on tasks. We are also dependent on others for knowledge, positive feedback, and social support, among other things. Thus interdependence can be an important part of group membership both for small working groups and for large social categories if the individuals use the group to provide information about appropriate behaviors and to validate their beliefs, values, and opinions.

Group Structure

Still other researchers have defined groups in terms of the development of a **group structure**—the stable rules and relationships that define the appropriate rules and behaviors for group members.

Interaction: Communication among group members.

Interdependence: The extent to which the group members are mutually dependent upon each other to reach a goal.

Group Structure: The rules that define group norms, roles, and status.

Norms

Group structure is based in part on the existence of *social norms* (Asch, 1952; Cialdini, Kallgren, & Reno, 1991; Reno, Cialdini, & Kallgren, 1993; Sherif, 1936; J. C. Turner, 1991). A **social norm** is a way of thinking, feeling, or behaving that is perceived by group members as appropriate (or NORMal). Norms include such things as customs, traditions, standards, and rules, as well as the general values of the group. Norms tell us what people actually do ("people in the United States are more likely to eat scrambled eggs in the morning and spaghetti in the evening, rather than vice versa") and also what we should ("do onto others as you would have them do onto you") and shouldn't do ("do not make racist jokes"). As we will consider more fully in chapter 4, norms develop because group members share their ideas and opinions, and this leads to a common set of shared beliefs.

Although there are many different types of norms, the most important are those that define the basic values of the group (Bar-Tal, 2000; Feldman, 1984), and without which the group would not have meaning. These norms define what the group members believe in as well as their underlying goals and purposes. For Boy Scouts the important norms are improving oneself and helping others, whereas for Catholics the norms involve following the teachings of the church. Individuals must follow group norms in order to be good and accepted group members.

Norms do not necessarily refer to clear-cut facts about what is good or bad, but more often indicate the values that the group places on certain opinions or behaviors. Thus the same behaviors that are seen as appropriate in one group are seen as inappropriate in another group, and a norm is only a norm because the members of the group agree on it and value it. Indeed, it appears that almost any possible behavior can be seen as normatively appropriate in some group, but as normatively inappropriate in another. For instance, in the United States people clap after they hear a lecture, whereas in Germany they knock their knuckles on the table. In some organizations, making sexist jokes is accepted behavior, whereas in others it is certainly not. And although many Americans love to eat beef, no member of the Hindu religion would ever do so. None of these norms are necessarily "right" or "wrong"—they are just different. But in each case the norm becomes an integral and essential part of the group's very existence. In this sense, even though the norm may not be based on any objective fact, it still has an important validity for the individuals in the group (Festinger, 1950). People believe in the norm and behave according to it because it seems right and proper to do so.

Social Norm: A way of thinking, feeling, or behaving that is perceived by group members as appropriate or normal.

Roles

Group norms that specify the behaviors expected to be performed by individual group members are known as **social roles**. Roles can include specific assigned duties (such as being the group's secretary or the treasurer), but may also be more abstract (for instance, the person who "presents new ideas," the one who "demands full discussion of the issues," or the one who "knows the rules and regulations"). We will see in chapter 6, however, that two of the most important and commonly found roles in social groups are the *task role* (to focus the group on getting the task done) and the *socioemotional* role (to make the group members happy).

Status

Still another type of group structure involves **status**—the amount of authority, prestige, or reputation that a group member has in the group. As we will discuss more fully in chapter 7, we can assess the status of individuals in many ways, for instance, by measuring the ability of the individual to influence the opinions of the other members of the group, by the extent to which the individual is perceived as helping the group meet its goals, or by looking at the patterns of communications among the group members. As an example, individuals with high status in a group tend to speak more frequently and are more likely to be allowed to interrupt the conversation of others (Meeker, 1990). Groups seem more grouplike to the extent that they have a defined status hierarchy.

Defining the Group: Entitativity

Now that we have considered some of the characteristics that seem important in creating groups, we must consider how we might put them all together to create a single definition of a group. One difficulty is that although each of the characteristics that we have considered is important in contributing to creating a group, none of them is alone sufficient. For instance, although similarity appears to be a necessary feature for groups, it is itself not sufficient to define a group. Social aggregates—such as the people sitting in the movie theater—are also similar to each other, both in terms of their interests and their physical location, and yet they do not seem to be a group. And although interaction and interdependence are frequently found in groups, they are also not themselves necessary or sufficient. Consider a large social category such as those who share a religious belief in Judaism. Because Jews are spread out throughout the world, there is little chance for direct interaction among them, and yet the group members may nevertheless perceive

Social Roles: A group norm that specifies the behaviors expected to be performed by individual group members.

Status: The amount of authority, prestige, or reputation that a group member has in the group.

themselves and be perceived by others as part of a meaningful group. In terms of interdependence, when the citizens of a country listen to a rousing speech given by their leader, they may feel a sense of pride in being a citizen of the country and thus feel an important part of this large group, even though they do not feel that they are interdependent upon each other to accomplish any particular goal. And while it is true that group structure, such as norms, roles, and status differences may frequently develop in small working groups, some groups (such as social categories or cultures) do not have explicit group structures, and yet they nevertheless appear to be groups.

Perceiving Entitativity

Social scientists have sometimes used the term **entitativity** to characterize the state of "groupiness" (Campbell, 1958; Hamilton & Sherman, 1996; Lickel et al., 2000), and this term can be used as part of a definition of a social group. Entitativity refers to the feeling or perception that a group of individuals is really a group. To give you an example of how groups vary in entitativity, consider the results of research by Brian Lickel and his colleagues, as shown in Table 1.3. In their research, 199 college students from the University of California at Santa Barbara were asked to rate 40 different groups according to how much each group seemed to them to be a group (from 1 = "not a group at all" to 9 = "very much a group"). Table 1.3 presents the average ratings of each of the groups as given by the students. As you can see, some groups, such as sport teams, families, and gangs were rated very high on entitativity, whereas others, such as those attending a movie or waiting at a bus stop were rated very low.

Let us return for a moment to the characteristics of groups that we listed in Table 1.1 and consider how they relate to entitativity. Although none of these characteristics may alone be sufficient to produce entitativity, each characteristic should nevertheless contribute to its perception. The more of each of the characteristics the group has, the more "groupy" it should seem to be. Indeed, this has been found to be the case. In their research, Lickel et al. (2000) also asked the students to rate each of the 40 groups on how similar the members were to each other, the extent of interaction among the group members, and their interdependence to reach their goals (although they did not have them rate group structure). They found that each of these variables related to the extent to which the group was seen as a group, although other variables (such as group size) did not.

If collections of individuals are seen as groups when they have entitativity, then this difference should show up in how entitative (versus non-entitative) groups are perceived and judged. Indeed, it has been found that our impres-

Entitativity: The feeling or perception that a collection of individuals is a social group.

TABLE 1.3
Perceived Entitativity of 40 Social Groups

Group	Entitativity Rating
Members of a professional sports team	8.27
Members of a family	8.16
Members of a rock band	8.16
Friends who do things together	7.75
Members of a local street gang	7.64
Members of a local environmental organization	7.28
People attending a support group	7.22
Members of an orchestra	7.21
Members of the cast of a play	7.16
Members of a university social club	7.12
Members of a student campus committee	6.95
Members of a labor union	6.89
Members of a jury	6.88
Students studying for an exam	6.70
A company committee designing a new product	6.60
Members of an airline flight crew	6.54
People having dinner together on a Saturday night	6.33
Coworkers assigned to a project	6.33
Two people in a romantic relationship	6.07
Roommates	5.62
Members of the same political party	5.59
Employees of a local restaurant	5.55
Jews	5.39
Students enrolled in a class	5.18
Women	5.16
Blacks	5.00
People living in a retirement home	4.86
People who live in the same neighborhood	4.78
Students at a university	4.75
Teachers	4.70
People who work in the same factory	4.63
Citizens of America	4.61
Doctors	4.39
Citizens of Poland	4.36
People who enjoy classical music	3.93
People attending an athletic contest	3.92
Plumbers	3.69
People in the audience at a movie	3.27
People at a bus stop	2.75
People in line at the bank	2.40

Note. The means indicate the extent to which college students perceived each of the listed collections of individuals as a group. Higher numbers indicate greater group perceptions. Data are from Lickel, B., Hamilton, D. L., Wieczorkowska, G., Lewis, A., Sherman, S. J., & Uhles, A. N. (2000). Varieties of groups and the perception of group entitativity. *Journal of Personality & Social Psychology, 78,* 223–246.

sions of entitative groups are more coherent in comparison to those we form about less entitative groups, and in some cases may be more extreme (Dasgupta, Banaji, & Ableson, 1999). Also, when we learn about one member of an entitative group, we tend to believe that all other members of the group are similar to that individual (Crawford, Sherman, & Hamilton, 2002; Picket, 2001; Stotland, Cottrell, & Laing, 1960). In short, as we will discuss more fully in chapter 5, it is easier to form stereotypes about entitative groups, in part because their members are perceived to be unified and coherent, and because they are expected to share group-relevant characteristics (Hilton & von Hippel, 1990; Yzerbyt, Corneille, & Estrada, 2001).

Because entitativity refers to the extent to which a collection of individuals is perceived as being a group, we can say that groups are groups to the extent that they have entitativity. *Therefore, we will define a* **social group** *as a collection of three or more individuals who are perceived, by themselves or others, to be a group.* What this definition means is that although there is no exact criterion for defining social groups, some collections of people seem more like groups than others because they have more entitativity, and it is this perception of entitativity that makes a group. Our definition of social groups is quite broad—including both small working groups and large social categories, crowds, and cultures. Yet this definition is justified because in each case the group is perceived as a group because it has entitativity.

Being Part of a Group: Group Cohesion and Social Identity

Our definition of the social group, based on entitativity, refers to how and when we perceive people as being a group. But groups are more than just our perceptions of individuals—groups also provide meaning for us by influencing how we feel about the group, about the members of the group, and about ourselves. Two variables that are used to describe the relationship between people and the groups they belong to are *group cohesion* and *social identity*.

Group Cohesion

One approach to assessing the meaning of groups for individuals is to assess the *cohesion* of the group. **Group cohesion** refers to the positive emotional attachment that group members have with the other members of the group. A group is said to be cohesive to the extent that the group members like the other group members, feel that they are part of the group, want to stay in the

Social Group: A collection of three or more individuals who are perceived, by themselves or others, to be a group.

Group Cohesion: The emotional attachment that group members have with the members of the group.

group, and find the group important to them (Cota, Evans, Dion, Kilik, & et al., 1995; Dion & Evans, 1992; Festinger, 1950; Festinger, Schachter, & Back, 1950; Hogg, 1992; Lott & Lott, 1965; Mudrack, 1989; Zander, Stotland, & Wolfe, 1960). In short, cohesion is a measure of the significance, importance, or attachment of group members to the group—the extent to which the group is likely to bond together and stick together. Groups in which the group members indicate high group cohesion are said to be cohesive groups.

In addition to their influence on perceived entitativity, many of the characteristics that we expect to contribute to creating a group also relate to perceptions of group cohesion. For instance, studies have found that members of groups who share similar beliefs and values also report more group cohesion than groups whose members are more dissimilar (Festinger, Schachter, & Back, 1950; Newcomb, 1956). Strong group interdependence, including the goals of attaining rewards and successfully performing group tasks, also relates to increased group cohesion. And groups that develop strong group norms and desire to maintain these norms also express more cohesion (Back, 1951; Festinger, 1950; Lott, 1961; McGrath, 1984; Roethlisberger & Dickson, 1939).

Cohesion and Group Behavior

Cohesive groups behave differently than do less cohesive groups (Hogg, 1992). For one, cohesion is associated with group satisfaction, including less anxiety, more positive group communication, and fewer absences from meetings (Seashore, 1954). Studies of military units have found that members of cohesive groups have better morale and express more trust in each other (Gal, 1986). Pepitone and Reichling (1955) found that cohesive groups vented more hostility to outsiders, whereas less cohesive groups vented more hostility within the groups. Individuals also care more about the positive and negative outcomes of the group when the group is cohesive (Brawley, Carron, & Widmeyer, 1987; Zander, 1971/1996).

In one laboratory study concerning cohesion, Zander, Stotland, and Wolfe (1960) created groups of college students who worked together on a project. However, the groups were created to be either high or low in cohesion. In the cohesive groups the research participants faced each other, were labeled by the experimenter as a "group," and selected a group name, whereas in the noncohesive groups the participants sat scattered about the room and were referred to by the experimenter only as "individuals." Demonstrating that the cohesive group members were more invested in the group, when the group members were informed that their group had succeeded on a task, the cohesive group members rated themselves very positively, but when they were informed that they failed, they rated themselves very negatively. On the other hand, the success or failure of the group had little impact for the members of noncohesive groups.

Cohesion, Norms, and Group Performance

As we will see in chapters 8 through 10, one question that has been of continuing interest to group researchers concerns the effectiveness of group performance. How well do groups perform on tasks, and under what conditions is this performance optimized? And one question of interest within this topic concerns the impact of group cohesion on task performance. On the one hand, it might seem that groups that are more cohesive, because the members like and have strong ties to each other, would be more productive than less cohesive groups. On the other hand, there is the potential that groups that are too cohesive will become too confident about the ability of their group to perform well and will not fully discuss the issues of importance or seek outside information to help them make decisions. Because the members like each other, cohesive groups may also spend so much time socializing that they do not fully engage in the task to be accomplished.

In fact, there is data to support both of these hypotheses. In some cases cohesion is related to better group performance and in some cases to worse (Bernthal & Insko, 1993; Callaway & Esser, 1984; Carron, 1980; Cratty, 1981; C. R. Evans & Dion, 1991; Flowers, 1977; Leana, 1985; Mullen & Copper, 1994; Swets & Bjork, 1990; M. E. Turner, Pratkanis, Probasco, & Leve, 1992; Zaccaro, 1995; Zaccaro, Gualtieri, & Minionis, 1995). One explanation for these conflicting results is that although group cohesion does not itself either increase or decrease performance, cohesion does increase conformity to group norms. As a result, whether cohesion increases or decreases performance will depend on the norm. If the norm is to work hard and to be productive, cohesion will increase performance. However, if the norm is to goof off, that, too, will happen (L. Berkowitz, 1954; Schachter, Ellertson, McBride, & Gregory, 1951; Stogdill, 1972).

Social Identity

You will recall that a basic principle of self-categorization theory is that people consider themselves sometimes as individuals and sometimes as group members. When we perceive ourselves as a member of a group, that group may begin to take on an importance for us. **Social identity** is defined as the part of the self-concept that results from our membership in social groups (Hogg & Abrams, 1988; Tajfel & Turner, 1979). Generally, because we prefer to remain in groups that we feel good about, the outcome of group membership is a

Social Identity: The part of the self-concept that results from our membership in social groups.

positive social identity—our group memberships make us feel good. Social identity might be seen as a tendency on the part of the individual to talk positively about the group to others, a general enjoyment of being part of the group, and a feeling of pride that comes from group membership. According to the social identity approach, then, people define themselves in part by the groups that they belong to (Oakes, Haslam, & Turner, 1994; J. C. Turner, 1987).

Although group cohesion and social identity represent similar ideas, they are not exactly the same thing, and it is important to be aware of the difference between them. Group cohesion refers primarily to strength of liking for the other group members in the group, whereas social identity refers to how much a part of the group the individual feels that he or she is or how important group membership is to him or her (Branscombe, Schmitt, & Harvey, 1999; Hogg, Hardie, & Reynolds, 1995; Prentice, Miller, & Lightdale, 1994). In short, social identity involves an attraction toward the group as a group more than an attraction to the particular individuals in the group. Although we probably generally like the members of the groups that we identify with, this might not always be the case. You might be able to imagine that the members of a sports team, for instance, might have a lot of identity with the team (particularly when the team is winning), even though they do not particularly care for the other team members. Or you might be able to think of a group that you belong to in which you enjoy the company of the other group members even though you do not identify particularly highly with the group itself. As we will see, social identity is extremely important for understanding groups, because feeling that one is part of a group has an important influence on a wide variety of group behaviors. At this point, however, we will defer our discussion, returning to it again in chapter 3.

Group Process Reconsidered

Before closing this chapter, one more important note should be made. Although our discussion to this point has focused on the extent to which the group characteristics of similarity, interaction, interdependence, and structure influence group outcomes, including identity, cohesion, and entitativity, this is really only half of the story. Although increases in a group characteristic (such as the perception of similarity among the group members) may increase group cohesion and social identity, the process is also likely to work in reverse. For instance, members of a group with a strong social identity will also be likely to see themselves as similar to and interdependent upon other group members, and such groups will be seen as entitative. Thus, there is a reciprocal relationship between the group characteristics of similarity, interaction, interdependence, and structure and the measures of group process—cohesion, identity, and entitativity. This relationship is diagrammed in Figure 1.1.

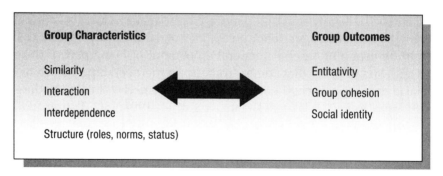

Group Characteristics	Group Outcomes
Similarity	Entitativity
Interaction	Group cohesion
Interdependence	Social identity
Structure (roles, norms, status)	

FIGURE 1.1. Group processes. This figure summarizes the reciprocal relationship between group characteristics and group outcomes. Group characteristics can influence group outcomes, including entitativity, cohesion, and social identity, and entitativity, cohesion, and identity can also influence group characteristics.

 Chapter Summary

Human beings spend a great deal of their time working and living together in social groups. We use groups to make decisions, to provide affiliation and belonging with others, and to create and validate our own attitudes and opinions. However, in some cases groups may also produce negative outcomes, such as poor decisions, riots, and wars. There are many different types of social groups, and they form for many different reasons. This makes studying them both difficult and exceedingly important. The goal of this book is to find common themes that can be used to understand all types of social groups.

Social groups are studied empirically by social scientists. They may be studied at either the group level or the individual level of analysis, and each approach has been found to provide important information about the behavior of social groups. Interactionist approaches involve taking into consideration both the individual and the group at the same time. The group dynamics approach is based on the ideas of Kurt Lewin, who proposed that the individual's behavior is a function of both his or her personality and his or her social environment. The self-categorization approach proposes that individuals can consider themselves either as individuals or as group members, and is based upon categorization into in-groups and out-groups.

Many researchers have attempted to determine what factors are important in changing a collection of individuals (known as an aggregate) into a real social group. Research has studied the characteristics common to social groups, including similarity, interaction, interdependence, and group structure (including roles, norms, and status). Each of these features increases the extent to which the group is seen as having entitativity, and thus we can define the group as a collection of individuals who are seen as being entitative.

Both cohesion and social identity have been used to assess the extent to which the individual group members care about and see the group as important to them. When individuals feel positively about the other group members, the group is said to be cohesive, whereas social identity refers to the positive feelings that individuals have about the group as a whole. There is a reciprocal relationship between group characteristics (similarity, interaction, interdependence, and structure) and group outcomes (group cohesion, entitativity, and identity).

Review and Discussion Questions

1. Why are social scientists interested in studying social groups, and why should people in general be?
2. What are the basic types of social groups that will be considered in this book, and what are the characteristics of each? Give an example, from your own experience, of each type of social group.
3. What does it mean to say that the study of social groups is empirical?
4. Explain the difference between the individual level and the group level of analysis in studying social groups.
5. Compare and contrast the group dynamics approach and self-categorization theory approach to studying groups. Why is each considered to be interactionist?
6. How do we know when a collection of individuals should be considered a social group?
7. Explain the importance of each of the group characteristics discussed in this chapter (similarity, interaction, interdependence, and group structure) as determinants of groups.
8. What are group cohesion and social identity, and how are they used to understand the meaning of groups for members of those groups? Do you belong to any groups in which you experience either group cohesion or social identity?
9. Give an example of the reciprocal influence of group characteristics and group outcomes on the basis of your personal experience with a social group.

Recommended Readings

A classic textbook on groups in social psychology:
Asch, S. E. (1952). *Social Psychology.* Englewood Cliffs: Prentice-Hall.

Why one psychologist is concerned about social groups:
Buys, B. J. (1978). Humans would do better without groups. *Personality and Social Psychology Bulletin, 4,* 123–125.

A research article that helps to define entitativity and considers its importance to group behavior:
Lickel, B., Hamilton, D. L., Wieczorkowska, G., Lewis, A., Sherman, S. J., & Uhles, A. N. (2000). Varieties of groups and the perception of group entitativity. *Journal of Personality and Social Psychology, 78,* 223–246.

Studying Groups Scientifically 2

As we have seen in chapter 1, social scientists are not content simply to speculate about them, but believe that a full and accurate understanding of groups must be based upon the systematic, empirical observation of individual and group behavior. Because empirical research forms the basis of this book, it is important to understand the methods that social scientists use to study groups. In this chapter we will discuss how research is used to study social groups, as well as the principles that social scientists use to guide research. Then, we will consider examples of the research techniques that are used to measure the perceptions and the behaviors of individuals in groups and will consider the research designs that are used to study group behavior. Finally, we will consider some of the potential difficulties in interpreting research and how scientists use research to draw overall conclusions about group behavior.

Basic and Applied Research

Before we begin to review the methods that are used by scientists when they conduct research, we should consider for a moment how they first get ideas for the research that they are going to conduct. Although a goal of empirical research is to make the study of social behavior objective, decisions about what is to be studied are made on the basis of the scientist's personal interests. As we have seen in chapter 1, scientists in many different fields study groups, and they have many different reasons for doing so. As a result, the types of groups and the types of settings in which they study groups will also vary. Furthermore, some scientists conduct research primarily to advance our general understanding of social behavior (*basic research*), whereas others conduct research that has the goal of gaining practical knowledge about a particular social issue or developing solutions to existing social problems (*applied research*).

Basic Research

Basic research is designed to answer fundamental questions about behavior, without a particular concern for how that knowledge will be used. For instance, one basic research question that has been studied, both within individuals and within social groups, concerns the conditions under which people's opinions and behaviors are influenced by the presence of others. As we will see in the chapters to come, this change—known as *conformity*—can occur in many ways and for many reasons. Conformity occurs, for instance, when people change their beliefs because they want to be similar to the other members of valued reference groups. It may also occur when an individual feels that the members of the social group have valid information that they were not aware of before.

> **Basic Research:**
> Research designed to answer fundamental questions about behavior, without a particular concern for how that knowledge will be used.

To learn about conformity, scientists have studied the characteristics of the people who are doing the influencing, the people who are being influenced, and the types of messages that are used to influence others. Among other things, this research has shown that people are more likely to conform to people who are more attractive, that people conform more to group members with whom they are highly identified, and that communicators who talk faster are more influential than those who talk slower.

The many studies that have investigated the conditions under which conformity is more or less likely to occur were performed in large part simply because the researchers were interested in better understanding it. However, although this research was not trying to solve any particular problems, or to help improve any particular social situations, it nevertheless provides a fundamental background of knowledge. Thus these studies represent basic research—research designed to learn about the fundamental underlying principles of behavior.

Applied Research

Applied research, on the other hand, is specifically designed to investigate issues that have implications for everyday life and to provide solutions to problems. Applied research has been conducted to study such issues as what types of group psychotherapy are most effective in reducing depression, under what conditions brainstorming groups are effective, how to reduce prejudice in young children, and how to predict who will perform well in leadership roles.

As one example of applied research, some researchers have been particularly interested in understanding whether courtroom juries can make good decisions and how the quality of these decisions is influenced by the characteristics and opinions of the group members who join them. These researchers have created "mock" (artificial) juries, frequently using college students, and studied their behavior as they discuss evidence about a fictitious case, with the goal of learning about jury decision making. Among other things, this research has found that jury decisions can usually be predicted by knowing the opinions of the jury members before the deliberation begins, that when they are unsure about guilt or innocence, juries are generally lenient on the defendant, and that jury members may vote differently when the vote is secret than they do when it is public (Kerr & MacCoun, 1985). We can say this research is applied research because it is designed specifically to understand the role of deliberation in juries and to learn how to make jury decision making more fair and accurate.

Although research usually has either a basic or an applied orientation, in many cases the distinction between the two types is not completely clear-cut. For instance, although research concerning the circumstances under which group members conform to the beliefs of others might be basic in orientation, the results of such research might also be used to understand how the members of juries influence each other during their deliberations. Correspondingly, scientists who are interested in applied issues such as the behavior of juries are

Applied Research: Research designed to investigate issues that have implications for everyday life and to provide solutions to problems.

well aware that knowledge gained through basic research can help them. Scientists frequently use the results of basic research, such as knowledge about fundamental properties of conformity, to help them understand how real groups work.

In short, applied and basic research inform each other, and both types are essential for the complete study of social groups (Lewin & Gold, 1999). The results of basic research provide underlying principles that can be used to solve specific problems, and applied research assessing specific problems gives ideas for the kinds of topics that basic research can study. Advances in the social sciences occur more rapidly when each type of research is represented in the enterprise. Accordingly, although our focus will be on basic research, we will discuss both approaches in this book.

Theories and Research Hypotheses

One of the important aspects of empirical research, including that conducted by social scientists, is that it is *cumulative*. That is, the research findings of one scientist do not stand alone, but rather are designed to build on, add to, and expand the existing research of other scientists. Over time, research findings are used to create a systematic set of knowledge about a given topic.

Theories as Organizing Principles

One method of assuring that scientific research fits together and thus accumulates in an organized manner is to attempt to organize the findings of many research projects into a coherent set of knowledge. This is done at least in part through the development of theories. A **theory** is an integrated set of principles that explains and predicts observed relationships within a given domain of inquiry. Thus theories about groups provide a basic organizing principle for the study of social groups.

As we have discussed in chapter 1, one important theory of group behavior is *self-categorization theory*. Self-categorization theory proposes that individuals may consider themselves and others, at various times and in various contexts, either as individuals or as members of social groups, and it makes specific predictions about the conditions under which one or the other level of perception will be most dominant, as well as the influence of changes in perceptions on people's behavior. This important theory has been developed and refined over many years through numerous empirical research projects that have tested it.

Consider two interesting predictions of self-categorization theory. First, the theory predicts that conditions that increase the tendency of people to perceive differences between their in-groups and out-groups (such as compe-

Theory: An integrated set of principles that explains and predicts observed relationships within a given domain of inquiry.

tition between the groups) will also increase the likelihood that they will categorize themselves as a member of the in-group (rather than as an individual), and that this self-categorization will heighten social identity with the in-group. Second, the theory predicts that this increase in social identity will increase liking for and cooperation with fellow in-group members, and also increase pressure toward uniformity within the group. Research has confirmed both of these predictions (J. C. Turner, 1987).

Self-categorization theory has contributed to the study of social groups because it provides an organized theme for conducting research designed to test its predictions. The theory not only explains how and when individuals perceive themselves as group members, rather than individuals, but also makes predictions about how people who are members of groups will feel and how they will respond to others. Self-categorization theory is thus an important theory for researchers studying social groups, both because it organizes many research findings about group behavior and because it provides ideas for future research.

As we will see in the chapters to come, there are many theories that are relevant to group behavior. These include such theories as social comparison theory, social exchange theory, social impact theory, and a number of theories of leadership. The theories vary widely in terms of the variables considered important to study and the types of groups that are relevant for testing them. Nevertheless, they all share the basic principles of a good theory.

The Research Hypothesis

Good theories allow the development of new predictions that can be tested through further research. These predictions are made in the form of a precise statement about the expected relationship between specific parts of the theory, and this statement is known as a **research hypothesis**. The research hypothesis can be defined as a specific prediction regarding the relationship between two or more **variables**, where a variable is anything that varies, for instance, among individuals or among groups.

Examples of Research Hypotheses

A research hypothesis states both that there is a relationship between or among the variables of interest and that there is a specific direction of that relationship. For instance, the research hypothesis

"Individuals who work in larger groups will perform tasks more efficiently"

predicts that there is a relationship between a variable called group size and another variable called task efficiency. Similarly, in the research hypothesis

Research Hypothesis: A specific prediction regarding the relationship between two or more variables.

Variable: Anything that varies, for instance, among individuals or among groups.

"Failure on a group task will increase group cohesion"

the variables that are expected to be related are group failure and group cohesion.

As we have seen, theories are frequently used to generate research hypotheses. For instance, self-categorization theory can be used to make many specific research hypotheses including:

"There will be a positive relationship between group members' perceptions of competition and their expressed social identity," and

"Individuals who categorize themselves as group members will be more likely to conform to group norms."

Falsifiability

Because the research hypothesis states both that there is a relationship between the variables, as well as the direction of that relationship, it is said to be *falsifiable*. Being falsifiable means that the outcome of the research can demonstrate either that the hypothesis is correct (that is that the relationship between the variables was correctly specified) or incorrect (that there is actually no relationship between the variables or that the actual relationship is not in the direction that was predicted). As an example, the research hypothesis that "larger groups will perform tasks more efficiently" is falsifiable because the research could show either that there was no relationship between group size and group efficiency or that larger groups were *less* efficient than smaller groups.

When a research hypothesis is shown to be incorrect on the basis of an empirical test, future research is frequently conducted to learn more about the specific conditions under which a relation might or might not be found. For instance, if initial research finds that there is no overall relation between group size and task efficiency, future research might continue to attempt to discover whether there was perhaps a relation only for some types of groups or for some types of tasks.

Measuring Groups

Once the researcher has created a research hypothesis, a decision must be made about how to measure the variables of interest. If a research hypothesis proposes that there is a relation between the size of the group and the efficiency of the group's performance, then we will need to have a way of measuring both of these variables. In some cases, measuring a variable is relatively straightforward—group size can be accurately determined simply by counting the group members. In other cases, however, the measurement of the variable is more complex. How exactly should we measure group efficiency in a study on group performance or group cohesion in a study assessing reactions to failure?

The Operational Definition

In scientific terms, the method that we use to measure a variable of interest is called an **operational definition**. For any variable that we might wish to measure, there are many different operational definitions, and which one we use is dependent upon such things as the goal of the research and the type of group we are studying. In a factory, group efficiency might be assessed by measuring how many units of a product the workers make in a day. For a decision-making group, on the other hand, efficiency might be measured by the quality of the group decisions, as rated by one or more expert judges.

Self-Report Measures

One approach to measuring group processes involves directly asking people about their perceptions using *self-report measures*. **Self-report measures** are measures in which individuals are asked to respond to questions posed by an interviewer or on a questionnaire. Generally, in order to provide a better measure, because any one question might be misunderstood or answered incorrectly, more than one question is asked, and the responses to the questions are averaged. For example, group cohesion could be measured by asking:

1. I enjoy the people in my work group

   Strongly disagree   1 2 3 4 5 6   Strongly agree

2. The people in my work group get along well together

   Strongly disagree   1 2 3 4 5 6   Strongly agree

3. The people in my work group help each other on the job

   Strongly disagree   1 2 3 4 5 6   Strongly agree

The operational definition would be the average of the responses across the three questions.

Although it is easy to ask many questions on self-report measures, they also have a potential disadvantage; people may not wish to or be able to tell

Operational Definition: The method used to measure a variable of interest.

Self-report Measures: Measures in which participants are asked to respond to questions posed by an interviewer or on a questionnaire.

the truth about their thoughts or feelings. When people are asked whether or not they are prejudiced, for instance, they may not want to admit it even if they are, and in research conducted in a factory, people might be afraid to express their dissatisfaction with their superiors for fear that they might be identified.

Behavioral Measures

An alternative to self-report that can sometimes provide more accurate measures is to directly measure behavior. Instead of asking people how much they identify with their group, we might instead measure social identity by assessing how much time people in the group spend together, or how many times they use the words "we" or "us" when they talk about the group. We might even measure how much the group members hug each other when the group disbands at the end of a session. There are a wide variety of behavioral measures that can be used in group research, such as:

Frequency (for instance, frequency of stuttering as a measure of anxiety in groups)

Duration (for instance, the number of minutes working at a task as a measure of task interest)

Intensity (for instance, how hard a person claps their hands as a measure of effort)

Latency (for instance, the number of days before beginning to work on a project as a measure of procrastination)

Speed (for instance, how long it takes a group to complete a task as a measure of efficiency)

Behavioral measures are useful because they provide information that is not available through self-report measures in which people are directly asked to report on their thoughts or feelings. And behavioral measures may also be more accurate than self-report measures, particularly if the participants are not aware that their behaviors are being measured (for example, if the participants are observed through a one-way mirror), and thus have no reason to alter their actions.

Measuring Group Interactions

As social scientists have studied groups, they have made many advances in measuring group behavior. Thus there are now many available self-report and behavioral measures that can be used to assess group processes. Although we cannot review all of those methods here, we can consider a couple of important examples.

Sociometric Methods

One approach to measuring group processes is to use a procedure known as a **network analysis**. Network analysis involves determining the relationships with, or feelings of each group member about, every other group member. The opinions can be obtained either through self-report, for example, by asking each person how much time people in the group spend together or how much each person would like to be friends with the other group members. Alternatively, behavioral measures can be used, perhaps, by observing how much time the group members spend with each other.

The outcome of a sociometric analysis is a visual display known as a **sociogram**, which represents a picture of the networks of relationships among the people in the group. One example, conducted using a classroom of fourth-graders, is presented in Figure 2.1. In the research, each of the students in the class was asked to indicate who hangs out together, and these ratings were the data for the analysis. The sociogram allows the researcher to visually inspect the patterns of relationships among the group members and to view subgroups within the overall group. In Figure 2.1 there are four subgroups. Some children belong to more than one group, and there is one dyad (group IV) that represents two good friends. Although there are none represented in this sociogram, in some cases there will also be *social isolates* (individuals who are rejected by all of the other group members).

Network analysis allows the researcher to get a picture of how the individuals in a group relate to each other and to determine the types of relationships that lead to effective group functioning. For instance, research on corporations has found that employees who have broader social networks, in the sense that they interact with many different people, make more effective managers, and research with children has shown that children who are aggressive tend to cluster together, as do those who smoke cigarettes (Ennett & Bauman, 1994) and those who are motivated to do well in school (Cairns, Cairns, Necerman, Gest, & Gariépy, 1988; Kindermann, 1993).

Analyzing Interactions: SYMLOG

In their quest to understand group behavior, researchers have also developed techniques for measuring interactions among the members of working groups. Perhaps the best known of these approaches is **SYMLOG (System of Multiple Level of Observation of Groups),** which was developed by Robert Bales (Bales, 1950, 1970, 1999).[1] The basic idea of SYMLOG is to observe the behaviors of a working group and to code the interactions among the group members into a

Network Analysis: A method of assessing group structure in which the relationships or feelings (usually assessed in terms of liking or time spent together) of each group member about each other group member are assessed.

Sociogram: A visual display of a social network.

SYMLOG (System of Multiple Level of Observation of Groups): A system of collecting data that involves observing the behaviors of a working group and coding the observed interactions into a limited number of types of activities.

---

1. SYMLOG is an update of an earlier approach to measuring group behavior known as *Interaction Process Analysis* (IPA).

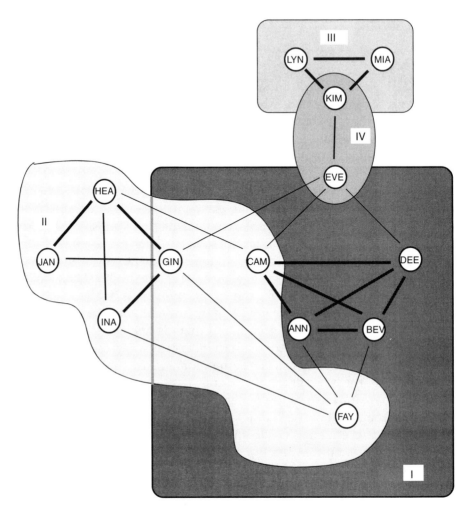

FIGURE 2.1. A sociogram. A sociogram showing the group memberships (groups I through IV) of 12 girls in a fourth-grade classroom. The data were derived from reports of the children in the classroom about "who hangs out together." Some children are in more than one group, and in this case all children belong to at least one group. The data are from: Kindermann, T. A. (1993). Natural peer groups as contexts for individual development: The case of children's motivation in school. *Developmental Psychology, 29*, 970–977.

limited number of types of activities, which can then be used in statistical analyses. Within SYMLOG, the interactions are classified by experienced raters into the categories of *task-oriented* (or *instrumental*) activities, *socioemotional* (or *relationship*) activities, and *power* (or *dominance*) activities.

The coding categories used by SYMLOG are presented in Table 2.1. As you can see, the categories are very detailed, and as a result virtually any type of verbal statement or group behavior can be coded into one of them. By systematically coding and analyzing the activities that are occurring in the group, the researcher can study the dynamics within the group, and can see how the

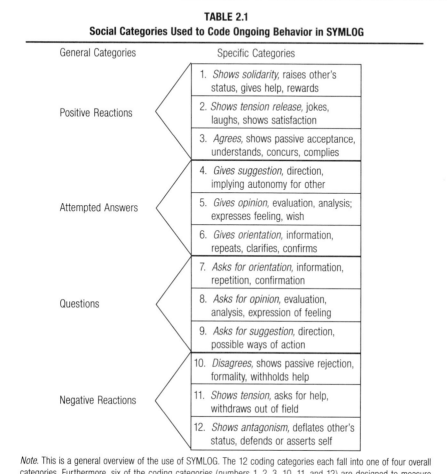

TABLE 2.1
Social Categories Used to Code Ongoing Behavior in SYMLOG

General Categories	Specific Categories
Positive Reactions	1. *Shows solidarity,* raises other's status, gives help, rewards
	2. *Shows tension release,* jokes, laughs, shows satisfaction
	3. *Agrees,* shows passive acceptance, understands, concurs, complies
Attempted Answers	4. *Gives suggestion,* direction, implying autonomy for other
	5. *Gives opinion,* evaluation, analysis; expresses feeling, wish
	6. *Gives orientation,* information, repeats, clarifies, confirms
Questions	7. *Asks for orientation,* information, repetition, confirmation
	8. *Asks for opinion,* evaluation, analysis, expression of feeling
	9. *Asks for suggestion,* direction, possible ways of action
Negative Reactions	10. *Disagrees,* shows passive rejection, formality, withholds help
	11. *Shows tension,* asks for help, withdraws out of field
	12. *Shows antagonism,* deflates other's status, defends or asserts self

Note. This is a general overview of the use of SYMLOG. The 12 coding categories each fall into one of four overall categories. Furthermore, six of the coding categories (numbers 1, 2, 3, 10, 11, and 12) are designed to measure socioemotional activity, whereas the other six measure task activity. At least two trained coders do the observation, which can result in reliable ratings of the group behaviors. Adapted from Bules, R. F. (1999). *Social interaction systems.* New Brunswick, NJ: Transaction, p. 165.

members' relationships change over time. The results of the SYMLOG analysis are usually used in conjunction with a group sociogram, not only to provide a picture of who is interacting with whom in the group, but also to understand what kinds of interactions are occurring.

SYMLOG represents an important approach to understanding group behavior, because it can be used to summarize the complicated interpersonal interactions that occur in a working group. Although the technique is difficult to use properly because it requires extensively trained interviewers, it has nevertheless been an important empirical approach for learning about relationships among the members of working groups.

Observational Research Designs

Now that we have considered some of the techniques used to measure the variables of interest to group researchers, we can turn to a review of the research designs that are used to study groups in action. The characteristics of these three designs, along with a list of their advantages and disadvantages, are outlined in Table 2.2.

"When Prophecy Fails"

The most basic research design, known as **observational research**, involves making observations of behavior and recording those observations in an objective manner. The observational approach, the oldest method of conducting research, is used routinely to study groups. One interesting observational study that has made an important contribution to understanding group behavior was reported in a book by Leon Festinger and his colleagues (Festinger, Riecken, & Schachter, 1956). In *When Prophecy Fails* they reported an observational study of the members of a doomsday cult. The cult members believed that they had received information, supposedly sent through "automatic writing" from a planet called "Clarion," that the world was going to end. More specifically, the group members were convinced that the earth would be destroyed, as the result of a gigantic flood, sometime before dawn on December 21, 1954.

When Festinger learned about the cult, he thought that it would be an interesting way to study how individuals in groups communicate with each

Observational Research: Research in which observations are made of behavior, and those observations are recorded in an objective manner.

TABLE 2.2
Summary of Research Designs

Research Design	Goal	Advantages	Disadvantages
Observational	Create a "snapshot" of the current state of affairs.	Provides a relatively complete picture of what is occurring at a given time.	Does not assess relationships among variables.
Correlational	Assess the relationships among two or more variables.	Allows testing expected relationships among variables and making predictions.	Cannot be used to draw inferences about the causal relationships among the variables.
Experimental	Assess the impact of one or more experimental manipulations on a dependent variable.	Allows drawing conclusions about the causal relationships among variables.	Many important variables of interest cannot be experimentally manipulated.

other to reinforce their (in this case, rather wacky) beliefs. He and his colleagues observed the members of the cult over a period of several months, beginning in July of the year in which the flood was expected. The researchers recorded the conversations among the group members, and interviewed them extensively. Festinger and his colleagues also recorded the reactions of the cult members, beginning on December 21, when the world did not end as they had predicted. This observational research provided a wealth of information about the indoctrination patterns of cult members and their reactions to disconfirmed predictions. Similar observational approaches have been used to study the behaviors of factory workers (e.g., Roy, 1959) and gang members in a city (e.g., Whyte, 1991).

Advantages of Observational Research

One advantage of observational research is that in many cases it is the only possible way to collect data about the topic of interest. A researcher who is interested in studying the impact of a hurricane on the residents of North Carolina, the reactions of New Yorkers to a terrorist attack, or the activities of a cult as it awaits the end of the world cannot create such situations in a laboratory, but must be ready to make observations when such events occur on their own. Thus, observational research allows the study of unique situations that could not be created by the researcher.

Ecological Validity

Because it is often conducted in the real world, observational research is said to have *ecological validity*. **Ecological validity** refers to the extent to which the research is conducted in situations that are similar to the everyday life experiences of the participants (Aronson, Ellsworth, Carlsmith, & Gonzales, 1990). Studies with high ecological validity are those that capture group behavior as it actually occurs, in everyday life. In observational research the people whose behavior is being measured are doing the things they do every day, and in some cases they may not even know that their behavior is being recorded.

Varieties of Data

Although observational research is normally conducted on people who are living their normal, everyday lives, it is also possible to create situations in which the research participants can be observed under special situations. In one well-known study of group behavior conducted by Philip Zimbardo (Haney, Banks, & Zimbardo, 1973), the researchers created a situation in which col-

Ecological Validity: The extent to which research is conducted in situations that are similar to the everyday life experiences of the participants.

lege students were assigned to role-play the behavior of prisoners and guards in a simulated "prison." Each student was randomly assigned to play the role of either guard or prisoner, and the prisoners were picked up at their homes in police cars and "arrested." At the simulated prison, they were given uniforms of the prisoners, whereas the guards were given uniforms of guards, and they began to play their roles. Over the course of several days, the students took the role-play very seriously. For instance, the "prisoners" went on a hunger strike and the "guards" punished them by placing some of them in solitary confinement. Eventually, the role-play had to be stopped because the students were taking it too seriously, and there was a potential for someone getting hurt. In this case the observational approach again allowed the researchers to study group behavior simply by observing behaviors in a specific setting. A full description of this observational study is available at www.zimbardo.com.

Disadvantages of Observational Research

Despite their advantages observational research designs also have some limitations. For one, although studies such as Festinger's observation of the doomsday cult can be used to assess how some particular people behaved in a particular situation, the results are generally limited to the particular group being studied. We do not know whether the group that he studied was typical of all cults. Furthermore, and even more important, because the data that are collected in observational studies are only a description of the events that are occurring, they cannot be used to test research hypotheses about which types of group behavior are related to or caused by which other variables. Thus, observational research is good for developing ideas that can be tested more fully using other research designs.

Correlational Research Designs

Correlational Research Design: A research design in which the goal is to search for and describe the relation among two or more variables.

Unlike observational research, which primarily provides a description of the ongoing behavior within a group, the goal of a **correlational research design** is to search for and to describe relations among two or more variables. In the simplest case, the association is between only two variables, such as that between group size and group cohesion, or between the number of men (versus women) on a jury and the outcome of the jury's decision making. There are many patterns of relations that can occur between two measured variables, and an even greater number of patterns can occur when more than two variables are assessed. It is this complexity, which is a part of everyday life, that correlational research designs attempt to capture.

The Research Hypothesis

In a correlational design, the research hypothesis is that there is an association (that is, a correlation) between the variables that are being measured. For instance, a researcher might hypothesize that the variable of group identity would be related to the variable of group effectiveness:

Group Identity ⟷ Group Effectiveness

Each of the variables would be measured with its own operational definition, and the researcher would specify the predicted direction of the relation—either that (*a*) as group identity increases, group effectiveness also increases, or that (*b*) as group identity increases, group effectiveness decreases (it is of course possible that there is no relation between group identity and group effectiveness, but this would not make a research hypothesis).

The Pearson Correlation Coefficient

A statistic known as the *Pearson Product-moment Correlation Coefficient* is frequently used to summarize and communicate the strength and direction of the association between two variables. The Pearson correlation coefficient, normally referred to simply as the "correlation coefficient," is designated by the letter r. The correlation coefficient is a number that indicates both the direction and the magnitude of the observed association. Values of the correlation coefficient range from $r = -1.00$ to $r = +1.00$.

The sign of the correlation coefficient indicates the direction of the relation. Positive values of r (such as $r = .24$ or $r = .47$) indicate that individuals who have higher values on one variable also tend to have higher values on the other variable. For example, the intelligence of a leader is positively correlated with his or her ability to influence others (Simonton, 1995), and (as we have seen in chapter 1) group cohesiveness is, at least in some cases, positively correlated with group productivity. Negative values of r (such as $r = -.31$ or $r = -.22$) occur when higher values on one variable are associated with lower values on the other variable. For example, as the number of individuals in a group increases, the responsibility that any one individual feels for the group output decreases. The distance of the correlation coefficient from zero (its absolute value) indexes the strength or magnitude of the relationship. Thus $r = .34$ is a stronger relationship than $r = -.11$, whereas $r = -.32$ is a stronger relationship than $r = .27$.

Advantages of Correlational Research Designs

As with any research design, correlational designs have both strengths and weaknesses, and it is important to be aware of these advantages and limitations when considering the results of research using them.

Ecological Validity

One advantage of correlational research designs is that, like observational research, they frequently have relatively high ecological validity. For instance, in research that has studied the relation between intelligence and leader effectiveness, the data have come from real-world settings, including leaders of businesses and past presidents of the United States. This high level of ecological validity assures us that the relation that we have found can be observed in everyday behavior (in comparison to experimental research designs in which the researcher frequently creates relatively artificial situations in a laboratory setting).

Making Predictions

Correlational research designs also have the advantage of allowing prediction. When two or more variables are correlated, we can use our knowledge of a person's score on one of the variables to predict his or her likely score on another variable. Because intelligence and leadership skills are positively correlated, if we know a person's intelligence we can make a prediction about his or her leadership skills. Similarly, if we know a person's college grade point average, as well as his or her achievement test scores, we can predict his or her likely performance in graduate school. These predictions will not be perfect, but they will allow us to make a better guess than we would have been able to if we had not known the person's score on the predictor variable ahead of time.

Disadvantages of Correlational Research Designs

Despite their advantages, correlational designs also have a very important limitation. This limitation is that they cannot be used to draw conclusions about the causal relation among the variables that have been measured. An observed correlation between two variables does not necessarily indicate that either one of the variables caused the other.

Reverse Causation

Let us imagine for a moment that a study has found a positive correlation between group cohesion and group performance and consider several possibilities about why these two variables might be correlated. Although one possibility is that increases in group cohesion caused better performance, another possibility is that the causal direction is exactly opposite to what has been hypothesized. Perhaps increased task performance caused the group to become more cohesive. There is no way to rule out the possibility of such *reverse causation* on the basis of this observed correlation.

Third Variables

Still another possible explanation for the observed correlation is that it has been produced by the presence of another variable that was not measured in the research (sometimes known as a *third variable*). Third variables refer to variables that are not part of the research hypothesis, but which cause both the predictor and the outcome variable, and thus produce the observed correlation between them. For instance, it has been observed that students who sit in the front of a class get better grades than those who sit in the back of the class. Although this could be because sitting in the front allows the student to take better notes or to understand the material better, the relationship is more likely to be caused by a third variable, such as the interest or motivation of the students to do well in the class. Because a student's interest in the class leads them both to do better and to sit nearer the teacher, seating position and class grade are correlated, even though neither one caused the other.

This possibility of third variables must always be taken into consideration when considering correlational research designs. For instance, in a study that finds a relationship between group cohesion and task performance, it is not impossible that a third variable, such as group identification or the skills of the group members, produced the relationship. Or consider a study that compares the performance effectiveness of two groups of office workers, one of which is composed of those who have signed up to take a motivational training course and one of which is composed of workers who have not taken the course. Even if the group that has taken the training has higher productivity than the group that did not, it must be kept in mind that there are likely to have been differences between the workers in the two groups before they took the course and that these differences may themselves have led some of workers to enroll and others to not enroll in the course. Again, a potential third variable (the motivation of the workers) might be causing the differences in performance, rather than the effects of the course itself.

When the two variables that have been measured are both caused by a third variable, the observed relation between them is said to be a **spurious relation.** In a spurious relation, the third variable produces and "explains away" the relation between the predictor and outcome variables. If the effects of the third variable were taken away, or controlled for, the relation between the predictor and outcome variables would disappear.

Spurious Relation: A relation between two variables that is caused by a third, but usually unmeasured, variable.

I like to think of third variables in correlational research designs as "mystery" variables, because their presence and identity is usually unknown to the researcher since they have not been measured. Because it is not possible to measure every variable that could possibly cause both the predictor and outcome variables, it is always possible that there is an unknown third variable. For this reason, we are left with the basic limitation of correlational research: "Correlation does not imply causation."

Experimental Research Designs

Although correlational research allows assessing the relation among variables, these designs do not allow making inferences about the causal relation among those variables. Yet the goal of much research in the social sciences is to understand such causal relations. We might want to know, for instance, whether group cohesiveness causes better group performance or whether group size causes decreases in perceived responsibility. The goal of experimental research designs is to provide more definitive conclusions about the causal relation among the variables in the research hypothesis than is available from correlational designs.

Characteristics of Experimental Designs

In an experimental design, as in correlational designs, the research hypothesis involves the relation between two or more variables. However, in experiments these variables are called the *independent variables* and the *dependent variable*.

The Experimental Manipulation

Experimental Research Design: A research design in which the independent variable is created by the experimenter through the experimental manipulation, and the research hypothesis is that the manipulated independent variable causes changes in the measured dependent variable.

In an **experimental research design** the independent variable or variables are created by the experimenter through the experimental manipulations, and the research hypothesis is that the manipulated independent variables cause changes in the measured dependent variable. For instance, consider the possibility of testing the hypothesis that increases in group cohesion cause increases in task performance. We might diagram the prediction like this, using an arrow that points in one direction to demonstrate the expected direction of causality:

Group Cohesion $\longrightarrow$ Task Performance
Independent Variable   *Dependent Variable*

To test this hypothesis the experimenter would create groups of research participants, some of whom are given manipulations designed to increase group cohesion (the high-cohesion condition), and some of whom are not (the low-cohesion condition). The experimenter would then assess the influence of this experimental manipulation on the task performance of the groups, with the expectation that the high-cohesion group would perform better. The design of this simple experiment is shown in Figure 2.2.

Equivalence and Control

In addition to guaranteeing that the independent variable occurs prior to measuring the dependent variable, the use of an experimental manipulation also allows the experimenter to rule out the possibility of third variables that cause both the independent and the dependent variable. In experimental designs, the influence of third variables is eliminated (or controlled) by creating equivalence among the participants in each of the experimental conditions before the manipulation occurs.

The most common method of creating equivalence among the experimental conditions is through *random assignment to conditions*. Random assignment (sometimes called *randomization*) involves determining, separately for each participant, which condition they will experience through a random pro-

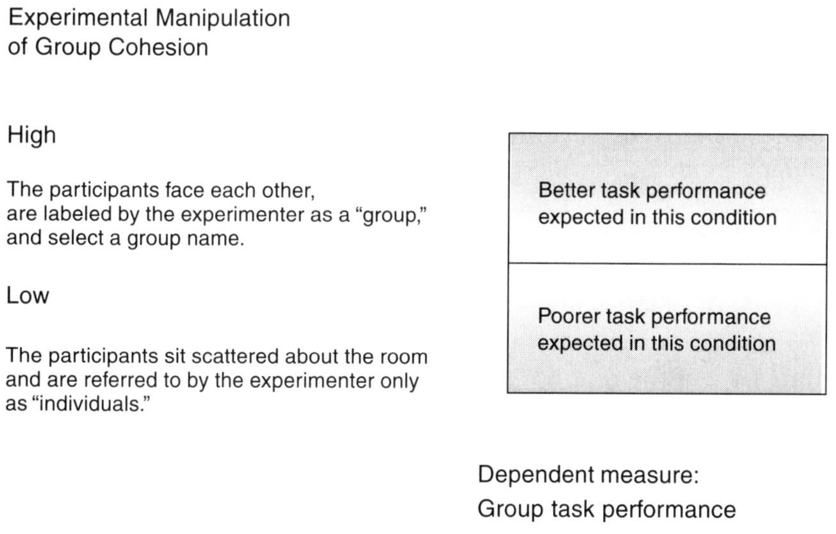

Experimental Manipulation
of Group Cohesion

High

The participants face each other,
are labeled by the experimenter as a "group,"
and select a group name.

Low

The participants sit scattered about the room
and are referred to by the experimenter only
as "individuals."

Better task performance expected in this condition
Poorer task performance expected in this condition

Dependent measure:
Group task performance

FIGURE 2.2. A one-way experimental design. In this hypothetical experiment the researcher manipulates the independent variable (group cohesion) and then measures the dependent variable. The prediction is that higher group cohesion will produce better task performance.

cess such as flipping a coin, drawing numbers out of an envelope, or using a random number table. The result of random assignment is that we can be confident that, before the experimental manipulation occurs, the participants in the different conditions are, on average, equivalent in every respect except for differences that are due to chance.

In our case, because they have been randomly assigned to conditions, the participants who were in the high-cohesiveness condition are, on average, equivalent to the participants who were in the low-cohesiveness condition in terms of every possible variable, including variables that are expected to be related to group task performance. Although random assignment does not guarantee that the participants in the different conditions are exactly equivalent before the experiment begins, it does greatly reduce the likelihood of differences. And the likelihood of chance differences between the conditions is reduced even further as the sample size in each condition increases. Because experiments create initial equivalence, if differences are observed on the dependent variable between the experimental conditions, we can draw the conclusion that it is the independent variable (and not some other variable) that caused these differences. The ability to say that the independent variable caused the dependent variable is called **internal validity**.

Factorial Experimental Designs

Many experimental designs have more than one independent variable. For instance, Figure 2.3 portrays an experimental design in which the research participants have been assigned to one of four experimental conditions. The conditions represent the assignment to either high- or low-cohesive groups and to high- or low-performance norms. Experiments that have more than one independent variable are called **factorial experimental designs.**

Normally, in factorial experimental designs the researcher predicts an *interaction* between the two variables. This means that the prediction is that both variables together influence the dependent variable, such that the influence of one of the variables is different in the different levels of the other. You can see in Figure 2.3 that the interaction prediction is that cohesion will increase the influence of the relevant social norm, such that when the norm is for high productivity, high group cohesion will increase performance, but when the norm is for low productivity, high group cohesion will decrease performance.

Hypothesis Testing in Experimental Designs

The goal of experimental research designs is to show that the experimental manipulation produced changes in the average scores on the dependent vari-

Internal Validity: The ability to draw the conclusion that the independent variable caused the dependent variable.

Factorial Experimental Design: An experiment that has more than one independent variable.

Productivity Norms

Group Cohesion	High	Low
High	Best task performance expected in this condition	Poorest task performance expected in this condition
Low	Better task performance expected in this condition	Poorer task performance expected in this condition

Dependent measure:
Group task performance

FIGURE 2.3. A two-way experimental design. In this hypothetical factorial experiment, the researcher manipulates two independent variables (group cohesion and group productivity norms) and then measures the dependent variable. The prediction is that higher group cohesion will produce better task performance when the productivity norm is high, but will produce poorer task performance when the productivity norm is low.

able across the different experimental conditions. The research hypothesis not only states that there is a difference among the conditions, but also, normally, states the specific direction of those differences. For instance, in our original example the research hypothesis was that high group cohesiveness will produce better task performance, whereas in the second example the research hypothesis is that increases in group cohesion will increase conformity to the prevailing social norm. To test the research hypothesis, the means of the dependent variable are generally compared using a statistical procedure known as the *Analysis of Variance* (abbreviated as ANOVA).

Advantages and Disadvantages of Experiments

The major advantage of experimental research designs is that they can be used to demonstrate causality. Because the researcher creates the independent variable (the experimental manipulation), we can be certain that it occurs before the dependent variable is measured. This eliminates the possibility of reverse causation. And because random assignment has created initial equivalence among the experimental conditions, we can also rule out the possibility of spurious relations between the variables. All possible third variables have been controlled.

Despite this major advantage, experiments do have some limitations. One is that, because they are usually conducted in laboratory situations rather than in the everyday lives of people, their ecological validity is low. We do not know whether results that we find in a laboratory setting will necessarily hold up in everyday life. However, in some cases experiments are conducted in everyday settings, for instance in schools or organizations. However, such **field experiments** are difficult to conduct, because they require a means of creating random assignment to conditions, and this is frequently not possible in natural settings. Second, and perhaps even more important, is that some of the most interesting and important social variables cannot be experimentally manipulated. If we want to study the influence of the size of a mob on the destructiveness of its behavior, or to learn about the relationship between differences in cultural background and individuals' self-concepts, these relationships must be assessed using correlational designs, because it is simply not possible to experimentally manipulate mob size or cultural background.

Interpreting Data

Although we do not have space in this book to fully cover all aspects of scientific data collection and interpretation, there are a couple of issues that we should consider, because they will be particularly important in understanding the research that is reported in this book as well as other research about group behavior that you might want to study.

Statistical Significance

As we have seen, both correlational and experimental research designs involve testing research hypotheses about the relation between two or more variables. The first question that must be asked, once the data are collected, concerns whether or not there really is a relation between the variables. That is, in a correlational design, are the two measured variables really correlated? Or, in an experimental design, did the experimental manipulation really produce changes in the dependent variable? There is unfortunately no easy way to be certain about the answers to these questions, because all data contain some random error. The presence of random error means that in some cases we might observe at least a small correlation between our measures of the two variables, or find at least small differences on the measured dependent variable across the experimental conditions entirely by chance, even though there was actually no real relationship.

Conclusions about the true existence of relation between variables are drawn through a calculation of the **statistical significance** of the relation. Technically, statistical significance is an assessment of how likely it is that the ob-

Field Experiment: An experiment that is conducted in an everyday setting, such as in a school or organization.

Statistical Significance: A method of testing the likelihood that the observed relationships between or among variables is due to chance.

served relation or relations among the variables occurred entirely as a result of chance. If the likelihood that the result is due to chance is very small (normally less than 5 percent of the time), then we say the result is statistically significant. However, if the likelihood that the result is due to random error is greater than 5 percent, then we say the result is nonsignificant. A statistically significant relation means that we can conclude that there is indeed a correlation between the measured variables, or that the conditions in an experimental design really do differ from each other, because the likelihood that the observed relations were due only to chance is quite small.

The Effect Size

Although statistical significance is used to determine whether or not there is a relation between two or more variables, a different statistic, known as the *effect-size statistic* is used to determine the size or magnitude of that relation. The **effect size** is a statistic in which zero indicates that there is no relation between the variables, and larger effect sizes indicate stronger relation. Generally, small effect sizes are about .20, medium effect sizes are about .50, and large effect sizes are about .80 (J. Cohen, 1992). Because it measures the size of a relation, the effect-size statistic provides important practical information that cannot be obtained from knowing the statistical significance of a relation.

In some cases, and particularly in applied research, the effect size of a relation may be more important than the statistical significance of the relation, because it provides a better index of a relation's strength. Consider, for instance, two researchers who were each attempting to determine the effectiveness of training programs designed to improve the quality of group decision making in a large corporation. The first researcher studies the effects of a month-long training program in which each employee travels to a distant city to learn decision-making skills. The second researcher studies the effects of showing and discussing a videotape on effective decision-making practices to the employees. This takes one hour of their time and is done right at the corporate headquarters. Furthermore, assume that both researchers find that the programs produce statistically significant increases in the ability of the group members to make effective decisions.

In such a case the statistical significance of the relation between the intervention and the outcome variable may not be as important as the effect size. Because the cost of one training program is much higher than that of the other program, the managers, in order to consider it worthwhile, would probably require that it have a much bigger impact on effective decision making. In this case, the effect-size statistic might be used to determine the impact of each program. Comparing the effect size of a relation with the cost of the interven-

Effect Size: A statistic that indicates the strength of a relationship between or among variables. Zero indicates that there is no relationship between the variables, and larger effect sizes indicate stronger relationships.

tion could help the managers determine whether each program is cost effective (Rossi & Freeman, 1993).

External Validity

No matter how carefully it is conducted or what type of research design is used, all research has limitations. For one thing, any research finding may be caused by random error rather than by real relations among the variables. Furthermore, any given research project studies only one set of participants, in one or a few settings, and assesses only one or a few dependent variables. But relations between and among variables are only really important if they can be expected to be found again when tested using other research designs, other operational definitions of the variables, other participants, other experimenters, or in other times and settings.

External validity refers to the extent to which relations can be expected to hold up when they are tested again in different ways. Science relies primarily upon replication—that is, the repeating of research—to test the external validity of research findings. Sometimes the original research is replicated exactly, but more often replications involve using new operational definitions of the independent or dependent variables or designs in which new conditions or variables are added to the original design. Replication allows scientists to test the external validity as well as the limitations of research findings.

Meta-analysis

External Validity: The extent to which relations observed in research can be expected to hold up when they are tested again in different ways.

Meta-analysis: A type of data analysis in which the data are drawn from the results of existing studies and combined to determine what conclusions can be drawn on the basis of all of the studies taken together.

Because each individual research project is limited in some way, many different studies are needed to draw clear conclusions about the true relation among variables. Over time, as more and more replications are conducted, more and more is learned about the topic, and more definitive conclusions can be drawn. In some cases the results of many different studies can be combined using a statistical technique known as a **meta-analysis**. In a meta-analysis, the data are the results of existing studies that are combined to determine what conclusions can be drawn on the basis of all of the studies taken together. A meta-analysis provides a relatively objective method of reviewing research findings because it specifies exactly which studies will or will not be included in the analysis, systematically searches for all studies that meet the inclusion criteria, and uses the effect-size statistic to provide an objective measure of the strength of observed relations. As we consider research that has studied group behavior in the chapters to come, we will frequently consider the results of meta-analyses that have been conducted to summarize it.

Chapter Summary

Research in the social sciences is empirical. This research is conducted either to gain knowledge or understanding of something (basic research) or to solve everyday issues or problems (applied research). The goal of accumulating research findings is accomplished in part through the development of theories that summarize and organize findings and make predictions for new research.

Theories are tested through the use of research hypotheses that make falsifiable predictions about the direction of relation between or among variables. The variables are measured using an operational definition. The measures can be based upon either self-report or behavioral measures, and there are advantages to each. Some important examples of measures of group research are network analysis and SYMLOG.

There are three basic research designs used to study group behavior. Observational research involves the study of everyday behavior. In many cases a large amount of information can be collected very quickly using observational approaches, and this information can provide basic knowledge about the phenomena of interest as well as providing ideas for future research. Observational research has high ecological validity because it involves people in their everyday lives. However, although the data can be rich and colorful, observational research does not provide much information about why behavior occurs or what would have happened to the same people in different situations, and it does not allow the testing of research hypotheses.

Correlational research is designed to test research hypotheses in cases where it is not possible or desirable to experimentally manipulate the independent variable of interest. Although correlational research often has high ecological validity, it is limited because it cannot generally be used to make inferences about the causal relations among variables.

Experimental research designs are used to allow the researcher to draw conclusions about the causal relation between one or more independent variables and a dependent variable. This is accomplished by manipulating, rather than measuring, the independent variable or variables. The manipulation guarantees that the independent variables occur prior to the dependent variable. The use of random assignment to conditions creates equivalence among the conditions and rules out the possibility that the relation was caused by a third variable. In experiments we can be more certain about the internal validity of the relation between the independent and dependent variables than we can in correlational designs, because equivalence has made it unlikely that there are differences among the participants in the different conditions except for the effects of the manipulation itself. Most experiments are conducted in labs, but some field experiments have been used to study group behavior.

Scientists test the results of research to determine whether relations among variables are likely to have been due to chance. If the likelihood that an observed result was due to chance is very small, we say that the result is statistically significant. However, the effect-size statistic provides a better indication of the strength of a relation, and is used particularly in applied research. Because all research has the possibility of error, it is important to replicate prior research to assure its external validity. Scientists summarize research, using such procedures as meta-analysis, to draw overall conclusions about the relations between variables.

 ## *Review and Discussion Questions*

1. What is meant by empirical, and what makes scientific research empirical?
2. What are the goals of basic research and applied research, and how do the two types of research relate to each other?
3. What are theories, and how are they used to guide research?
4. What is a research hypothesis, and how does it relate to a theory?
5. What are network analysis and SYMLOG, and how are they used in group research?
6. What are the goals of observational, correlational, and experimental research? What are the advantages and disadvantages of each research approach?
7. Describe a correlational and an experimental research design that someone might use to test the research hypothesis that increases in social identity are related to (or cause) increases in conformity to group norms.
8. What is external validity, and how does a meta-analysis help us understand whether a result is likely to generalize to new populations and settings?

Recommended Readings

A recent analysis of where research on groups is being published:

Sanna, L. J., & Parks, C. D. (1997). Group research trends in social and organizational psychology: Whatever happened to intragroup research? *Psychological Science, 8,* 261–267.

An introduction to research methods in the behavioral sciences, written by an exceptional author!

Stangor, C. (2003). *Research Methods for the Behavioral Sciences, Second Edition.* Boston: Houghton Mifflin.

Groups and Their Functions 3

*H*aving considered the methods social scientists use to study social groups, we are now ready to return to our analysis of group behavior. In this chapter we will consider why we join groups and why groups have meaning for us. Most simply, we can say that people join groups for the benefits that the groups provide them, and they leave groups (if they can) if those benefits are not greater than the costs that accrue from being a group member. The goals of this chapter are to consider how people make these decisions and to review the costs and benefits that come with group membership.

Benefits of Group Membership

If we accept the fundamental assumption that people form and remain in social groups to obtain benefits from the group, it then becomes important to specify what those potential benefits are. Although we gain many different rewards from our memberships in different groups, we can effectively summarize these benefits in terms of a smaller set of underlying needs that groups meet for individuals (Mackie & Goethals, 1987; Moreland, 1987). I have summarized these benefits in Table 3.1. But before we begin to consider the specific benefits that groups provide, let us first consider a method for specifying how costs and benefits are shared within groups.

Social Exchange

Relationships among group members (and among people, more generally) can be considered as a type of *social exchange* (Blau, 1964; Homans, 1961; Schutz, 1958; Thibaut & Kelley, 1959). **Social exchange** refers to the sharing of social

TABLE 3.1
Some Benefits of Social Groups

Group Function	Example
Survival	Groups help us find appropriate mates, facilitate food gathering and production, and enhance security.
Anxiety reduction	Groups allow us to assess danger through social comparison, and help reduce anxiety.
Positive self-esteem	Downward comparison with others who are worse off allows us to feel good about ourselves.
Social accuracy	Social comparison allows us to validate our opinions, particularly regarding important social values.
Social identity	Identifying with other in-group members results in positive feelings about our group membership.
Productivity	Groups help us develop new ideas and accomplish important tasks. They may also help us have the power to produce social change.
Social support mental	Groups provide feelings of love, caring, and value, which produce better and physical health.
Belonging	Groups help prevent loneliness through the development of positive, enduring relationships with other people.

Social Exchange: The sharing of social rewards and social costs among people.

rewards and social costs among people. Social rewards include such things as the attention, praise, affection, love, and even the financial support that we receive from others. Social costs, on the other hand, include, for instance, the frustrations that accrue when disagreements with others develop, the guilt that results if we perceive that we have acted inappropriately toward others, and the effort involved in developing and maintaining harmonious interpersonal relationships.

You might imagine a first-year student at your college or university who is trying to decide whether or not to pledge a fraternity. Joining the fraternity has costs, in terms of the dues that have to be paid, the requirement of making friends with each of the other fraternity members and attending fraternity meetings, and so forth. On the other hand, there are also potential benefits of group membership, including having a group of friends with similar interests and a social network to help find activities to participate in. To determine whether or not to pledge, the student has to weigh the costs and benefits before coming to a conclusion.

Research has supported the idea that people consider their group memberships in terms of social exchange. For instance, in a descriptive research study, Moreland, Levine, and Cini (1993) asked first-year college students to indicate which campus groups they were thinking about joining and to indicate the rewards and benefits that those groups might provide. The students listed such rewards as enhancing their self-esteem, developing self-discipline, making new friends, learning new skills, and having fun. But they also mentioned costs such as financial constraints, potential conflicts with other group members, finding the group boring, and having to spend too much time in the group.

Assumptions of Social Exchange

The idea of social exchange is based upon two basic assumptions about how individuals interact with each other. First, individuals are assumed to be *interdependent*, in the sense that they rely upon each other both to gain rewards and to reach goals. In some cases this interdependence may reflect a type of overt cooperation, such as when two students take notes for each other in classes that they miss or when a group of friends simply enjoy each other's company. In other cases, however, the individuals in social relationships may not even realize that they are exchanging rewards. A kindergarten teacher may inadvertently reward a problem child by paying attention to him when he misbehaves. The child is rewarded by the attention and therefore continues or even increases the negative behavior, although the teacher may not realize (at least at first) that the attentive behaviors are rewarding him.

Secondly, social exchange assumes that people prefer to develop and maintain interpersonal relationships that result in *positive outcomes* for them, where positive outcomes are said to occur when the rewards received from the relationship are greater than the costs incurred in maintaining the relationship. In essence, people maintain relationships, including their group memberships, that have the greatest rewards and the fewest costs.

Staying and Leaving

In terms of group behavior, social exchange theory thus makes a very basic prediction—people will join and remain in groups that provide positive outcomes, whereas they will (if possible) leave groups that do not provide positive outcomes. For instance, Ellemers, Spears, and Doosje (1997) found that individuals who showed low levels of social identity with their groups (an indication that they were not getting many rewards from them) were more likely to want to leave the group in comparison to those who were highly identified. Although this prediction seems straightforward, it is nevertheless the case that people end up belonging to groups from which they receive virtually no positive, or perhaps even some negative, outcomes. Sometimes this occurs when they cannot leave the group, even though they may well want to. For example, the members of a low-status high school clique who are teased and bullied by others may want to be accepted into a higher-status group and yet may not be able to.

In still other cases, however, individuals may stay in groups that they could leave even though the costs of group membership clearly outweigh the benefits. You may know someone who a remains working at a low-paying, demeaning job, even though she could probably receive other, better job offers if she made the effort to search. And couples may remain together in romantic relationships that don't seem to benefit either of them. Remember, however, that social exchange suggests only that people will attempt to maximize their outcomes and not that they will necessarily obtain a lot of them. In addition to evaluating the outcomes that one gains from a given group membership, the individual also evaluates the potential costs of moving to another group or not being in a group at all. We might stay in a romantic relationship, even if the benefits of that relationship are not high, because the costs of being in no relationship at all are perceived as even higher. Or a member of a low-ranking fraternity might prefer to be in a better one, but prefer even the low rank to nothing. Social exchange can explain both why we prefer groups that provide benefits to us and why we may stay in groups in which the benefits are low (Rusbult, 1980; Rusbult, Zembrodt, & Gunn, 1982).

Survival

Human beings have survived as a species for thousands of years. Furthermore, humans have lived in social groups during all of this time. Thus it is reasonable to assume that social groups are helpful in survival and to ask how groups might promote survival and how humans have evolved as a result of their group experiences.

Evolutionary Psychology

Evolutionary psychology (Buss & Kenrick, 1998; Tooby & Cosmides, 1992; an overview can be found at http://www.psych.ucsb.edu/research/cep/primer.html) is a theoretical approach that addresses these questions by assuming that the behavior of all living things is determined by attempts to meet the goals of survival and successful reproduction. According to this approach, people have inherited, as a result of natural selection and evolutionary adaptation, specialized skills that allow us to efficiently perform tasks that are important for survival, including those related to mating, security, and social interaction.

Furthermore, since humans have always lived together in small groups, evolutionary psychology predicts that many of these fundamental skills will relate to group behavior. For instance, the ability to recognize other people is an important skill that should be part of our repertoire. Indeed, it has been found that babies who are less than one hour old have this skill: they are able to differentiate faces from scrambled patterns (Johnson, Dziurawiec, Ellis, & Morton, 1991). Similarly, being aware of the processes of social exchange, and particularly being willing to cooperate with others by exchanging benefits would also be expected to be very adaptive, and so it is expected that people will be good at this too.

In fact, research has found that people do cooperate with others, and that they also have well-developed routines that allow them to be sure that people respect their commitments in social exchange. For instance, if I help you by taking notes for you in class, I expect that you would do the same in the future. If you do not reciprocate, it is to my advantage to quickly stop being altruistic to you. In their research, Cosmides and Tooby (1989, 1992) gave research participants tasks to solve that either involved reasoning about abstract problems or gave them the same problems framed in a way that involved violations of social exchange. Consistent with the predictions of evolutionary psychology, people were much better at solving the task when it concerned social exchange than when it was framed in other ways.

Evolutionary Psychology: A theoretical approach based on the assumption that the behavior of all living things is determined by attempts to meet the goals of survival and reproduction.

The Advantages of Groups

Group memberships provide important benefits toward the survival of the group members. For one, groups help us reproduce successfully by providing a set of readily available and acceptable mates. The group also provides for security and defense, allowing group members to divide guard duties and create armies (Alexander, 1987). Groups allow better opportunities for food gathering and production, helping to create a stable food supply. Over the course of human development, the groups needed for survival have, of course, changed. For the major part of human existence, we lived in small nomadic groups, specialized for hunting. Larger social groups, such as extended families, communities, and villages, formed more recently as humans turned to agricultural living. Technology and commerce later brought individuals into cities in which still other types of groups formed. Social groups are likely to remain an important vehicle for survival, although the format and function of those groups will probably continue to change over time.

Accomplishing Goals

Another important function of social groups is providing the ability to accomplish specific task-related goals. There are a lot of things that can't be done alone—we rely on groups to play baseball and basketball, to have a dance party, and to explore outer space. And there are other things—such as watching a sporting event or playing cards—that, though they can be done alone, simply aren't as much fun as they are in groups. Sometimes we use the group to provide benefits for ourselves, as when we join a fraternity in order to develop friendships or join a business club to make business contacts. In other cases we may use groups to help others, as when we join a political party or volunteer in the Peace Corps in order to work toward positive social changes. Perhaps most important, we frequently use working groups to make important decisions, both because we think that these decisions will be better than those that we make alone and because the group can be useful in assuring that the decisions are properly implemented. However, the question of whether groups actually perform better or make better decisions than individuals is a complicated one, and we will return to it in subsequent chapters.

Social Affiliation and Attachment

In addition to helping provide the fundamental needs of survival and task attainment, group membership also provides benefits to our psychological well-being in the form of affiliation and acceptance by others.

Belonging and Ostracism

Friendship and companionship—the formation of positive, enduring relationships with other people and a sense of belonging—is a fundamental need of human beings (Barash, 1982; Baumeister & Leary, 1995; Baumeister & Tice, 1990; Freud, 1922; R. M. Lee & Robbins, 1995; Rook, 1984; Schachter, 1959; Shaver & Buhrmester, 1983). That people find it important to be accepted by their social groups is not surprising, given the importance of the social group in promoting survival and the potential costs of being rejected by the other group members. In fact, it has been proposed that our feeling about own worth — our *self-esteem*—is in large part a measure of how much we feel we are accepted by others (Leary, Tambor, Terdal, & Downs, 1995). According to this idea, self-esteem rises when we feel accepted and seen as worthy by others, and it falls when we feel rejected or devalued.

Perhaps the most obvious sources of acceptance are our reference groups. The support and caring provided by family and friends produces a feeling of comfort and belonging in which we can thrive. In addition to our families, we may also search out other groups that provide affiliation. Therapy and support groups are designed, in part, to provide a sense of belonging and self-worth. Even a baseball team or a study group can provide feelings of acceptance, in addition to the opportunity to engage in specific tasks. People who do not feel that their social relationships are adequate are lonely—a highly unpleasant state for most people (DiTommaso & Spinner, 1997; Kraus, Bazzini, Davis, Church, & Kirchman, 1993; Rubenstein & Shaver, 1982; Russell, Curtona, Rose, & Yurko, 1984; Weiss, 1974; Wheeler, Reis, & Nezlek, 1983).

Ostracism

Because affiliation is so important to group members, groups may sometimes withhold affiliation from or ostracize group members in order to force them to conform to the norms of the group. When individuals of the Amish religion violate the rulings of an elder, they are placed under a *Meidung*. During this time, and until they make amends, they are not spoken to by community members. And an angry boyfriend or girlfriend may use the "silent treatment" to express disapproval of a partner's behavior (Gottman & Krokoff, 1989; K. D. Williams, Shore, & Grahe, 1998). The use of ostracism has also been observed in parents and children, and even on Internet games and chat rooms (K. D. Williams, Cheung, & Choi, 2000).

The "silent treatment" and other forms of ostracism are popular because they work! Withholding social communication and interaction is a powerful weapon for punishing individuals and forcing them to change their behaviors. Individuals who are ostracized report feeling alone, frustrated, sad, and unworthy, have lower self-esteem, and may feel jealous about the fact that others are included in the group whereas they are not (K. D. Williams, 1997).

As part of an experiment on ostracism, Kipling Williams and his colleagues (2000) created a website and advertised it as a psychology experiment. It turned out that 1,486 participants from 62 countries accessed the webpage to participate in the research. When individuals arrived at the site, they were asked to play a game in which they tossed an imaginary Frisbee among themselves and two other "players." Although the participants thought that they were playing online with two other participants, the other players were actually computer-generated and controlled to act in a preprogramed manner.

To create different experimental levels of belonging or ostracism, the computer implemented an experimental manipulation such that the participants were randomly assigned to be either "overincluded" (the "others" threw the Frisbee to the participant most—67 percent—of the time), "included" (the "others" threw the Frisbee to the participant 33 percent of the time), "partially ostracized" (the "others" threw the Frisbee to the participant 20 percent of the time), or "completely ostracized" (the "others" never threw the Frisbee to the participant). The participants then indicated the extent to which they felt that they belonged to their group and reported their current self-esteem. As shown in Figure 3.1, the participants who were more ostracized also reported less belonging to the group and lower self-esteem.

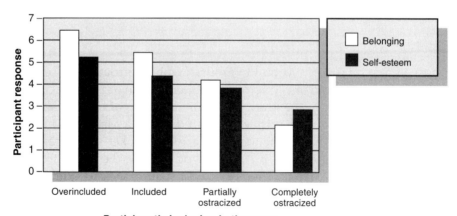

FIGURE 3.1. The effects of cyber-ostracism. In this online experiment participants believed that they were playing a game with other participants, but the behaviors of the "others" were actually preprogramed. As the participants were more ignored by the supposed other players, they rated themselves as being less accepted by the group (belonging), and their self-esteem also decreased. Data are from Williams, K. D., Cheung, C. K. T., & Choi, W. (2000). Cyberostracism: Effects of being ignored over the Internet. *Journal of Personality and Social Psychology, 79,* 748–762.

Social Groups on the Internet

Although the experiment by Williams et al. (2000) could have been conducted in a laboratory rather than on the Internet, it does bring up an interesting question concerning the extent to which communicating with others online can produce a sense of belonging. On one hand, people report that the ability to contact many people easily and frequently through e-mail has increased their contact with relatives and friends (Pew, 2000), and it has also been shown that people can and do easily develop close friendships with people they meet online (McKenna & Bargh, 1998, 2000). On the other hand, Kraut, Patterson, Lundmark, Kiesler, Mukopadhyay, and Scherlis (1998) found that people who had used the Internet for just a year or two were more likely to report being depressed and lonely, and argued that this was because using the Internet reduces the time that people spend in person with their family and friends. Although future research is needed to determine the impact of the Internet on social relations, it may be the case that, at least in the long term, Internet relationships do not provide the same degree of belonging, affiliation, and self-esteem that can be provided by direct contact with others.

Affiliation and Anxiety

Being with other people provides a sense of security and acceptance and reduces anxiety. When we are sad or afraid, or when we are unsure what to do or how to feel, we frequently turn to others (S. Cohen & Wills, 1985; Gerard, 1963). In one well-known research program, Stanley Schachter (1959) conducted experiments to test the hypothesis that people who were feeling anxious would prefer to be with others rather than to be alone, because having others around would reduce their anxiety. In one of his experiments, female college students at the University of Minnesota volunteered to participate for extra credit in their introductory psychology class. They arrived at the experimental room to find a scientist dressed in a white lab coat standing in front of a large array of electrical machinery. The scientist introduced himself as Dr. Zilstein of the Department of Neurology and Psychiatry and told the women that they would be serving as participants in an experiment concerning the effects of electrical shock. Dr. Zilstein stressed how important it was to learn about the effects of shocks, since shock was being used more and more commonly in electroshock therapy and because the number of accidents due to electricity was also increasing!

At this point the experimental manipulation occurred. For one-half of the sessions (the high-anxiety condition) the women were told that the shocks would be "painful" and "intense," although they were assured that they could do no permanent damage. The other half of the women (those in the low-anxiety condition) were also told that they would be receiving shocks, but that they would in no way be painful—rather the shocks were said to be mild and would resemble a "tickle" or a "tingle." Of course, the respondents were randomly assigned to conditions to assure that the women in the two conditions were, on average, equivalent except for the experimental manipulation.

The women were then told that before the experiment could continue the experimenter would have to prepare the equipment and that they would have to wait for a while until he was finished. And he asked them if they would prefer to wait alone or to wait with others. The outcome of Schachter's research was clear—while only 33 percent of the women who were expecting mild shocks preferred to wait with others, 63 percent of the women expecting to get painful shocks wanted to wait with others. This was a statistically significant difference, and Schachter concluded that the women chose to wait with each other in order to reduce their anxiety about the upcoming shocks.

Attachment Styles

Although even strangers can provide some comfort, the family provides the most safety and security, and this is provided at a time when we are most vulnerable—as infants and children. It is therefore probably not surprising that social science research has demonstrated that children learn skills for relating to others in large part through their early family experiences.

Research has suggested that young children develop either a healthy or an unhealthy *attachment style* with their parents (Ainsworth, 1989; Bowlby, 1969, 1979; Cassidy & Shaver, 1999). **Attachment style** is a description of the different types of relationships that people may have with other individuals, and particularly with one's parents. Most children develop healthy or *secure* attachment styles. These children perceive their parents as safe, available, and responsive caregivers and are able to relate easily to them. For these children the family successfully creates appropriate feelings of affiliation and security. However, for children with unhealthy attachment styles, the family does not provide these needs. Some children develop an *insecure* attachment style, becoming overly dependent upon the parents, and continually seeking more affection from them than they can give. Still other children become unable to relate to the parents at all, becoming distant, fearful, and cold (the *fearful* style) or simply rejecting the parents' role in a desire to demonstrate independence (the *dismissing* style). These difficulties seem to be caused in part by characteristics of the child and in part by characteristics of the family structure.

In addition to influencing how the child responds to his or her parents, attachment styles are also correlated with the ability of the individual to create stable, healthy interpersonal relationships with other individuals later in life. Indeed, R. Chris Fraley (2002) conducted a meta-analysis of 27 studies that

Attachment Style: A description of the different types of relationships that people may have with other individuals, and particularly with one's parents.

had studied the relationship between attachment behavior in infants and in adults over 17 years of age, and found that the correlation between the two measures was .27 (a moderate effect size). The relationship appeared to be due to the fact that the people studied were influenced by their early family experiences and these experiences continued to play a role in their interactions with others as adults.

In short, children who have developed secure attachment styles have better and more fulfilling relationships with others, and these relationships are characterized by more security and trust, in comparison to children who have developed unhealthy attachment styles. However, children's attachment styles do not predict everything. People have many experiences as adults, such as accidents, divorce, illnesses, and so forth, and these things also have profound influences on their ability to relate with others. Nevertheless, the ability to successfully relate to others appears to be learned at least in part during childhood, and is related to people's behavior later in life.

Social Support

When people find themselves in novel, difficult, or unpleasant circumstances, they frequently turn to others for help. In some cases, for instance, when a freshman pledges a fraternity, the "others" are a formal group. In other cases, the links are more informal, for instance, when friends get together over a cup of coffee to talk about their personal lives. Regardless of whether the group is formal or informal, however, being with others can make us feel better.

Social support refers to the approval, assistance, advice, comfort, and other aid that we receive from those with whom we have developed stable positive relationships, including our families, as well as romantic partners, siblings, friends, neighbors, and other acquaintances (Wellman, 1992; Coyne & Downey, 1991). Social support can be given in a wide variety of ways, including both task-related support, such as taking care of someone who is ill by cooking and cleaning their house, as well as emotional support, such as talking to people about their problems and providing comfort (Barrera & Ainlay, 1983; Folkman & Lazarus, 1980; Finch et al., 1997; Harlow & Cantor, 1994; Thoits, 1986). When we experience social support, we feel loved and cared for, esteemed and valued, and part of a network of important others. People with social support can turn to their support networks when they face difficulties, and these groups have substantial positive influence on mental and physical health.

Social Support: The approval, assistance, advice, comfort, and other aid that we receive from those with whom we have developed stable positive relationships.

Mental Health

People who feel that they have adequate social support (in comparison to those who feel that they do not have a network of others that they can turn to) report being happier (Harlow & Cantor, 1996; Cohen & Wills, 1985; Hartup & Stevens, 1997) and have also been found to have fewer psychological problems, including criminal behavior, eating disorders, and mental illness (Sampson & Laub, 1993; Sours, 1974; Thoits, 1993). And, supporting a research hypothesis originally proposed by Durkheim (1951), correlational research designs have found that people with more social support (for example, those who are married and employed in comparison to those who are single and unemployed) are also less likely to commit suicide (Rothberg & Jones, 1987; Trout, 1980).

Social support also buffers people against stress (S. Cohen, Sherrod, & Clark, 1986; Cutrona, 1989). For instance, research has found that military veterans who are lonely and perceive that they have little social support are more likely to experience post-traumatic stress disorder than those who have greater perceived social support (Solomon, Waysman, & Mikulincer, 1990). Indeed, one of the goals of effective psychotherapy is to help people generate better social support networks, because such relationships have such a positive effect on mental health (Lindt & Pennal, 1962).

Physical Health

In addition to having better mental health, people who have adequate social support are also more physically healthy. They have fewer diseases (such as tuberculosis, heart attacks, and cancer), engage in fewer dangerous behaviors, and live longer (M. S. Stroebe, 1994; W. Stroebe & Stroebe, 1996; Sugisawa, Liang, & Liu, 1994; Uchino, Cacioppo, & Kiecolt-Glaser, 1996; Wills & Cleary, 1996). Sports psychologists have even found that individuals with higher levels of social support are less likely to be injured playing at sports and recover more quickly from injuries they do receive (Hardy, Richman, & Rosenfeld, 1991; Williams & Anderson, 1998). These differences appear to be due to the positive effects of social support upon physiological functioning, including the immune system.

Social Comparison

The influence of group memberships on health and well-being represents only the beginning of the many benefits that we derive from our groups. Perhaps even more fundamentally, the other people in our social environment—and particularly those with whom we share important group memberships—also provide the means by which we develop our entire self-concept (Cooley, 1909; Festinger, 1954; C. Hardin & Higgins, 1996; James, 1890; Rosenberg, 1979).

Social Comparison Theory

The assumption that we learn about ourselves through comparison with others represents the fundamental prediction of social comparison theory (Festinger, 1954; Goethals & Darley, 1977; Suls & Miller, 1977). According to this theory, we learn about our abilities and skills, about the appropriateness and validity of our opinions, and about our relative social standing through **social comparison**—the process of comparing our own attitudes, beliefs, and behaviors with those of others.

One of the important uses of social comparison is to come to a consensual understanding about both how things are and how they should be. The problem is that many of our important beliefs and values are not based upon direct knowledge, but rather are norms that are defined only through social convention. Although we can test whether one chair feels more comfortable than another by sitting in both of them, we are more likely to learn how much punishment is appropriate to give a child or whether we are "good" at golf by comparing our own opinions and abilities with those of relevant others. As Leon Festinger (1954) put it, we use others to provide a social reality (C. Hardin & Higgins, 1996; J. C. Turner, 1991). Sharing opinions and values, or at least knowing how our beliefs compare to those of others, provides a basic sense of understanding.

Abilities

In some cases we use social comparison to help us determine our skills or abilities—how good we are at performing a task or doing or job, for example. When a student looks at another student's paper to see what grade they got, or when we join a tennis club to compare our performance and progress with those of others, we are evaluating our abilities through social comparison. The outcomes of these comparisons can have a substantial impact on our feelings, our attempts to do better, and even on whether or not we want to continue performing the activity. When we compare positively with others, we feel good about ourselves, enjoy the activity, and work harder at it. When we compare negatively with others, however, we are more likely to feel poorly about ourselves, enjoy the activity less, and even stop performing it entirely.

Opinions

In other cases social comparison is used, not to determine our abilities, but rather to help us develop and validate our beliefs, opinions, and values. This type of social comparison occurs primarily on dimensions upon which there is no objectively correct answer, and thus in which we can only rely on the be-

Social Comparison:
The process of learning about our own abilities and opinions by comparing them with the abilities and opinions of others.

liefs of others for information. Answers to questions of values, such as "what should I wear to the formal" or "what kind of music should I have at my wedding?" are frequently determined at least in part by using other others as a basis of comparison.

The extent to which individuals use social comparison to learn how they should feel about something was demonstrated in Stanley Schachter's subsequent research concerning the influence of anxiety on the desire to be with others. As we have discussed earlier, in his initial study Schachter had found that women expecting to undergo severe shock were more likely to want to wait with other women, whereas women who were expecting only a mild shock were more likely to want to wait alone. But in his subsequent research Schachter found that the research participants who were under stress did not want to wait with just any other people. Rather, they were more likely to want to wait with other women who were expecting to undergo the same severe shock than they were than to want to wait with women who were supposedly just waiting to see their professor. Schachter concluded that this was because, although other people might reduce our anxiety just because they were around, we also use others who are in the same situation as we are to help us determine how to feel about things. As Schachter (1959) put it, "Misery doesn't just love any kind of company, it loves only miserable company" (page 24). In this case the women were expecting to use the others to determine how afraid they should be of the upcoming shocks. In short, as predicted by social comparison theory, people use each other to help them understand what is happening to them and to find out how they should feel and respond to their social situations (Gerard, 1963; H. Gerard & Rabbie, 1961; Rofe, 1984).

Equity and Relative Deprivation

People believe that they should be treated fairly, in comparison to other members of their group, and social comparison is used to determine whether this is happening. **Equity** refers to the perception that things are fair, in the sense that people feel that they are receiving rewards that are proportionate to the contributions they make to the group. As an example, in organizations there are often substantial differences in the amount that employees are paid. However, there are also differences in the contribution that the employees make to the group, including the number of years that they have worked for the company, how many hours per week they work, and the level of skill required of them. Equity results when there is a perceived balance between what people contribute to the group and what they get back from it.

When individuals perceive that relationships are equitable, they are generally satisfied, but when they perceive inequity, they are generally dissatis-

Equity: The perception that things are fair, in the sense that people are receiving rewards that are proportionate to the contributions they make to the group.

fied. This disappointment is particularly strong when we feel we are getting less than we deserve (although people who feel they are unfairly getting *more* than they deserve may also feel uncomfortable). One of the potential outcomes of social comparison is the discovery that we (or our in-group) do not compare as well as we might like with a relevant other, given the amount that we (or our group) are perceived to be contributing. In this case of perceived inequity, we say that the person is feeling **relative deprivation** (Adams, 1965; Crosby, 1976; Runciman, 1966). Individual-level or *egoistic* relative deprivation occurs when the individual feels dissatisfaction with his or her own position in comparison to the other members of his or her ingroup. Group-level or *fraternalistic* relative deprivation occurs when the feelings of dissatisfaction arise regarding the position of one's in-group in society as a whole, in comparison to the position of other groups.

Perceived relative deprivation can have a profound influence on thoughts, feelings, and behavior. At the individual level, if individuals believe that they are not receiving the benefits they deserve from their group, they are likely to react in ways that attempt to restore equity. An employee who feels egoistic deprivation may first demand a pay increase, but if this is not successful, he or she may react in other ways, for instance, by not working as hard, by being absent from work more frequently, or by stealing from the corporation (Dittrich & Carrell, 1979; Geurts, Buunk, & Schaufeli, 1994; Oldham, Kulik, Stepina, & Ambrose, 1986).

In terms of group-level, fraternalistic, deprivation, if people feel that their group is being deprived, they may react with negative feelings and attempt to restore equity through social action designed to improve the status of their group. In research studying the attitudes of African Americans, for instance, it has been found that perceptions that blacks are not receiving the outcomes they deserve, in comparison to whites and other competing groups, is a powerful predictor of discontent, militancy, and voting to change the social status (Dion, 1986). We will discuss the process of social change more fully in chapter 11.

To Whom Do We Compare?

The principles of social comparison suggest that, if we have a choice, we will attempt to choose the people (or groups) we use for comparison. When we want to assess our own abilities, we normally prefer to compare to others who are similar to us on relevant dimensions, and yet who are slightly better than us on the dimension being compared. To learn about your skills as a tennis player, for example, you would want to compete with another who is about the same age as you, and who has had about the same amount of experience

Relative Deprivation:
The perception that we (or our in-group) do not compare as positively as we might like with a relevant other or other group.

and training in tennis, because these characteristics are predictive of the ability being compared (Goethals & Darley, 1977). However, you might also want to play with someone who is a bit better than you in order to fully demonstrate your skills and have an opportunity to improve.

When comparing with others to determine our important values, on the other hand, social comparison is particularly likely to be made with members of relevant reference groups (Kelley, 1952). For example, we would likely choose members of our family, peers, or a religious group to help us validate our opinions about the appropriateness of our religious beliefs because we respect and admire these people and their opinions.

Using Others to Feel Good

Although we use social comparison in part to come to accurate conclusions about our abilities and to determine the validity of our opinions, in other cases we may use others not so much for gaining an accurate picture, but rather to determine how to feel emotionally about ourselves. When we are able to compare ourselves favorably with others, we feel good, but when the outcome of comparison suggests that others are better, or better off than we are, we are likely to feel bad.

Because most people naturally want to feel good, we frequently attempt to make positive social comparisons with others. When we are able to create a positive image of ourselves through favorable comparisons with others who are worse off than we are, the process is known as *downward social comparison* (Goethals & Darley, 1977; Wood, 1989). Downward social comparison helps us deal with situations by making our own circumstances seem less negative. For example, Morse and Gergen (1970) had students apply for a job, and they also presented the students with another individual who was applying for the same job. When the other candidate was made to appear to be less qualified for the job than they were, the students reported higher self-esteem (presumably as a result of the downward comparison) than they did when the other applicant was seen as a very highly competent job candidate. Also demonstrating the tendency for downward comparison, Wood, Taylor, and Lichtman (1985) found that women who were suffering from breast cancer preferred to compare their condition with other individuals whose current condition and likely prognosis was worse than their own.

Although downward comparison provides us with positive feelings, *upward social comparison* (when we compare ourselves with others who are better off than we are) is also possible. Upward comparison is useful because it can provide information that can help us do better, and gives us hope (C. Snyder, Cheavens, & Sympson, 1997; S. E. Taylor & Lobel, 1989). But upward comparison can of course lead us to feel bad about ourselves, particularly when the comparison is with another person who excels on a task or dimension that we find important. We may be able to enjoy the success of others who are close to us when they excel in domains that we do not care about, but nevertheless feel jealous and insecure when others do better than we do on dimensions that are important to our self-concept (Lockwood & Kunda, 1997; Tesser, 1988; Tesser & Campbell, 1983).

The Trade-off

In some cases the two goals of social comparison—obtaining an accurate picture of ourselves and our social world and gaining positive self-esteem—work hand in hand. Getting the best grade in the class on an important exam produces accurate knowledge about our skills in the domain as well as positive self-esteem. But doing poorly on an exam produces conflicting, contradictory outcomes. The poor score indicates that we have not mastered the subject, but at the same time makes us feel bad.

In these cases of conflict, one or other of the goals may well override the other. Sometimes the goal of feeling good overrides the accuracy goal. For example, Major, Sciacchitano, and Crocker (1993) found that when male college students were told that they had outperformed other students on an important task, they used downward social comparison to bolster their self-esteem, regardless of whether they thought the other students were members of their own group or members of an out-group. However, when the men were told that they had performed more poorly than the other students, they only made the relevant upward comparison when they thought the other students were similar to them. Thus it appeared that the men were taking advantage of the opportunity to bolster self-esteem when downward comparison was beneficial, regardless of the similarity of the other, but used the differences between themselves and the comparison others to avoid having to make social comparisons when doing so would have brought negative feelings and low self-esteem.

Social Identity

To this point we have primarily considered the processes of social comparison in terms of single individuals comparing their opinions or abilities with those of another individual. Although we have seen that these comparisons are often made with members of important reference groups, we have not yet considered the possibility that individuals might use their group memberships—and comparisons of their group with other groups—to create positive self-esteem. One method of gaining positive self-esteem is to be a member of one or more social groups that make us feel good about ourselves. And being a member of an important and valued social group is best achieved when those groups compare positively to other groups.

Creating Social Identity

As we have seen in chapter 1, social identity refers to the part of the self-concept that is derived from our membership in social groups and our attachments to those groups (Branscombe, Wann, Noel, & Coleman, 1993; Deaux, 1996; Ethier & Deaux, 1994; P. Oakes & Turner, 1980; Oakes, Haslam, & Turner, 1994; M. Rubin & Hewstone, 1998; Tajfel, 1981). Normally, social identity results in positive feelings, which occur because we perceive our own groups, and thus ourselves, in a positive light. If you are a "Midwesterner at heart," or if you live in the "best fraternity house on campus," being part of this group is part of what you are, and it makes you feel good about yourself.

Eliot Smith and his colleagues (E. R. Smith & Henry, 1996) tested the hypothesis that people's thoughts about their in-groups would become linked in memory to their thoughts about themselves. In the research, college students first described themselves and their in-groups according to 90 different traits. Then, at a later experimental session the participants sat at a computer and judged, by answering either yes or no, whether each of those traits was descriptive of themselves, while the computer recorded how long it took them to make each decision. As shown in Figure 3.2, the results showed that participants were significantly faster at responding to traits that they had earlier described as descriptive of both themselves and their in-groups, in comparison to the traits that they thought were true of themselves but not of the in-group. Furthermore they were also significantly faster at rejecting traits that

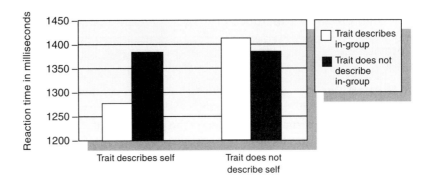

FIGURE 3.2. The in-group becomes part of the self. Reaction times to traits that are or are not descriptive of the self and that are or are not descriptive of an important in-group. The data are from Smith, E. R., & Henry, S. (1996). An in-group becomes part of the self: Response time evidence. *Personality and Social Psychology Bulletin, 22*, 635–642.

were not true of themselves or the in-group than at rejecting traits that were not true of the in-group but were true of themselves. These results suggest that beliefs about the self and beliefs about the in-group had become linked in memory—that the in-group had indeed "become part of the self."

Social Identity and Self-esteem

Because being a member of a valued social group can increase our self-esteem, we may go out of our way to emphasize these memberships (C. R. Snyder, Lassegard, & Ford, 1986). Robert Cialdini and his colleagues (Cialdini et al., 1976) conducted an observational study in which they observed the clothes and clothing accessories that university students at different U.S. universities wore to classes on Mondays during the fall semester. When the university football team had won its game on Saturday, students were likely to emphasize their university memberships by wearing clothing, such as sweatshirts and hats, with the symbols of their university on them. However, they were significantly less likely to wear university clothing on the Mondays that followed a football loss. Furthermore, in a study in which students from the university were asked to describe a victory by their university team, they frequently used the term "we," whereas when asked to describe a game in which their school lost, they used the term "we" significantly less frequently. Emphasizing that "we're a good school" and "we beat them" evidently provided a social identity for these students, allowing them to feel good about themselves.

Varieties of Self-categorization

The findings of Cialdini and his colleagues are important not only because they show that we use our group memberships to create positive self-esteem, but also because they indicate how flexibly we do it. The students in this study differentially emphasized or downplayed their membership as students at their university, depending upon the extent to which that group membership was able to provide them with a positive social identity. When their team had won, they emphasized their group membership with the university, but when it lost, they did not. Thus people creatively use their group memberships to help them gain positive self-esteem. It has even been found that people will change the language, accents, or slang that they use in conversation in order to emphasize their group memberships and their differences from others (Bourhis, Giles, Leyens, & Tajfel, 1979; Sachdev & Bourhis, 1990).

Which of our many category identities is most important varies from day to day, as a function of the particular situation we are in. Seeing an American flag hanging outside a post office may remind of us our national identity, whereas walking across campus and seeing the school library may remind us of our college identity. Identity can also be heightened when our identity is threatened by conflict with another group—such as during an important sports game with another university.

Which Groups Provide Social Identity?

The ability to be flexible is enhanced because each individual has multiple potential self-categorizations, including school and religious memberships, sports, hobbies, and fraternities, as well as many other social categories, each of which is a potential source of social identity (Deaux, Reid, Mizrahi, & Ethier, 1995; Hinkle & Brown, 1990). As a result, which of the many group memberships a person emphasizes at a given time will depend on the situation as well as the person's goals in that situation (Stryker & Serpe, 1994). In one descriptive study, Kay Deaux and her colleagues (1995) asked college students to sort a list of social identities. As shown in Figure 3.3, the students sorted them into a variety of categories, including personal relationships, ethnic and religious groups, political affiliations, occupations and hobbies, and stigmatized groups.

Limits to Social Identity

Although people generally enjoy being in groups, in part because they can gain social identity from their group memberships, not all groups produce social identity for all people all of the time.

Does Everyone Identify?

Although it is assumed that most people gain at least some positive social identity through their group memberships, individuals differ in the extent to which they use their group memberships to create social identity. We might say that some people are primarily individual-oriented, gaining their self-esteem from their own personal accomplishments, whereas others find their group memberships more important to them and base their personal self-worth on those memberships. Differences in group identification can be assessed through self-report measures, such as the one shown in Figure 3.4 (Luhtanen & Crocker, 1992).

One advantage of being highly identified with a group is that people may in some cases be able to gain self-esteem from their group memberships even when their own individual outcomes are not very positive. Schmitt, Silvia, and Branscombe (2000) had groups of female college students perform a creativity task, and then gave them feedback indicating that, although they themselves had performed very poorly, another woman in their group had performed

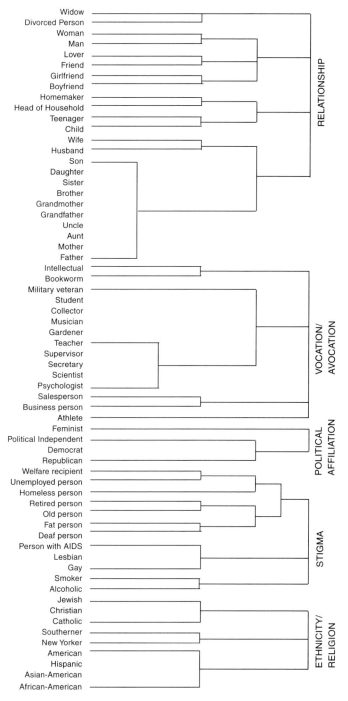

FIGURE 3.3. Varieties of social identities. This figure represents some of the many social identities reported by a sample of college students. Data are from Deaux, K., Reid, A., Mizrahi, K., & Ethier, K. A. (1995). Parameters of social identity. *Journal of Personality and Social Psychology, 68*, 280–291.

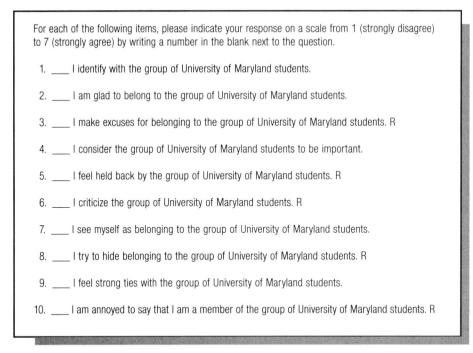

For each of the following items, please indicate your response on a scale from 1 (strongly disagree) to 7 (strongly agree) by writing a number in the blank next to the question.

1. ___ I identify with the group of University of Maryland students.

2. ___ I am glad to belong to the group of University of Maryland students.

3. ___ I make excuses for belonging to the group of University of Maryland students. R

4. ___ I consider the group of University of Maryland students to be important.

5. ___ I feel held back by the group of University of Maryland students. R

6. ___ I criticize the group of University of Maryland students. R

7. ___ I see myself as belonging to the group of University of Maryland students.

8. ___ I try to hide belonging to the group of University of Maryland students. R

9. ___ I feel strong ties with the group of University of Maryland students.

10. ___ I am annoyed to say that I am a member of the group of University of Maryland students. R

FIGURE 3.4. A measure of social identity. This 10-item scale is used to measure identification with students at the University of Maryland, but it could be modified to assess identification with any group. The items marked with an R are reversed before the average of the scale is computed The scale was originally reported in Luhtanen, R., & Crocker, J. (1992). A collective self-esteem scale: Self-evaluation of one's social identity. *Personality and Social Psychology Bulletin, 18*, 302–318.

very well. Furthermore, in some experimental conditions the women were told that the research was comparing the scores of men and women (which was designed to increase categorization by gender). In these conditions, rather than being saddened by the upward comparison with the other woman, participants used the successful performance of the other woman to feel good about themselves, through their identification with the social category of women.

Low Status Groups

A person who is overweight may see himself as a member of a group that includes other overweight people, but may not gain any social identity from this categorization—in fact, the categorization may provide more costs than benefits. And people who are not earning much money in their current job may envy other people who belong to groups that have more money or prestige. What do people do when they find themselves in a group that has low status, and which therefore does not provide them with a positive social identity?

As predicted by social exchange theory, one approach is to simply leave the group, assuming that is possible. If you can lose weight, find a better job, or make friends with higher-status people, you'll likely do that. Of course, leaving isn't always that easy. People cannot change their racial group membership, and losing weight or moving to a higher-status clique are also difficult, if not impossible, tasks. If the individual cannot physically leave the group, he or she may attempt to leave it psychologically, by attempting to distance himself or herself from it (Gibbons, Gerrard, Lando, & McGovern, 1991), perhaps attempting to convince him or herself that he or she is not a member of the group after all ("I'm really not that fat!")

If leaving the group doesn't work, another approach is to try to perceive the group as positively as possible, perhaps by focusing on dimensions upon which the group does not compare so unfavorably. African Americans, who are frequently the target of negative beliefs in U.S. society, may decide that their cultural background is a positive aspect of their personality. Or someone who is overweight may emphasize his or her sense of humor. Finally, as we will see in chapter 11, in some cases the individuals may try to change the situation through social action, such as civil rights activities, the development of social movements, or revolutionary activity (Tajfel, 1978; Tajfel & Turner, 1979).

Optimal Distinctiveness

Although individuals do gain social identity from their group memberships, people do not want *only* to be seen as a group member. According to the principle of **optimal distinctiveness** (M. B. Brewer, 1991), there is a dynamic tension between drives for distinctiveness (considering oneself as a unique individual) and inclusiveness (feeling part of a group). Therefore individuals desire not only to identify with social groups, but also to maintain their own personal identities. When we are made to feel too much like a part of an interchangeable group member, we attempt to emphasize our uniqueness. On the other hand, when we are made to feel too different from others, we attempt to recapture our group connections.

In short, although group identity is important, it is not everything. People do not get a great deal of identity out of large social groups, because they become too "lost" in the group. On the other hand, being completely different from others is also not desirable. It seems that smaller groups, in which our needs for uniqueness and our needs for social acceptance are balanced, produce the most social identity (Mullen, Brown, & Smith, 1992; Simon & Brown, 1987; Simon & Pettigrew, 1990). Although we all desire a balance between thinking of ourselves as unique individuals (our personal identity) and thinking of ourselves as group members (our social identity), some people

Optimal Distinctiveness: The tendency of individuals to prefer to maintain both their independent as well as their interdependent cultural orientations.

nevertheless derive more of their self-esteem from their social identities than others do.

 ## *Chapter Summary*

Social groups exist because they provide important benefits both to the group and to the members of those groups. According to social exchange theory, group members exchange social rewards and costs with each other, each attempting to maximize their outcomes by increasing the benefits and reducing the costs of group membership. Although individuals may leave groups that do not provide positive outcomes for them, this will only occur when the perceived costs of leaving the group are not seen as even more negative than staying in the group.

One type of benefit provided by groups is to help in survival by allowing efficient use of resources and providing defense. We also use groups to accomplish goals, such as completing tasks and making decisions. Social groups also serve to reduce anxiety by allowing us to learn how others are reacting to potentially dangerous situations. Developing a satisfactory attachment style with one's family members as a child improves the ability to have meaningful relationships with others as an adult. And individuals who perceive that they have adequate social support, in the form of stable, positive relationships with others, have both better mental and physical health. The lack of support, which may occur when people are ostracized or ignored by others, produces loneliness.

We also use other people to help us validate our opinions and to learn about our own abilities through the process of social comparison. We determine our abilities by comparing with others who are similar on relevant dimensions, but are likely to validate our opinions through comparison with appropriate reference groups. In some cases the goal of gaining accurate knowledge and the goal of obtaining positive self-esteem may be in conflict, and the individual must prioritize one goal or the other.

Social identity involves using our group memberships to feel good about ourselves. This occurs when we see the groups that we belong to as better than groups that we do not belong to. Individuals differ in the extent to which they identify with social groups and in the extent to which they gain their personal self-esteem through their group memberships. The ability to gain positive social identity is enhanced by the flexible use of the wide variety of group memberships available to us. When our group memberships do not provide social identity, we may either leave the group or attempt to use social creativity strategies to regain positive identity.

Although people do enjoy being part of their social groups, they prefer a balance between their group memberships and their individual personalities.

When we feel too similar to other group members, we attempt to enhance our uniqueness, but when we feel too different from others, we attempt to emphasize our group memberships.

 Review and Discussion Questions

1. Why, according to social exchange theory, do individuals join and leave social groups?
2. Review the benefits of joining groups. Then consider some groups that you belong to and how they fulfill these needs.
3. Do you think that the friendships developed over the Internet are as rewarding as those developed in person? Why or why not?
4. What are attachment styles, and how do they influence how people behave in groups?
5. What is social support, and what benefits does it provide? Who provides you with social support?
6. What are the functions of social comparison, and how do we use it to learn about ourselves? Consider a time when downward social comparison made you feel good about yourself or when upward social comparison made you feel bad.
7. How do people use their group memberships to create social identity? Complete the items on the collective self-esteem scale shown in Figure 3.4 and consider whether you are a person who is likely to create self-esteem through social identification.
8. Do people always prefer to maximize their social identities? Which people are most likely to do so, and under what circumstances?

Recommended Readings

Evolutionary psychology and its influence on group behavior:
Buss, D., & Kenrick, D. (1998). Evolutionary social psychology. In D. T. Gilbert & S. T. Fiske & G. Lindzey (Eds.), *Handbook of Social Psychology* (4th ed., Vol. 2, pp. 982–1026). Boston: McGraw-Hill.

The original formulation of social comparison theory:
Festinger, L. (1954). A theory of social comparison processes. *Human Relations, 7*, 117–140.

A summary of social categorization theory:
Turner, J. C. (1987). *Rediscovering the Social Group: A Self-Categorization Theory*. Oxford: Blackwell.

Social
Influence 4

As we have seen in chapter 1, one of the most fundamental assumptions about social groups is that the members of those groups will be similar to each other, in the sense that they share important values and beliefs (Asch, 1955; Bar-Tal, 1990, 2000; Festinger, Schachter, & Back, 1950; Newcomb, 1943, 1961, 1963; Sherif, 1936; J. C. Turner, 1991). Although this sharing occurs in part because similar individuals are likely to initially join or form groups, similarity is also increased as the group functions, through the tendency for group members to act in ways that lead other group members to come to share their beliefs. The focus of this chapter is on when and how this sharing—or *social influence*—occurs. We will see that social influence is a ubiquitous part of social life, occurring both in small working groups as well as in large social categories.

Social Influence

Social influence refers to the processes through which individuals or groups change the thoughts, feelings, and behaviors of others. Although social influence is a broad concept that is discussed in every chapter of this book, including processes such as social comparison, social categorization, and the influence of others on decision making and task performance, we will focus in this chapter on one particular type of social influence—the influence that leads individuals to adhere to group norms.

Social influence is usually in a direction such that the individual's beliefs become more similar to those of the other group members, and thus the outcome of social influence is a general tendency for members of social groups to share important beliefs and values (Festinger et al., 1950). In some cases social influence occurs in a passive sense, without any obvious intent of one person to change the other. In essence, passive social influence involves learning about and adopting the norms of the groups that we are part of and accepting those norms simply because we are part of the group. Passive social influence occurs when a young child learns the beliefs and values of his or her parents, and when we laugh at a joke that we don't even find funny just because everyone else is laughing. The outcome of passive social influence is that the group members end up sharing social norms—holding similar beliefs and values and engaging in similar behaviors. In many cases passive social influence occurs even though neither the individuals who provide the influence nor the persons who are being influenced are aware of it.

In other cases social influence involves one or more individuals actively attempting to change the beliefs of others, with the explicit goal of getting them to accept the social norms, even though the person they are attempting to persuade may not initially want to change. In this case both parties are likely to be aware of the influence attempt, and those who are being influenced may try to resist the pressure to change their beliefs. Such active social influence ranges from the attempts of the members of a jury to get a dissenting member to change his or her opinion to the brainwashing techniques used on prisoners of war. Successful active influence requires communicating the beliefs that it is desired the others adopt, monitoring whether the others have

Social Influence: The processes through which individual or groups change the thoughts, feelings, and behaviors of others.

acted in accord with the communication, and using methods for punishing or reprimanding individuals who are not in accord, for instance, by threatening ostracism or rejecting the individual from the group entirely (Israel, 1956; J. M. Levine, 1980; Orcutt, 1973; Schachter, 1951). The change in opinion or behavior that is the result of social influence is known as **conformity** (Allen, 1965; Crutchfield, 1955; Deutsch & Gerard, 1955; Festinger et al., 1950; Kelman, 1961; J. M. Levine & Russo, 1987; J. C. Turner, 1991).

Some Examples of Influence

One way of understanding the variety of types of social influence is to consider some concrete examples. In the following section we will consider four examples of social influence as it has been captured in classic social science research. And we will see that these examples vary both in terms of whether the conformity involves opinions or behaviors and whether the influence is active or passive.

The Development of Social Norms

In a series of important studies on social influence, Muzafer Sherif (1935, 1936) used a perceptual phenomenon known as the *autokinetic effect* to study the outcomes of passive social influence on the development of group norms. The autokinetic effect is caused by the involuntary movements of our eyes that occur as we view objects, and which allow us to focus upon stimuli in our environment. However, when individuals are placed in a dark room that contains only a single small point of light, these eye movements produce an unusual effect for the perceiver—they make the point of light appear to move.

Sherif took advantage of this effect to study how group norms develop in ambiguous situations. In one of his studies, college students were placed in a room with the point of light and asked to indicate, each time the light was turned on, how much it appeared to be moving. Some participants first made their judgments alone. Sherif found that although each participant made estimates that were within a relatively narrow range (as if they had developed their own "individual" norm), there were wide variations in the size of these judgments among the different participants he studied.

Sherif also found that when individuals who initially had made very different estimates were then placed in groups with one or two other individuals, and in which all of the group members gave their responses on each trial aloud (each time in a different random order), the initial differences in judgments among the participants began to disappear, such that the group members eventually began to make very similar judgments. This pattern is shown in Figure 4.1.

Conformity: The change in opinion or behavior that is the result of social influence.

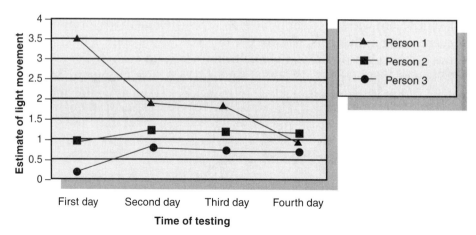

FIGURE 4.1. The development of group norms. As participants who initially have different beliefs begin to share them with other group members, a common group norm develops. This figure shows the estimates of light movement made by a group of three participants who met together on four days. Data are from Sherif, M. (1936). *The psychology of social norms.* New York: Harper & Row.

Furthermore, and indicating that the participants had really changed their opinions, these group norms continued to influence judgments when the individuals were later again tested alone. The participants did not revert back to their initial opinions, even though they were quite free to do so, but rather stayed with the new group norms. Interestingly, these conformity effects appear to have been passive, because they were out of the awareness of most participants. Sherif (1936, p. 108) reports that the majority of the participants indicated after the experiment was over that their judgments had *not* been influenced by the judgments made by the other group members.

In other studies Sherif created norms within small groups of participants by placing in the group a confederate who gave unusual responses (by estimating extremely large movements for the light). He found that these responses also influenced the group norm, such that the norms in the group tended to cluster around the large estimates made by the confederate. And these norms again continued to influence the judgments of the other group members (the research participants) when they were moved into new groups of individuals who were also judging the light movement. The norms persisted through several "generations" (Jacobs & Campbell, 1961; MacNeil & Sherif, 1976), and could influence individual judgments up to a year after the individual was last tested (Rohrer, Baron, Hoffman, & Swander, 1954).

Binge Eating in Sororities

Whereas Sherif studied conformity in a relatively artificial laboratory situation, Christian Crandall (1988) studied conformity using a correlational research design in a more ecologically valid setting—among members of sororities on a college campus. Crandall was interested in how norms influenced the prevalence of a behavior known as bulimia. Bulimia is a cycle of binge eating followed by self-induced vomiting that can cause severe health consequences. Unfortunately, many college women practice this dangerous behavior.

Crandall gave out questionnaires to the women in two different sororities at the University of Florida, asking them about both their binge eating behavior and about their friendships and friendship preferences within the sorority. On the basis of their responses, Crandall determined that the two sororities differed in the prevalence of binge eating. Bingeing was very frequent among the members in one sorority, but was not as common in the other. On the basis of the friendship data, Crandall also created a sociometric measure indicating the popularity of each of the members of each sorority.

Crandall then created a measure that indicated, for each member, how far from the norm was each woman's binge eating behavior. Thus, any woman could be at about the average, above the average, or below the average of her sorority in terms of her frequency of bingeing. The important finding was that the correlation between a woman's popularity and her correspondence to the sorority norm was positive, and statistically significant, in both sororities. The more popular girls, as measured by the sociometric measure, were closer to the norm, regardless of whether the norm was for a lot of bingeing or only a small amount. In short, bingeing was not a good thing in itself, but being close to the norm was. Although the study is based on correlational data, making causal conclusions difficult to draw, the results are consistent with the hypothesis that the girls in both sororities binged (or didn't binge) because it was the normative thing to do. To be popular, the girls had to engage in the behavior that was normative within their group.

Reacting to Opinion Deviance

Although the research of Sherif and Crandall focused on passive conformity, research conducted by Stanley Schachter (1951) was designed to test a basic principle of social influence—that group members will use (in this case very active) influence to bring deviant group members into line with group norms. Schachter invited men to participate in small "clubs" that were discussing current topics. The task given to the groups was to discuss a legal case that involved a runaway teenager named Johnny Rocco. The case information explained that Rocco had begun to get in trouble with the police, and the men in the discussion club were asked to decide on a course of treatment for him that could range from very mild to very harsh punishment for his transgressions.

Schachter placed three confederates in each group session who provided either agreeing or dissenting opinions during the group discussion. In each

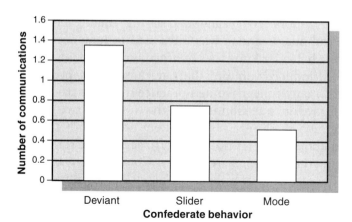

FIGURE 4.2. Modes, sliders, and deviants. Group members directed more comments toward other members who held positions that were deviant from the group norm than they did toward individuals who either acted in accord with group norms (the "mode") or those who were slowly coming to agree with the group norm (the "slider"). Data are from Schachter, S. (1951). Deviation, rejection and communication. *Journal of Abnormal and Social Psychology, 46,* 190–207.

group, one of the confederates always expressed opinions that were in complete agreement with the group's initial opinion (Schachter called this confederate the "mode"). If the group opinion shifted in any direction, the mode always went along with it. Another confederate played the role of the "deviant" by adopting a position that was opposite of the group's overall opinion and never changing this position. Finally, the third confederate played the role of the "slider" by initially arguing against the group's opinion and then slowly shifting his position to agree with the majority as the conversation continued.

Schachter measured two dependent variables in his experiment. First, he assessed the amount of attempted social influence, in the form of communication, which was directed at each of the confederates. As shown in Figure 4.2, Schachter found that more communication was directed toward the deviant than to the other confederates, reflecting the desire to bring his opinions into line with the rest of the group (there were some cases, however, in which the group members rejected the deviant entirely, gave up on the possibility of ever persuading him to agree with the rest of the group, and in these cases the amount of communication directed toward him therefore decreased). Secondly, after the discussion ended, the group members were asked to rate their liking for each person, as well as recommending them for nomination for various committees. The results showed that the deviant was particularly disliked, in comparison to the mode and the slider, and that the deviant was also assigned to lower status committees.

Group Persuasion

An important set of experiments by Kurt Lewin (Lewin & Gold, 1999, chapter 10) was designed to compare several methods of encouraging American housewives to engage in behaviors that they would not normally engage in, such as serving unusual meats (kidneys and hearts) to their families and feeding cod liver oil to babies. This research had a particular applied focus, because it was conducted during World War II, and the behaviors that were encouraged were expected to have a positive influence on the United States' war effort.

Small groups of about 15 housewives were gathered to hear a lecture emphasizing the importance of these behaviors to the U.S. economy and the war effort as well as presenting information about the nutritional value of the food items. In some of the experimental conditions, in addition to hearing the lecture, the women also then discussed the issue among themselves with the goal of coming to agreement on their opinions about the appropriateness of the behavior. The women were then asked to indicate whether or not they expected to actually engage in the behavior in the near future. The results showed that the women were significantly more likely to indicate that they would engage in the behavior when they had discussed the issue with the others than when they had only heard the lecture. In short, the group discussion, including the goal of coming to a common agreement, changed group norms about the appropriate behaviors and also encouraged the women to conform to the new norms (Festinger et al., 1950; Lott, 1961).

Motives for Conformity

As you can see from these examples, social influence can take a variety of forms. But in each case, the people conform to the influence because doing so provides some benefits, either for those who are conforming, for those who are doing the influencing, or for both of the parties. Let us now consider in more detail the reasons that people might conform to others.

Informational Conformity

Sometimes we conform to others because we believe that they have valid knowledge about an opinion or issue. The change in opinions that occurs as a result of a desire for accurate knowledge is known as *informational conformity* (Deutsch & Gerard, 1955). As we have seen in chapter 3, informational conformity is the end result of social comparison, a process that involves comparing one's own opinion to those of others to gain an accurate appraisal of the validity of an opinion. Social comparison and its resulting informational conformity provide much of our knowledge about the world around us (Festinger et al., 1950; Hardin & Higgins, 1996; Orive, 1988; Turner, 1991). We base our own beliefs on those presented to us by reporters, scientists, doctors, counselors, and lawyers because we believe they have more expertise in certain fields than we do. Thus, one reason for conformity is to develop and inform our opinions, and we do so because we believe that the knowledge or opinions held by others are correct and accurate.

Because the goal of social comparison is to understand and have accurate opinions, conformity to others perceived to be knowledgeable is likely to be real, in the sense that the opinions of the individual are changed to be in line with the beliefs of others. Thus, the result of informational influence is **private acceptance**, or real change in opinions on the part of the individual (Allen, 1965; Eagly & Chaiken, 1993; Kaplan & Miller, 1987; C. A. Kiesler & Kiesler, 1969).

Normative Conformity

In other cases conformity occurs not so much from the pursuit of valid knowledge, but rather to gain social rewards, such as the pleasure of belonging and being accepted by a group that we care about, and to avoid social costs or punishments, such as being ostracized, embarrassed, or ridiculed by others (Deutsch & Gerard, 1955; Kelley, 1952). *Normative conformity* occurs when we express opinions or behave in ways that help us to be accepted or that keep us from being isolated or rejected by the group. It is no surprise that individuals wish to conform to the group norms, because group members frequently withhold rewards from or even punish those who are deviant, even when this deviance is not particularly important for meeting the group's goals.

In contrast to informational conformity, in which the opinions of the individual change to match that of the influencers, normative conformity often represents *public compliance* rather than private acceptance. **Public compliance** involves a change in behavior (including the public expression of opinions) that is not accompanied by an actual change in one's private opinion. Thus, compliance represents what people do or say in public, even though they believe something different in private. We may obey the speed limit or wear a tie (behavior) to conform to social norms, even though we may not necessarily believe that it is appropriate to do so (opinion). However, behaviors that are originally performed out of a desire to be accepted (normative conformity) may frequently produce changes in beliefs to match them, and the result becomes private acceptance (for instance, a child who begins smoking to please his friends, but soon convinces himself that it is the right thing to do, or a prisoner of war who eventually accepts the political beliefs of his captor).

Private Acceptance: Conformity that involves real change in opinions on the part of the individual

Public Compliance: A change in behavior (including the public expression of opinions) that is not accompanied by an actual change in one's private opinion.

Differentiating Motives for Conformity

Although in some cases conformity may be purely informational or normative, it is probably safe to conclude that motivations to be accurate and motivations to be liked often go hand in hand, and thus that informational and normative conformity often occur at the same time. For instance, in Sherif's studies using the autokinetic effect, individuals probably changed their opinions to match those of other group members both because they thought that the others had valid information about the actual movement of the light, and also because they wished to avoid having to express opinions that were different from everyone else's. Similarly, in Crandall's research on bulimia, the sorority women probably conformed to the eating norms of their sorority to be liked, but they may also have decided that, since so many others were engaging in the behaviors, those behaviors were appropriate and valid.

Although informational conformity can usually be expected to lead to private acceptance, normative conformity may produce either compliance or acceptance (the latter occurring when the behaviors that were initially performed merely to avoid rejection later become to be seen as correct or appropriate). Therefore, it has been argued (e.g., Turner, 1991) that the distinction between informational and normative conformity is more apparent than real and that it may not be possible to fully differentiate them.

Majority Influence

Although social influence occurs whenever group members change their opinions or behaviors as a result of the actual or expected presence of others, it has been traditional to divide such influence into two major types. **Majority influence** is said to occur when a larger number of individuals in the current social group (the *majority subgroup*) attempt to change the opinions or behaviors of a smaller number of individuals (the *minority subgroup*). On the other hand, **minority influence** is said to occur when the minority attempts to change the majority.

Solomon Asch's Line Perception Studies

Solomon Asch (1952, 1955) conducted some of the best-known studies demonstrating the power of majority social influence. In contrast to autokinetic effect experiments conducted by Sherif, in which the task to be judged was very ambiguous, Asch used tasks in which the correct and incorrect answers to the judgments were very clear. In these studies the research participants were male college students who were told that they were to be participating in

Majority Influence:
Influence that occurs when a larger subgroup produces change in a smaller subgroup.

Minority Influence:
Influence that occurs when a smaller subgroup produces change in a larger subgroup.

a test of visual abilities. The men were seated in a small semicircle in front of a board that was to display the visual stimuli to be judged. They were told that there would be 18 trials during the experiment, and on each trial they would see two cards. One card, called the standard card, had a single line that was to be judged in comparison to the three lines on the test card:

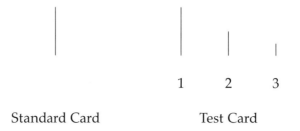

Standard Card   Test Card

The task of the men was simply to indicate which line on the test card was the same length as the line on the standard card. Note that in this case the correct answer is unambiguous. As you can see in the example above, there is no question that correct answer is line 1. In fact, Asch found that people did not make mistakes on the task when they made their judgments alone.

On each trial the participants were to each state their answer out loud, beginning with one end of the semicircle and moving down the row. Because the participant was seated next to last in the row, he always made his judgment following most of the other group members. Unbeknown to him, however, the other group members were actually not participants, but experimental confederates who gave predetermined answers on each trial. Although on the first two trials the confederates each gave the correct answer, on the third and on eleven of the subsequent trials, they had been instructed to all give the same wrong choice. For instance, even though the correct answer was line 1 they would all say it was line 2. Thus, when it became the participant's turn to answer, he could either give the clearly correct answer or conform to the incorrect responses of the confederates. Remarkably, in this study about 76 percent of the 123 men who were tested gave at least one incorrect response when it was their turn. This is indeed evidence for the power of social conformity. However, conformity was not absolute—in addition to the 24 percent of the men who never conformed at all, only 5 percent of the men conformed on all 12 of the critical trials.

Determinants of Influence

That fact that at least some people will conform to the majority opinion even when it means making an obviously incorrect judgment provides support for a basic assumption of the group dynamics approach—there is a general pressure toward similarity in groups. However, although this study does point out the power that some situations have to produce conformity, conformity is nevertheless more likely in some groups than in others, and the social factors that produce it are well known.

Number of Persons in the Majority

As the number of people in the majority increases, relative to the number of persons in the minority, pressure on the minority to conform also increases (Latané, 1981; Mullen, 1983). Asch conducted replications of his original study in which he varied the number of confederates (the majority subgroup members) who gave initial incorrect responses from 1 to 16 people, while holding the number in the minority subgroup constant at one (the single research participant). You may not be shocked to hear the results: the bigger the majority, the more likely it was that the lone participant gave the incorrect answer.

Increases in the size of the majority increase conformity, regardless of whether the conformity is informational or normative. In terms of informational conformity, if more people express an opinion, the listener will assume that they have more information and that their position is therefore more valid. Thus, bigger majorities should result in more informational conformity. But larger majorities will also produce more normative conformity, because being different will be harder when the majority is bigger, due to the fact that the individual's differing behavior will be more obvious. As the majority gets bigger, the individual giving the different opinion becomes more aware of being different, and this produces a greater need to conform to the prevailing norm.

Social Impact

Although increasing the size of the majority does increase conformity, this is only true up to a point. The increase in the amount of conformity that is produced by adding new members to the majority group (known as the **social impact** of each group member) is greater for initial majority members than it is for later members (Latané, 1981). This pattern is shown in Figure 4.3, which presents data from a well-known experiment by Milgram, Bickman, and Berkowitz (1969) that studied how the number of people gawking on a city street increases the number of people who stop to gawk themselves. The research was an experimental design in which confederates in groups ranging from 1 to 15 gathered on 42nd Street in New York City, in front of the Graduate Center of the City University of New York, and craned their necks, looking up at a window on the 6th floor of the building. A video camera in the room recorded the behavior of 1,424 pedestrians who passed along the sidewalk. As

Social Impact: The increase in the amount of conformity that is produced by each new member added to a group.

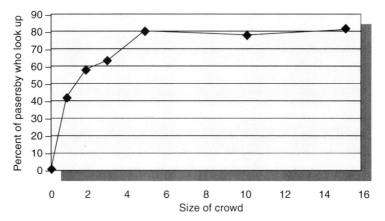

FIGURE 4.3. Social impact. This figure shows the average number of trials on which there was conformity in different conditions of Stanley Milgram's study on the streets of New York. You can see that the amount of conformity increases dramatically until there are five participants, after which it levels off. Similar patterns have been found in many other studies of conformity. Data are from Milgram, S., Bickman, L., & Berkowitz, L. (1969). Note on the drawing power of crowds of different size. *Journal of Personality and Social Psychology, 13,* 79–82.

shown in Figure 4.3, increases in the number of confederates increased the number of passersby who also stopped and looked up, but the influence of each additional confederate was less than it was for the individual before that.[1] In short, just as turning on the first light in an initially dark room makes more difference in the brightness of the room than turning on the second, third, and fourth lights does, adding more and more people to the majority tends to have less and less effect on conformity.

Group size is an extremely important variable that influences a wide variety of behaviors of the individuals in the group. For instance, people leave proportionally smaller tips in restaurants as the number in their party increases, and people are less likely to help as the number of bystanders to the incident increases (Latané, 1981). Furthermore, as we will see in chapters to come, the number of group members also has an important influence on individuals' performance in the group. In each case, this influence of group size on behavior is found to be in a relationship very similar to that shown in Figure 4.3.

Perceptions of the Group

As you can see in Figure 4.3, the ability of new individuals in the group to create more social influence eventually levels off entirely, such that adding more people to the majority after that point makes essentially no difference.

---

1. The relationship between the number of individuals and influence can be mathematically expressed as a power function: Influence = (number of individuals)^t where t is between 0 and 1.

This peak usually occurs when the majority has about 4 or 5 persons. One reason that the impact of new group members decreases so rapidly is because, as the number in the group increases, the individuals in the majority quickly become to be seen more as a group, rather than as separate individuals. When there are only a couple of individuals in the majority, each person is likely to be seen as an individual, holding his or her own unique opinions, and each new individual adds to the impact. As a result, two people are more influential than one, and three more influential than two. However, as the number of individuals grows, and particularly when those individuals are perceived as being able to communicate with each other, it becomes more and more likely that the individuals will be seen as a group rather than as individuals and so adding new members does not change that perception. Regardless of whether there are four, five, or more members, the group is still just a group. As a result, the expressed opinions or behaviors of the group members no longer seem to reflect their own characteristics so much as they do that of the group as a whole, and thus they are less able to influence.

To demonstrate that group perceptions are important determinants of conformity, David Wilder (1977) presented research participants with information about others' judgments in a fictitious court case before they were asked to give their own opinion. Furthermore, he varied both the number of other individuals whose opinions were available and the number of groups that these individuals were supposedly working in. The individuals all expressed support for one of the defendants in the case, and the dependent measure was the extent to which the participants adopted this position. Wilder found that, overall, and as predicted by social impact theory, more individuals produced more conformity. But individuals also had more influence when they presented their opinions as individuals than they did when they presented the same opinions as a member of a group. For instance, in one condition of the experiment, six individuals gave their opinions, but they were said to be either six individuals working alone, six individuals working in two groups of three members, or six individuals working in three groups of two members. As shown in Figure 4.4, conformity was greater to six individuals than to three individuals in two groups or to two individuals in three groups. Evidently, the participants did not treat the arguments of the six individuals as independent when they were part of a group. Similar results were found by Harkins and Petty (1987).

Still another reason that larger and larger majorities may not produce as much conformity as expected is that, as predicted by the principle of optimal distinctiveness (see chapter 3), after there are a lot of people in the majority, individuals may feel the need to maintain their individual identity rather than losing their individuality by conforming to the group. For instance, a recent federally funded report on the effectiveness of "virginity pledges" among high

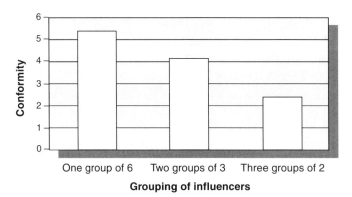

FIGURE 4.4. Conformity to individuals and groups. In this research, research participants showed more conformity to individuals who were said to have reached their decisions alone than to the same arguments presented by individuals who were said to be members of social groups. Data are from Wilder, D. A. (1977). Perception of groups, size of opposition, and social influence. *Journal of Experimental Social Psychology, 13,* 253–268.

school students showed that the pledges did not hold when only one teenager in a classroom took them, but that it required the support of like-minded classmates. However, the pledges' effectiveness began to decline and teenagers stopped delaying sex when the percentage of students signing virginity pledges increased to more than 30 percent of the class (Schemo, 2000). Although the results are correlational, they appear consistent with the hypothesis that taking a public stand on turning down sex offers teenagers an identity, much the way joining a club does. But once the virginity pledge became more popular and less unique, teenagers were less inclined to find it appealing.

Unanimity of the Majority

Although the number in the group is an important determinant of conformity, the *consistency* or *unanimity* of the group members is even more so (Allen & Wilder, 1980). In Asch's study, for example, conformity occurred not so much because many confederates gave a wrong answer, but rather because each of the confederates gave the *same* wrong answer. In fact, in one follow-up study Asch increased the number of confederates to 16, but had just one of those confederates give the correct answer. He found that in this case, even though there were 15 incorrect and only one correct answer given by the confederates, conformity was nevertheless sharply reduced—to only about 5 percent of the participants' responses.

Although you might not be surprised to hear that conformity decreases when one of the group members gives the right answer, you may be more surprised to hear that conformity is reduced even when the dissenting confederate gives a different *wrong* answer. For example, conformity is reduced

dramatically in Asch's line-judging situation, such that virtually all participants give the correct answer (assume it is line 3 in this case), even when the
majority of the confederates have indicated that line 2 is the correct answer
and a single confederate indicates that line 1 is correct! In short, conformity is
reduced when there is *any* inconsistency among the members of the majority
group—even when one member of the majority gives an answer that is even
more incorrect than that given by the other majority group members.

Why should unanimity be such an important determinant of conformity?
For one, when there is complete agreement among the majority members, the
individual who is the target of influence stands completely alone and must be
the first to break ranks by giving a different opinion. Being the only person
who is different is potentially embarrassing, and participants may naturally
want to avoid this. Second, when there is complete agreement, the participant may become less sure of his or her own perceptions of the lines. When
such doubt occurs, the individual may be likely to conform due to informational conformity. Finally, when one or more of the other group members
gives a different answer than the rest of the group (so that the unanimity of
the majority group is broken), that person changes from being part of the
majority group to being (along with the participant) part of the group being
influenced. You can see that another way of describing the effect of unanimity
is to say that as soon as the individual has someone who agrees with him or
her (a supporter or ally), they no longer need to conform. Having one or more
supporters who challenge the status quo validates one's own opinion and makes
disagreeing with the majority less fearful (Allen, 1975; Boyanowsky & Allen,
1973).

Task Importance

One other determinant of the amount of conformity that occurs on group
tasks is the perceived importance of the decision. The studies of Sherif and
Asch have been criticized because the decisions that the participants made—
for instance, judging the length of lines—seem rather trivial. Although you
might think that conformity would be less when the task becomes more important (perhaps because people would feel uncomfortable relying on the judgments of others and want to take more responsibility for their own decisions),
the influence of task importance actually turns out to be more complicated
that that.

This was demonstrated in an experiment conducted by Baron, Vandello,
and Brunsman (1996) that used a slight modification of the Asch procedure to
assess conformity. Participants completed the experiment along with two other
students, who were actually experimental confederates. The participants
worked on several different types of trials, but there were 26 that were rel-

evant to the conformity predictions. On these trials a photo of a single individual was presented first, followed immediately by a "lineup" photo of four individuals, one of whom had been viewed in the initial slide (but who might have been dressed differently):

The participants' task was to call out which person in the lineup was the same as the original individual using a number between 1 (the person on the left) and 4 (the person on the right). In each of the critical trials the two confederates went before the participant and they each gave the same wrong response.

Two experimental manipulations were used. First, the researchers manipulated task importance by telling participants in the high-importance condition that their performance on the task was a verified measure of eyewitness ability and that the participants who performed most accurately would receive $20 at the end of the data collection (a lottery using all of the participants was actually held at the end of the semester, and some participants were paid the $20). Participants in the low-importance condition were told that the test procedure was part of a pilot study. Second, task difficulty was varied by showing the test and the lineup photos for 5 and 10 seconds respectively (easy condition) or for only 0.5 and 1 second respectively (difficult condition). The conformity score was defined as the number of trials in which the participant offered the same (incorrect) response as the confederates.

As shown in Figure 4.5, an interaction between task difficulty and task importance was observed. On easy tasks, participants conformed less when they thought that the decision was of high (versus low) importance, whereas on difficult tasks, participants conformed more when they thought the decision was of high importance. It appears that when participants are confident about their decisions (because the task is easy), they rely on their own decisions when they think it is important to be accurate. On the other hand, when the situation is more ambiguous and the judgments cannot be verified objectively (in the difficult conditions), individuals engage in social comparison—becoming increasingly reliant on the judgments of others to inform their own views.

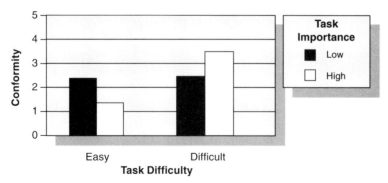

FIGURE 4.5. Task importance, task difficulty, and conformity. On easy tasks, participants conformed less when they thought that the decision was of high (versus low) importance, whereas on difficult tasks, participants conformed more when they thought the decision was of high importance. Data are from Baron, R. S., Vandello, J. A., & Brunsman, B. (1996). The forgotten variable in conformity research: Impact of task importance on social influence. *Journal of Personality and Social Psychology, 71*, 915–927.

Minority Influence

To this point, our discussion of majority influence might make it seem that individuals always prefer to conform to the opinions of others. But the assumption that all social behavior is driven by goals of conformity is problematic. For one, there are clear cases in which a smaller number of individuals (a minority group) is able to influence the opinions or behaviors of a larger group of individuals (Moscovici, Mucchi-Faina, & Maass, 1994; Moscovici, Mugny, & Van Avermaet, 1985). Teachers are able to change the beliefs of their students, and political leaders are able to change the behavior of their followers. And when we look back on history, we find that it is the unusual, divergent, innovative minority groups or individuals, who—although frequently ridiculed at the time for their unusual ideas—end up being respected in the end for producing positive changes. Although conformity to majority opinions is essential to provide a smoothly working society, if individuals only conformed to others there could never be any new ideas or social change.

Minority Influence in Action

The French social psychologist Serge Moscovici was particularly interested in the situations in which minority influence might occur. In fact, he argued that all members of all groups are able (at least in some degree) to influence others, regardless of whether they are in the majority or the minority. To test whether minority group members could indeed produce influence, Moscovici, Lage, and Naffrechoux (1969) essentially created the reverse of Asch's line perception study, such that there was now a minority of confederates in the group (two) and a majority of experimental participants (four). All six individuals viewed a series of slides depicting colors, supposedly as a study of color perception, and as in Asch's research, each gave an opinion about the color of the slide out loud.

Although the color of the slides varied in brightness, they were all clearly blue in color. Moreover, demonstrating that the slides were unambiguous, just as the line judgments of Asch had been, participants in a control condition who were asked to make judgments alone called the slides a different color than blue less than one percent of the time (when it happened, they were called green).

In the experimental conditions, the two confederates had been instructed to give one of two patterns of answers that were different from the normal responses. In the *consistent-minority* condition, the two confederates called the slides green on every trial. In the *inconsistent-minority* condition, however, the confederates called the slides green on only 25 percent of their responses, and called them blue on the other 75 percent.

As shown in Figure 4.6, Moscovici found that the presence of a minority who gave consistently incorrect responses influenced the judgments made by the experimental participants. When the minority was consistent, 32 percent of the participants said green at least once and 8 percent of the responses of the majority group were green. However, the inconsistent minority had virtually no influence on judgments. Thus, just as Asch found in his line-matching studies, the unanimity of the influencing group was critical.

In another version of the study, participants were again exposed to the consistent or inconsistent confederates in the initial perception phase but then completed what they thought was a different study conducted by a different

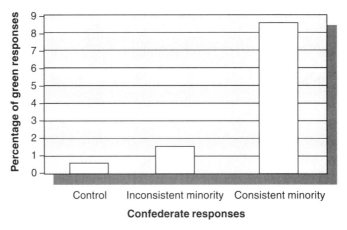

FIGURE 4.6. Consistent and inconsistent minorities. Only a consistent minority (in which each individual gives the same incorrect response) is able to produce conformity in the majority participants. Data are from Moscovici, S., Lage, E., & Naffrechoux, M. (1969). Influence of a consistent minority on the responses of a majority in a colour perception task. *Sociometry, 32*, 365-380.

experimenter. In this study they viewed ambiguous color stimuli that could also be seen as either blue or green, and were asked to label the colors of these stimuli in private. In the experimental condition in which the confederates had only called the slides green on 25 percent of the trials the participants were not influenced by the discrepant judgments—there were hardly any green responses on the later private judgments. However, in the consistent minority condition, where the confederates had called all of the slides green, participants were significantly more likely to make green judgments in private. And these changes in perception were found to occur even for those participants who did not publicly give a green response in their initial public judgments of the slides in front of the confederates (Moscovici & Personnaz, 1980, 1986; Sorrentino, King, & Leo, 1980).

On the basis of this research, Moscovici argued that minorities could indeed have influence over majorities, provided they gave consistent (that is, unanimous) responses. Furthermore, the fact that the participants who had been exposed to unanimous minorities frequently called the slides green not only in public, but also in private, led Moscovici to argue that minorities, when they were successful at producing influence, were able to produce strong and lasting attitude change—true acceptance—rather than simply public compliance, as might be expected as a result of majority influence (Crano & Chen, 1998).

Minority Influence and Creative Thinking

In addition to being able to change their opinions, minorities have been found to have another, and potentially even more important, effect on the opinions of majority group members. Minority groups can make majorities engage in more divergent, innovative, and creative thinking about the topics being discussed (Mugny, 1982; Nemeth & Kwan, 1987; Nemeth, Mosier, & Chiles, 1992; Nemeth & Wachtler, 1983).

In one study that demonstrated this outcome, Charlan Nemeth and Julianne Kwan (1987) had participants work in groups of four on a creativity task in which they were presented with letter strings such as "tdogto" and asked to indicate which word came to their mind first as they looked at the letters. The judgments were made privately, which allowed the experimenters to provide false feedback about the responses of the other group members. All participants actually indicated the most obvious word (in this case, "dog") as their response on each of the initial trials. However, the participants were told (according to experimental condition) either that three of the other group members had also reported seeing "dog" and that one had reported seeing "god," or they were told that three out of the four had reported seeing "god," whereas only one had reported "dog." Participants then completed some other similar word strings on their own, and their responses were studied.

Results showed that when the participants thought that the unusual response (for instance, "god" rather than "dog") was only given by a minority of one individual in the group, rather than a majority of three individuals, they subsequently answered more of the new word strings using novel solutions, such as finding words made backward or using a random order of the letters. This outcome is predicted from the assumption that behavior that comes from minority groups leads individuals to think about the behaviors more carefully, in comparison to the same behaviors performed by majority group members. This, along with other research showing similar findings, was interpreted by Nemeth and Kwan as indicating that messages that come from minority groups can produce innovative, creative thinking in majority group members.

Comparing Majority and Minority Influence

Although it is now clear that conformity can occur to either majorities or minorities, there is nevertheless disagreement among researchers about whether it is necessary to consider the conformity that results from majority and minority influence as representing fundamentally different processes, or whether it is more accurate to consider conformity as conformity, regardless of whether it is initiated by a majority or a minority.

Single-Process Approaches

The principle of parsimony (that is, preferring the simplest possible explanation) suggests that, if possible, we should assume that majority and minority influence are caused by the same underlying factors. This is the prediction of the *single-process* approach, which assumes that the situations that produce conformity to majorities and minorities are the same (Chaiken & Stangor, 1987; Kruglanski & Mackie, 1990; Latané, 1981; Tanford & Penrod, 1984).

Mathematical Models of Social Influence

Several theorists have proposed mathematical models designed to summarize the impact of individuals on conformity based on the assumption that influence is influence, regardless of its source (Tanford & Penrod, 1984). We have already considered one of these approaches—social impact theory—in our prior discussion (Latané, 1981; Wolf, 1987). According to social impact theory, conformity depends upon three separate variables: S (the strength of the majority, such as its status and expertise), I (the physical closeness or *immediacy* of the majority to the person or persons being influenced), and N (the number of people in the majority). The model is expressed as a mathematical equation, such as:

$$\text{Influence} = f(\text{SIN})$$

According to this formula, calculating the ability of individuals to influence others is similar to calculating the amount of light that a series of lightbulbs shines on the walls of a room. The influence is determined by the strength of each individual to influence the others (the brightness of the light), the distance of the individual from the others (the distance of the lightbulb from the wall), and the number of individuals (the number of lights).

A second approach to mathematically modeling the observed effects of social impact is provided by Brian Mullen (1983). In his approach, the size of both the majority and the minority are important, and the equation that represents influence is written as

$$\text{Influence} = \frac{\text{Number in Majority}}{\text{Number in Majority} + \text{Number in Minority}}$$

The idea here is that when there are relatively fewer members of the minority group in comparison to the majority group, majority influence is greater. In these conditions, minorities become more focused on themselves and their discrepant opinions, which makes them more conscious about the necessity of behaving according to social norms, and thus more likely to conform to the majority (e.g., Carver & Scheier, 1981).

Both of these models are able to explain when and how minorities (and majorities) are influential. But though both of these models seem appropriate, it is difficult to know which is more adequate, as there is little research attempting to differentiate their predictions.

Research Supporting the Single-Process Approach

There are several empirical reasons to favor the single-process approach. For one, the variables that determine the amount of influence toward majorities and minorities seem to be quite similar, which would not be expected if different processes were operating. For instance, the number of individuals giving the same response increases conformity, regardless of whether the influence comes from majority or minority groups (Arbuthnot & Wayner, 1982; C. Nemeth, Wachter, & Endicott, 1977). And, as we have seen, the consistency or unanimity of the expressed opinions of the influencing group is also critical in producing conformity from both majorities and minorities.

Dual-Process Approaches

In direct contrast to the single-process approach, Moscovici (Moscovici & Lage, 1976; Moscovici et al., 1985) argued that there were substantial and important differences between majority and minority influence, and thus that the single-process approach was inaccurate. According to him, when a message comes from a majority group it is easily accepted as being valid, simply because so many people believe it. Thus, majority influence does not really involve any thinking about the message itself, but the focus rather is on the *source* of the message (the majority). In this case the strategy seems to be "if they all say so, it must be right."

Persuasion attempts that come from the minority, on the other hand, do not have the advantage of number. Rather, the minority can only produce influence by convincing the majority that their opinions are valid. Therefore, Moscovici argued that arguments from minorities lead people to focus on the *message*, as if they were wondering, "why would those few people be saying something like that?" According to Moscovici, the cognitive activity involved in listening to and evaluating the message given by minorities may lead to its acceptance, whereas majorities can only produce compliance.

In short, then, according to this dual-process approach, information coming from a majority group triggers compliance to social norms without real change in opinion (normative conformity), whereas information coming from a minority group triggers a "validation" process in which the message is processed and potentially accepted (informational conformity). Based on this theory, Moscovici gave advice to individuals in minorities who were attempting to change opinions. Specifically, they should argue their positions forcefully and consistently, in order to draw attention to their arguments (Wood, Lundgren, Ouellette, & Busceme, 1994).

Research Supporting the Dual-Process Approach

Some data have been interpreted as supporting Moscovici's dual-process approach. Most importantly, it has been found that when individuals make their responses in public, the majority is more effective in producing opinion change than the minority. This would be expected because the majority is producing normative influence that appears on public measures. On the other hand, when responses are made privately, the minority is relatively more effective (e.g., Maass & Clark, 1983, 1986; Maass & Clark, 1984; Moscovici, 1980). Indeed, Wood, Lundgren, Ouelette, and Busceme (1994) used a meta-analysis to summarize the results of 97 studies that had looked at minority and majority influence; they found that minorities had greater impact on private measures of opinion than on public measures. These findings suggest that, as Moscovici proposed, minority influence is more likely to produce true acceptance of the opinion (as assessed in private), whereas majority influence is more likely to produce (public) compliance.

Limits to the Dual-Process Approach

Despite these findings, there is little empirical evidence to support another of the basic predictions of the dual-process approach, namely that the type of cognitive processes produced by majorities and minorities will be different (Kruglanski & Mackie, 1990). Research has found few differences in the amount of attention paid to messages that come from majority or minority sources or the amount of cognitive activity elicited by majorities versus minorities. That minorities promote more creative thinking than majorities is, however, consistent with the idea that they stimulate more cognitive activity. These differences would be expected from the dual-process perspective.

Summary

Taking all of the data together, it does not appear that the dual-process approach is well supported. Indeed, in a summary of this literature Kruglanski and Mackie (1990) argued that, based on current data, there is no strong reason to believe that the processes by which majorities influence minorities are different than the processes by which minorities influence majorities. In essence, they argue that it is not the size of the group that makes a difference in terms of its ability to produce conformity or even creative thinking, but that other characteristics of the group are more relevant. What is important are factors such as the relative power or status of the group, the validity of the group's expressed opinion, and the relationship of the opinion to existing group norms. In some cases the majority group may have more power and more status, but in other cases the minority group may have more power and status. Similarly, the opinions of either the majority or the minority may be more valid or more consistent with prevailing social norms. Thus, it is these variables, rather than the group's numerical size, that are most important, and they determine the ability of the group to influence. In short, as proposed by the single-process model, influence is influence, regardless of its source.

Limits of Conformity

To this point in the chapter we have presented a substantial amount of data suggesting that individuals are influenced to share (or at least to publicly express) the beliefs and opinions of others even when the others may be perceived to hold incorrect positions. And conformity to the norms and opinions of others is probably quite adaptive overall, both for the group itself and for the individual group members. Knowing that others share our views and opinions allows us to predict what they are going to do and helps maintain a smoothly functioning society. If only half of the people in your neighborhood thought it was appropriate to stop on red and go on green and the other half thought the opposite, there would be problems indeed!

Although we have focused to this point on the situational determinants of conformity, such as the number of people in the majority and their unanimity and status, we have not yet considered the question of which people are likely to conform and which people are not. Even in cases in which the pressure to conform is strong, and in which a large percentage of individuals do conform (such as in Asch's line judging research), not everyone does so. There are usually some people willing and able to go against the prevailing norm. In Asch's study, for instance, 24 percent of the participants never conformed on any of the trials.

Personality Variables

Some research has attempted to discover the personality characteristics of individuals who are more or less likely to conform, and some differences have been found. People with lower self-esteem are more likely to conform in comparison to those with higher self-esteem, and people who are dependent on and who have strong needs for approval from others are also more conforming (Bornstein, 1992; Crutchfield, 1955; M. Snyder & Ickes, 1985). Recent research by Visser and Krosnick (1998) studied the influence of age on conformity and found a curvilinear relationship, such that individuals who are either very young or very old were more easily influenced than individuals who were in their thirties and forties. And, perhaps not surprisingly, people who highly identify with, or who have a high degree of commitment to, the group are also more likely to conform to group norms (Jetten, Spears, & Manstead, 1997; Terry & Hogg, 1996). As we will discuss more fully in chapter 11, there are also differences in the amount of conformity observed in different cultures. However, although there are some differences among people in terms of their tendency to conform, research has generally found that the impact of person variables on conformity is smaller than the influence of situational variables, such as the number and unanimity of the majority.

Gender Differences in Conformity

In Asch's study, only men were used. You might ask yourself what might have happened had women been included. In fact, several reviews and meta-analyses of the existing research on conformity in men and women have now been conducted (Eagly & Carli, 1981; Eagly & Chrvala, 1986). The overall conclusions from these studies is that there are only small differences between men and women in the amount of conformity they exhibit, and these differences do not show up in every case. For instance, in a meta-analysis by Alice Eagly (1978), 68 percent of the reviewed studies found no male-female differences. On the other hand, of the studies that did find differences, 34 percent found that women conformed more than men but only 3 percent found that men conformed more than women. Overall, the difference between men and women was very small.

Eagly's meta-analysis showed that the difference between men and women was observed primarily in situations in which the opinions were expressed publicly rather than privately. In public conditions women tend to show more conformity than men, whereas this difference does not appear when the opinions are expressed privately. Eagly (1978) argued that this discrepancy seemed to be the result of differences in the overall orientations and roles of men and women in groups. Because, on average, men are more concerned about appearing independent to others than are women, they resist changing their beliefs in public, even if not doing so has some costs to group harmony and agreement. On the other hand, women are more concerned with maintaining group harmony (the socioemotional role), and thus are more likely to conform to others in public situations.

Although differences in social roles are important, there are also other reasons that women might conform more than men. For one, despite changes in stereotypes over the past years in Western cultures, men still generally have higher social status in groups. Individuals with high status are less likely to conform, and this also explains, in part, why women are more likely to conform to men than men are to conform to women. Finally, the nature of the topic being discussed appears to play at least some role, such that both men and women are less likely to conform on topics that they know a lot about, in comparison to topics on which they feel less knowledgeable (Eagly & Chrvala, 1986). Thus, it appears that the observed differences between men and women is at least in part based on informational influence.

Psychological Reactance

A full understanding of who conforms to whom, and under what conditions, involves a careful consideration of the motivations of the individual being influenced. If we feel that we have the choice to conform or not conform, we may well choose to do so in order to be accepted or to obtain valid knowledge. On the other hand, if we perceive that others are trying to force our conformity, and yet that person's authority is perceived as illegitimate or if he or she is not in the position to actually demand the conformity, the influence pressure may backfire, resulting in the exact opposite of conformity.

Consider an experiment conducted by Pennebaker and Sanders (1976), who attempted to get people to stop writing graffiti on the walls of campus restrooms. In some restrooms they put a sign that read "Do not write on these walls under any circumstances!" whereas in other restrooms they placed a sign that simply said "Please don't write on these walls." Two weeks later, the researchers returned to the restrooms to see if the signs had made a difference. They found that there was much less graffiti in the second restroom than in the first one. It seems as if people who were given strong pressures to not engage in the behavior were less likely to conform to the demands than were people who were given a weaker message.

When individuals feel that their freedom is being threatened by influence attempts, and yet that they also have the ability to resist that persuasion, they may develop a strong emotional state, known as **psychological reactance,** and not conform at all. Reactance represents a desire to restore freedom that is being threatened (Brehm, 1966). A child who feels that his or her parents are forcing him to eat his asparagus may react quite vehemently with a strong refusal to touch the plate. And an adult who feels that he is being pressured by a car salesman might feel the same way and leave the showroom entirely, resulting in the exact opposite of the salesman's intended outcome. Of course, parents are sometimes aware of this potential, and even use "reverse psychology"—telling a child that she should not go outside when they really want her to, hoping that reactance will occur.

 Chapter Summary

One of the basic predictions of the group dynamics approach is that individuals who share group memberships will also share important opinions and values. As a result, there is a pervasive tendency in groups for group members to adopt the prevailing group norms. This process, known as social influence, occurs both actively and passively, and the resulting change in opinions and beliefs is known as conformity.

Conformity allows both the group and the individual to meet important goals. From the point of view of the individual, conforming to group norms allows one to feel that he or she has obtained valid information and avoids the possibility of rejection or ridicule. Conformity to gain accurate knowledge is known as informational conformity, whereas conformity to avoid ridicule is known as normative conformity.

Psychological Reactance: A reaction to conformity pressures that results from a desire to restore threatened freedom.

In some cases, social influence may lead to unexpected behaviors, such as in Asch's line perception study, in which individuals gave obviously inaccurate judgments in public. The variables that increase the likelihood of conformity have been extensively studied and include the number of individuals who are doing the influencing, the number of individuals who are being influenced, the unanimity of the positions of the influencers, and the importance of the topic to the individual.

Influence can come from the minority group as well as the majority group. Indeed, minority influence is powerful, because it produces private acceptance of the message, and real opinion change. Minority influence may also increase creative thinking about a topic. There has been debate regarding whether the process of majority and minority influence are the same (the single-process approach) or different (the dual-process approach).

Although there is a general tendency for conformity in most groups, not everyone conforms all of the time. Some personality variables, such as self-esteem and dependence, are important in this regard. There are few overall sex differences in conformity. When the attempt to influence is very blatant, and the target of the influence feels that he or she is being pressured, psychological reactance may result, in which the individual moves his or her belief or behavior in the opposite direction from the source of influence.

 *Review and Discussion Questions*

1. What is the difference between normative and informational social influence? Consider which is most likely to have been occurring in the studies discussed in this chapter (for instance, Crandall, Sherif, Asch, and Milgram). Is it possible to be certain whether conformity is caused by informational or normative social influence? Why or why not?
2. What is the difference between compliance and private acceptance? How can we tell which one is occurring? What is the relationship between the compliance-acceptance distinction and the normative-informational influence distinction?
3. Consider a time when you complied with a social norm, and a time when you accepted one. What feelings did you experience in each case?
4. If you wanted to create a social situation that would be most likely to produce conformity, how would you arrange it?
5. When and how can minorities influence majorities? And what are the outcomes of such influence?

6. Do majority and minority influence represent two different underlying pro-
    cesses, or one common process? What research evidence supports your opinion?
7. Is conformity good or bad? Justify your answer.

Recommended Readings

A classic introduction to group dynamics:
Cartwright, D., & Zander, A. (Eds.). (1968). *Group Dynamics: Research and Theory* (3rd
    ed.). New York: Harper & Row.

An approach to social influence based on self categorization theory:
Turner, J. C. (1991). *Social Influence.* Pacific Grove, CA: Brooks Cole.

Social
Categorization 5

*O*ur focus in chapter 4 was on group process in small working groups in which the group members are able to directly communicate with each other. In this chapter we turn to another type of group process—*social categorization*—that allows us to increase the range of groups that we can study, because it is applicable not only to small working groups, but also to large social categories such as those based on gender, race, age, social class, and religion. Social categorization occurs when people think about themselves and others as members of a social group (Eiser & Stroebe, 1972; Tajfel, 1981; S. T. Fiske & Neuberg, 1990; Stangor & Lange, 1994; Turner, 1987). Social categorization influences the thoughts, feelings, and behaviors of the people doing the categorizing as well as those who are categorized.

Although they generally address similar issues, there is nevertheless a fundamental difference between the social influence and the social categorization approaches to group behavior. According to the social influence approach, what is important are the (active and passive) social pressures applied by others that lead an individual to hold and express an opinion and potentially to behave in accord with or counter to these beliefs. In the social categorization approach, however, the emphasis is upon perceiving individuals as members of groups and the results of these perceptions on our cognitions and behavior.

Social categorization is relevant to the study of groups not only because it allows us to better understand social categories and the relationships among their members, but also because memberships in social categories frequently intersect with memberships in working groups, and these relationships are, unfortunately, as likely to be destructive as they are to be productive. Demographic trends in the United States and in other Western countries are leading to a more diverse workforce (S. E. Jackson & Ruderman, 1995). Older people are working longer, women are becoming more equally represented in various fields of employment, and the ethnic mix of most occupations is also increasing. People from minority groups now account for about half of the U.S. workforce and most of the growth in its labor force (Goldstein & Gilliam, 1990). As a result, employers and workers are increasingly required to work in multilingual, multicultural workplaces, in which people's identities are derived both from their work groups as well as their social category memberships. An understanding of the efficient function of working groups must therefore include knowledge about how group members respond to others on the basis of their social category memberships.

Social Categorization

Social categorization occurs when we think about someone—either ourself or another person—as a member of a meaningful social group. This categorization can be based on physical features (skin color, physical attractiveness, clothing, or hairstyle), as well as other types of categories (for instance, if we know that an individual is Vietnamese, a lottery winner, an alcoholic, or a schizophrenic). Social categorization occurs, for example, when a college professor notices that the person knocking on the door is a student, rather than another faculty member, or when a student thinks about his or her instructor as one who seems "too old to still be teaching."

Although social categorization can occur on the basis of virtually any sort of group membership, in this chapter we will be primarily concerned with

Social Categorization:
The process of thinking about someone as a member of a meaningful social group.

social categorization on the basis of group memberships that are difficult or impossible to change, such as one's sex, race, ethnicity, and age. We will also consider a special case of social categorization—**self-categorization**—that occurs when a person thinks about himself or herself (rather than thinking about another person) as a member of a social group. Self-categorization involves comparisons between groups that we belong to (in-groups) and the ones that we don't belong to (out-groups).

Spontaneous Social Categorization

One of the reasons to be interested in social categorization is that it occurs very quickly when we first see another person, and without any real intention on the part of the person who is doing the categorizing. This quick categorization is sometimes said to be *automatic* or *spontaneous,* meaning that it occurs quickly and without the conscious intention of the individual (Uleman & Bargh, 1989).

   One research methodology that has been used to demonstrate spontaneous social categorization is the *name-confusion paradigm* (Arcuri, 1982; Brewer, Weber, & Carini, 1995; Spears & Haslam, 1997; Stangor, Lynch, Duan, & Glass, 1992; S. E. Taylor, Fiske, Etcoff, & Ruderman, 1978). In these studies, the research participants are first shown a videotape or a slide show of some people from different social categories interacting in a discussion group and then asked to identify who made each of the discussion statements. For instance, Shelley Taylor and her colleagues (1978, experiment 2) showed their research participants a slide and tape presentation of three male and three female European-American college students who had supposedly participated in a discussion group. During the presentation the members of the discussion group each made some suggestions about how to advertise a college play. The statements were controlled so that, across all of the research participants, the statements made by the men and the women were of equal length and quality. Furthermore, one-half of the participants were told that when the presentation was over they would be asked to remember which person had made which suggestion, whereas the other half of the participants were told merely to observe the interaction without attending to anything in particular.

   After they had viewed all of the statements made by the individuals in the discussion group, the research participants were given a memory test (this was entirely unexpected for the participants who had not been given memory instructions). The participants were shown the list of all of the statements that had been made, along with the pictures of each of the discussion group members, and were asked to indicate who had made each of the statements. The research participants were not very good at this task, and when they made

Self-categorization: The social categorization of oneself as a member of a social group.

mistakes, they were very systematic. These mistakes were such that the statements that had actually been made by a man were more frequently wrongly attributed to another man in the group than to another woman, and the statements actually made by a woman were more frequently attributed to other women in the group than to a man. The participants evidently categorized the speakers by their gender, leading them to make more within-gender than across-gender confusions. Interestingly, the instructions that the participants had been given made absolutely no difference. There was just as much categorization for those who were not given any instructions as for those who were told to match individuals to statements. The name-confusion paradigm and other techniques have been used in many other studies to demonstrate that people do spontaneously categorize each other on the basis of their social group memberships, including race, academic status (student versus teacher), social roles, as well as other social categories (E. R. Smith & Zárate, 1990; Stangor et al., 1992; S. E. Taylor et al., 1978; A. P. Fiske, Haslam, & Fiske, 1991).

Spontaneous social categorization is probably a natural tendency of human beings. To promote safety, and to help find acceptable mates, animals develop a natural tendency to socialize with other members of their own species, and to avoid contacts with members of other species. Although humans certainly think more complexly about categorizations than do animals, categorizing people according to their physical appearance may be a "hard-wired" tendency for humans that is difficult for us to avoid, even when we want to (Caporael, 1991; Schaller & Conway, 2000).

The Goals of Social Categorization

Social categorization is evidently a very basic part of perceiving others, and one that humans are well equipped to perform. Indeed, the idea that social categorization occurs spontaneously suggests that people may have difficulty *not* thinking about others in terms of their social categories (you might recall the *Saturday Night Live* skits in which people became confused and upset when they were not able to determine the gender of another person). But why exactly should social categorization occur so readily in human beings?

Stereotypes, Prejudice, and Discrimination

Perhaps the most fundamental underlying reason for social categorization is that we believe that categorizing others provides information about the characteristics of the person being categorized. For instance, we categorize people by race in part because we believe that people from different races are somehow different, and thus that we can learn something about the individual by knowing his or her social category. Beliefs about the characteristics of social groups and the members of those groups are known as **social stereotypes** (S. T. Fiske, 1998; Hamilton & Sherman, 1994; Stangor & Lange, 1994). Stereotypes are frequently in the form of traits (for instance, the beliefs that "Italians are romantic" or that "college professors are absent-minded"). In addition to stereotypes, people may also have positive or negative attitudes toward members of different social groups. **Prejudice** refers to unjustifiable negative attitudes toward an out0group, or toward members of that out-group. Prejudice includes negative feelings toward group members—dislikes, anger, fear, disgust, discomfort, and even hatred. Although negative stereotypes and prejudice are problematic, we are concerned about them primarily because they relate to **discrimination**—unjustified negative behaviors toward members of out-groups based on their group membership—for instance, when an individual is denied housing or job opportunities because of his or her group membership.

Stereotypes and prejudice are learned through direct contact with members of the categorized group, through communication from parents and peers (Aboud & Doyle, 1996), and from the media (Brown, 1995; Ruscher, 2001). Research has shown that even four-year-old children have stereotypes about the appropriate activities for boys and girls (Brown, 1995; Ruble & Ruble, 1982). And there is often good agreement about the stereotypes of social categories among the individuals within a given culture. For instance, one study assessing stereotypes (Katz and Braly, 1933) presented U.S. college students with a list of 84 trait terms and asked them to indicate for which groups each trait seemed appropriate. The participants tended to agree about what traits were true of which groups, and this was true even for groups of which the respondents were likely to never have met a single member (Arabs and Russians). Although there is at least some evidence that some stereotypes are fading, even today there is good agreement about the stereotypes of members of many social groups, including men and women (Locksley, Borgida, Brekke, & Hepburn, 1980; Martin, 1987; Ruble & Ruble, 1982) and racial and ethnic groups (Devine & Elliot, 1995).

As shown in Figure 5.1, stereotypes can be thought of as being linked, in the memory of individuals, to the social categories. Thus stereotypes are "pictures in our heads" of social groups (Lippmann, 1922). When we think about Italians, for instance, stereotypes about them (perhaps "romantic" and "sensuous") quickly come to mind. These cognitive mental representations are frequently referred to as cognitive *schemas* or *prototypes* (Stangor & McMillan, 1992; S. E. Taylor & Crocker, 1981). People may also have images of particular individual members of the category, for instance media figures (Bill Cosby or

Social Stereotypes: Beliefs about the characteristics of social groups and the members of those groups

Prejudice: An unjustifiable negative attitude toward an out-group, or toward members of that out-group.

Discrimination: Unjustified negative behaviors toward members of out-groups that are based on their group membership.

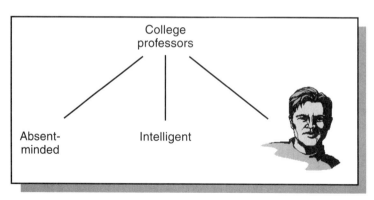

FIGURE 5.1. A stereotype representation. This figure represents a hypothetical person's cognitive representation of the social category "college professors." It includes both positive and negative stereotypes as well as an exemplar of a college professor.

Michael Jordan as African Americans) or other people they have known. These images, known as *exemplars,* may also be brought to mind when the individual thinks about members of the social category, and the activation of exemplars may influence judgments of new individuals (Bodenhausen, Schwarz, Bless, & Wanke, 1995). Prejudice is also linked to category labels in memory, such that negative feelings may automatically occur in the presence of group members (Greenwald, McGhee, & Schwartz, 1998).

The strength of cognitive beliefs can be assessed using reaction-time measures, by assessing how quickly activation of the category label in memory activates the associated stereotypes (Dovidio, Evans, & Tyler, 1986). For instance, in one relevant study investigating the development of mental representations of social groups, Sechrist and Stangor (2001) demonstrated that the strength of individuals' stereotypes is determined by their perceptions of appropriate social norms. White participants first indicated their stereotypes about African Americans, and then were told, according to random assignment to conditions, either that 80 percent or that only 20 percent of other college students agreed with their beliefs. Then, in a second session, conducted on a computer, they were presented on a series of trials with either the word *black* or with a neutral word (*chair*), before being immediately presented with a word that was either stereotypical or nonstereotypical of African Americans. We found that participants who had been led to believe that most other college students agreed with their stereotypes were able to respond to stereotypical words faster than those who had learned that the others did not share their beliefs, and that this was only true after being exposed to the word *black*. We interpreted this finding as support for our hypothesis that the participants' stereotypes of African Americans (conceptualized as the links between the category label *blacks,* and the stereotypical traits) were strengthened when they learned that others held similar beliefs.

Accurate Information

In some cases, thinking about others in terms of their social category memberships might occur because it is informative, in the sense that it provides the perceiver with information about the characteristics of people who belong to certain social groups or categories (Lee, Jussim, & McCauley, 1995; P. Oakes & Turner, 1990). For instance, if you found yourself lost in a city, you might look for a police officer or a taxi driver to help you find your way. In this case, social categorization would probably be useful, because a police officer or a taxi driver might be particularly likely to know the city streets.

Of course using social categories will only be informative to the extent that the stereotypes held by the individual about that category are accurate. If police officers were actually not that knowledgeable about the city layout, then using this categorization would not be informative. It has been argued that there is a "kernel of truth" in most stereotypes, and this truth may come in part from the roles that individuals play in society (Lee et al., 1995). The stereotypes that women are "nurturant" and that men are "dominant" may occur in part because, on average, men and women find themselves in different social roles within a culture (Eagly, 1987; Eagly & Steffen, 1984). In most cultures men are more likely to be in high-status occupations, such as doctors and lawyers, whereas women are more likely to play the role of homemakers and child-care workers. In this sense the stereotypes are at least partly "true" for many of the members of the social category, in terms of their actual behaviors, although they do not necessarily imply any truth about underlying personality differences. In short, we may find categories informative because we believe there are important differences among the members of the different groups. As we will see, comparisons that involve distinguishing the groups that we belong to (in-groups) from groups that we do not belong to (out-groups) are particularly important in this regard.

Cognitive Economy

Although we may sometimes categorize others to learn something about them, another reason for doing so is because we may not have time to do anything more thorough. Thus using our stereotypes to size up another person might simply make our life easier (G. W. Allport, 1954; S. T. Fiske & Taylor, 1991; Macrae, Hewstone, & Griffiths, 1993; Macrae, Milne, & Bodenhausen, 1994; Tajfel & Forgas, 1981; Van Knippenberg & Van Knippenberg, 1994). According to this approach, thinking about other people in terms of their social category memberships is a functional way of dealing with the world—things are complicated, and we reduce complexity by categorizing others.

If categorizing others makes things easier for us, then we should be particularly likely to rely on it in situations where there is a lot of information to learn or when we have few cognitive resources available to process information. In a demonstration of the role of cognitive economy in stereotyping, Galen Bodenhausen (1990) presented research participants with information about a court case in a jury trial. The trial information that the participants read was arranged such that stereotypes about the defendant (for instance, that student athletes would be likely to cheat on exams) implied that he would be guilty, but the actual information presented at the trial was more ambiguous. Furthermore, Bodenhausen had obtained self-reports from the participants about whether they considered themselves to be primarily "morning people" (those who feel better and are more alert in the morning) or "evening people" (those who are more alert in the evening). As shown in Figure 5.2, Bodenhausen found that participants were more likely to make use of their (negative) stereotypes, thereby judging the defendant as guilty, at the time of day when the participants acknowledged that they were normally more fatigued. People who reported being most alert in the morning stereotyped more at night, and vice versa. This experiment thus provides substantial support for the idea that stereotypes serve, in part, to make our lives easier and that we rely on them when we are cognitively overloaded (for instance, when we are tired).

Categorization versus Individuation

Social categorization is a basic part of social life occurring regularly and often

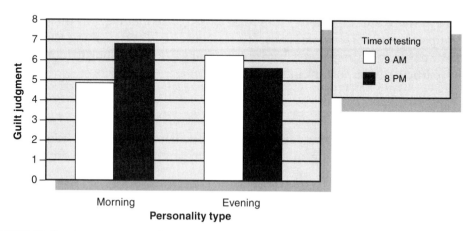

FIGURE 5.2. Stereotypes as energy savers. Participants were asked to judge the degree to which a defendant was guilty of a crime for which he was accused (however unfairly), and for which the crime fit the stereotype (for instance, that student athletes were likely to cheat on exams). Participants had previously indicated whether they were "morning people" or "night people" on a questionnaire and were tested in either the morning or the evening. Results showed that people used their stereotypes to a greater extent at times when they were more likely to be fatigued. Data from Bodenhausen, G. V. (1990). Stereotypes as judgmental heuristics: Evidence of circadian variations in discrimination. *Psychological Science, 1,* 319–322.

without our conscious intent. And once social categorization has occurred, stereotypes, as well as other feelings about the person who has been categorized, are activated (S. T. Fiske, 1982, 1998). However, we do not always think only about other people in terms of their group memberships. Rather, although we may normally begin our perception of others by categorizing them, we may (hopefully, most often) go beyond this initial step, getting to know the person as an individual rather than simply as a member of a social group. Whether or not we do so will depend on our current relationship with the other person, such as whether we think that the other person is interesting or important enough to warrant further processing (M. B. Brewer, 1988; S. T. Fiske & Neuberg, 1990). In short, we may use our stereotypes almost exclusively when the category is all the information we have about someone (Brodt & Ross, 1998), or if we are not particularly interested in getting to know the person better. In other cases, when we know the individual well (for instance, as classroom teachers know their students), we may ignore people's group memberships almost completely, responding to them entirely at the individual level (Madon et al., 1998).

Subtyping

One potential outcome of the continued processing of information about the person being categorized is **subtyping**. Subtyping occurs when the individual recategorizes the individual into a lower-level group membership (M. B. Brewer, Dull, & Lui, 1981; Deaux & Lewis, 1984; S. E. Taylor, 1981; R. Weber & Crocker, 1983). For instance, although we may have originally categorized a new co-worker as a man, we might later find it more useful to think of him as a "sports jock" or a "culture enthusiast." Subtyping is thus a logical extension of social categorization, one that provides even more information about the person than do broader social categories (Devine & Baker, 1991; Stangor et al., 1992).

Individuation

In other cases, it may not be possible to classify the individual into a subtype, and we proceed to consider them as individuals. In this case *individuation* or *personalization* occurs (Brewer, 1988; S. T. Fiske & Neuberg, 1990). Individuation is particularly likely when a category is accompanied by other information that makes the original categorization seem inappropriate. For instance, if we found out that a new female coworker was also an amateur weight lifter and a member of the Ku Klux Klan, we might need to completely abandon our use of the initial category. In this case the initial category (that she is female) becomes only one piece of information that we use in our attempt to understand the individual. In some cases, learning about others as individuals will

Subtyping: In the process of social categorization, recategorizing an individual into a lower-level group membership.

completely overwhelm the influence of their group memberships on our impressions of them (Locksley et al., 1980).

When Do We Individuate?

Whether we consider others in terms of their social categories or on the basis of other personal features will depend in part on our goals and motivations—that is, what we want to get out of the interaction. Motivations may lead to either categorization or individuation, depending on what the motivation is and who controls the desired outcome. In one relevant study (Neuberg & Fiske, 1987), research participants played a game with another person who was described as being a recovered mental patient (an "ex-schizophrenic"). In some cases the participants were dependent upon the other person for rewards, in the sense that they had to work together with the other person on the game to win a prize. In another experimental condition the research participants worked in the same room with the other person, but each person was competing on their own for the prize. Neuberg and Fiske found that the participants paid much more attention to information about the person when they were dependent upon him to win the prize, causing them to learn more about him—and particularly to find out his positive characteristics (things that they had not expected to be true of ex-schizophrenics). The participants who worked on the task to gain their own prize, however, didn't pay much attention to the other person, categorized him as a schizophrenic, and (although they had seen information that should have disconfirmed this expectation) perceived him negatively. In short, people are more likely to individuate others when they are interested in learning about them or when they need to accurately predict their behaviors.

Which Categories?

Because people are members of many different social categories, and because almost any characteristic of a person can become a category that could potentially be used for social categorization, it becomes important to attempt to understand which categories are used by which people under which circumstances to categorize others. Most generally, there are two answers to this question—categorization might be influenced by the characteristics of the person who is being categorized or by the characteristics of the person doing the categorizing.

Category Salience

We are more likely to categorize people using categories that are *salient*, meaning that they are immediately apparent when we see someone. Social categorization occurs frequently on the basis of people's sex, race, age, and physical attractiveness, in part because these features are immediately physically apparent to us when we see other people (M. B. Brewer, 1988). Although some categories, such as race and gender, are highly salient overall, categories are also likely to become particularly salient when individuals are in the context of members of other, different categories—that is, when they are *solos* (the only member of their group present) or when they are in the minority (Cota & Dion, 1986; Kanter, 1977; S. E. Taylor, 1981; P. J. Oakes, Turner, & Haslam, 1991; S. E. Taylor & Crocker, 1981). For instance, Taylor, Fiske, Etcoff, and Ruderman (1978) had people watch a discussion group in which there were either 3 men and 3 women, or in which there was only 1 woman and 5 men. They found that the same woman was more likely to be stereotyped when she was in a group of men than when she was with a group of women because her group membership became more salient. When individuals are infrequent representatives of their social categories—for instance, a senior citizen attending college or the only man in a ballet class—that category becomes contextually salient and the members of the category become particularly likely to be thought about in terms of their category membership.

Category Accessibility

Although the categories that are used to think about another person are determined in part by the salience of the category, characteristics of the individual who is doing the categorizing are also important. People vary in the categories that they find important to use when judging others such that some are more highly *accessible* (that is, more likely to be used in information processing) than are others. For instance, members of minority groups (such as African Americans) might find ethnicity to be a more important category than members of majority groups (European Americans), and, because it is highly accessible, these individuals might be particularly likely to think about others in terms of their ethnicity. Similarly, highly prejudiced people may also be particularly likely to categorize by race (Stangor et al., 1992), and women who are active in the feminist movement might be particularly likely to think about people in terms of gender (Bem, 1981; Pinel, 1999).

Outcomes of Social Categorization

There would be no particular reason to be concerned that social categorization routinely occurs in our interactions except that categorization has such important outcomes for the individuals whom we categorize. The problem is that, although thinking about others in terms of their social category memberships has some potential benefits for the person who does the categorizing, categorizing rather than individuating others may have some particularly negative outcomes for those who are categorized.

Social Categorization and Stereotyping

One potentially negative outcome of social categorization occurs because, once another person has been categorized, the stereotypes that are associated with the category may also be activated. Because the stereotypes are so closely associated with the category label, they may be activated spontaneously, without our even intending for them to be, and it may be difficult or impossible to stop the activation (Devine, 1989; Dovidio, Evans, & Tyler, 1986; Fazio, Jackson, Dunton, & Williams, 1995; Wittenbrink, Judd, & Park, 1997). Once the individual is categorized and the stereotypes associated with that category are activated, we may respond to the individual on the basis of the stereotypes.

It is known that stereotypes frequently color our judgments of those we categorize (M. B. Brewer, 1996; Cantor & Mischel, 1977; Duncan, 1976; Hamilton & Rose, 1980; Sagar & Schofield, 1980; Secord, Bevan, & Katz, 1956). For instance, Bodenhausen and Lichtenstein (1987) had research participants read about a courtroom trial in which a person had been accused of either a violent crime (murder) or a white-collar crime (embezzlement). Furthermore, the ethnicity of the person who had been accused of the crime was said to be either Hispanic or white. These researchers found that the sentences given were harsher when the crime was stereotypical of the person—Hispanics were given harsher sentences for the violent crime, whereas whites were given harsher sentences for the embezzlement. These negative outcomes of stereotyping are not only found in the lab, but also occur to real people who hold important positions (see, for instance, Fiske, Bersoff, Borgida, Deaux, & Heilman, 1991, for a case that went to the U.S. Supreme Court).

Research has also documented effects of stereotypes on hiring and medical decisions. In one study that investigated the prevalence of sex discrimination in hiring among major businesses in the United States, Glick and his colleagues (1988) sent bogus résumés to 212 business professionals. They found significant gender discrimination, even among these expert and supposedly impartial employment officers. Stereotypes have also been found to influence medical health treatment and outcomes. For example, black patients are less likely to receive major therapeutic procedures for many conditions and often do not receive necessary treatments, have delayed diagnoses, or fail to manage chronic diseases (Williams & Rucker, 2000). In one recent study, Bach, Cramer, Warren, and Begg (1999) found that blacks die from one form of lung cancer more often than whites, possibly as the result of their lower rate of surgical treatment, and similar problems have been identified for other minorities.

Although in some cases the stereotypes that are used to make judgments might actually be true of the individual being judged, in many other cases they are not. Thus stereotyping is problematic when the stereotypes held about a social group are inaccurate overall or when they do not apply to the individual who is being judged (Stangor, 1995). Although it may be difficult, individuals who wish to avoid stereotyping may be able to do so (S. T. Fiske, 1989; Lepore & Brown, 1997; Monteith, 1993; Monteith, Sherman, & Devine, 1998). For instance, many people in contemporary society hold egalitarian beliefs and feel that the use of stereotypes is inappropriate and unwarranted. These people have been found to be less likely to activate and use stereotypes in comparison to those who do not endorse egalitarian beliefs as strongly (Moskowitz, Wasel, Schall, & Gollwitzer, 1999; Monteith, Ashburn-Nardo, Voils, & Czopp, 2000). However, in many cases the person who is doing the judging may not even realize that he or she is being influenced by stereotypes, and thus is of course unable to correct for them.

Perceptual Accentuation

Henri Tajfel was an influential British social psychologist who studied the perception of both objects and people. In 1963 Tajfel and Wilkes performed a simple experiment that provided a picture of the potential outcomes of categorization (see also Marchand, 1970). As you can see in Figure 5.3, Tajfel and Wilkes' experiment involved having research participants judge the length of six lines. In one of the experimental conditions participants simply saw six

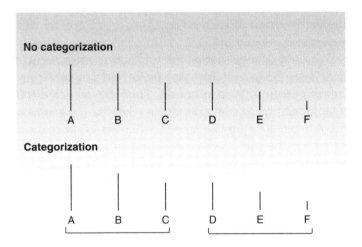

FIGURE 5.3. Perceptual accentuation. Tajfel and Wilkes (1963) showed how categorizing objects into groups could produce perceptual group differentiation. Line C and D were seen as the same length in the noncategorized condition, but line C was perceived as longer than line D when the lines were categorized into two groups.

lines, whereas in the other condition the lines were systematically divided into two groups—one comprising the three shorter lines and one comprising the three longer lines.

Tajfel made two predictions about how the individuals would perceive the lines. First, he expected to find *group differentiation*. Group differentiation occurs when the differences between members of two groups are exaggerated, such that the members of the two groups are seen as more different from each other (because they belong to different groups) than they actually are. Supporting this hypothesis, the results of his experiment showed that although lines C and D (which are actually the same length) were perceived as being of equal length when the lines were not categorized, line D was perceived as being significantly longer than line C in the condition in which the lines were categorized into two groups. In short, Tajfel found that the categorization into two groups—the "short lines group" and the "long lines group"—produced a perceptual bias such that lines C and D were actually seen as different lengths.

Tajfel also expected to find evidence for *group homogeneity*—the tendency for members of the same group to be seen as more similar to each other than they actually are. Although the findings of this study were more supportive of the group differentiation than the group homogeneity hypothesis, subsequent research has showed that both processes may operate in perception. Tajfel called this phenomenon by which individuals misperceive characteristics of groups of objects, **perceptual accentuation.**

Out-group Homogeneity

The important demonstration of Tajfel's study is that our perception of objects can frequently be distorted in such a way that we see greater differences between categories, and greater similarity within categories, than is actually the case. But Tajfel did not believe that perceptual accentuation only occurred for objects—rather, he expected to find that perception of social groups would also be subject to perceptual accentuation. Thus, he expected that social categorization would lead us to see individuals who share a group membership (such as women) to be more similar to each other than they really are, whereas differences between the members of different groups (men versus women) would be exaggerated.

Although there is at least some research evidence for the exaggeration of group differences (Ford & Stangor, 1992), there is even more evidence showing perceptions of group homogeneity. Although the perceptual accentuation perspective suggests that members of all social categories would be seen as similar when they are categorized as group members, it turns out that the tendency to see all members of a given social group as similar to each other is particularly strong for members of groups that the individual does not belong to. This

Perceptual Accentuation: The tendency to amplify perceived between-group differences and within-group similarities.

phenomenon, in which people view members of out-groups as being more similar to each other than they do members of in-groups is called the perception of **out-group homogeneity** (Jones, Wood, & Quattrone, 1981; Linville, Salovey, & Fischer, 1986; Ostrom & Sedikides, 1992; Park & Rothbart, 1982).

In a series of demonstrations of the out-group homogeneity effect, Patricia Linville and her colleagues (Linville & Jones, 1980; Linville et al., 1986) gave research participants a series of trait characteristics and asked them to think about a group of people and to place the trait terms into piles that represented different types of people in the group. The results of the studies were clear—for many different social groups people perceived the out-group as more homogeneous than the in-group. Thus men made fewer piles of traits when they were judging women than men, and women made fewer piles when they were judging men than women. Similarly, young people rated elderly people as more similar to each other than they did other young people, and students rated members of other universities as more similar than members of their own university.

There are a number of different potential causes for out-group homogeneity, each of which probably contributes at least in part to its occurrence. For one, people don't have as much contact with out-group members as they do with in-groups (Linville et al., 1986), and the quality of that interaction may be more superficial. In addition to learning less about them because we see and interact with them less, we also routinely categorize out-group members, thus reducing opportunities to individuate them and learn about their individual characteristics (S. A. Haslam, Oakes, & Turner, 1996). Furthermore, once we have stereotypes, we are likely to judge out-group members in terms of their social categories, leading interactions to remain at the group level, rather than the individual level.

In-group Homogeneity

Although research suggests that there is a general tendency toward perceived out-group homogeneity (Ostrom & Sedikides, 1992), there are also some cases in which in-groups are seen as more homogeneous than out-groups. This occurs particularly when the size of the in-group is small in relationship to the out-group (Simon & Brown, 1987), and when the in-group is particularly organized or the members have high social identity—for instance, when they are threatened by the presence of a larger, more powerful group. In these cases the members of the group perceive themselves as a unified, and therefore, similar group in relation to the larger (and hence more diverse) comparison group (Doosje, Ellemers, & Spears, 1995; Simon & Hamilton, 1994; Simon, Pantaleo, & Mummendey, 1995). The result is the perception of in-group, rather than out-group, homogeneity.

Out-Group Homogeneity: The tendency to view members of out-groups as extremely similar to each other.

Stereotype Maintenance

Once they become established, stereotypes are difficult to change. In part, this resistance is due to the use of the stereotypes themselves. Individuals who hold stereotypes may respond to members of stereotyped categories as if they already know what they are like, and this may confirm their existing beliefs. Supporting this idea, Trope and Thompson (1997) found in a laboratory experiment that individuals addressed fewer questions to members of categories about which they had strong stereotypes (as if they already knew what these people were like), and the questions that they did ask were likely to confirm the stereotypes they already had (see also Johnston & Macrae, 1994). In other cases stereotypes are maintained because information that confirms our stereotypes is better remembered than information that disconfirms them. Indeed, there is substantial research evidence indicating that, when processing information about social groups, individuals tend to better remember information that confirms their stereotypes (Fyock & Stangor, 1994; Sagar & Schofield, 1980; M. Snyder & Uranowitz, 1978; A. Van Knippenberg & Dijksterhuis, 1996). And stereotypes are also maintained because when people get together in groups they talk about out-groups in ways that tend to express confirming stereotypes (Harasty, 1997; Ruscher & Duval, 1998; Schaller & Conway, 1999).

Perhaps the most damaging aspect of stereotypes for the people who are being categorized, and a major factor making stereotypes so difficult to change, is that stereotypes about the members of social groups may actually influence the behavior of the individuals who are being categorized, such that the stereotypes are made to come true. A **self-fulfilling prophecy** occurs when people behave in ways toward members of groups about which they have expectations such that they make those expectations come true (Darley & Fazio, 1980; Hilton & Darley, 1985; Jussim, 1989, 1991; Jussim, 1996; R. Merton, 1948; D. T. Miller & Turnbull, 1986). In one study, Rosenthal and Jacobson (1968) informed some elementary school teachers that they had identified some of the students in their classes as "late bloomers." According to the researchers, these students could be expected to show sudden and dramatic increases in IQ over the course of the school year. These students had, in fact, been selected at random. When the researchers measured the achievement of the students at the end of the year, they found that, especially for younger children, the "late bloomers" had actually gained more in IQ than the other students, even though there was actually nothing special about them. Somehow the teachers' expectations about the children influenced how they behaved toward them, and this made their expectations come true. Self-fulfilling prophecies have also been found to maintain people's stereotypes about ethnicity, gender, social class, and physical attractiveness making it very difficult for people who are

Self-fulfilling Prophecy: The outcome of behaving in accordance with one's expectations so that those expectations come true.

stereotyped to disconfirm the existing beliefs about them (M. Snyder, 1981; M. Snyder, Tanke, & Berscheid, 1977; Word, Zanna, & Cooper, 1974).

Categorization into Us and Them

We have now seen that social categorization occurs whenever we think about others in terms of their category memberships rather than on the basis of other more individuating information about the person. And we have seen that social categorization can have negative consequences for the individuals who are the targets of stereotyping and prejudice. But social categorization becomes even more important, and has even more powerful effects upon our reactions to others, when the categorization involves *self-categorization* into a group to which we belong, as opposed to groups to which we do not belong.

In-group Favoritism

Although Henri Tajfel's important demonstration of the perceptual accentuation between groups fostered much research on perceptions of social group members and became the foundation of recent work on social categorization, Tajfel also conducted another important study involving self-categorization, and it is just as important for understanding group behavior.

Creating Social Groups

As we have seen, Tajfel was interested in how people perceive both objects and people. And he felt that both processes had similar characteristics. However, he noted that one important difference is that, in contrast to objects, people can be members of the groups that they categorize. In his research (Tajfel, Billig, Bundy, & Flament, 1971), groups of eight high school students came to his laboratory for a study supposedly concerning "artistic tastes." The students were first shown a series of paintings by two contemporary artists, Paul Klee and Wassily Kandinski. On the basis of their preferences for each painting, the students were divided into two groups (they were called the X group and the Y group). Each boy was told which group he had been assigned to and was told that different boys were assigned to different groups. But none of the children were told the group memberships of any of the other individual boys.

The boys were then given a chance to allocate small amounts of money to other boys in the in-group and the out-group (but never to themselves), using a series of charts, such as those shown in Figure 5.4. The charts divided a given number of points between two boys, and the task was to choose which

| In-group | 19 | 18 | 17 | 16 | 15 | 14 | 13 | 12 | 11 | 10 | 9 | 8 | 7 |
| Out-group | 1 | 3 | 5 | 7 | 9 | 11 | 13 | 15 | 17 | 19 | 21 | 23 | 25 |

| In-group | 23 | 22 | 21 | 20 | 19 | 18 | 17 | 16 | 15 | 14 | 13 | 12 | 11 |
| Out-group | 5 | 7 | 9 | 11 | 13 | 15 | 17 | 19 | 21 | 23 | 25 | 27 | 29 |

| In-group | 7 | 8 | 9 | 10 | 11 | 12 | 13 | 14 | 15 | 16 | 17 | 18 | 19 |
| Out-group | 1 | 3 | 5 | 7 | 9 | 11 | 13 | 15 | 17 | 19 | 21 | 23 | 25 |

| In-group | 11 | 12 | 13 | 14 | 15 | 16 | 17 | 18 | 19 | 20 | 21 | 22 | 23 |
| Out-group | 5 | 7 | 9 | 11 | 13 | 15 | 17 | 19 | 21 | 23 | 25 | 27 | 29 |

FIGURE 5.4. Examples of matrices used in the minimal intergroup studies of Tajfel and his colleagues. From Tajfel, H. (1970). Experiments in intergroup discrimination. *Scientific American, 223*, 96–102.

division to use. In some cases the division was between two boys in the in-group, in other cases the division was between two boys in the out-group, and in still other cases (as shown in Figure 5.4) the division was between a boy in the in-group and a boy in the out-group. The boys' point choices allowed Tajfel to make inferences about the goals that the boys were using when dividing up the points.

A comparison of the boys' choices in the different matrices showed that they allocated money between two boys in the in-group or between two boys in the out-group in an essentially fair way—so that each boy got the same amount. However, fairness was not the predominant approach when dividing points between in-group and out-group. In this case, rather than exhibiting fairness, the boys displayed **in-group favoritism**, such that they gave more points to other members of the in-group in relation to out-group members. For instance, the boys might assign 8 points to the in-group boy and only 3 points to the out-group boy, even though the matrix also contained a choice in which they could give the in-group and the out-group boys 13 points each. In short, the boys preferred to maximize the relative gains of the other boys in their own group, in comparison to the boys in the out-group, even if that meant giving their own group members fewer points than they could other-wise have received.

In-group Favoritism:
Expressing more positive attitudes, or behaving more positively toward in-group members than toward out-group members.

The Minimal Intergroup Effect

Perhaps the most striking part of Tajfel's results is that in-group favoritism was found to occur on the basis of arbitrary and unimportant groupings, such as perferences for paintings. Indeed, in-group favoritism even occurs when the assignment to groups is on a completely random basis and when there is little similarity among the members within a group (Locksley, Ortiz, &

Hepburn, 1980). When in-group favoritism occurs in groups that are not very meaningful, it is known as the **minimal intergroup effect** (M. B. Brewer, 1979; Wilder, 1981). The minimal intergroup effect represents a powerful demonstration of a very important group process—namely, that groups exist simply because individuals perceive those groups as existing. Even in a case where there really is no group (at least no meaningful group in the sense of interdependence or group structure), people still perceive the groups and demonstrate in-group favoritism.

Outcomes of Categorization into In-groups and Out-groups

Since the important studies of Tajfel and his colleagues, many other studies have been conducted to better understand in-group favoritism. In-group favoritism has been found for many different types of categories, in many different settings, on many different dimensions, and in many different cultures. A recent meta-analysis confirmed that people generally have an inclination to perceive the in-group favorably in comparison to relevant out-groups, and that the effect is of moderate magnitude (Mullen, Brown, & Smith, 1992). In addition to point allocation, in-group favoritism also occurs on trait ratings, such that in-group members are rated as having more positive characteristics than out-groups (Hewstone, 1990). People also talk differently about their in-groups than their out-groups. For instance, it has been found that people describe the in-group and its members as having broad positive traits (such as "generous" or "friendly") but describe negative in-group behaviors in terms of specific behaviors ("Bill hit someone") (Maass & Arcuri, 1996; Maass, Ceccarielli, & Rudin, 1996; Von Hippel, Sekaquaptewa, & Vargas, 1997). This allows them to spread positive aspects to all members of the in-group but reserve negative aspects for individual members. People also take credit for the successes of other in-group members (R. Brown, 1986), remember more positive information about in-groups (J. W. Howard & Rothbart, 1980), and are more critical of the performance of out-group than of in-group members (Wayne & Ferris, 1990).

Why In-group Favoritism?

There are a number of explanations for in-group favoritism, many of which probably simultaneously determine its occurrence (M. B. Brewer, 1979; Cadinu & Rothbart, 1996; Diehl, 1989). First, differentiating in-groups from out-groups helps us to simplify and structure our environment. In fact, people who report that they have strong needs for simplifying their environments also show more in-group favoritism (Shah, Kruglanski, & Thompson, 1998; Stangor & Thompson, 2002), and creating situations that require people to think simply (for

Minimal Intergroup Effect: In-group favoritism that occurs in groups that are not very meaningful.

instance, because they are under time pressure to make a decision) also increases in-group favoritism (Kruglanski & Freund, 1983). Secondly, there is a generalized and consensual norm among individuals to favor their in-groups over their out-groups. This occurs in part because people expect out-group members to act competitively, and they prepare for this by favoring in-group members. And in-group favoritism also occurs at least in part simply because (as we have seen in chapter 3) the self is part of the in-group, but not part of the out-group (Cadinu & Rothbart, 1996; E. R. Smith & Henry, 1996). Because we like people who are similar to ourselves (and other in-group members are perceived as similar to us), we end up favoring other members of our in-group, particularly when we differentiate them from members of out-groups.

Perhaps most importantly, in-group favoritism is the result of attempts to create a positive social identity by evaluating one's own groups positively (M. B. Brewer, 1979). Identification with a meaningful social group helps us maintain our personal and collective self-esteem (Phinney, Cantu, & Kurtz, 1997; Platow, Howard, & Stringer, 1996; Postmes, Branscombe, Spears, & Young, 1999; Spears & Manstead, 1997; J. C. Turner, 1987). Supporting this prediction, individuals have been found to express higher self-esteem after they have been given the opportunity to derogate out-groups (Fein & Spencer, 1997; Hogg & Abrams, 1988; Lemyre & Smith, 1985; M. Rubin & Hewstone, 1998), suggesting that in-group favoritism does increase personal self-worth. Furthermore, when individuals feel that the value of their in-group is being threatened, they respond by expressing more positive attitudes about in-groups and more negative out-group attitudes (Branscombe, Wann, Noel, & Coleman, 1993; Spears, Doosje, & Ellemers, 1997). In-group favoritism also increases when competition between groups is increased (Andreoli & Folger, 1977; M. B. Brewer et al., 1995; Coser, 1956), and particularly for the group that is doing more poorly in the competition (A. Kahn & Ryen, 1972; Wilson & Miller, 1961).

Exceptions to In-group Favoritism

Although there is a general tendency to show in-group favoritism, in at least some cases this does not occur. One situation in which in-group favoritism is less likely to be found is when the members of the in-group are clearly inferior on an important dimension. The players on a baseball team that has not won a single game all season are unlikely to be able to feel very good about themselves as a team, and are pretty much forced to concede that the out-groups are better, at least as far as playing baseball is concerned. In fact, a number of studies have shown that members of low-status groups show less in-group favoritism than do members of high-status groups and may even display out-group favoritism, in which they admit that the other groups are better than they are (K. Clark & Clark, 1947; Crocker & Luhtanen, 1990; C. Seta, Seta, & Donaldson, 1992; J. J. Seta & Seta, 1996). If individuals from low-status groups cannot gain positive social identity through their group memberships, it is likely that they may seek to leave the in-group entirely (Ellemers, Van Knippenberg, & Wilke, 1990; Lalonde & Silverman, 1994; D. M. Taylor & McKirnan, 1984; D. M. Taylor & Moghaddam, 1994; Wright, Taylor, & Moghaddam, 1990), and the group may therefore disband. We will discuss how individuals respond to being a member of a low-status group more fully in chapter 11.

 ## *Chapter Summary*

Social categorization refers to the use of social categories when judging other people. This often occurs spontaneously and without any real awareness or effort on the part of the person doing the judging. We categorize others because it is easy and because it can provide some information about them. Social categorization is at least in part the result of biological tendencies, but they are also determined by the salience and the accessibility of the categories. In many cases we are able to get beyond our initial categorizations, for instance, by using subcategories or (even better) by considering the individual characteristics of the person. Whether or not we do so depends upon our motivations and the time we have or are willing to spend.

In addition to producing stereotypes, prejudice, and even discrimination, social categorization also results in perceptual accentuation—the tendency to see members of in-groups and out-groups as more similar to each other than they are and to see bigger differences between groups than warranted. Because we do not interact as frequently with them, and because we use our stereotypes to judge them, perceptions of out-group homogeneity are particularly strong. In-group homogeneity results only in some relatively unusual situations, such as when a small in-group is threatened or of low status. Stereotypes are difficult to change once they are developed, due to memory and information-seeking biases as well as self-fulfilling prophecies.

Perhaps the most important outcome of social categorization is the tendency to favor our in-groups over out-groups. This occurs even in minimal situations, and even at the cost of absolute rewards for the in-group. In-group favoritism occurs in part because the self is a member of the in-group, but also results in part from the desire to increase social identity. In some cases, such as when the in-group is low status or obviously inferior on an important dimension, we may evaluate out-groups more positively than in-groups.

Review & Discussion Questions

1. What is social categorization? Which categories do you think are the most frequently used by the students at your university? Why are these categories so important to them?
2. Consider a time when you unfairly categorized another person and a time when you felt that another person unfairly categorized you. How did these experiences make you feel and behave?
3. What is self-categorization? Why does it occur, and what are its outcomes? What self-categories are most important to you?
4. What is outgroup homogeneity, and why does it occur? Under what circumstances are in-groups seen as homogenous?
5. What factors help make stereotypes and prejudices so difficult to change?
6. What is in-group favoritism and why does it occur? Do you think that in-group favoritism is a natural part of everyday life, or can people avoid it?
7. What is the minimal intergroup effect, and why does it occur?

Recommended Readings

A summary of social identity theory:
Hogg, M. A., & Abrams, D. (1988). *Social Identifications: A Social Psychology of Intergroup Relations and Group Processes*. London: Routledge.

A classic book concerning stereotyping, prejudice and discrimination:
Allport, G. W. (1954). *The Nature of Prejudice*. Reading, MA: Addison-Wesley.

A recent review of the difficulties of promoting harmonious relations among social groups:
Brewer, M., & Brown, R. (1998). Intergroup relations. In S. Fiske, D. Gilbert & G. Lindzey (Eds.), *Handbook of Social Psychology* (4 ed., Vol. 2, pp. 554–594). Boston: McGraw-Hill.

Group Development and Structure

6

*T*o this point we have investigated the elementary processes of group behavior. We have reviewed the basic principles of social influence and social categorization and considered why people join groups as well as the benefits that they can expect to receive from them. Now that we have developed a background for our study of groups, we can turn in this section to focus on the day-to-day behavior of active, working groups. We will begin our analysis in this chapter by considering how groups develop and change over time and how they begin to take on a structure. This structure includes group norms and the specific roles that different group members play in the group, as well as differences in status among group members.

Group Development

Although many groups seem to be mired in an existence that stays the same day in and day out, other groups are more dynamic—they change from year to year, month to month, or even from day to day. In fact, in almost all groups there is at least some change; new members come and go, the group may become more or less cohesive, and the goals of the group may also change. And even groups that have remained relatively stable for long periods of time may suddenly make dramatic changes, for instance when they face a crisis such as a change in task goals or the loss of a leader. And some groups may become more effective over time, as they adapt to their task demands and as the group members become more knowledgeable and proficient in meeting the group goals (Insko, 1982). On the other hand, groups may also lose their cohesion and identity as they meet the goals they initially set out to accomplish.

Regardless of their exact form, changes are important for both the group itself as well as for the individual group members. If the group is successful, other people will desire to become part of the group, because doing so allows them to receive the benefits of group membership. And in order to survive and continue to meet its goals, the group itself must maintain a sense of cohesion, keeping the members actively identified with the group and willing to work. In order to keep going the group may wish to recruit new members or to reject old ones. Thus the process of group development is a classic example of an interactionist phenomenon—the group changes to allow individual group members to contribute to the well-being of the group and to allow the group to provide benefits to its members.

Models of Group Development

How to understand and quantify the changes that occur in groups over time is a question that has long been of interest, and there have been many different proposed theories about how groups develop (Arrow, 1997; A. P. Hare, Borgatta, & Bales, 1965; J. M. Levine & Moreland, 1994; McGrath & Gruenfeld, 1993; Moreland & Levine, 1982; Tuckman, 1965; Worchel, Coutant-Sassic, & Grossmann, 1992). Although all of these theories share the common assumption that groups are dynamic rather than static, and that it is important to understand these changes, they differ in the level of analysis they have used to understand the problem.

Group-Level Approaches

Some models of group development have been framed at the level of the group. These models propose that groups pass through a series of states or stages over time. Some of these models assume that the stages of group development are sequential—that is, that all groups will pass through the same series of stages in a predetermined sequence. However, the patterns of changes in groups may not always be that well organized, and acknowledging this, other models suggest that different groups reach different stages in different orders, that some stages may be skipped, and that groups may also return to earlier stages over time.

Some researchers who favor sequential models of group development have compared the stages of group functioning to stages in the development of human beings. Just as a human being progresses from birth, through childhood, adolescence, adulthood, old age, and eventual death, so a social group, such as a musical group, a club, or a business may also pass through a series of sequential stages. During these stages the group members will initially get to know each other, develop group norms, and begin to work together. They will cooperate with each other and perhaps compete with other groups. During this time new members may join the group and current members may leave. Finally, if the members decide or are forced to disband—perhaps to form a new group or groups—the group may even die. Such sequential changes are observed in many different types of groups, including working groups that meet for only a relatively short time to accomplish relatively limited goals.

Interactionist Approaches

Other researchers have been critical of the group-level approach to understanding changes in groups over time, arguing that it is necessary to take into consideration not only the changes in the group, but also changes in relationships between the individual and the group (J. M. Levine & Moreland, 1994; Moreland & Levine, 1982). These authors suggest that a full understanding of group growth must take into consideration that groups and individuals are sometimes in harmonious relationships, but that at other times their relationships are more strained. For instance, in some cases an individual may be highly committed to being a group member, but the group is not so committed to the individual. The group may therefore be in a position to demand changes from the person in order for him or her to remain in the group. In other cases, when the group is more interested in having the individual as a member than the individual is in remaining part of the group, the balance of power may shift such that the individual may demand changes in the group in order to remain a member. Thus group development involves not just changes in the group as a group, but rather the evolution and change of the relationships between the group and its individual members.

In this chapter we consider some of the stages that many groups are likely to pass through and the characteristics that are likely to be found in groups at

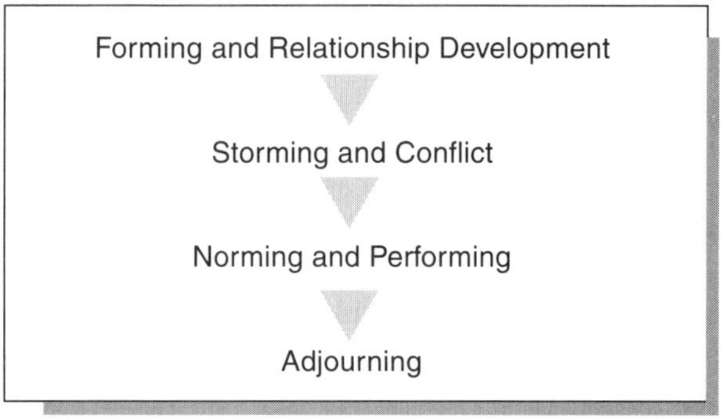

FIGURE 6.1. Stages of group development. This figure represents a general model of the phases of group development—beginning with group formation and ending with adjournment. It should be kept in mind, however, that the stages are not necessarily sequential, and it is not necessary that all groups pass through all stages.

each stage. We will organize our discussion in terms of a sequential model at the group level, as shown in Figure 6.1. However, we will also assume that these stages are rather loosely defined, that not all stages necessarily occur in all groups, and that the stages may not always occur in the order that we discuss them. Furthermore, we will explicitly consider the reciprocal relationship between the group and the individual at each of these stages.

Group Formation

The *group formation* stage occurs when the members of the group come together and begin their existence as a group. In some cases, such as when a new group such as a jury forms to accomplish a goal, the formation stage occurs relatively quickly, and is appropriately considered to be the group's first stage. In other cases, however, the process of group formation occurs continuously over a long period of time, such as when factory workers leave their jobs and must be replaced by new employees, or when a fraternity or sorority recruits new members every year to replace the old ones that leave at the end of each school year.

Developing New Relationships

Group formation involves the development of new relationships between the group and the individual group members. This development is important for both the new members as well as for the group itself. During this time the group and the individual will exchange knowledge about appropriate norms, including the existing group structures, procedures, and routines. This process may be difficult, because the individual and the group are in effect strangers to each other. The individual will need to learn about the group and determine how he or she is going to fit in. And the group may be inspecting the individual to discover his or her characteristics and appropriateness as a group member. This initial investigation process may end up with the individual rejecting the group or the group rejecting the individual.

Sometimes this get-acquainted process has a formal structure. Some groups, such as a classroom or a therapy group, will already have a leader who is skilled in integrating new members. The leader may have the participants engage in some formal activities that allow the group members to get to know each other, such as asking each of the participants to reveal something about themselves to the group. The group may also provide a mentor or sponsor who helps the individual adapt to the group, and the incoming members may also help each other during the initiation stage (Kram & Isabella, 1985).

The process of group formation is perhaps even more difficult when a new group is being formed. In this case the new group may not have a leader and must first decide whether there should be one. If so, they will need to determine procedures for choosing him or her. Because the group usually agrees that this should be done in a democratic manner, and yet the group may have no mechanisms in place for making such decisions, this decision may take a long time and involve much discussion and potential disagreement among the group members.

Behaviors of New Group Members

Although research into the behavior of individuals as they first join a group is not plentiful, there is some evidence about this process. In one experiment, Richard Moreland (1985) divided 50 male and 50 female undergraduates into five-member same-sex discussion groups that met once a week for three weeks to discuss issues of interest to students. Within each group, two randomly selected participants were told that they were "newcomers" and led to believe that they were entering a long-standing group. The other three participants assumed (correctly) that everyone was new to the group. Results showed that the individuals who thought they were new group members in an existing group expressed more anxiety, talked more than did the other participants, and agreed more with the other group members. As would be expected, this tendency was strongest at the first meeting, but over time the "new" participants began to blend in and behave more similarly to the other group members.

Initial Social Categorization

One problem in the group formation stage is that, because group members know little about each other as individuals, judgments are likely to be made on the basis of the members' social categories, resulting in stereotyping (S. T. Fiske & Neuberg, 1990). Salient social categories such as sex, race, and age are likely to play an important role at this stage, and group members may also be categorized as "new members" versus "old members." This problem is compounded in cases in which decisions about roles need to be made under time pressure. If the group needs to quickly elect a leader, for instance, this decision may be based almost exclusively on the social category memberships of the group members, because that is the only information that is available about them. As a result, women may be less likely to be chosen for leadership roles than men because of stereotypes about the superior leadership abilities of men over women (Eagly & Wood, 1982), and African Americans and other minorities may similarly receive lower-status positions. Unfortunately, once these stereotypes are used to make initial role assignments, the individuals may later find it very difficult to overcome them.

Initiation into Existing Groups

In other cases the group formation process is ongoing. The group has existed for a time, but it is continually losing members and needing to replace them. In this case the group formation process is somewhat different because, whereas in a new group the group members essentially define the group and create its norms, in an ongoing group it is more likely that the group will demand that the new members conform to existing group norms.

Some groups require that new members go through a strong initiation process before they are admitted. In extreme cases, such as fraternity or military hazing, the initiation may be so extreme as to become dangerous to the individuals. However, a more moderate initiation process can have positive outcomes, both for the individual and for the group. For one, an initiation period allows the group to learn about the individual and the individual to learn about the group. The initiation period may also provide a time period for the new individual to work together with the group members in order to learn new skills and to develop a good match between group and individual.

An initiation can in some cases be used to increase the loyalty, commitment, or investment of the individual to the group. For instance, in one classic experiment, Aronson and Mills (1959) had women perform an embarrassing procedure (reading sexually oriented passages from a novel in public) before they were allowed to join a group. The women who had gone through this experience subsequently reported more liking for the group than those who had not (see also Gerard & Matthewson, 1966, who found that being given mild electrical shocks as part of an initiation process had the same effect). Aronson and Mills argued that the more effort an individual expends to become a member of the group (for instance, a severe initiation), the more they will become committed to the group in order to justify the effort they have put in during the initiation.

Storming and Conflict

If the group formation stage can be compared to childhood, there is no doubt that the next stage—storming—can be compared to adolescence. As they begin to form and get to know each other, the group members may not always find that they agree on everything. In this stage the group members may attempt to make their own views known, expressing their independence and attempting to mold the group into accepting their own ideas. Although storming may occur as the group first gets started, it may recur at any point during the group's development, particularly if the group experiences a time of stress caused by a negative event such as a setback in progress toward the group goal. In some cases the conflict may be so strong that the group members decide that the group is not working at all, and the group disbands. In fact, field studies of real working groups have shown that a large percentage of new groups never get past the forming and storming stages before breaking up (Kuypers, Davies, & Hazewinkel, 1986).

    Although storming can be harmful to group functioning and thus groups must work to stop it, some conflict among the group members may in fact be helpful to the group. The most successful groups are sometimes those that have successfully passed through a storming stage, because, unless the conflict becomes so extreme that the group disbands prematurely, conflict may actually increase the productivity of the group (Coser, 1956; Hare et al., 1965; Tuckman, 1965). As we will see in chapter 8, members of groups that experience no conflict at all may be unproductive, because the members are bored, uninvolved, and unmotivated, and because they do not think creatively or openly about the topics of relevance to them. In order to progress, the group needs to develop new ideas and new approaches, and this requires that the members discuss their different opinions about the decisions that the group needs to make. The approaches the group uses to be creative and productive must be developed through conversation and interaction, which may be accompanied by some conflict.

Norming and Performing

Assuming that the storming does not go too far, the group will move into a stage in which norms and roles are developed, allowing the group to establish a routine and effectively work together. At this stage the individual group members may report great satisfaction and identification with the group, as well as strong group cohesion. Groups that have reached this stage have the ability to meet goals and survive challenges. However, in some cases the optimal stage for effective performance takes a long time to develop, and groups often do not reach this stage until near the end of the group's proposed time period.

In one interesting observational study studying the group development process, Connie Gersick (1988) observed a number of teams (ranging from student study groups to community fundraising committees) as they worked on different projects. The teams were selected so that, though they were all working within a specific time frame, the time frame itself varied dramatically—from 4 to 25 meetings held over periods ranging from 11 days to 6 months. Despite this variability, Gersick found that each of the teams followed a very similar pattern of norming and performing. In each case the team established well-defined norms regarding its method of attacking its task in its very first meeting. And each team stayed with this approach, with very little deviation, during the first half of the time it had been allotted. However, midway through the time it had been given to complete the project (and regardless of whether that was after 2 meetings or after 12 meetings), the group suddenly had a meeting in which it decided to change its approach. Then, each of the groups used this new method of performing the task during the rest of its allotted time. It was as if there was a sort of an alarm clock that went off at the halfway point that led each group to rethink its approach.

Adjourning

Most groups eventually come to an end. In some cases this occurs because the task for which the group was formed has been completed, whereas in other cases it occurs because the group members have developed new interests outside the group. In any case, because people who have worked in a group have often developed a strong identification with the group and the other group members, the adjournment phase is often stressful, and participants may resist the breakup. Faced with these situations, individuals frequently plan to get together again in the future, exchanging addresses and phone numbers, even though they may well know that it is unlikely that they will actually do so. In some cases it is useful for the group to work ahead of time to prepare the group members for the breakup.

Group Structure

As we have discussed in chapter 1, there are several indications that an initial aggregate of individuals has developed into a true social group. One such marker is group structure. Group structure refers to the relatively stable relationships among group members, including lines of communication, procedures, and decision rules, distribution of labor, as well as the types of roles that different group members take on. In some cases the structure in a group is formal, as in the power hierarchy of a large corporation. In other cases the structure is more implicit—for instance the relationships within a family or among a group of friends.

Group structure develops in part for efficiency. Specialized social roles—for instance having a president, a secretary, and a treasurer—allow an efficient division of labor. In other cases, structure may occur because of the characteristics of the individual group members. Members who have similar interests or who share a social category membership may tend to work and socialize together and form a subgroup within the larger group. In still other cases structure occurs just to make people happy—we prefer to know what our own roles and the roles of others are (Bales, 1950).

Social Roles

As we have seen in chapter 1, roles refer to the behaviors that individual group members are expected to perform. Roles reflect, in essence, the parts that we play in a group, just as an actor has a role to play in a movie or on the stage (Biddle, 1986; Parsons, 1951; Simmel, 1920). In some cases the roles are assigned to us, and in some cases we choose them. Some roles are rather well defined—for instance, the role of boss versus employee or that of teacher versus pupil. In other cases, the roles are less clear—for instance, the different roles that men and women are expected to play on the basis of social stereotypes. In every case, however, the roles matter because the group members perceive them, and these roles determine how the individual relates to the group.

In short, roles represent norms or expectations that apply to the jobs or positions of individuals in the group (E. P. Hollander, 1964; McGrath, 1984; Newcomb & Charters, 1950). Social roles are defined not only by what the individual thinks he or she should do, and what he or she prefers to do, but also in terms of what the group members think that the individual should believe or do (which may or may not match the person's own beliefs). The role expectations both define as well as limit the range of appropriate behaviors for a person. Thus, although social roles have a great advantage for the group, because they allow the group members to specialize and provide for lines of communication among the group members, the need to adopt a particular role may not always be in the best interests of the individual.

Task Roles and Socioemotional Roles

A number of research projects have discovered that in many working groups individuals tend to fall into two commonly occurring social roles (Bales, 1950;

Benne & Sheats, 1948). These roles are not usually assigned to the individual (although they may be), but rather represent differences in the preferred way that individuals relate to the other group members. The *task-oriented role* refers to a set of behavior patterns that involve working toward production and goal achievement. Individuals who assume task-oriented roles assign tasks, coordinate activities, and monitor and criticize the performance of others. The *socioemotional role*, on the other hand, involves behaviors that provide support to group members and attempts to keep group interactions harmonious. Those who assume the socioemotional role consider the feelings of the other group members, which is accomplished through open, friendly communications.

Although it is not impossible that the two types of roles could be found in the same person, usually different people will do these jobs. One reason for this is that the two roles demand different types of responses to group members (either assigning tasks, monitoring, and criticizing for the task-oriented role or being friendly and helpful for the socioemotional role), and it is difficult for the same person to engage in both types of behavior. The distinction may be particularly strong when the group is under stress. A large number of studies have now documented that these two roles can account for the behavior patterns of many group members. Indeed, as we have seen in chapter 2, Bales built his system of analyzing group behavior (SYMLOG) to assess the extent to which the group members displayed these two primary roles.

Role Ambiguity

Although roles are important for defining the functions of group members and coordinating group activities, the need to fulfill roles may in some cases cause problems for the group and its members. One potential difficulty occurs when the group expects the individual to perform a role but at the same time does not provide sufficient information about how to do it. **Role ambiguity** occurs when the goals and objectives of the role are not clear to the person and he or she is unsure what is demanded. This might occur when a group member is elected to chair a committee to suggest changes in group process or structure, but it is not clear to him or her what changes would be effective or whether the group wishes to change at all. In this case the group may be expecting the individual to fulfill a given role and may perhaps even punish them if they do not do so, and yet the individual cannot really do the job because the demands of the role are not clear or there is no support from the rest of the group for engaging in it. Role ambiguity may be a particular problem for new group members or for those who have been given new positions until the roles become clear for them.

Role Ambiguity: A situation in which goals and objectives of one's role are not clear to the person and he or she is unsure what is demanded.

Role Conflict

Another role-related problem is *role conflict.* **Role conflict** occurs when the individual is expected to fulfill more than one role or when the demands from one set of people compete with those of another set of people. Role conflict can occur when the individual is expected to play two separate and yet competing roles (trying to be both a manager and a friend to subordinates) or when playing the same role produces conflicting demands (when a manager struggling to keep costs down must fire valued coworkers). It has been argued that women in contemporary society are suffering from role conflict when they are required to play the role both of mothers and of working women. And in other cases individuals within a working group may feel competing loyalties to other members of their ethnic or racial groups and to the corporation as a whole (Thomas-Hunt & Gruenfeld, 1998).

Because role ambiguity and role conflict create great sources of stress for the individual, they will eventually harm the group's productivity (Flaherty, Dahlstrom, & Skinner, 1999). As a result, it is important for group leaders to make the requirements of each group member very clear to all of the individuals in the group by providing explicit information about which demands a group member must put ahead of others (Brief, Aldag, Russell, & Rude, 1981; Van Sell, Brief, & Schuler, 1981) and by not assigning individuals to conflicting roles.

Gender Roles

On average, women and men differ in both their preferences for and likelihood of engaging in task-oriented versus socioemotional roles. When asked to report about their own characteristics, men tend to show more task orientation, whereas women report having a greater socioemotional orientation (Dion, 1979; Hare, 1976). And observations of the behaviors of men and women show that men and women take on different roles in social groups, particularly when the group is under stress (L. R. Anderson & Blanchard, 1982).

Although there are differences, on average, between men and women in their preferences for playing one role or the other, not all women prefer to take socioemotional roles, and not all men prefer task-oriented roles. However, stereotypical perceptions may force individual men and women to play their appropriate sex roles even when this might not be their preferred approach.

This problem is particularly acute for women, because expectations about their appropriate social roles conflict with the behaviors required for the role of effective leaders or managers. The difficulty is that women are expected to be socioemotional, rather than task-oriented. When women act assertively, or attempt to give orders to others, they are seen as acting out of their gender

Role Conflict: A situation in which the individual is expected to fulfill more than one conflicting role or when it is difficult to fulfill one's role because the demands from one set of people compete with those of another set of people.

role, which frequently leads them to be disliked. However, it is exactly these behaviors that are required of effective leaders and managers, and women who do not take on the task role may not be able to gain the respect and promotions that they deserve (S. T. Fiske et al., 1991).

Furthermore, because it is more natural for them, women frequently perform the behaviors required of them in the group by engaging in socioemotional activities—cooperating, helping others, and encouraging group interaction—rather than by overtly commanding and supervising. As a result, women may not be seen as effective group members by their superiors, and this may prevent their accomplishments from being recognized (Tannen, 1995). Women must learn to negotiate these role conflicts (Rojahn & Willemsen, 1994; Rudman & Glick, 1999), and effective work groups must work to be sure that competent women are allowed and encouraged to contribute to the group process.

Social Status

In addition to differences among group members in their expected roles, in many groups a structure is also created around status differences. As we have seen in chapter 1, status refers to a group member's authority, prestige, or reputation, in relationship to the other members of the group (Sachdev & Bourhis, 1987; Tajfel, 1978; D. G. Wagner & Berger, 1993). Although status always involves relative prestige, it nevertheless takes somewhat different forms in different groups. At a societal level, for instance, status is known as *socioeconomic status* or *SES,* and is determined by a combination of factors, including household income and educational background. In small working groups, on the other hand, status is normally determined by the ability of the individual to influence others or to help the group reach its goals. Status in working groups is usually measured either using self-report, or though behavioral measures such as speaking time, eye contact, and the tendency to interrupt others (Stiles et al., 1984), all of which are allotted to greater degree to those with higher status.

As we have seen earlier, when a group is first forming, individuals' social category memberships play a large role in determining their status (D. G. Wagner & Berger, 1993). The status that one accrues as a result of his or her social category memberships is called **diffuse status.** In most cases, men have more diffuse status than women (Eagly, 1983; Riordan, 1983), older people have more diffuse status than younger people, those with high-paying occupations have more diffuse status than those with low-paying occupations and (at least in the United States) whites have more diffuse status than blacks. Thus, older white male individuals, and particularly those with high-prestige occupations, are likely to be afforded status (Meeker, 1990).

The effects of diffuse status are problematic for working groups when

Diffuse Status: The status that one accrues as a result of one's social category memberships.

group members make inferences about the likely performance of an individual on the basis of his or her status characteristics. Driskell and Mullen (1990) conducted a meta-analysis summarizing existing studies that had tested the influence of status on expectations and behavior by experimentally manipulating the diffuse status of one or more of the members of a social group. These manipulations included variation in such status characteristics as race, gender, and education. Their analysis showed that, across the studies, the experimental manipulations did significantly influence the expectations that other group members held about the individuals, and that these expectations in turn significantly influenced group task performance. In each case individuals with low status were perceived as less effective group members, and this in turn led them to perform more poorly.

Unfortunately, diffuse status may well have no relationship to the individual's actual ability to help the group reach its goals, and thus decisions made on the basis of these categories may be counterproductive (Ridgeway, 1997). If the younger black female is actually a better leader than the older white male, then the influence of diffuse status on group performance will be negative. Furthermore, status afforded on the basis of social categories has another drawback—it constrains how people will behave in groups. Because women have low status in many groups, they participate less and engage in fewer active behaviors in comparison to men. They are also interrupted more often, speak less, and tend to be less influential than men overall (Dovidio, Brown, Heltman, Ellyson, & Keation, 1988; Pugh & Wahrman, 1983; W. Wood & Karten, 1986). In addition, women (and other lower- status individuals) recognize their lower status, report more dissatisfaction about it (E. G. Cohen, 1982; McCranie & Kimberley, 1973), and must work harder to gain status (Foschi, 1996). Again, leaders of effective work groups must assure that those with low diffuse status are encouraged to contribute to the group process.

Getting and Keeping Status

Although the initial assignment of status in working groups is likely to be based on diffuse status, as the group members get to know each other and as the group starts to work to accomplish its goals, other characteristics will come into play that determine who gets status and who gets to keep it. There are a number of theories that have been developed to explain these processes.

Dominance Contests

Because status hierarchies are also found in animals, it has been argued that humans may gain status, at least in part, as animals do, by expressing and earning their dominance over others in social interaction (M. T. Lee & Ofshe,

1981; Mazur, 1985; Strayer, 1995). Supporting this hypothesis, people who talk more and louder, and who initiate more social interactions, are afforded higher status, even when their contribution to meeting the group goals is not actually greater than that of others (Dovidio et al., 1988; Mullen, Salas, & Driskell, 1989). A businessman who adopts a strong handshake and a direct gaze does so to gain status, and those who speak out strongly for their opinions in group discussions may be doing so as well. Although such "dominance contests" occur in large part in normal social behavior, they may at times escalate into events in which the taller or stronger individual uses physical or verbal threat to attempt to get his or her way—for instance, by shouting, commanding, or aggressively staring at others. Furthermore, taller people may have more status because they are perceived as being more dominant, and this may have something to do with why men frequently have higher status than women.

One interesting empirical finding that is quite consistent with this line of reasoning is that taller people tend to be more likely to be perceived as leaders in comparison to shorter people. For instance, with two exceptions (Jimmy Carter and George W. Bush), in every election for U.S. president back to Abraham Lincoln, the taller candidate has won. Although this could be coincidence, the likelihood of its occurring by chance is very small.

Specific Status

Over the long run, status will be determined not only by winning dominance contests, but also by the individual's perceived ability to lead the group toward its goals. Status that is gained through effective and competent performance on the group tasks is called **specific status.** Those who have particular knowledge or skills that are needed for effective group functioning, or who come up with new ideas or plans, will be accorded specific status within the group.

Because having the ability to help the group reach its goals will give people status, even those who initially have low diffuse status may eventually be able gain prestige through successful performance. However, the expectation on the part of other group members is that these individuals do not have such skills. As a result of the many processes that make it difficult to change stereotypes (see chapter 5), it is therefore difficult for people to disconfirm these initial expectations, and the burden of proof rests on the ability of the low-diffuse-status individual to overcome these negative expectations and demonstrate that they are incorrect. Faced with these problems—and unless the group works to prevent this from occurring—low-diffuse-status individuals may simply accept their existing position and give up trying to convince others that they do have appropriate skills and abilities (Jost & Banaji, 1994).

Specific Status: Status that is gained through effective and competent performance on group tasks.

Conformity to Group Norms

Still another method of earning status is by engaging in behaviors that are approved of by the group—for instance, by conforming to group norms or by publicly expressing positive feelings about the group and its opinions (E. P. Hollander, 1958; E. P. Hollander & Julian, 1970). In one study demonstrating this effect, Hollander (1960) created work groups of four students and one confederate. The task was to choose, on each of 15 trials, and on the basis of a complicated matrix that the experimenter provided, which outcome would achieve the most points for the group. The confederate was given answers ahead of time that allowed him to do better than any of the other group members could do. On each block of 5 trials the confederate either acted in accordance with group norms by following the speaking and decision rules of the group or else broke with convention by talking out of turn or questioning the group's decision-making procedures. The dependent measure was the number of trials on which the group decided to use the confederate's decision.

The results made it clear that just having the proper information (and thus being able to help the group reach its goals) did not always help the confederate to gain status. Rather, the way the confederate made use of this information was critical. The confederate's decision was used significantly more often on trials after which he had initially conformed to group norms than on trials in which (although he gave the correct answer) he had earlier violated the norms. Thus the confederate was able to convince the others to accept his decision partly on the basis of his skills, but also partly on the basis of conforming, on a previous trial, to group norms. Hollander argued that those who wish to gain status must first build up a type of "credit" with the other group members by demonstrating that they were aware of and willing to follow group norms, and that only then would they be able to exert their influence.

Consequences of Status

Perhaps not surprisingly, people enjoy having status and generally try to attain it. For one, the high-status individual is in a better position to assert influence on the other group members. In a study using simulated juries, Strodtbeck and Lipinski (1985) found that high-status forepersons had more influence in jury outcomes than did low-status forepersons. In addition to being able to get their way, research has also found that higher-status individuals have higher self-esteem, are also better liked by the other group members, and are more satisfied with their group relations (Lovaglia & Houser, 1996). However, because the group relies upon high-status members to help it reach its goals, individuals with high status who hurt the groups' performance can be treated very negatively. Wiggins, Dill, and Schwartz (1965) found that when a high-status person made a decision that had only a minor negative effect upon the group, he was given more leeway than a lower-status person. However, when the poor decision involved grave negative consequences for the group, the high-status person was disliked even more than a group member with low or medium status who had made the same poor decision.

Social Networks

In addition to developing a formal structure with defined roles and status, groups also develop a more informal set of communication patterns that determine how information is shared among the group members. A **social network** is a set of individuals within a group who are connected through social relationships, such as friendship, and who thus communicate frequently and influence each other. As we have seen in chapter, 2 social networks can be diagrammed using a sociogram that indicates the patterns of communication within the group (Wellman & Berkowitz, 1988). Larger groups generally have several small subgroups or cliques of individuals who communicate frequently, and may also have some outcasts and isolates who are rejected or neglected by other group members. Variation in status among group members also influences social networks. For instance, high-status individuals frequently form subgroups from which they exclude those of lower status, and communication is generally directed from high-status members to low-status members more often than in the reverse direction. However, social networks are also based to large extent upon liking—people tend to communicate with people they like. Social networks have an important influence on how groups develop, their likelihood of remaining together, and their ability to get work done (Reagans & Zuckerman, 2001; Leavitt, 1951).

The Physical Environment

The organization of people in space helps determine their communication patterns and the development of social networks (Sommer, 1969). People who are physically closer to each other in their everyday environments (those who sit nearest each other in an office or who live nearest each other in a neighborhood, for example) are likely to communicate more frequently and end up influencing each other. In one experiment Festinger, Schachter, and Back (1950) studied the development of friendships among married couples living in a student apartment complex. Although the couples had been randomly assigned to their buildings and apartments, the researchers found that over time people reported that their best friends lived nearer to them. This makes sense, because people are more likely to see and have access to others who are nearby,

Social Network: A set of individuals within a group who are connected through social relationships, such as friendship and social influence, and thus who communicate frequently with one another.

and being near to people makes it easier to become friends with them. The same patterns develop in schools and organizations—individuals who are in physical proximity tend to develop subgroups and cliques.

Because people who are nearer each other physically are more likely to develop friendly relationships, social networks end up being structured in large part as a result of the situations in which people find themselves. A small group that works in an office environment may well develop clear, stable, and open social networks among coworkers, because they are in constant contact with each other, and communication is easy. A larger corporation, on the other hand, in which different workers are located on different floors in an office building, is likely to develop cliques made up of the members who work on the different floors. And emergency workers who spend their time out in the field, and who are rotated from shift to shift into different teams, may develop much less complete social networks—perhaps becoming close to only one or two other coworkers.

The physical features of the group's work environment may influence the development of networks in other ways as well. One example of the importance of the physical relationship among group members is that people who sit at the head of a table in a working group are afforded more status than the other people around the table. This is in part because people who have leadership skills are more likely to choose to sit at the head of the table. It is also possible that the people who sit at the head of the table are perceived as having higher status, in part, because the attention of other group members is directed toward them (Nemeth & Wachtler, 1974).

Information Sharing and Networks

Social networks are important because they determine the flow of information among the individuals within the group, and access to information is important for good decision making. Information does not flow equally to all members. Individuals who are central in the group structure, in the sense that they communicate frequently with others and have access to important group-related information, will have more power and influence in the organization. Individuals with less access to information, on the other hand, can feel isolated and dissatisfied, and are less likely to have much influence or status (Lovaglia & Houser, 1996).

In some working groups the communication patterns are relatively limited, and information is sent primarily to and from one or a few individuals. Often these communications are from those with higher status to those with lower status. For instance, a manager may receive information from his or her workers, consider that information, and relay his or her decisions and new orders back to the managers, but the managers may not communicate among themselves at all. This pattern represents a more *centralized* network, in which one or a few persons control access to most of the information and in which information primarily flows in one direction. Such centralized networks include the "star" structure, in which all of the information must flow through one central individual (for instance a manager):

and the hierarchical structure, in which information flows from lower-status to upper-status workers, but the workers at any one level do not share information.

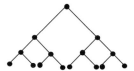

In other cases, however, the flow of communication in the group may be more open, *decentralized,* and lateral—for instance, if the workers are all encouraged to share information directly with each other:

There may be advantages to each type of network. A centralized network may be more useful when the task is relatively simple and it is important to keep track of information and relay orders quickly. A decentralized network, on the other hand, may be better for more complex tasks that require creative solutions that can only occur with increased information flow (Shaw, 1964).

Social networks develop in large social groups such as organizations just as they do in smaller social groups. Some of these networks are prescribed by the defined structure of the company's organizational chart and include work groups, committees, and teams. But informal social networks of friendship structures also develop. As in smaller groups, it is possible to assess the networks within an organization, and we can use the resulting sociograms to compare the structure of different organizations (Baker, 1992). For instance, many traditional corporations have a hierarchical and highly structured network, beginning with a small number of powerful individuals at the top and opening up to a larger number of less powerful individuals at the bottom. In these cases communication and influence is primarily hierarchical, moving from the less powerful to the more powerful and vice versa.

Many contemporary firms, on the other hand, attempt to develop a more lateral or horizontal network. In these situations the communication is more decentralized, based on informal interactions, and the flow of influence is broader. The ability to develop such informal structures has been enhanced by advances in communication technology, and many of these communications are developed and maintained through e-mail. Again, although centralized organizations may be useful in some situations, decentralized networks may have some advantages, for instance, in crisis situations, because the flow of information is greater.

Because those with more access to information have more power, individuals will work to gain it—a process generally known as *networking* (Guetzkow & Simon, 1955). It has been found in investigations within organizations that individuals who have more contacts with others—for instance, because they have made friendships across a wide variety of people from different areas within the organization—also have more power and status (Brass, 1984; Thomas-Hunt & Gruenfeld, 1998). In some cases members of lower-status social categories, such as ethnic minorities and women, may be isolated from some of the important social networks within the organization, and this may limit their ability to gain status (Linehan, 2001). In many organizations men may have informal networks that revolve around sports and other interests, and women and minorities may not be included in these. To help retain and improve their status with the organization, women and minorities may develop their own networks, in part to share information and increase their social influence (Ibarra, 1993; Thomas-Hunt & Gruenfeld, 1998).

 Chapter Summary

This chapter has been concerned with how groups develop over time and the structure that they take on as they do so. We have taken an interactionist perspective, considering both how the individual influences the group as well as how the group influences the individual.

Over time many groups follow similar patterns of development, although these may be either sequential or cyclical in nature. During the forming stage the group provides information to the group members who are first joining the group, and the new members learn about the group and what to expect once they join it. In some cases the formation involves an initiation of group members, often used to increase loyalty to the group. During the forming stage stereotypes about new group members are likely to form, and these may frequently impact the outcome of initial group interactions.

Once the initial stage has passed, the group can begin its work. Frequently the next stage involves storming and conflict, in which the group members compete to get their ideas accepted. The storming stage can have benefits for the members as they get to know each other better and learn to work prematurely together, but it can also be dangerous if conflict escalates and the group disbands. The next stage of group development is norming, in which the group develops appropriate guidelines and structure to do its work. The new structure allows the group to enter the performing stage, in which it efficiently meets its goals. Finally, many groups end in an adjournment stage, in which the group disbands.

Group structure involves the creation of social roles and social status— rules of preferred activities perceived as appropriate for a specific group member or members. Two common types of social roles are task roles and socioemotional roles. Frequently men tend to perform task roles and women to perform socioemotional roles. Roles can help define the appropriate behavior for the individual, yet in other times they can force individuals into performing unwanted behaviors, or result in role ambiguity or role conflict.

Social status refers to the extent to which the group member has prestige and respect. Diffuse status is determined by the social category memberships of the individual. Although diffuse status influences the initial assignment of status, performance-based (specific) status and conformity to group norms are more important in obtaining and maintaining status during later stages of group development. Having status has both positive and negative consequences for the group member.

Social networks refer to the lines of communication and influence within a group. Individuals who are able to access information generally have higher status in the group, and therefore people frequently attempt to develop strong social networks. The ability to form networks is influenced by the physical features of the group setting as well as by one's social category memberships and the relevant group norms and group structure.

 ## Review and Discussion Questions

1. Consider the group and the interactionist approaches to understanding group development.
2. What are the normal stages of group development? Do all groups go through similar stages?

3. What kinds of social roles are played in social groups, and how does role-playing relate to status and power? Consider some groups that you belong to and the roles you play in them.
4. What is status? How do we know when someone has it, and how is it gained? How is status determined among the students at your college or university?
5. What is the relationship between one's gender and ethnicity and one's status?
6. What are social networks, how are they developed, and why are they important for groups and group members?

Recommended Readings

Why an initiation process can produce group cohesion:
Aronson, E., & Mills, J. (1959). The effect of severity of initiation on liking for a group. *Journal of Abnormal and Social Psychology, 59,* 171–181.

Here are two different theories of group development that can be compared:
Levine, J., & Moreland, R. (1994). Group socialization: Theory and research. In W. Stroebe & M. Hewstone (Eds.), *European Review of Social Psychology* (Vol. 5, pp. 305–336). Chichester, UK: Wiley.
Tuckman, B. (1965). Developmental sequences in small groups. *Psychological Bulletin, 63,* 384–399.

Power and Leadership 7

*I*n the last chapter we considered how groups change over time and how group structures develop that differentiate group members into various roles and status levels within the group. In this chapter we will extend our discussion of group structure by more fully considering group status hierarchies, with a focus on the issues of *social power* and *leadership*. When a jury picks a foreperson to be the spokesperson and coordinator of the group's activities, when a corporation names a new chief executive officer, or when we vote for a school council president, we are determining who will have social influence. Thus, power and leadership are part of the role and status structures that define the patterns of social influence in the group.

People who have power over others, such as those who are in positions of leadership, can produce either positive or negative outcomes for the group as a whole. An effective military leader or the coach of a football team can motivate the group to produce outstanding achievements. On the other hand, a poor leader can lead a group into ruin. Because leaders have such powerful influence on group behaviors, much research effort has been devoted to understanding the issues of power and leadership. Let us begin by analyzing the types of power that individuals may wield over other group members and then turn to an analysis of how leaders may make use of this power.

Social Power

One of the fundamental aspects of virtually all social groups is that some individuals have more influence than others. These differences create the group structure and are essential for group process. **Social power** can be defined as the ability of one individual to create behavioral or opinion changes in another person, even when the person being influenced may attempt to resist those changes (French & Raven, 1959; Raven, 1992; Sachdev & Bourhis, 1985; Sachdev & Bourhis, 1991). In short, then, power refers to the process of social influence itself—those who have power are those who have the ability to influence others.

Milgram's Studies on Obedience to Authority

A classic example of the ability of those in authority to control others was demonstrated in a remarkable set of studies performed by Stanley Milgram (1974). Milgram was interested in the extent to which a person who presented himself as an authority would be able to produce obedience, even to the extent of leading that person to cause harm to others.[1] Like many other researchers who were interested in conformity, Milgram's interest stemmed in part from his desire to understand the ability of one influential leader—Adolph Hitler, the German dictator who ordered the killing of millions of Jews during World War II—to produce obedience in his followers.

Using newspaper ads, Milgram recruited men (and a few women) from a wide variety of professions to participate in his research (Milgram did not find any gender differences in obedience). When the research participant arrived at the lab, he was introduced to another man who was ostensibly another research participant, but who actually was an experimental confederate. The

Social Power: The ability of one individual to create behavioral or opinion changes in another person, even when the person being influenced may attempt to resist those changes.

---

1. Milgram called his participants' behavior *obedience,* and we will use this term, but obedience can be considered as a type of compliance toward authority figures.

experimenter explained that the goal of the research was to study the effects of punishment on learning. After the participant (and the confederate) both consented to participate, it was explained that one of them would become the teacher, and the other the learner. They were each given a slip of paper and asked to open it and to indicate what it said. In fact, both papers read "teacher," which allowed the confederate to pretend that he had been assigned to be the learner and thus assured that the participant always became the teacher.

While the research participant (now the teacher) looked on, the learner was taken into the adjoining shock room and strapped to an electrode that was to deliver the punishment. The experimenter explained that the teacher's job would be to sit in the control room and read a list of words pairs to the learner. After the teacher read the list once, it would be the learner's job to remember which words went together. For instance, if the word pair was "blue-sofa" the teacher would say the word "blue" on the testing trials, and the learner would have to indicate which of four possible words ("house," "sofa," "cat," or "carpet") was the correct answer by pressing one of four buttons in front of him.

After the experimenter gave the "teacher" a moderate shock to demonstrate that the shocks really were painful, the experiment began. The research participant first read the list of words to the learner, and then began testing him on his learning. The shock panel, as shown in Figure 7.1, was presented in front of the teacher, and the learner was not visible in the shock room. The experimenter sat next to the teacher and explained to him that each time the learner made a mistake he was to press one of the shock switches to administer the shock. Moreover, the switch to be pressed increased the shock by one level with each mistake, so that each mistake produced a stronger shock. The researcher was interested in how far the participant would go, as the learner continued to make mistakes, before demanding that the experiment stop.

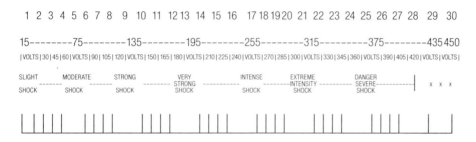

FIGURE 7.1. Diagram of the shock panel used in Milgram's obedience study. This is a representation of the shock panel used by the teachers in Milgram's (1974) studies on obedience. There are 30 switches, each marked by the number of volts supposedly administered as well as a description of the shock. From Milgram, S. (1974). *Obedience to authority: An experimental view.* New York: Harper and Row, page 28.

Once the learner-confederate was alone in the shock room, he brought out a tape recorder that he used to play a prerecorded series of responses that the teacher could hear through the wall of the room. The teacher heard the learner say "ouch" after the first few shocks. After the next few mistakes, when the shock level reached 150 volts, the learner was heard to exclaim, "Let me out of here. I have a heart condition!" As the shock reached 250 volts, the protests of the learner became more vehement, and after 300 volts the learner proclaimed that he was not going to answer any more questions. From here on the learner was silent, although the experimenter urged the participants to continue by reading the question and applying increasing shock when the learner did not respond.

The Shocking Results!

The results of Milgram's research were themselves quite shocking. Although all of the participants gave the initial mild levels of shock, responses varied after that. Some refused to continue after about 150 volts, despite the insistent demands of the experimenter to continue to increase the shock level. Still others, however, continued to present the questions and to administer the shocks under the pressure of the experimenter, who demanded that they continue. In the end, 65 percent of the participants continued giving the shock to the learner all the way up to the 450 volts maximum, even though that shock was marked as "danger: severe shock" and there had been no response at all heard from the participant for several trials.

What Produces Obedience?

Although it might be tempting to conclude that Milgram's experiments demonstrate that people are evil creatures who are ready to shock others to death, Milgram did not believe that this was the case. Rather, he felt that it was the social situation, and not the people themselves, that was most important. To demonstrate this, Milgram conducted fifteen variations on his original procedure, each of which demonstrated that changes in the situation could dramatically influence the amount of conformity. Some of these variations are summarized in Table 7.1.

In the initial study the authority's status and power was maximized—the experimenter had been introduced as a respected scientist at Yale University. As we have seen, in this case 65 percent of the participants were fully obedient (delivering all 450 volts of shock). However, in replications of the study in which the experimenter's authority was decreased, this level of obedience also declined. In one replication (experiment 10 in his series) the status of the experimenter was reduced by having the experiment take place in a building

TABLE 7.1
Authority and Obedience in Stanley Milgram's Studies

Experimental replication		Percent obedience
Experiment 1:	Initial study: Yale University men and women	65
Experiment 10:	The study is conducted off campus, in Bridgeport, CT	48
Experiment 7:	The experimenter communicates by phone from another room	20
Experiment 13:	An "ordinary man" (presumably another research participant) gives orders	20
Experiment 3:	The teacher is in the same room as the learner	40
Experiment 4:	The participant must hold the learner's hand on the shock pad	20
Experiment 17:	Two other research participants refuse to give shock	10
Experiment 15:	One experimenter indicates that the participant should not shock	0
Experiment 11:	The teacher chooses his own preferred shock level	2

This table presents the percentage of participants in Stanley Milgram's (1974) studies on obedience who were maximally obedient (that is, who gave all 450 volts of shock) in some of the variations that he conducted.

located in Bridgeport, Connecticut, rather than at the labs on the Yale campus. In this variation the research was said to be conducted by the "Research Associates of Bridgeport." Less obedience was observed in this replication, leading Milgram to conclude that the observed obedience was caused in large part by the perceived authority of the experimenter, which was greater when he was associated with a prestigious university.

Other variations that reduced the perceived authority of the experimenter also reduced obedience. Obedience was reduced to 20 percent when the experimenter's ability to express his authority was limited by making him more distant from the teacher. In this variation (experiment 7) the experimenter sat in an adjoining room and communicated to the teacher by telephone. Similarly, when the experimenter left the room and had a lower status "ordinary man" (an experimental confederate) give the instructions for him, conformity was reduced to 20 percent.

Milgram also found that obedience was determined in part by the psychological distance between the teacher and the learner. When the teacher gave the shock in the same room that the learner was in, and thus could see his distress, obedience was reduced to 40 percent. And when the teacher sat next to the learner and was forced to wear an insulated glove and to hold the learner's hand on the shock pad as he administered the shock, obedience was only 30 percent.

In addition to the role of authority, Milgram's studies also confirmed the role of unanimity in producing conformity. When another research participant (again an experimental confederate) began by giving the shocks, but then later refused to continue and the participant was asked to take over, only 10 percent were obedient. And if two experimenters were present and only one proposed shocking while the other argued for stopping the shocks, all of the research participants took the more benevolent advice and did not shock.

Finally, in the experiment that is perhaps most informative about his procedure, in experiment 11 of his series, Milgram let the participants choose their own shock level, rather than having it specified by the experimenter. Demonstrating that it was the situation, and not the people that were important, in this experiment where the choice was up to them, the majority of the subjects delivered the very lowest shocks to the victim, although there was one participant (out of the 40 tested) who did choose the maximum shock level.

In short, Milgram's research represents a classic demonstration of the power of the social context on behavior. When the experimenter was viewed as an authority who claimed that he would take full responsibility for their behavior no matter how reprehensible it was, obedience was high. When the power or salience of the authority was reduced, or when there were others present who argued for disobeying the orders, obedience decreased. Clearly, individuals with power can have remarkable effects on others, and those who dissent can break the influence.

A Theory of Power

Although Milgram's study provides an extreme example, power also occurs in more subtle forms. One of the best-known and most influential theories of power was developed by Bertram Raven (French & Raven, 1959; Raven, 1992). Raven argued that a full understanding of power requires studying both the person who is using the power and the person who is being influenced. He thus defined the power of a person A over another person, B, as:

Power of A over B = Maximum force   –   Maximum resistance
                    A can exert on B   B can offer against A

Part of the reason that this approach has been so influential is that it is also very specific about the different types of social influence that could be brought to bear on others. As summarized in Table 7.2, Raven argued that there were six basic types of power, each of which involves a different type of social influence. The types differ in terms of whether the outcome of the use of power is likely to be public compliance or private acceptance. We will discuss these types of power, beginning with those that are most likely to produce compliance (a change in behavior only) and moving on to those that are more likely to produce private acceptance (a change in both behavior and opinions).

> **TABLE 7.2**
> **Types of Power**
>
> | | |
> |---|---|
> | Reward power | The ability to distribute positive or negative rewards. |
> | Coercive power | The ability to dispense punishments. |
> | Legitimate power | Authority that comes from a belief on the part of those being influenced that the person has a legitimate right to demand compliance. |
> | Referent power | Influence based on identification with, attraction to, or respect for the power-holder. |
> | Expert power | Power that comes from other's beliefs that the power-holder possesses superior skills and abilities. |
> | Informational power | Power that comes from the ability to use information to persuade others. |

Reward Power

Reward power occurs when one person is able to influence others by providing them with positive outcomes. Bosses have reward power over employees because they are able to increase their salary and job benefits, and teachers have reward power over students because they can assign grades. The variety of rewards that can be used by the powerful is almost endless, including verbal praise or approval, the awarding of status or prestige, and even direct financial payment.

The ability to wield reward power over those we desire to influence is, however, not absolute, but is contingent upon the needs of the person being influenced. Power is greater to the extent that the person being influenced has a strong desire to obtain the reward, and power is less to the extent that the individual does not need the reward or is able to get the same or equivalent reward somewhere else. A boss will have more influence on an employee who has no other job prospects than on one who is being sought after by other corporations, and expensive presents will be more effective in persuading those who cannot buy the items with their own money. Because reward power is based entirely on conformity to gain rewards, it is more likely to produce compliance than acceptance.

Coercive Power

Coercive power is closely related to reward power, although it is based on the ability to punish, rather than to reward, others. Bosses have coercive power over employees if they are able (and willing) to punish the employees by reducing their salary, demoting them to a lower position, embarrassing them, or firing them. And friends can coerce each other through teasing, humiliation, and ostracism. As with reward power, coercive power is only effective when

Reward Power: The ability of one person to influence others by providing them with positive outcomes.

Coercive Power: Power based on the ability to punish others.

the person being influenced is dependent upon the power-holder. Furthermore, coercion only works if the person being influenced does not leave the group entirely; people who are punished too much are likely to look for other situations that provide more positive outcomes.

In many cases power-holders use reward and coercive power at the same time, for instance, both by increasing salaries as a result of positive performance and by threatening to reduce them if the performance drops. However, because it has such negative consequences, coercion is less likely to be used than is reward (Molm, 1997). For one, coercion may be more difficult to employ, since it often requires energy to keep the person from avoiding the punishment by leaving the situation altogether. And coercive power is less desirable for both the power-holder and the person being influenced, because it creates an environment of negative feelings and distrust that is likely to make interactions difficult and undermine group satisfaction for everyone involved.

As with reward power, coercive power is more likely to produce compliance than acceptance. Furthermore, in both cases the effective use of the power requires that the power-holder continually monitor the behavior of the target to be sure that he or she is complying. This monitoring may itself lead to a sense of mistrust between the two individuals in the relationship. The power-holder feels (perhaps unjustly) that the target is only complying due to the monitoring, whereas the target feels (again perhaps unjustly) that the power-holder does not trust him or her.

Legitimate Power

Whereas reward and coercive power are likely to produce compliance, other types of power, which are not so highly focused around reward and punishment, are more likely to create changes in attitudes as well as behavior (private acceptance). In many ways, then, these sources of power are stronger, because they produce real belief change. **Legitimate power** is vested in those who are appointed or elected to positions of authority, such as teachers, politicians, policemen, and judges, and their power is effective because members of the group accept it as appropriate. We accept that governments can levy taxes and that judges can decide the outcomes of court cases because we see these groups and individuals as valid parts of our society. Individuals with legitimate power can exert substantial influence on their followers. In fact, those with legitimate power may not only create changes in the behavior of others, but also have the power to create the norms themselves.

In some cases legitimate power is given to the authority figure as a result of laws or elections or as part of the norms, traditions, and values of the society. The power that the experimenter had over the research participants in Milgram's study on obedience seems to have been primarily the result of his

Legitimate Power: Power that is successful because members of the group accept it as appropriate.

legitimate power as a respected scientist at an important university. In other cases legitimate power comes more informally, as a result of being a respected group member. As we have seen in chapter 6, those who contribute to the group process and follow group norms gain status within the group, and therefore earn legitimate power.

Interestingly, in some cases legitimate power can even be used successfully by those who do not seem to have much power. For example, because people believe to a large extent in equity and fairness, people who do not have as much as others (for instance, those who are very poor) may have some power to demand resources from those who have more. This might not always work, but to the extent it does it is a type of legitimate power—power that comes from a belief in the appropriateness or obligation to help others who are in need.

Referent Power

People who hold **referent power** have still greater ability to influence others, because they can lead others to identify with them. In this case, the person who provides the influence is a member of an important reference group—someone we personally admire and attempt to emulate—or perhaps a charismatic, dynamic, and persuasive leader. A young child who mimics the opinions or behaviors of an older sibling or a famous baseball player, or a churchgoer who follows the advice of a respected church leader, are influenced by referent power. Referent power generally produces acceptance rather than compliance (Kelman, 1961).

The influence brought by referent power generally occurs in a passive sense, because the person being emulated does not necessarily attempt to influence others, and the person who is being influenced may not even realize that the influence is occurring. In other cases, however, the person with referent power (such as the leader of a cult) may make full use of his or her status as the target of identification or respect to produce change. In either case, however, referent power is a particularly strong source of influence because it is likely to result in the unconditional private acceptance of the opinions of the power-holder.

Expert Power

French and Raven's next source of power is **expert power.** Experts have knowledge or information, and conforming to those whom we perceive to be experts is useful for making decisions about topics in which we are not ourselves proficient. Expert power thus represents a type of informational influence based on the fundamental desire to obtain valid and accurate information.

Referent Power: Power that comes from identification with the power-holder.

Expert Power: Power that is based on expertise.

Conformity to the opinions of doctors, lawyers, and computer experts are examples of expert influence. We assume that these individuals have valid information about their areas of expertise, and we accept their opinions based upon this perceived expertise (particularly if their advice seems to be successful in solving problems). Indeed, one method of increasing one's power is to become an expert in a domain. Expert power is increased for those who possess more information about a relevant topic than others do, because the others must turn to these individuals to gain the information.

Informational Power

French and Raven proposed one last type of power, which is based upon the ability of people to influence others by providing information and convincing them that their beliefs are accurate. Informational power leads to informational conformity, private acceptance of new beliefs as a result of gaining new information.

Power Tactics

Although French and Raven's analysis considers the underlying types of influence that power-holders may use over others, it does not directly consider what types of power tactics the power-holder might use to assert influence. Powerful individuals have a choice of power tactics available to them and are likely to choose among them wisely (Cialdini, 1993; Eagly & Chaiken, 1993; Howard, Blumstein, & Schwartz, 1986; J. C. Turner, 1991; Yukl, 2002).

Choosing Tactics

Different tactics will be more or less appropriate for influencing different types of people. For instance, reward and coercive power may work well with subordinates who are in a position of dependency, whereas expertise is likely to work better when we are trying to influence our peers or our superiors (Deutsch, 1973; Kipnis, 1984). In some cases, it may matter how the demand for power is presented and how extreme that demand is. For instance, coercive power may be more effective if it is presented in a softer, friendlier mode than when it is presented in a harsh, demanding tone, and referent power may only be successful if it is not so extreme that it reduces the subordinate's identification with the power-holder.

In some cases it may be necessary for the power-holder to do some background preparation before trying to assert influence. When using coercive power, it would be useful to demonstrate that one was really willing to punish the transgressor, perhaps by reminding the person of others who have been subject to the punishment in the past. A person trying to use expert power may wish to first demonstrate his or her expertise in the area, which would build a basis for subsequent persuasion.

Different people prefer to use different tactics. For instance, there is evidence that people with low self-esteem are more likely to use the "harder" forms of influence (for instance, coercion), because they do not believe that they would be able to influence others through more moderate forms, such as expertise. It has also been found that men are more likely to use the direct tactics of reward and coercive power, whereas women are more likely to use other less forceful approaches (Raven, 1992). And, as a result of different social norms, different types of power are differentially used and differentially effective in different cultures (Wosinska, Cialdini, Barrett, & Reykowski, 2001).

Because there are so many different ways to influence others, ranging from the direct use of reward and coercive power to relying on methods of referent power and expertise, it is not surprising that effective leaders make efficient use of many different strategies as well as combinations of different strategies (Kipnis, 1984). An effective influencer might dispense both rewards and threats, while learning more about the topic so that he or she is perceived as an expert, coordinating each of these potential types of influence together, particularly taking into consideration the characteristics of the person he or she is trying to influence. Gary Yukl (2002) has created a list of potential tactics that people have been found to use when trying to influence others, and these are summarized in Table 7.3.

Does Power Corrupt?

Although people prefer to have power rather than to not have it, a little power goes a long way, and having too much can be dangerous, both to the targets of the power and to the power-holder. This idea was made famous in the statement by the European writer Lord Acton who in 1887 said "Power tends to corrupt, and absolute power corrupts absolutely. Great men are almost always bad men." This suggests that power-holders may use all of the power tactics available to them, even if that is not really necessary.

In an experiment designed to see if this was really the case by David Kipnis (1972), college students thought that they were supervising other college students who were supposedly working on a task (the others did not really exist, although the "supervisors" received feedback indicating that they did). One-half of the "supervisors" were able to influence the workers through legitimate power, by sending them messages attempting to persuade them to work harder. However, the other half of the supervisors were given increased power. In addition to attempting to persuade the "workers" to increase their output through the messages, they were also given both reward power (the

---

TABLE 7.3
Influence Tactics

Apprising. The agent explains how carrying out a request or supporting a proposal will benefit the target personally or help advance the target person's career.

Coalition tactics. The agent seeks the aid of others to persuade the target to do something or uses the support of others as a reason for the target to agree.

Collaboration. The agent offers to provide relevant resources and assistance if the target will carry out a request or approve a proposed change.

Consultation. The agent encourages the target to suggest improvements in a proposal, or to help plan an activity or change for which the target person's support and assistance are desired.

Exchange. The agent offers an incentive, suggests an exchange of favors, or indicates willingness to reciprocate at a later time if the target will do what the agent requests.

Ingratiation. The agent uses praise and flattery before or during an influence attempt or expresses confidence in the target's ability to carry out a difficult request.

Inspirational appeals. The agent makes an appeal to values and ideals or seeks to arouse the target person's emotions to gain commitment for a request or proposal.

Legitimating tactics. The agent seeks to establish the legitimacy of a request or to verity authority to make it by referring to rules, formal policies, or official documents.

Personal appeals. The agent asks the target to carry out a request or support a proposal out of friendship, or asks for a personal favor before saying what it is.

Pressure. The agent uses demands, threats, frequent checking, or persistent reminders to influence the target person.

Rational persuasion. The agent uses logical arguments and factual evidence to show a proposal or request is feasible and relevant for attaining important task objectives.

From Yukl, G. A. (2002). *Leadership in organizations.* Upper Saddle River, NJ: Prentice Hall, page 160.

---

ability to give small monetary rewards) and coercive power (the ability to take away earlier rewards).

Although the "workers" (who were actually preprogrammed) performed equally well in both experimental conditions, the participants who were given more power took advantage of it by more frequently contacting the workers and more frequently threatening them. In short, they relied almost exclusively on reward and coercive power rather than attempting to use their legitimate power to develop positive relations with the subordinates. Furthermore, at the end of the study, the participants who had been given extra power rated the "workers" more negatively, were less interested in meeting them, and felt that the only reason the workers did well was to obtain the rewards.

Kipnis concluded that having power leads people to use it, even though it may not be necessary, which then leads them to believe that the subordinates are only performing because of the threats. Although using excess power may be successful in the short run, autocratic power, based exclusively on reward and coercion, is not likely to produce a positive environment for either the power-holder or the subordinate. As we will see in the section on leadership, the best leaders are those who are willing to use their power, but do so in what appears to be a fair and friendly manner.

Gender and Power

In most U.S. corporations and other places of business, there are more men than women, and the men generally have higher status—they have higher-level positions and earn more money. Thus the balance of power often lies with men, and it may be difficult for women to gain power. Furthermore, the norms for what constitutes success in corporate life are usually defined in masculine terms, including assertiveness or aggressiveness, self-promotion and perhaps even macho behavior. It is difficult for women to gain power, because to do so they must conform to these masculine norms, and often this goes against their personal beliefs about appropriate behavior (Rudman & Glick, 1999). And when women do take on male models of expressing power, it may "backfire" on them; they end up being disliked because they are acting nonstereotypically for their gender. Indeed, in a recent court case a woman account executive argued that she was denied promotion (although she was a top performer) because she acted too "masculine," even though the same behaviors were required for the success of the male coworkers (S. T. Fiske et al., 1991). In short, women are caught in a double bind in which they must take on masculine characteristics to succeed, but if they do so they are not liked, at least in part because masculine behavior by women many be threatening to the power and status of the male leadership. As a result, each woman is in effect forced to adapt to the double bind in her own way.

Leadership

Now that we have considered what power is, it is time to consider those who have power or who are perceived by others to have power. People who have power are often considered to be leaders. In fact, leaders can be thought of as those people who have power over others in the sense that they are able to influence them.

Defining Leadership

There are many different types of leaders, and a leader can influence the group in many different ways. Some leaders actively attempt to influence others, because that is part of their social role—the manager of a workgroup or the strongest member of a gang are examples. In other cases, however, leadership involves more passive influence—the person who is able to figure out how to use the new software programs in an office may be seen as a leader, and we may speak of leaders as those who develop new and creative ideas, who perform their assigned roles particularly effectively, or who espouse visions that motivate the group to achieve. Leaders may in some cases produce undesirable outcomes for the group, but in other cases the group may rely completely on its leaders for effective group performance.

As you can imagine from our prior discussion concerning the types of power that are effective in creating influence, leaders have many different influence techniques at their disposal. As a result, even the most active forms of leadership are much more than just giving orders and making sure they are obeyed. Rather, effective leadership involves the creative use of social influence to produce desired outcomes. Although in some cases the leader may give commands and enforce them with reward or coercive power, in most cases he or she will also rely on legitimate, referent, or expert power, thereby attempting to keep the group satisfied and leading the followers to accept his or her position. Indeed, people frequently voluntarily comply with the demands of their leaders, at least when they see their positions as legitimate. And leaders generally share their power with others—for instance, cabinet members, advisors, and managers. Good leaders often get their followers to participate in the leadership. Thus leadership does not represent so much of a power struggle as a mutually cooperative and beneficial relationship in which the goal of the leader is to work with others to reach common goals (Bass, 1985; Tyler & Lind, 1992). We can define **leadership** as the process of influencing others to effectively obtain group goals.

The study of leadership is currently conducted by researchers in psychology, sociology, business, political science, and other fields. There is, however, good agreement across these fields about the characteristics of leaders. We will consider two basic models of leadership effectiveness that, together, encompass virtually all current approaches to understanding leadership. One approach studies the characteristics of people that allow them to emerge as leaders, under the assumption that some people are born with the personality necessary to be a good leader whereas others are not. The second approach is interactionist in the sense that it assumes that people are not "born leaders," but rather that the social situation in which they find themselves is critical. These theories assume that some types of leaders are more effective in some situations than in others.

Measuring Leadership

Leadership: The process of influencing others to effectively obtain group goals.

Two general types of dependent measures have been used in most research studying leadership. One involves assessing the actual effectiveness of leaders, as measured by group performance. If the group is successful at performing its task, then it is assumed that the leader has been, at least in part, the cause of this success. A second approach involves assessing the perceptions of the effectiveness of a leader by his or her followers. According to this approach, a leader is a good leader if the followers in the group like or respect the leader and feel that he or she is doing a good job. It is useful to consider these two measures separately, because, although they are usually correlated (effective leaders are seen that way by followers), they are not exactly the same.

In general, groups have expectations about what makes a good leader, and more effective leaders will be those who fit with these expectations. Indeed, the *leadership categorization theory* of Robert Lord (Cronshaw & Lord, 1987) explicitly proposes that the way groups perceive their leaders determines leader effectiveness, perhaps even more so than the leaders' actual behaviors. This theory proposes that leaders will be effective to the extent that they are aware of what is expected of them, and that leaders who deviate from these expectations will have difficulty being effective. Supporting this idea, research has shown that individuals who are perceived as typical of their groups, in the sense that they express appropriate norms, are more likely to be perceived as leaders (Hains, Hogg, & Duck, 1997; Hogg, 2001; Fielding & Hogg, 1997; Nye & Forsyth, 1991).

Characteristics of Leaders

One approach to understanding leadership is to study the types of people who make—or who are perceived as making—good leaders. *Personality theories of leadership* suggest that some people are simply "natural leaders," because they possess one or more personality characteristics that make them effective. For instance, leaders who are better able to get along with others might be more likable, and leaders who are intelligent might be better able to develop and communicate good ideas. And at least some relationships have been found between the measured personality traits of leaders and measures of leadership skills, as assessed either on the basis of group performance or on the basis of followers' ratings of leadership effectiveness.

Intelligence

One trait that would seem to be useful for leaders is intelligence, and some studies have found a relationship between intelligence (or education) and leader effectiveness. In several research projects, Dean Simonton (1987, 1988, 1994, 1995) has investigated the personalities of past leaders, including past presidents of the United States. He found that across all of the leaders he studied, the correlation between intelligence and leadership effectiveness was significant and positive, suggesting that being intelligent does help one lead. However,

Simonton found that there is a limit to the amount of intelligence that is useful for a leader. Leaders must also be able to communicate effectively with their followers, but a leader who is too intelligent may communicate in a manner that is not easily understood by the average person, making it difficult to obtain their allegiance. The presidential candidates Adlai Stevenson (who lost to Dwight Eisenhower) and George McGovern (who lost to Richard Nixon in a landslide) are examples of extremely well-educated and intelligent individuals who seem to have alienated voters, perhaps in part by their intelligence. In the end, Simonton concluded that it was the versatility of the leader (that is, his or her ability to effectively adapt to changes in situations) that is more important than intelligence itself as a determinant of leadership effectiveness.

Task-Oriented and Relationship-Oriented Leaders

Other researchers investigating the characteristics of good leaders have argued that there is not one, but rather two types of individuals who make effective leaders. Stogdill and his colleagues (S. Kerr, Schreisheim, Murphy, & Stogdill, 1974; R. G. Lord, 1977) have studied this question by administering the Leader Behavior Description Questionnaire to group members and asking them to rate their leaders on a number of items. Results from this approach show that people generally see their leaders as having one of two distinct personalities, and these follow the task-oriented and socioemotional roles that we have discussed in earlier chapters. The *task-oriented leader* is focused on goal achievement and derives satisfaction from seeing the group successfully meet its task goals. Task-oriented leaders attempt to get all of the group members to work toward the goal, and under situations of pressure or stress they tend toward more directive or structuring leadership. *Relationship-oriented leaders*, on the other hand, are more concerned with social acceptance and gaining positive regard from the group members. They work to support group harmony through openness, participation, and communication, particularly when under pressure.

Other Traits

Some other traits have also been found to be important in leadership, at least in the sense that they relate to perceptions of what makes a good leader. Kenny and Zaccaro (1983) found that a leader's social skills, such as the ability to accurately perceive the needs and goals of the group members, were important to being perceived as a leader. Sociability is likely to influence leadership perceptions and effectiveness in part because people who participate more in group discussions are more likely to be seen as leaders. Group members who do not contribute to the group process, perhaps because they are naturally shy, may be perceived as less influential and have difficulty gaining leadership positions. Sorrentino and Field (1986) found that a combination of achievement motivation and affiliation motivation (sociability) was most effective in producing the perception of effective leadership.

In one interesting experiment supporting the idea that sociable people are more likely to be seen as leaders, Sorrentino and Boutillier (1975) manipulated both the number and the quality of the comments given by a confederate who was playing the role of a group member. Although the quality of the comments influenced perceived differences on such variables as competence, influence, and contribution to the group's goal, only the number of comments made by the confederates (regardless of whether the comments were useful or not) predicted perceived differences in leadership. People who are able and willing to participate in group discussions may be seen as motivated to contribute to the group's outcomes, as well as willing to take responsibility for those outcomes, and this may lead us to perceive them as leaders.

Other variables that have been found to relate to leadership effectiveness include achievement orientation, verbal skills, creativity, self-confidence, emotional stability, internal locus of control, need for affiliation, and dominance (Cronshaw & Lord, 1987; Lord, de Vader, & Alliger, 1984; Simonton, 1988; Yukl, 2002). And, of course, the individual's skills at the task at hand are important. A person who has at least some relevant skills is more likely to be seen as a leader than someone who is not capable.

Charismatic and Transformational Leaders

Because so many characteristics seem to be related to leader skills, some researchers have attempted to account for leadership not in terms of individual traits, but rather in terms of a package of traits that successful leaders seem to have. Some have considered this in terms of *charisma* (Beyer, 1999; Conger & Kanungo, 1998; Strange & Mumford, 2002). Charismatic leaders are those who are enthusiastic, committed, and self-confident; who tend to talk about the importance of group goals at a broad level; and who make personal sacrifices for the group. Charismatic leaders express views that primarily support existing group norms, but which also contain a vision of what the group could or should be. Charismatic leaders create a lot of social identity in their followers, and they therefore have the ability to uplift and inspire others as a result of their referent power. Some research has found a positive relationship between charisma and effective leadership performance (Simonton, 1988).

Another trait-based approach to leadership is based on the idea that leaders take either *transactional* or *transformational* leadership styles with their subordinates (Burns, 1978; Podsakoff, MacKenzie, Moorman, & Fetter, 1990; Bass, 1999; Judge & Bono, 2000; Judge, Bono, Ilies, & Gerhardt, 2002). Transactional leaders are the more regular leaders, who work with their subordinates to help them understand what is required of them to get the job done. Transformational leaders, on the other hand, are more like charismatic leaders—they have a vision of where the group is going and attempt to stimulate and inspire their workers to move beyond their present status and to create a new and better future.

Overall, there is at least some support for the idea that charismatic and transformational leaders are effective. However, this research is primarily correlational, and it is therefore difficult to draw causal conclusions about the influence of charisma on leadership. In many cases the definitions of charisma and transformational leadership are not well defined, which also limits the ability to carefully and fully test predictions.

Status, Gender, and Ethnicity

As you would expect on the basis of our discussion of status in chapter 6, individuals who have more status are also more likely to be perceived as effective leaders. This is true both for specific, attained status, as well as for the diffuse status that is ascribed on the basis of physical features and social categories. Thus, people who have been in the group longer have more status and are more likely to be seen as leaders, at least in part because they have attained it by virtue of their prior contributions to the group. Similarly, individuals with diffuse status—such as men, older individuals, and those who are taller and bigger, are also more likely to be perceived as leaders as a result of their status.

Men are more likely to be leaders across a wide variety of group settings. For instance, in the U.S. Senate in 2003, 87 percent of the members are men. And the percentages also favor men in the U.S. House of Representatives (86 percent) and the Supreme Court (78 percent). Similar differences are found in the legislatures of almost all countries. There are also more men than women in leadership roles, and particularly in high-level administrative positions, in many different types of businesses and other organizations. Women are not promoted to positions of leadership as fast as men are in real working groups, even when actual performance is taken into consideration (Geis, Boston, & Hoffman, 1985; Heilman, Block & Martell, 1995).

Overall, research has found that men who are in the role of leaders are perceived more favorably than are female leaders, particularly when women adopt a task-oriented (and thus stereotypically inconsistent) role. However, the tendency to dislike female leaders is greater for men than for women (Eagly, Makhijani, & Klonsky, 1992). There is also evidence that men are more likely to emerge and act as leaders in small groups, even when other personality characteristics are accounted for (Bartol & Martin, 1986; Megargee, 1969). In one experiment, Nyquist and Spence (1986) had same-sex and mixed-sex pairs of students interact. In each pair there was one highly dominant and one low dominant individual, as assessed by previous personality measures. They found that in pairs in which there was one man and one woman, the dominant man became the leader 90 percent of the time, but the dominant woman became the leader only 35 percent of the time. The emergence of men as leaders is probably in part because men are more likely to take active task-directed roles in groups, by giving instructions and voicing their opinions, whereas women are more likely to take more socioemotional roles, for instance, by agreeing with others and acting in a friendly manner (Eagly & Johnson, 1990; Eagly et al., 1992; W. Wood, 1987).

It must be kept in mind, however, that the fact that men are perceived as effective leaders, and are more likely to become leaders, does not necessarily mean that they are actually better, more effective leaders than women. Indeed, a meta-analysis studying the *effectiveness* of male and female leaders did not find that there were any gender differences overall (Eagly, Karau, & Makhijani, 1995). And Eagly and Johnson (1990) found that in organizations, female leaders took on task-oriented roles as frequently as did their male counterparts. Women did differ from men, however, in their tendency to adopt a more democratic or participatory leadership style. That is, women were more likely than men to invite subordinates to participate in the decision-making process, whereas men tended to have an autocratic, directive style, giving orders rather than soliciting suggestions. As a result, the effectiveness of male and female leaders was particularly influenced by the task that the group was performing. When the task was defined in masculine terms (for instance, in military roles), men were more effective leaders than were women, but in roles that were defined in less masculine terms, women were more effective.

Lewin, Lippitt, and White's Research

Although most studies assessing the relationship between leader characteristics and leader performance have been correlational in nature, the differential effectiveness of different leadership styles was also studied in an important field experiment by Kurt Lewin and his colleagues (Lewin, Lippitt, & White, 1939; White & Lippitt, 1968). These researchers studied 10- and 11-year-old children working in after-school clubs. The experimenters acted as the leaders for the different clubs, but were trained to act in different ways toward the children in the different clubs in order to assess the effectiveness of different leadership styles. For some clubs the experimenter played the role of the *autocratic leader*. The autocratic leader took no input from the group members, emphasized his authority, and assigned group projects arbitrarily. In other clubs the experimenter played the role of the *democratic leader*. The democratic leader discussed the proposed activities with the group members before assigning them and allowed the children to make their own decisions. He encouraged the development of an egalitarian atmosphere. Finally the *laissez-faire* leader rarely intervened in the group activities, but rather let the group members work by themselves without much supervision.

Results of this experiment showed clear differences in both group satisfaction and performance across the children who had experienced the three leadership styles. In terms of the amount of time that the children spent working on the group activities (rather than goofing off), the groups with an autocratic leader spent as much time working on their projects as did the democratic groups, but the laissez-faire groups (who were not supervised) spent less. When the leader left the room, however, work in the autocratic group dropped off, stayed the same in the democratic groups, and increased in the laissez-faire groups. Thus it appears that the democratic leaders were able to produce a type of acceptance of the rules and norms, whereas the authoritarian leaders produced only compliance. In addition, the children who worked under autocratic leaders showed more reliance on the leader, complained more, and made more demands for attention. On the other hand, the children in the democratic groups were friendlier to each other and reported more satisfaction with the group. A recent meta-analysis of 19 studies that compared democratic and autocratic leadership styles has confirmed these results, although the observed effect size was small (Foels, Driskell, Mullen, & Salas, 2000).

Limitations to Personality Theories

Despite the fact that a number of different traits have been found to relate to perceptions of leadership effectiveness, at least to some degree, there are substantial problems with personality theories of leadership. For one, it has generally been found that, overall, personality is not a particularly good predictor of actual leadership effectiveness. Thus, although we tend to like people who have positive personalities and think that they are good leaders, this is more perception than reality. Only intelligence, out of all of the potential traits that have been studied, seems to predict leadership effectiveness, and even this relationship is not strong (remember that extremely intelligent individuals do not seem to be the best leaders). The relationships between other traits and leadership effectiveness are also weak, although combining many traits together (for instance, in the idea of the "charismatic" or "transformational" leader) can increase prediction (Kenny & Zaccaro, 1983).

Secondly, although personality variables may relate to a leader's ability to influence, they do not necessarily relate to the quality of his or her leadership. Charismatic leaders, for instance, may be able to persuade their followers. But they can be just as persuasive when they are leading them down the wrong path and into disaster as they are when they are leading them toward effective group functioning.

Still another problem with personality theories of leadership is that, although some personality styles, such as intelligence or charisma, may be important overall, the effect of these personality variables on leadership effectiveness is strongly influenced by the situation in which the leader finds himself or herself. Simonton's research on U.S. presidents, for example, found that the events that occur during president's term (Was there a war? Did major scandals occur?) are much better predictors of his effectiveness than are any of the many measured personality variables (Simonton, 1986). As Hollander (1964) put it, "Leaders are made by circumstance even though some come to those circumstances better equipped than others" (p. 5).

Interactionist Approaches

Despite the fact that there appear to be some personality traits that relate (at least to some extent) to leadership ability, you will probably not be surprised to hear that some of the most important approaches to understanding leadership are interactionist, in the sense that both the personality characteristics of the leader as well as the situation in which the leader is operating are assumed to be jointly important in determining the leader's success.

In general, the interactionist approach assumes that different situations are likely to require both different types of leaders and different amounts of leadership input. For instance, when groups face a crisis, they will be more likely to choose strong leaders (and particularly those who are charismatic) than they are in more benign situations. And larger groups are more likely to need leaders to help them coordinate their activities than are smaller groups (Mullen, Symons, Hu, & Salas, 1989). In other words, when groups are functioning routinely and normally and the individuals are happy at their work, show respect for each other, and are well coordinated, leaders are simply less necessary.

The Contingency Model

One of the best-known interactionist approaches to understanding leadership effectiveness is the **contingency model of leadership effectiveness** (Ayman, Chemers, & Fiedler, 1995). The general idea of the contingency model is based on the fact that most people are more comfortable adopting either a task-oriented leadership style or a relationship-oriented leadership style. Furthermore, different types of groups are assumed to demand different types of

Contingency Model of Leadership Effectiveness: A theory of leadership effectiveness based on the interaction between individual's leadership style and the group's task demands.

leaders. Therefore, a relationship is expected between the type of leader and the type of task that needs to be done, such that some people will be better leaders of some groups than of others.

Fred Fielder conceptualized the leadership style of the individual as a relatively stable personality variable and measured it by having people describe their *least preferred coworker (LPC)*. This measure asks the individual to consider all the people they have ever worked with and to think about the person with whom they had the "hardest time getting a job done" (that is, their least preferred coworker). They then rate this individual on some personality traits, including how "pleasant," "interesting," and "friendly" the person was. The answers to the questions determine whether the individual is primarily a task leader or primarily a relationship leader. Those who indicate that they pretty much liked even their LPC (high LPC individuals) are relationship-oriented types, who are motivated to have close personal relationships with others, whereas those who indicated that they did not like this person (low LPC individuals) are task leaders, motivated primarily by getting the job done.

In addition to classifying individuals according to their leadership styles, Fiedler also classified the situations in which groups had to perform their tasks, both on the basis of the task itself and on the basis of the leader's relationship to the group members. Specifically, as shown in Figure 7.3, Fiedler thought that three aspects of the group situation were important:

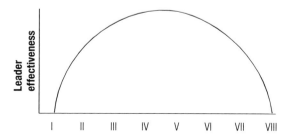

Favorable situational control				**Unfavorable sitational control**			

Leader-member relations	Good	Good	Good	Good	Bad	Bad	Bad	Bad
Task structure	Structured		Unstructured		Structured		Unstructured	
Leader's position of power	Strong	Weak	Strong	Weak	Strong	Weak	Strong	Weak

FIGURE 7.3. Predictions from the contingency model of leadership effectiveness. Predicted effectiveness of high LPC (relationship-oriented) leaders in group work situations that range from very favorable (left) to very unfavorable (right). The high LPC leaders are expected to be most successful when the group structure is neither extremely favorable nor extremely unfavorable. Predictions are from Fiedler, F. E. (1967). *A theory of leadership effectiveness*. New York: McGraw-Hill.

1. The degree to which the leader already has a good relationship with the group and the support of the group members (*leader-member relations*).
2. The extent to which the task is structured and unambiguous (*task structure*).
3. The leader's level of power or support in the organization of which the group is a member (*position power*).

Furthermore, Fielder believed that the above factors were ordered in terms of their importance, such that leader-member relationships were more important than task structure, which was in turn more important than position power. As a result, he was able to create eight levels of the "situational favorableness" of the group situation, which roughly range from most favorable to least favorable for the leader. The most favorable relationship involves good relationships, a structured task, and strong power for the leader, whereas the least favorable relationship involves poor relationships, an unstructured task, and weak leader power.

The contingency model is interactionist, because it proposes that individuals with different leadership styles will be differentially effective in different group situations. Specifically, low LPC, task-oriented leaders are expected to be most effective in situations in which the group process is very favorable, because this gives the leader the ability to move the group forward, and in situations in which the group situation is very unfavorable, and in which the extreme problems of the situation require the leader to engage in decisive action. However, in the situations of moderate favorableness, which occur when there is a lack of support for the leader, or when the problem to be solved is very difficult or unclear, the more relationship-oriented (high LPC) leader is expected to be more effective. In short, the contingency model predicts that task-oriented leaders will be most effective either when the group climate is very favorable, and thus there is no need to be concerned about the group members' feelings, or when the group climate is very unfavorable, and the task-oriented leader needs to take firm control.

To test his hypothesis, Fiedler (1967) looked at over a dozen studies that had measured the correlation between LPC and leader effectiveness in groups ranging from army tank crews to basketball teams and found some support for the contingency model. And other researchers have also concluded that, overall, the model does predict some aspects of leader behavior (Chemers, Hays, Rhodewalt, & Wysocki, 1985). The results of meta-analyses, which have analyzed the results of hundreds of studies testing the model, however, do not provide a clear picture. Although Strube and Garcia (1981) found overall support for the basic predictions of the theory, an analysis by Peters, Hartke, and Phlomann (1985) found that the predicted relationships were more likely to hold up in laboratory than in field studies, whereas Schriesheim, Tepper, and Tetrault (1994) found little support for the theory.

One difficulty with the contingency model is that many people cannot be classified into either high or low LPC leaders, and the theory does not make predictions for these "medium" LPC leaders. It is not impossible, however, that these individuals might be particularly effective, at least in some conditions. In fact, although the model proposes that people are either high or low LPC leaders, it is not unreasonable to assume that some people may be able to take on both styles and that this flexibility in leadership ability might be useful (Kenny & Zaccaro, 1983; Sorrentino & Field, 1986; Zaccaro, Foti, & Kenny, 1991). In sum, although there are some difficulties with the contingency model, it appears that, at least in laboratory situations, the model is somewhat predictive of leadership effectiveness. Further tests and modifications of the theory are still underway (Ayman et al., 1995).

Alternatives to the Contingency Model

Other researchers have provided other variations on the contingency model, but they are nevertheless based on the interactionist approach (for a review, see Yukl, 2002). Similar to the contingency model, the *path-goal theory* of leadership (M. G. Evans, 1970; House, Filley, & Gujarati, 1971; House & Mitchell, 1974) divides individuals into two basic personality types—those who are *directive*, in the sense that they prefer to provide structure for the group members (such as providing specific tasks and reducing role ambiguity), and those who are *supportive*, in the sense that they consider the needs and satisfaction of the workers (two other leadership types, *participative* and a*chievement-oriented* have also been proposed).

Similar to the contingency model, this theory assumes that different types of leaders will be differentially effective in different situations. For instance, directive leaders will be most effective when the roles and task assignments are unclear, because they are able to reduce role ambiguity and provide appropriate rewards for successful task completion. On the other hand, supportive leaders will be most effective when the task is stressful or tedious, and thus group member satisfaction needs to be increased or maintained. Although the path-goal theory has provided an important conceptual model for understanding leadership, research testing the theory is mixed (Podsakoff, MacKenzie, Ahearne, & Bommer, 1995; Wofford & Liska, 1993).

Still another similar approach is Vroom and Yetton's *normative decision model* (Vroom & Yetton, 1973; Vroom & Jago, 1988). Also similar to the contingency model, and echoing the styles of leadership used in Lewin's study on leadership, this approach defines leaders in terms of the basic approach they take toward groups, ranging from "authoritarian" (essentially a directive approach), through "consultative" (more open to inputs of others) to "group oriented" (democratic). Again, the prediction is that some types of leaders will be more effective in certain situations, and the theory makes practical suggestions for existing leaders about which approaches will be better under which conditions, to help them determine which type of leadership behavior is likely to be most effective. Although the amount of research testing this model is not large, some research has supported it (T. E. Hill & Schmitt, 1977; Jago & Vroom, 1980).

The *leader-member exchange model* (Graen & Uhl-Bien, 1998) is based on the idea that the leader develops better relationships with some subordinates than with others, and that those who have good relationships with the leader are treated better, get more freedom on the job, and produce high-quality output. The individuals the leader does not get along with, on the other hand, are treated more formally, are given less interesting assignments, and as a result are less satisfied in their positions. There is substantial research support for this prediction (Fairhurst, 1993; Liden & Graen, 1980).

Finally, Fiedler himself has developed a new interactionist approach to leadership known as *cognitive resource theory* (Ayman et al., 1995; Fiedler & Garcia, 1987). The major situational variable in cognitive resource theory is the stress that the leader is experiencing as he or she attempts to lead. For instance, when leaders have good, anxiety-free relations with their groups, their intelligence scores correlate highly with performance while their leadership experience (e.g., time on the job) correlates negatively with performance. However, when stress is high, these variables are less predictive.

In sum, although they vary in their specifics, each of the contingency approaches shares the basic idea that leaders are not equally effective in all situations and that effective leaders are those who are aware of the needs of the group. Research has not been as supportive of these models as we might hope, but they are still popular and generating research attention that is likely to refine and improve them.

Chapter Summary

Social power refers to the ability of an individual to influence others, even when those others might attempt to resist that influence. Stanley Milgram's important studies on obedience demonstrated the extent to which the power vested in an authority figure can produce conformity and obedience, even in cases where the outcome of the behavior was ostensibly harmful to another. The power that an individual may have over others varies in terms of its ability to elicit compliance or acceptance. Examples of the types of power that individuals may use include reward, coercive, legitimate, referent, expert, and informational power. Effective influencers use a wide variety of tactics to produce change in their subordinates.

One type of power comes in the form of leadership. Leaders are those who are able to influence others. There is some evidence that personality traits, such as intelligence and sociability, predict leadership perceptions and effectiveness, at least to a small degree. Other variables that include a combination of personality traits, such as charisma and transformational leadership, have also been found to predict leadership perceptions and, to a lesser extent, leadership effectiveness. Taken together, however, a leader's personality seems to have only a small influence on his or her success as a leader. There is also little evidence that men make better leaders than women, even though they are found more frequently in leadership roles.

The interactionist approach to leader effectiveness proposes that leaders are effective to the extent that their preferred leadership style matches the needs of the group. The contingency model is the best-known interactionist approach, although there are other similar approaches, including the path-goal theory of leadership, the normative decision model, and cognitive resource theory. Some research has supported the predictions of these interactionist models, but they still need further refinement to be strongly predictive of leadership effectiveness.

 Review and Discussion Questions

1. What is social power, and what does it mean to have it? Give some examples of times that you have used power to influence others, or in which others have influenced you.
2. What types of power are there, and what effects do they have on those being influenced? Which types of power are most effective in which situations?
3. Give an example of a specific individual who has each of French and Raven's types of power.
4. What are the personality variables that have been found to predict leadership abilities and perceptions? Can you think of other personality types that might be important?
5. Consider the types of strategies that leaders have been shown to use, and indicate how and when you think each would be most effective.
6. What types of leadership do you personally respond best to, and why?
7. What are the differences in leadership abilities between men and women?

8. What are the most important interactionist models of leadership effectiveness and what are their underlying assumptions? Give an example of a group situation in which each of the proposed leadership styles would likely be most effective.

Recommended Readings

The contingency model of leadership effectiveness, and its original empirical tests:
Fiedler, F. E. (1967). *A Theory of Leadership Effectiveness*. New York: McGraw-Hill.

The original formulation of the various types of power:
French, J. R. P., & Raven, B. H. (1959). The bases of social power. In D. Cartwright (Ed.), *Studies in Social Power* (pp. 150–167). Ann Arbor, MI: Institute for Social Research.

Studies of great leaders using historical data:
Simonton, D. K. (1994). *Greatness: Who Makes History and Why*. New York: Guilford.

Group
Decision Making

8

▶ *Contents at a Glance*

*N*ow that we have considered the formation and structure of working groups, it is time to turn to study of these groups in action, when they are doing the work that they have been formed to accomplish. We will begin our discussion in this chapter by outlining how social scientists study the performance of groups and how they compare group performance to individual performance. We will also consider how to classify the tasks that groups perform. We will then focus in on a common type of group task—group decision making. In chapter 9 we will investigate another type of group performance—how groups work together to create tangible products.

Understanding Group Performance

When important decisions need to be made, or when tasks need to be performed quickly or effectively, we frequently create groups to accomplish them. Many people believe that groups are effective for making decisions and performing other tasks, and such a belief seems commonsensical. After all, because groups have many members, they will also have more resources, and thus more ability, to efficiently perform tasks and to make good decisions. Many heads must be better than one, and many arms must be stronger than two. And in many ways they are. Barns are raised and cars are built faster when there are many people at hand, and at least some decisions are better made in groups.

However, although groups sometimes do perform better than individuals, this outcome is not guaranteed. Group performance will only be better than individual performance to the extent that people continue to exert effort toward meeting the relevant goals when they are in the group, and if the group is able to efficiently coordinate the efforts of the group members. And group decisions will only be better than individual decisions if at least some of the group members bring information or expertise that other group members do not have and if that information is fully discussed and made use of. Because these things do not always happen, groups often produce very poor outcomes. In fact, as we will see, group performance is almost never as good as we would expect, given the number of individuals in the group, and may even in some cases be inferior to that which could have been made by one or more members of the group working alone (Buys, 1978; G. W. Hill, 1982; Steiner, 1972).

Some of the most interesting and important questions about group performance concern when and why groups do better or worse than individuals and how we can improve the functioning of groups. Group performance is another example of an interactionist phenomenon, because it depends both on the skills of the group members and on the way these resources are combined in the group itself (J. H. Davis, 1969; Laughlin, 1996). Understanding these questions is important precisely because groups are used so frequently to perform tasks and make important decisions, both in informal life (as when a study group must decide how and when to prepare for an exam or the individuals preparing a party must coordinate the work to be done) and in industry, government, and business (as when managers attempt to get an assembly line to work to its full potential or a surgical team performs a complex operation).

Task Classifications

Ivan Steiner (1966, 1972) argued that to fully understand group performance, the particular task that the group needed to accomplish must be considered.

To better understand the nature of the tasks that groups might have to perform, and thus to better understand when and how groups performed better or worse than individuals, Steiner developed a system for classifying group tasks. The idea that we can better understand group performance by classifying tasks has guided subsequent research, and in this section we consider some of the distinctions that have been found to be useful, both by Steiner and by others (J. Hackman & Morris, 1975; McGrath, 1984; Shaw, 1981). These classifications are summarized in Table 8.1.

Task Division

One basic distinction concerns whether the task can be divided into smaller subtasks or whether it has to be done as a whole. Building a car on an assembly line or painting a house are **divisible tasks**, because each of the group members working on the job can do a separate part of the job at the same time. Groups are likely to be particularly productive on divisible tasks when the division of the work allows the group members to specialize in those tasks that they are best at performing. Writing a group term paper is facilitated if one group member is an expert typist, another is an expert at library research,

---

TABLE 8.1
Classifying Group Tasks

Task Division
   Divisible. A task in which the work can be divided up among individuals.
   Unitary. A task in which the work cannot be divided up among individuals.

Task Combination
   Additive. A task in which the inputs of each of the group members are added together to create the group performance.
   Compensatory. A task in which the group input is combined such that the performance of the individuals is averaged.

Group Member Performance
   Disjunctive. A task in which the group's performance is determined by its best group member.
   Conjunctive. A task in which the group's performance is determined by its worst member.

Task Assessment
   Maximizing. A task that involves performance that is measured by how rapidly the group works, or how much of a product they are able to make.
   Intellective. Tasks that involve the ability of the group to make a decision or a judgment.

Task Clarity
   Criterion. Tasks in which there is a clearly correct answer to the problem that is being posed.
   Judgmental. Tasks in which there is no clearly correct answer to the problem that is being posed.

Divisible Task: A task in which the work can be divided up among individuals.

and so forth. Climbing a mountain or lifting a piano, on the other hand, are **unitary tasks**, because they have to be done all at once and cannot be divided up. In this case specialization among group members is not useful, because each group member has to work on the same task at the same time.

Task Combination

Another way of classifying tasks is by the way the contributions of the group members are combined. On **additive tasks** the inputs of each of the group members are added together to create the group performance, and the expected performance of the group is the sum of group members' individual inputs. A tug of war is a good example of an additive task, because the total performance of a team is expected to be the sum of all of the team members' individual efforts.

On **compensatory tasks**, however, the group input is combined so that the performance of the individuals is averaged rather than added (Sniezek & Henry, 1988). Imagine that you wanted to estimate the current temperature in your classroom, but you had no thermometer. One approach to getting an estimate would be to have each of the individuals in your class make an estimate of the temperature and then average the estimates to create a group judgment. On decisions such as this, the average group judgment is likely to be more accurate than that made by most individuals.

Group Member Performance

Another task classification involves comparing tasks in which the group performance is dependent upon the abilities of the *best* member or members of the group to tasks in which the group performance is dependent upon the abilities of the *worst* member or members of the group. When the group's performance is determined by the best group member, we call it a **disjunctive task.** When a group is given a complicated problem to solve and thus, the correct answer to the problem is not immediately apparent, each of the group members will attempt to solve the problem. With any luck, one or more of the group members will discover the correct solution, and when that happens the other group members will be able to see that it is indeed correct. At this point the group as a whole has correctly solved the task, and the performance of the group is thus determined by the ability of the best member of the group.

On **conjunctive tasks**, however, the group performance is determined by the ability of the group member who performs most poorly. Imagine an assembly line in which each individual working on the line has to insert one screw into the part being made, and that the parts move down the line at a constant speed. If any one individual is substantially slower than the others,

Unitary Task: A task in which the work cannot be divided up among individuals.

Additive Task: A task in which the inputs of each of the group members are added together to create the group performance.

Compensatory Task: A task in which the group input is combined in such a way that the performance of the individuals is averaged.

Disjunctive Task: A task in which the group's performance is determined by its best group member.

Conjunctive Task: A task in which a group's performance is determined by its worst member.

the entire speed of the line will need to be slowed down to match the capability of that individual. As another example, hiking up a mountain in a group is also compensatory, because the group must wait for the slowest hiker to catch up.

Task Assessment

Still another distinction among tasks concerns the specific product that the group is creating and how that group output is measured. **Intellective tasks** generally involve the ability of the group to make a decision or a judgment and are measured by studying either the processes that the group uses to make the decision (such as how a jury arrives at a verdict) or the quality of the decision (such as whether the group is able to solve a complicated problem). **Maximizing tasks**, on the other hand, are those that involve performance that is measured by how rapidly the group works, or how much of a product they are able to make (such as how many computer chips are manufactured on an assembly line, how many creative ideas are generated by a brainstorming group, or how fast a construction crew can build a house). It is convenient and traditional to consider these two types of tasks separately. Therefore, we will consider decision-making (intellective) tasks in this chapter and consider group performance (maximizing tasks) in chapter 9.

Task Clarity

Finally, within the category of intellective (decision-making) tasks, we can differentiate problems for which there is an objectively correct decision from those in which there is not a clear best decision. On **criterion tasks**, the group can see that there is a clearly correct answer to the problem that is being posed. Some examples would be finding solutions to mathematics or logic problems.

On some criterion tasks the correct answer is immediately seen as the correct one once it is found. For instance, what is the next letter in each of the following two patterns of letters?

JFMAM _

OTTFF _

In criterion problems such as these, as soon as one of the group members finds the correct answer[1] the problem is solved, because all of the group members can see that it is correct. Criterion tasks in which the correct answer is obvious once it is found are known as "Eureka!" or "Aha!" tasks (Lorge &

Intellective Task: Tasks that involve the ability of the group to make a decision or a judgment.

Maximizing Task: A task that involves performance that is measured by how rapidly the group works or by how much of a product they are able to make.

Criterion Tasks: Tasks in which there is a clearly correct answer to the problem that is being posed.

---

1. The correct answer for the first line is J, for June, because the pattern represents the first letters of the days of the months (and I'm sure you can now get the second line!).

Solomon, 1955), named for the response that we have when we see the correct solution.

In other types of criterion-based tasks there is an objectively correct answer, although that answer is not immediately obvious. In this case there is a correct answer, but it may not be apparent to the group participants, even when it is proposed by one or more of the group members (for this reason we might call this a "non-Eureka" task). In fact, in one study using this problem only 80 percent of the groups in which the correct answer was considered actually decided upon that answer as the correct one after they had discussed it together.

In still other criterion-based tasks there is an objectively correct answer, but it is not at all obvious, and experts must be used to assess the quality or creativity of the group's performance. One such task involves asking groups of individuals to imagine themselves as a group of astronauts who are exploring the moon, but who have become stranded away from their base (you can read more about the problem at http://www.teleometrics.com/nasa02.htm). The problem is to determine which of the available equipment (for instance, oxygen bottles, a rope, a knife) they should take with them as they attempt to reach the base. Experts on the difficulties of living in space make judgments about the quality of the group decisions. Non-Eureka tasks represent an interesting challenge for groups, because even when they have found what they think is a good answer, they may still need to continue their discussion to convince themselves that their answer is the best they can do, and that they can therefore stop their deliberation. In contrast to criterion tasks, in **judgmental tasks** there is no clearly correct answer to the problem. Judgmental tasks involve such matters as deciding the innocence or guilt of an accused person in a jury or making an appropriate business decision. Because there is no objectively correct answer on judgmental tasks, the research approach usually involves studying the processes that the group uses to make the decision rather than measuring the outcome of the decision itself. Thus the question of interest on judgmental tasks is not "do groups get the right answer," but rather "how does the group reach its decision?"

Summary

In sum, there are a number of useful ways that we can classify tasks. These classifications help us understand group performance, because the advantages or disadvantages of working in groups rather than as individuals will depend on the specific task being performed. Many real-life tasks represent clear examples of one or more of the task classifications discussed here, and understanding these characteristics can help us understand how groups will perform

Judgmental Tasks: Tasks in which there is no clearly correct answer to the problem that is being posed.

these tasks. Furthermore, the type of task that the group is asked to perform will also determine the research approach that is taken to understand it. Assessing groups' performance on maximizing tasks will be different than assessing their performance on intellective tasks, and judgments about the effectiveness of a group decision will vary depending on whether the task is a criterion or a judgmental task.

Predicting Group Performance

In addition to the characteristics of the task itself, a group's effectiveness will also be influenced by the traits, skills, and abilities of the group members, as well as by the ability of the group members to work together efficiently. We can use information about these two factors to predict group performance.

Member Characteristics

Member characteristics refer to the traits, skills, or abilities of the individual group members. On a rope-pulling task, for instance, the member characteristics refer to the ability of each of the group members to pull on the rope on their own, whereas on the horse-trading problem the member characteristics refer to the ability of the individual group members to solve the problem at hand. Furthermore, it is assumed that the performance of the group as a whole— known as the *potential group productivity*—will be related to the member characteristics. On a maximizing, additive task such as rope pulling, the potential group productivity (the strength with which the group should pull when working together) would be calculated as the sum of all of the individual inputs, whereas on a criterion-based disjunctive task, the potential group productivity (the ability of the group to solve the problem) might be calculated as the ability of the best group member to solve the problem.

Group Process

Although the member characteristics define the expected productivity of the group, the *actual productivity* of the group (the amount that the group is actually able to pull, or whether the group actually solves the problem) will generally be different than the potential productivity. The difference between the expected productivity of the group and the actual productivity of the group is determined by the **group process**, defined as the events that occur while the group is working together on the task. When the outcome of the group performance is more or better than would be expected on the basis of the member characteristics we speak of a **process gain**, whereas when the outcome of the

Member Characteristics: The traits, skills, or abilities of the individual group members.

Group Process: The events that occur while the group is working together on the task.

Process Gain: When the outcome of the group performance is more than would be expected on the basis of the member characteristics.

group performance is less or worse than would be expected on the basis of the member characteristics we speak of a **process loss**. Mathematically, we can write the following equation to express this relationship.

Actual productivity = potential productivity – process loss + process gain.

Measuring Group Effectiveness

Determining the extent to which groups are influenced by process losses and process gains involves making comparisons between the abilities of individuals and groups and among different types of groups. Imagine, for instance, that we were interested in knowing whether groups pull harder on a rope than do individuals or whether students do better on class assignments when they work in small groups than they do when they work in larger groups. The answer to these questions will depend on how the comparisons are made.

Group Size

One approach to comparing groups with individuals is to directly assess the outcomes of a group of individuals working together with the performance of one individual working alone on the same task. For instance, on a maximizing, additive task, such as lifting a weight, we could compare the ability of a group of individuals to lift the weight versus the ability of any one individual to lift it. Or, on a compensatory task, we could compare the accuracy of a group of individuals (for instance, their average estimate of the temperature of a room) to that of a single individual.

In one example of research making this type of comparison Marjorie Shaw (1932) gave the a disjunctive Eureka-type problem to 21 individuals who worked alone and to 5 groups of 5 individuals working together. Shaw found that only 3 out of the 21 individuals who were given the problem to work on alone were able to solve it (14 percent), but that 3 out of the 5 groups who were assigned the problem solved it (60 percent). Shaw concluded that groups were more effective than individuals, and the results of other similar studies (Laughlin & Adamopoulos, 1980) led to similar conclusions.

If you think about this comparison for a minute, however, you might discover that the conclusion is not as straightforward as it might seem, because it does not take into consideration the number of people who were working on the problem. Shaw used a disjunctive, Eureka-type task. This means that the correct answer will be clearly seen as correct when it is discovered, and the performance of the group is therefore based on the performance of the best member in the group. Indeed, the likelihood that a group has at least one person who can solve the problem can be calculated on the basis of the likeli-

Process Loss: When the outcome of the group performance is less than would be expected on the basis of the member characteristics.

hood that any one individual will find the solution (which we know was 14 percent) and the number of people in the group (5).[2] This calculation results in the prediction that 53 percent of the groups will be able to solve the problem correctly, a prediction that is very close to the number that was actually found for groups (60 percent).

Considered this way, it's not clear that there was any real advantage to using groups at all. In fact, on tasks such as weight lifting, temperature estimation, and problem solving, it is generally the number of group members that matters (that is, the member characteristics) and not anything particular about the group process. In these cases our conclusion would be that larger groups perform better simply because they are bigger, but that the fact that they are a group may not make much difference. In fact, it's not impossible that on these tasks the individual workers might actually have been impeded by being in the group and that a process loss, rather than a process gain, occurred. Perhaps the individuals who were lifting the weight together each slacked off at least a bit in comparison to how hard they would have worked alone, and those who could get the problem correct might even have been able to solve the problem faster if they hadn't had to listen to the other, incorrect, solutions proposed by the other group members.

Nominal Groups

An alternative, and potentially fairer, approach to comparing groups and individuals does not involve comparing group performance with that of single individuals, but rather compares individuals working together interactively in a group to the *same number* of individuals working alone. This comparison equates the number of people contributing to the group output (the member characteristics) and thus allows assessment of the group process itself. For example, we might compare the performance of ten individuals working together in a group to the performance of ten people working alone but whose efforts are pooled together. In this case we call the individuals who work alone a **nominal group**, because they are considered a group by the researchers even though they work separately as individuals. As we will see, the nominal-group approach is frequently used to compare the abilities of groups and individuals.

Decision Schemes

Still another approach to understanding group effectiveness is based on assessing the group process itself. In this case the question is not whether the

Nominal Group: A group of individuals who work as individuals but who are considered a group by the researchers.

---

2. The formula used to make the prediction is: $P_g = 1 - (1-P_i)^r$ where P_g is the probability that the group will solve the problem, P_i is the probability that an individual can solve the problem, and r is the group size.

group gets the right answer, but how it reaches whatever decision it makes. This approach is particularly useful on intellective, judgmental tasks—that is, those in which a decision has to be made, but in which there is no way to know whether the final decision was the correct one. When using this approach, researchers usually compare group and individual performance in a rather different way—by polling the individuals ahead of time about their individual opinions, letting them work together in a group to discuss the issue, and then comparing the group decision to the individuals' initial opinions. And we might test the individuals again after the group discussion to see whether group discussion actually produced acceptance of the ideas generated by the group. This approach thus studies the outcomes of the decision-making process, but in doing so focuses to a large extent on the group process itself—what techniques do the group members use when making the decision?

Analyzing Group Discussion

One approach to understanding how groups work on problems or make decisions is to directly observe groups in action (Dabbs & Ruback, 1987; Fisek, Berger, & Norman, 1991; Stasser & Taylor, 1991; Stasser & Vaughan, 1996). As the group members begin discussing the issue, they normally don't completely agree with one another, and to reach consensus there will probably be arguments, counterarguments, perhaps even some open conflict, and (hopefully, at least) some compromise. It is this give-and-take that becomes the data for the analysis.

Some researchers have attempted to make a relatively complete analysis of the conversations that group members engage in as they attempt to come to consensus on a decision, for instance, by coding the conversations using Bales's SYMLOG. One difficulty with this approach is that there is a lot of conversation that occurs in a group, and much of it may be about topics that are not particularly relevant to the decision that is being made. Therefore, using a simplifying approach, researchers sometimes create groups that are assigned to discuss a given issue that they do not know much about ahead of time and give to each participant some particular information about the topic at hand. As the group discusses the issue, the researcher can measure the extent to which each of these particular pieces of information is discussed during the group deliberation. This approach, in which only discussion of the particular information given ahead of time is of interest, reduces the amount of information that needs to be analyzed. As we will discuss in chapter 10, this approach has been particularly useful for studying how information is shared in groups.

Because analyzing the discussions of group members is time consuming, even when the information available is constrained by the experimenters, other simplifying approaches have also been developed. One approach to understanding group problem solving is to assume that each of the group members makes an equal contribution to the final decision and to attempt to predict the group decision on the basis of the initial opinions of the individuals without actually observing the group process itself. In this approach, the initial opinions of the individuals are first measured and then a **decision scheme** is used to predict how the groups will combine their opinions together to reach consensus (Crott & Werner, 1994; J. H. Davis, 1969; Hastie, Penrod, & Pennington, 1983; Laughlin & Ellis, 1986; C. E. Miller, 1989; Stasser et al., 1989). As summarized in Table 8.2, there are many potential decision schemes that might serve as the basis of group decision making, and which one is most predictive of the group decision depends on the specific task being performed.

Demonstrating the Correct Solution

On Eureka tasks in which the correct answer is obvious once it has been found, we can predict the likelihood that the group will find the solution on the basis

---

TABLE 8.2
Decision Schemes

Decision Scheme	Definition	Likely Occurrences
Truth wins	Group solves the problem if any single member finds the correct answer.	Criterion-based tasks in which the correct answer is clear (Eureka tasks).
Truth-supported wins	Group solves the problem if any two members agree on which answer is correct.	Criterion-based tasks in which the correct answer is not obvious (non-Eureka tasks).
First shift	Accept a decision as soon as one group member changes his or her opinion to accept it.	
Majority wins	The group votes, and chooses it if an option is agreed upon by over 50 percent of the group members.	Judgmental tasks such as jury trials.
Unanimity	All group members must agree on the decision, or no decision can be made.	Some jury trials.
Random selection among alternatives	Group members randomly select one out of the potential alternatives.	Very difficult tasks where there are several proposed alternatives and no correct answer is apparent.
Turn-taking among proposed alternatives	Group members choose a different one of the alternatives at different times.	

Decision Scheme: A rule that predicts how groups will combine their opinions together to reach consensus.

of the *truth wins* decision scheme (Laughlin & Ellis, 1986). To make this prediction, we simply calculate the probability that any individual can get the problem correct (by having some individuals do the task alone), and adjust this probability by the number of individuals in the group (see footnote 2). The result is taken as the probability that the group as a whole will find the answer. If there is a process gain, then the group will be more likely to find the answer than expected on the basis of this prediction, whereas if there is a process loss, the group will be less likely to find the answer than was predicted.

In criterion-based tasks in which the correct answer is not apparent, it might be assumed that the group as a whole will accept the decision only if someone else in the group also supports a solution proposed by one person. In this case we can predict that the group will get the answer correct when at least two people in the group get the correct answer, and this decision scheme is called *truth-supported wins*. This scheme might be particularly likely to be used when the group is unfamiliar with or uncertain about the decision and requires the added confidence provided by a second advocate (Parks & Cowlin, 1996). The calculations and the resulting probabilities of correct group judgment can be adjusted when making the prediction.

Voting among Proposed Alternatives

On judgmental tasks in which there is no clearly correct answer, the decision scheme used to reach consensus frequently involves voting among proposed alternatives, with the goal of selecting the one that is most popular. Because there is no objectively correct answer, this agreement is considered to provide the best answer that the group can come up with. Voting may also be used on criterion-based but non-Eureka tasks when there is no clear support for any of the proposed solutions and thus the correct solution is not apparent to the group.

When the voting approach is used, the decision scheme is the number or percentage of votes for one alternative that allows the group to stop its deliberations. The opinions of each of the group members are assessed before they begin their deliberations (for instance, do they believe that the defendant is guilty or innocent?), and the group decision is predicted on the basis of this information. In some cases only a majority of the group members is required to support a decision, and thus the appropriate rule is the *majority wins* decision scheme. Figure 8.1 shows the results of decisions that were made by mock juries using the majority decision scheme. As expected, the decision initially favored by the majority is almost always the decision also favored by the group. Another commonly used voting-based decision scheme is *two-thirds majority wins*. In this rule the group discusses until two-thirds of the group agree on a

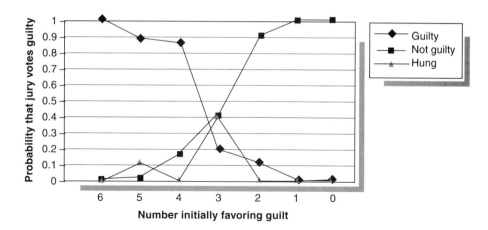

FIGURE 8.1. Conformity to the majority in mock jury trials. This figure shows the results of six-member mock jury decisions that were operating under a majority-rules decision scheme. When the majority of the six initially favored voting guilty, the jury almost always voted guilty, and when the majority of the six initially favored voting innocence, the jury almost always voted innocence. The juries were frequently hung (could not make a decision) when initial split was three-three. Data are from Stasser, G., Kerr, N. L., & Bray, R. M. (1982). The social psychology of jury deliberations: Structure, process and product. In N. L. Kerr & R. M. Bray (Eds.), *The psychology of the courtroom* (pp. 221–256). New York: Academic Press, page 239.

decision, and then it stops. This rule has been shown to predict the outcomes of group judgments on mock jury trials (J. H. Davis, 1975).

In some cases the group decides or is forced by the rules that govern it to use a *unanimous* decision scheme. This frequently requires taking repeated votes, followed by more discussion and more voting, until all group members agree on the decision. In the United States, juries that are deliberating criminal trials are usually required to reach a unanimous decision. Such an extreme decision scheme is presumed to be useful because a unanimous decision implies that the evidence in favor of guilt is strong and "beyond a reasonable doubt." Research has shown that groups that are required to make a unanimous decision do discuss the information more fully (Hastie et al., 1983). Furthermore, requiring a unanimous decision forces the group to listen to the opinions of each of the group members. In a situation in which a jury is split 11 to 1, for instance, the opinions of the single dissenter become most important, and the group must listen carefully to his or her arguments. On the other hand, there are also potential costs to working under a unanimity rule. One difficulty is that there is more conformity pressure directed at those who hold different opinions.

Other Decision Schemes

In some cases the outcome of the group decision is best predicted by still other decision schemes. For instance, in some groups there are multiple correct alternatives, and the group is in a position to try them all. Therefore either a *turn-taking* decision scheme is used in which the different proposed choices are used sequentially, or a *random* decision scheme is used in which one of the proposed alternatives is selected at random. Alternatively, a *first shift* rule can be followed, in which the group accepts a decision as soon as one group member changes his or her opinion, indicating that he or she has been persuaded by the group discussion.

Limitations of the Decision Scheme Approach

In sum, the social decision scheme approach involves using knowledge about the ways that groups come to consensus to predict their final decisions. The predictions are made based on the initial opinions of the group members and the potential decision schemes that the group operates under. The approach has been useful in helping to understand how groups come to decisions and, at least in some cases, in helping understand whether and when group performance is better than individual performance. This approach works well when the task is to choose among a relatively limited number of discrete alternatives, but it is more difficult to apply when the decision involves a quantity, such as how much a company should be willing to spend to purchase another company or how many years in prison a defendant should receive. There are, however, some recent decision-making models, based on the social decision scheme approach, that may be useful in predicting such judgments (Crott & Werner, 1994; Davis, 1996; Hinsz, 1999).

Although the decision scheme approach to group decision making has been important in understanding group dynamics, it also has some limitations in terms of its ability to account for all types of group processes. One limitation is that, in contrast to approaches that observe the group process directly, the problem-solving approach does not fully consider the dynamics among group members. By assuming that each individual has an equal input to the decision-making process, the approach ignores differences in status and power among group members, which can influence the persuasive ability of the group members (Kirchmeyer, 1993; Stasser & Taylor, 1991). Thus the desision scheme approach simplifies the situation, which in some, but probably not all, cases, may be appropriate.

Groupthink

Groups will only make effective decisions when they are able to make use of the advantages that come with group decision making, such as the ability to pool information and to test out contradictory ideas through group discussion. Thus, the basic idea that group decisions are better than individual decisions is based on the assumption that the group members act carefully and rationally, considering all of the evidence and coming to an unbiased, fair, and open decision. However, these conditions are not always met in real groups. One example of a group process that can lead to poor decisions is **groupthink**. Groupthink occurs when a group, which is made up of members who may actually be very competent and thus quite capable of making excellent decisions, nevertheless ends up, as a result of a flawed group process and strong conformity pressures, making poor ones (Janis, 1972; Janis, 1982; M. E. Turner & Pratkanis, 1998). Groupthink is more likely to occur in groups in which there is very high group cohesiveness and social identity, when there is a strong and directive leader, and in times of stress and crisis. Groups suffering from groupthink are unwilling to seek out or discuss discrepant or unsettling information about the topic at hand, and they do not express contradictory opinions. Because the group members are afraid to express opinions that contradict the prevailing group norms, the group is prevented from making a fully informed decision. Figure 8.2 summarizes the basic causes and outcomes of groupthink.

It has been suggested that groupthink was involved in a number of well-known and important, but very poor, decisions made by government and business groups, including Israel's lack of preparedness for the October 1973 war

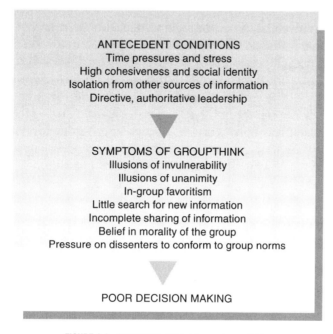

ANTECEDENT CONDITIONS
Time pressures and stress
High cohesiveness and social identity
Isolation from other sources of information
Directive, authoritative leadership

▼

SYMPTOMS OF GROUPTHINK
Illusions of invulnerability
Illusions of unanimity
In-group favoritism
Little search for new information
Incomplete sharing of information
Belief in morality of the group
Pressure on dissenters to conform to group norms

▼

POOR DECISION MAKING

FIGURE 8.2. Antecedents and outcomes of groupthink.

Groupthink: A process that occurs when a group makes poor decisions as a result of flawed group process and strong conformity pressures.

in the Middle East and the Carter administration's failed attempt to use military force to rescue Iranian hostages. Several examples of the occurrence of groupthink in important decisions made by real groups have been analyzed, and these examples give an idea of the potential negative outcomes of groupthink. One example involves the decision of President John Kennedy and his very competent advisors to commit U.S. forces to help with an invasion of Cuba, with the goal of overthrowing Fidel Castro in 1962. The Bay of Pigs invasion resulted in the loss of lives, a great embarrassment to the United States government, and likely led to the attempt by the Soviet Union to place nuclear missiles in Cuba a short time later, an event that created a very dangerous confrontation with the United States (Janis, 1972). Another example was the decision, made in 1986 by NASA and the chemical company Morton Thiokol, to launch the space shuttle *Challenger* in weather that was too cold. The decision led to an explosion and the death of the astronauts as well as the loss of the shuttle. Analyses of the decision-making process in this case have shown that rather than obtaining unbiased information from all of the relevant individuals, many of those in the know were pressured to give a yes response. Furthermore, the decision to launch was made by a yes vote among only four of the responsible decision makers, and the opinions of the others were ignored.[3]

Causes of Groupthink

Irving Janis's analysis of the planning and decision making that led up to the Bay of Pigs found that President Kennedy met for many sessions with his advisors, and at each session they became more and more convinced of the viability of their plan. Janis argued that despite the fact that they met regularly, the ability of the group to make a good decision was nevertheless severely limited by the nature of the group process used during these meetings. Although he based his analysis on this particular group making this particular decision, he argued that groupthink could occur in almost any decision-making group, and that it was the result of a specific, and all too common, set of group processes.

Conformity Pressures

Groupthink is the result of high conformity pressures in the group, frequently brought on by the group leader or leaders, which keeps the group members

---

3. There are a number of Web sites related to the disaster and the decisions that led up to it. For instance, www.fas.org/spp/51L and www.colostate.edu/Depts/Speech/rccs/theory16.

from expressing contradictory opinions. Often the group process seems to be arranged to maximize the amount of conformity rather than to foster free and open discussion. In the meetings of the Bay of Pigs advisory committee, for instance, President Kennedy sometimes demanded that the group members give a voice vote regarding their individual opinions before the group actually discussed the pros and cons of a new idea. Such a procedure, in which Kennedy sometimes voted first, has great similarities to the Asch line-judging procedure that was discussed in chapter 4, and which is known to produce extremely high levels of conformity. The result of these conformity pressures is a general unwillingness to express ideas that do not match the group norm.

The high conformity pressure in groups suffering from groupthink limits discussion and produces an apparent unanimity in opinion among the group members. Members who are known to have conflicting views may not be given an opportunity to speak, and the other group members may ridicule their comments. Often, only a few group members are actually involved in conversation, whereas the others do not express any opinions. Because little or no dissent is expressed in the group, the group members come to believe that they are in complete agreement. In some cases the leader may even select individuals (known as *mindguards*) whose job it is to help quash dissent and to increase conformity to the leader's opinions.

Social Identity

An outcome of the high levels of conformity found in these groups is that the group begins to see itself as extremely valuable and important, capable of making high-quality decisions, and invulnerable. In short, the group members develop extremely high levels of social identity. Although this social identity may have some positive outcomes in terms of a commitment to work toward group goals, it also tends to result in illusions of invulnerability, leading the group members to feel that they are superior and that they do not need to seek outside information. Such a situation is conducive to terrible decision making and resulting fiascos.

Isolation, Time Pressure, and Stress

Conformity to the prevailing opinion, and thus groupthink, is more likely to occur when the group does not discuss the issues fully. Frequently, because they are so confident of their own opinions, the group feels that they do not need to consult anyone else, and this isolation may prevent the group from obtaining up-to-date and potentially contradictory information. Groupthink is also more likely in situations of crisis and stress, and particularly when there is pressure to make the decision quickly. All too often groups make their decisions at the last minute, when they are suffering a lot of anxiety about it, the group members are tired, and there is therefore little opportunity for full discussion. In short, decisions are better when the group discusses the issues fully, and groups tend to make poorer decisions when they are rushed (Kruglanski & Webster, 1991; Staw, Sandelands, & Dutton, 1981).

Studying Groupthink

Most research that has studied groupthink has been based on descriptive analyses of real groups that have made poor decisions, such as those concerning the Bay of Pigs or the launching of the *Challenger*. And these studies have generally found that the quality of important decisions is negatively related to the number of groupthink-related symptoms, including simplistic thinking, strong leadership, conformity pressures, the presence of mindguards, and time pressure (McCauley, 1989; Moorhead & Montanari, 1986; Tetlock, 1979). However, although the existing research is generally supportive of the occurrence of groupthink, and the negative outcomes that result from it, it should nevertheless be kept in mind that these studies have exclusively focused on situations in which groups have already made poor decisions. As a result, these reviews may selectively ignore situations in which highly cohesive groups made good decisions.

More definitive conclusions about the effects of groupthink-related symptoms on decision making come from experimental research, and at least some experimental findings have been interpreted as supporting the basic principles of groupthink (Callaway & Esser, 1984; Flowers, 1977; Leana, 1985; Moorhead, 1982; M. E. Turner, Pratkanis, Probasco, & Leve, 1992). For instance, Flowers (1977) found that strong and directive leadership decreased group discussion and led groups to reach decisions sooner. And Marlene Turner and her colleagues (1992) found support for the prediction that highly cohesive groups would experience poor decision making. In this research members of high cohesive groups also reported symptoms of groupthink, such as a feeling of invulnerability and a failure to reconsider information. However, one of the most important predictions regarding groupthink—that highly cohesive groups should be more subject to groupthink than are less cohesive groups—has not always been supported. Indeed, Leana (1985) found that highly cohesive groups shared *more* information than did noncohesive groups, and also did not make more risky decisions (cf. Choi & Kim, 1999). In fact, as we have seen in chapter 1, high group cohesiveness does not always relate to poor group performance, but may in fact lead to good decisions if the group norms are to be creative and to spend time making the decision.

Preventing Groupthink

Research concerning the occurrence and symptoms of groupthink provides information about the methods that might be used to prevent it from occurring. Most generally, as summarized in Figure 8.3, these techniques involve making sure that the initial causes of groupthink are not present.

One important method of preventing groupthink is to assure that the group has plenty of time to make its decision and that it is not rushed to do so. Of course, such a luxury is not always possible, but better decisions are likely to be made when there is sufficient time. Having plenty of time allows a full discussion of the issues and prevents the group from coming to premature consensus and making an unwise choice. Time to consider the issues fully also allows the group to gain new knowledge by seeking information and analysis from outside experts.

One approach to increasing full discussion of the issues is to have the group break up into smaller subgroups. This increases the amount of discussion and allows more group members to air more ideas. In some decision-making groups it is standard practice to set up several independent groups that consider the same questions, each carrying on its deliberations under a separate leader. The subgroups then meet together to make the final decision.

Within the group itself, conversation can be encouraged through the use of a *devil's advocate*—an individual who is given the job of expressing conflicting opinions and forcing the group (in a noncombative way) to fully discuss all

1. Tell group members about groupthink, its causes and consequences.
2. The leader should be impartial and should not endorse any position.
3. The leader should instruct everyone to critically evaluate the statements made by others and should encourage objections and doubts.
4. One or more members should be assigned the role of "devil's advocate."
5. From time to time subdivide the group. Have the subgroups meet separately and then come together to air differences.
6. When the issue concerns relations with a rival group, take time to survey all warning signals and identify various possible actions by the rival.
7. After reaching a preliminary decision, a "second-chance" meeting should be called at which each member is asked to express remaining doubts.
8. Outside experts should attend meetings on a staggered basis and be asked to challenge the group's views.
9. Each group member should air the group's deliberations with trusted associates and report their reactions.
10. Several independent groups should work simultaneously on the same question.

FIGURE 8.3. Ten prescriptions for preventing groupthink. Adapted from "Counteracting the Adverse Effects of Concurrence-Seeking in Policy-Planning Groups: Theory and Research Perspectives" by I. L. Janis. In H. Brandstätter et al. (Eds.). *Group Decision Making*. New York: Academic Press, 1982. pp. 477–501.

of the alternatives. Because his or her opinions challenge the group consensus, and thus may hinder quick group decision making and group identity, the individual who takes the job as the devil's advocate may not be particularly popular in the group. For this reason, the leader should formally assign the person to the role and make it clear that this role is an essential part of group functioning. The job can profitably be given to one of the most qualified group members and may sometimes rotate from person to person. In other cases, it may be useful to invite an expert or another qualified individual who is not a regular member of the group to the decision-making meetings to give his or her input. This person should be encouraged to challenge the views of the core group.

The leader is important in fostering norms of open discussion. Effective leadership in decision-making groups involves making sure that the leader does not state his or her opinions early, but rather allows the other group members to express their ideas first and encourages the presentation of contrasting positions. This allows a fuller discussion of pros and cons and prevents simple agreement by conformity. Some decision-making groups even have "second-chance" meetings before a final decision is made. In this final meeting the goal is to explicitly consider alternatives and to allow all lingering doubts to be expressed.

Group Polarization

One common task of groups is to come to a consensus on a judgment or decision, such as whether a defendant at trial is innocent or guilty or how much money a corporation should invest in a new product. As we have discussed earlier, one way to understand how groups reach consensus is to predict the judgment of the group using the group members' initial individual opinions. As you can see in Figure 8.1 on page 178, the power of the majority is very strong. Whenever a majority of the members in the group favors a given opinion, even if that majority is very slim, the group is likely to end up adopting that majority opinion. Of course, such a result would be expected since, as a result of conformity pressures, the group's final judgment should reflect the average of group members' initial opinions (or perhaps a weighted average if some members are more persuasive than others). Although group decision making does involve conformity, the tendency to side with the majority after group discussion turns out to be even stronger than this—in fact, it is commonly found that groups make even more extreme decisions, in the direction of the existing norm, than we would predict they would, given the initial opinions of the group members. **Group polarization** is said to occur when, after discussion, the attitudes held by the group members are more extreme than

Group Polarization: A tendency for group members' opinions to become more extreme as a result of group discussion.

they were before the group began discussing the topic (Lamm & Myers, 1978; Moscovici & Zavalloni, 1969; Myers, 1982; Myers & Lamm, 1976).

Group polarization has been studied, primarily using experimental designs, by comparing the outcome of a group decision with knowledge of the opinions of the individual group members before the group discussion began. To consider one example, in an experiment by Myers and Kaplan (1976) mock juries made up of U.S. college students were asked to assess the guilt or innocence of defendants in felony traffic cases. The researchers also manipulated the strength of the evidence against the defendant, such that in some groups the evidence was strong and in other groups the evidence was weak. This resulted in two groups of juries—some in which the majority of the students initially favored conviction (on the basis of the strong evidence), and others in which a majority initially favored acquittal (on the basis of only weak evidence). The researchers asked the individuals to express their opinions about the guilt of the defendant both before and after the jury deliberated.

As shown in Figure 8.4, the opinions that the individuals held about the guilt or innocence of the defendants were found to be more extreme after discussion than they were, on average, before the discussion began. That is, members of juries in which the majority of the individuals initially favored conviction became more likely to believe the defendant was guilty after the discussion, and members of juries in which the majority of the individuals initially favored acquittal became more likely to believe the defendant was innocent after the discussion. Similarly, Myers and Bishop (1970) found that groups of college students who initially had racist attitudes became more rac-

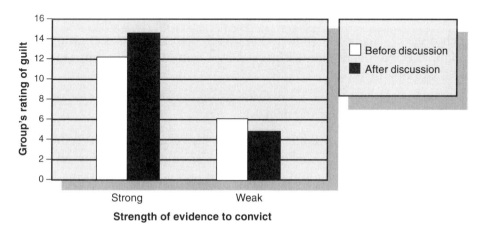

FIGURE 8.4. Group polarization. The juries in this research were given either strong or weak evidence of the guilt of a defendant and then were allowed to discuss the evidence before making a final decision. Demonstrating group polarization, the juries that discussed the case made significantly more extreme decisions than did the juries that did not discuss the case. Data are from Myers, D. G., & Kaplan, M. F. (1976). Group-induced polarization in simulated juries. *Personality & Social Psychology Bulletin, 2*(1), 63–66.

ist after group discussion, whereas groups of college students who initially had antiracist attitudes became even less racist after group discussion. Similar findings have been found for groups discussing a very wide variety of topics, and across many different cultures.

Group polarization does not occur in all groups and in all settings but tends to happen when two conditions are present. First, the group members must have an initial leaning toward a given opinion or decision. If the group members generally support liberal policies, their opinions are likely to become even more liberal after discussion. But if the group is made up of both liberals and conservatives, group polarization would not be expected. Secondly, group polarization is strengthened by discussion of the topic. For instance, in the research by Myers and Kaplan (1976) reported above, in some experimental conditions the group members did not discuss the issue, and these groups showed less polarization than groups that discussed the issue.

Although group polarization may occur in decision-making groups in businesses or courtroom settings, it may also occur in other situations. It has been argued that terrorists groups, for instance, develop their extreme positions, and may engage in violent behaviors, as a result of the group polarization that occurs in their everyday interactions (McCauley, 1991). As the group members, all of whom initially have some radical beliefs, meet and discuss their concerns and desires, their opinions polarize, allowing them to become progressively more extreme. Because they are also away from any other influences that might moderate their opinions, they may eventually become mass killers.

What Causes Group Polarization?

Much research has been conducted to understand the causes of group polarization, and it appears that it is caused by a number of different group processes working together.

Diffusion of Responsibility and the Risky Shift

Group polarization was initially observed using problems in which the group members had to indicate how an individual should choose between a risky but very positive outcome and a certain but less desirable outcome (Stoner, 1968). For example, consider the following question:

> Mr. A has a secure job with a large, secure company. His salary is adequate but unlikely to increase. He's offered a high-paying job with an unknown small company in which the likelihood of failure is higher than that in the large company. What is the minimum probability of the small company's

success that you would find acceptable to make it worthwhile for Mr. A to take the job (choose one)?

1 in 10   3 in 10   5 in 10   7 in 10   9 in 10

Research found group polarization in these types of decisions, such that the group recommendation was more risky (in this case requiring a lower probability of success of the new company) than the average of the individual group members' initial opinions. In fact, because this type of problem had been used in the research, the observed polarization was initially known as the *risky shift* and was explained in terms of *diffusion of responsibility* (Kogan & Wallach, 1967). According to this explanation, because the group as a whole is taking responsibility for the decision, the individual may be willing to take a more extreme stand, since if the risky decision does not work out, he or she can share the blame with other group members.

Social Comparison and Normative Conformity

Although originally demonstrated in groups that were initially leaning toward making a risky choice, further research soon showed that group discussion can produce shifts toward more cautious choices if the group is initially leaning in the cautious direction (Fraser, Gouge, & Billig, 1971) and that group polarization can occur on opinions that have nothing to do with risk or caution, such as opinions about the attractiveness of individuals, political attitudes, and responses to evidence in jury trials (Isenberg, 1986; Moscovici & Zavalloni, 1969; Myers & Lamm, 1976).

Because diffusion of responsibility does not seem to be an appropriate explanation to account for polarization on decisions that are not risky, other explanations for the effect were soon proposed. One idea was based on social comparison theory and conformity to group norms (Jellison & Riskind, 1970; Lamm & Myers, 1978; Sanders & Baron, 1977). According to this idea, the group members first compare their own opinions to those of others and in so doing discover the norms of the group. At this point, they attempt to match their opinion to the norm.

However, although conformity certainly plays a major role, it cannot by itself account for group polarization. This is because conformity would lead to a consensus being developed around the group norm—which is the average of the group members' initial opinions. Therefore, something else has to happen in addition to social comparison to produce polarization, because polarization involves group decisions that are more extreme than the norm. One possibility is that the group members erroneously perceive the group norm to be more extreme than it actually is, or erroneously perceive their own views to be less extreme than the norm, and therefore shift to be more extreme. Alternatively, the norm could itself be polarized through group discussion if the opinions of group members with more extreme views are seen as more valuable or if the advocates of extreme alternatives are more persuasive. Still another possibility is that extreme positions, in any direction, are seen as more important or valuable, and individuals attempt to match their opinions to them. At least some research has supported each of these potential causes of group polarization.

Self-Categorization Theory

Perhaps a better explanation for group polarization, and one that can well explain why individuals go past the group norm to adopt relatively extreme positions, is based on the predictions of social identity and self-categorization theory (Hogg, Turner, & Davidson, 1990; Mackie, 1986; Mackie & Cooper, 1984). According to this approach, group polarization involves conformity to group norms, and in this sense the explanation is very similar to that proposed by social comparison theory. However, self-categorization theory provides an elegant explanation for polarization by proposing that, because the group initially leans in one direction, the "ideal" norm of the group will be more extreme than the average of the group members' initial opinions (the "true" norm). This occurs because the group members, in their desire to create positive social identity, attempt to differentiate their group from other implied or actual groups by adopting extreme beliefs. Thus the amount of group polarization observed is expected to be determined not only by the norms of the in-group but also by a movement away from the norms of other relevant out-groups. In short, this explanation says that groups that have well-defined (extreme) beliefs are better able to produce social identity for their members than are groups that have more moderate (and potentially less clear) beliefs.

In addition to explaining group polarization, the social identity approach also makes some unique predictions about the contexts in which group polarization is most likely to occur. For one, it is expected that the perceived norms of groups will be seen as more extreme, and that the resulting change in opinion toward those norms will be greater, when the group members identify with the group, and this prediction has been supported in several studies (Abrams, Wetherell, Cochrane, & Hogg, 1990; Hogg et al., 1990; Mackie, 1986). High group identification is expected to increase both conformity to in-group norms and a motivation to differentiate the in-group from other groups.

In one relevant experiment, Diane Mackie (1986) had participants listen to three people discussing a topic, supposedly so that they could become familiar with the issue themselves to help them make their own decisions. However, the individuals that they listened to were said to be either members of a group that the participants would be joining during the upcoming experi-

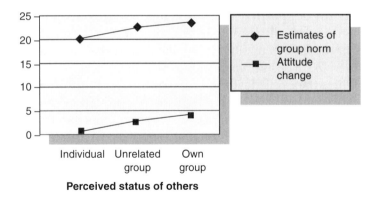

FIGURE 8.5. Social identity and group polarization. When individuals believed that they would later be joining a group (the own-group condition), they estimated that the group norm was more extreme and were more influenced by the group members' arguments. From Mackie, D. M. (1986). Social identification effects in group polarization. *Journal of Personality & Social Psychology, 50*(4), 720–728.

mental session, members of a group that they were not expecting to join, or some individuals who were not a group at all. As shown in Figure 8.5, Mackie found that the perceived norms of the (future) in-group were seen as more extreme than those of the other (unrelated) group and the individuals and that the participants were more likely to agree with the arguments of the in-group. This finding supports the idea that the group norm is perceived as more extreme for a group that people identify with (in this case because they were expecting to join it in the future). Another experiment by Mackie (1986) also supported the social identity prediction that the existence of a rival out-group increases polarization as the group members attempt to differentiate themselves from the other group by adopting more extreme positions.

Persuasive Arguments Theory

The explanations presented for group polarization to this point have primarily involved normative influence. According to the social comparison and social identity explanations, group polarization occurs because group members want to be accepted and valued, and the studies we have reviewed seem to support this expectation. However, group polarization also occurs in part simply because the group discussion presents the group members with new arguments that they have not heard before—a type of informational influence.

The general idea of *persuasive arguments theory* is that there is a set of potential arguments that support any given opinion and another set of potential arguments that refute that opinion. Furthermore, an individual's current opinion about the topic is predicted to be based on the arguments that he or she is currently aware of. During group discussion, the group members each present arguments supporting their own individual opinions. Because the group members are initially leaning in one direction, it is expected that there will be many arguments generated that will support the initial leaning of the group members. As a result, each group member is exposed to new arguments supporting the initial leaning of the group, and this predominance of arguments leaning in one direction polarizes the opinions of the group members. Supporting the predictions of persuasive arguments theory, research has shown that the number of novel arguments mentioned in discussion is related to the amount of polarization (Ebbesen & Bowers, 1974; Kaplan, 1977; Vinokur & Burnstein, 1978b).

In one experiment testing the predictions of persuasive arguments theory, Vinokur and Burnstein (1978a) placed six participants in a single group where they were asked to discuss a decision regarding whether an individual should make a risky or a cautious choice. Three of the individuals were initially known to favor the "cautious" decision whereas the other three were known to originally have "risky" opinions. Furthermore, in half of the groups the subgroup membership was made explicit by placing a card in front of each individual that indicated whether they were pro-risk or pro-caution. In the other half of the groups the participants' initial opinions were not indicated by the nametags.

This is a very interesting experiment because different theoretical explanations for group polarization make different predictions about the expected results. Specifically, the social identity approach predicts that the cautious and the risky groups will polarize, each becoming more extreme in their own direction (toward caution and risk respectively), and that this polarization will be particularly strong when the differences between the two initial groups are made salient by the nametags. However, the results of this study did not find this polarization, but rather showed moderation of each group's opinions. That is, the members of the initially cautious group became more risky, whereas the members of the originally risky group became more cautious, and this did not depend upon whether the group memberships had been made salient or not. Vinokur and Burnstein argued that this could easily be explained by persuasive arguments theory, as the members of the cautious group were exposed to risky arguments made by the other group members and as the members of the risky group were exposed to cautious arguments.

Repeated Expression Theory

There is still another approach to understanding group polarization, which is again based upon informational influence. Brauer and Judd (1996) argued that it is not so much hearing the expressions of others that is critical, but rather that simply expressing one's own beliefs during the group discussion makes people's beliefs more extreme. According to *repeated expression theory*, in the group discussion people present their own arguments to the group, and doing so increases one's belief in the argument. And, as the arguments are repeatedly expressed, they become simpler and sound less tentative and more certain. Furthermore, when people hear their own arguments picked up and repeated by other group members, they become more confident in them themselves. In one study testing this hypothesis, Brauer and Judd (1996) independently manipulated both the number of times that the participants heard others express their beliefs as well as the number of times the participants expressed their own beliefs in the group, in a series of face-to-face interactions. Supporting repeated expression theory, the results showed that the best predictor of opinion polarization was the number of times that the individuals expressed their own beliefs.

Summary

In summary, laboratory research has found that group polarization occurs frequently, and that it is the result of both normative and informational conformity (Isenberg, 1986; Laughlin & Earley, 1982). Although there is little research in this regard, it seems likely that the occurrence of group polarization depends upon many factors, including the structure of the group and the type of task being discussed. For instance, when the task involves important values and high group cohesion or identity, normative conformity is perhaps most likely as the group members coalesce around a perceived norm. On the other hand, informational influence may be more important in task-focused groups, when cohesion and identity are lower. It has also been suggested that group polarization may be more likely to be found in tasks in which the individual group members are not themselves involved in the outcome of the decision (Baron et al., 1974), perhaps because they are more willing to make extreme decisions for others than they are for themselves. Unfortunately, group polarization has primarily been studied using laboratory experiments, and much less frequently in real world settings. Thus it is not clear how frequently group polarization occurs in everyday life.

 ## *Chapter Summary*

It is customary to divide the tasks performed by working groups into various types. These types specify the dimensions that are likely to be important in determining the relative performance of groups versus individuals. Some of the important distinctions include unitary versus divisible tasks, additive versus compensatory tasks, disjunctive versus conjunctive tasks, maximizing versus intellective tasks, and criterion versus judgmental tasks. Most tasks fall into one or more of these basic classifications.

In general, larger groups are better able to perform tasks than are smaller groups. However, when the productivity of groups is compared with the productivity of nominal groups—collections of the same number of individuals working alone—the advantages of groups are not so apparent. In fact, in most cases the process losses that occur in working groups are greater than the process gains.

One approach to understanding group decision making is to assess the processes that groups use as they reach their decisions. In addition to analyzing the conversations that occur in groups, the outcome of group discussion can be predicted on the basis of decision schemes that the group uses to come to consensus. In some cases these decision schemes involve the demonstration of correct solutions, whereas in other cases they involve voting on the best alternatives. Knowing the decision scheme used by the group is helpful in predicting the group's final decision.

Groupthink is a process that occurs in groups when there are strong pressures for conformity, the group is isolated from other sources of information, and the group has to make a decision under time pressure or stress. Groups that experience groupthink are prone to make poor decisions, because they do not carefully consider all of the potential alternatives to the decision they are making. Reducing conformity pressures in the group and encouraging the group to seek outside information may help reduce the tendency toward groupthink.

Group polarization occurs when groups, through discussion, become more extreme, in the direction of the initial leanings of the group, than they were initially. Group polarization has been observed in many different types of groups and on many different topics. The causes of group polarization include diffusion of responsibility, the tendency for individuals to attempt to match (and sometimes exceed) the norms of the group, and the tendency of groups to differentiate themselves from other groups. However, group polarization may also be the result of informational influence, following the expression and repeated expression of novel arguments.

 Review and Discussion Questions

1. What are process losses and process gains? Consider the situations under which each is most likely to occur and the reasons that they do. Have you been in a group that experienced either a process loss or gain? If so, what caused it?

2. How should group performance be compared to that of individuals, and how do process gains and losses fit into such comparisons?
3. How is group effectiveness likely to be influenced by the types of tasks that the group members are asked to perform?
4. What is groupthink? Are "groupthought" decisions always bad? How can groupthink be prevented?
5. What is group polarization? What factors are necessary for group polarization to occur?
6. Discuss and explain three different theoretical approaches that can explain group polarization. What research supports each of these explanations?
7. Given the information in this chapter, what general conclusions can you draw about if and when groups should be allowed to make decisions?

Recommended Readings

A current summary of decision-making and performance in working groups:

Levine, J. M., & Moreland, R. L. (1998). Small groups. In *The Handbook of Social Psychology* (4th ed., Vol. 2, pp. 415–469). New York: McGraw-Hill.

A meta-analysis of group polarization:

Isenberg, D. J. (1986). Group polarization: A critical review and meta-analysis. *Journal of Personality and Social Psychology, 50*, 1141–1151.

The original formulation of groupthink:

Janis, I. (1982). *Groupthink* (2nd Ed.). Boston: Houghton-Mifflin.

Group Perfomance and Productivity 9

Now that we have considered some of the variables that influence group performance on decision-making tasks, we turn in this chapter to a discussion of maximizing tasks—those in which the performance of the group is measured in terms of the amount or quality of a product that is produced. Many applied researchers have found that group process is particularly important in determining the production of working groups and is frequently even more important than member characteristics, the working conditions or technology available to the workers, or the incentives offered to them. In this chapter we consider some of the ways that group process influences the performance of individuals in groups, in some cases by facilitating or improving performance, but also (and more frequently) by hindering it.

Social Facilitation and Social Inhibition

Perhaps the most interesting question concerning the influence of groups on the performance of maximizing tasks is whether and when people perform such tasks better while working with others (for instance, in groups), and when they perform such tasks better working alone. As we will see, the presence of others has powerful effects on task performance and can produce either process gains or process losses. When the influence of others on the performance of maximizing tasks creates process gains, this is known as **social facilitation,** and when the influence of others results in process losses, this is known as **social inhibition.**

Process Gains in Group Performance

Social Facilitation: Process gains on the performance of maximizing tasks that are caused by the influence of others.

Social Inhibition: Process losses on the performance of maximizing tasks that are caused by the influence of others.

One of the earliest social psychology experiments studying group performance was conducted by Norman Triplett in 1898. Triplett was interested in performance on many different types of tasks, and in the course of his research he investigated the records of over 2,000 race times that had been recorded for bicycle racers. These data showed that, altogether, racers who were competing with other bicyclers on the track rode significantly faster than bicyclers who were racing alone, against the clock. The results of this research led Triplett to conduct an experiment testing the hypothesis that the presence of others could produce social facilitation. In this experiment children were given a fishing line with a small flag on the end and were told to reel the flag in as fast as they possibly could. Confirming his expectations, and matching his findings for the bicyclers, Triplett found that the children reeled in the lines significantly faster when they were working with another child in the room than they did when they were performing alone.

Subsequent findings validated Triplett's results, and indeed many experiments have shown that the presence of others can increase performance on maximizing tasks (Dashiell, 1930), even in situations in which there does not appear to be great pressures for the individuals to compete against each other. For example, Floyd Allport (1924) found that participants performed faster on word identification tasks, wrote more rebuttals to arguments, and solved more multiplication problems when they were in the presence of other individuals, even when those individuals were only present in the room in which the individuals were working and there was no apparent competition among them. Similar findings occurred for jogging, shooting pool, lifting weights, and working on math and computer problems (Geen, 1989; Guerin, 1983; Robinson-Staveley & Cooper, 1990; Strube, Miles, & Finch, 1981).

Process Losses in Group Performance

Although process gains are commonly found when people work on tasks together, other research has demonstrated that working with others does not always turn out to help performance and that the presence of others may sometimes even result in process losses. In fact, in some cases both social facilitation and social inhibition could be found in the same research. For instance, Allport (1924) found that while working with others increased the *quantity* of behaviors that were performed, the *quality* of those behaviors sometimes decreased when others were present.

In one relevant study, Hazel Markus (1978) gave research participants both easy tasks (putting on and taking off their shoes) and unfamiliar, and thus more difficult, tasks (putting on a lab coat that tied in the back) and had them perform these tasks either alone or with a confederate present who either watched or sat in the corner of the room, repairing a piece of apparatus. As shown in Figure 9.1, Markus found that when there was another person

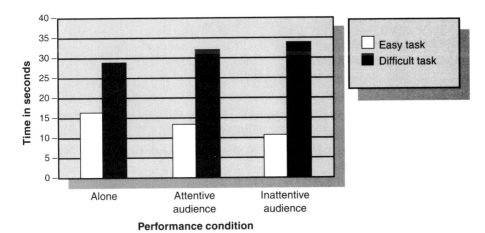

FIGURE 9.1. Performance on easy and difficult tasks. In this experiment, participants were asked to perform either well-learned tasks (putting on and taking off one's own shoes) or poorly learned tasks (putting on a lab coat that tied in the back). Overall, the poorly learned responses take longer to perform. However, regardless of whether the other individual was paying attention or not, poorly learned responses took longer and well-learned responses took less time when an audience was present. Data are from Markus (1978), The effect of mere presence on social facilitation: An unobtrusive test. *Journal of Experimental Social Psychology, 14,* 389–397.

present in the room the participants performed the easy tasks faster, but the more difficult tasks were performed slower, in comparison to when the tasks were performed alone. Furthermore, this occurred regardless of whether the confederate was paying attention to the performance of the research participant or just happened to be in the room working on another task. These results convincingly demonstrated that working around others could produce both process losses and process gains.

Explaining Social Facilitation and Social Inhibition

For many years, it was not well understood why or when the presence of others sometimes increased and sometimes decreased individual performance. However, a number of explanations have now been proposed to account for these findings, and it appears that they each have some validity.

Drive Arousal

Perhaps the most complete and best-studied explanation of the influence of others on task performance was proposed in 1965 by Robert Zajonc (his last name rhymes with *science*). Zajonc's theory is outlined in Figure 9.2. Zajonc made use of the concept of **drive arousal** (Cottrell, 1968; Weiss & Miller, 1971), which refers to the excitement and energy that occurs when other individuals

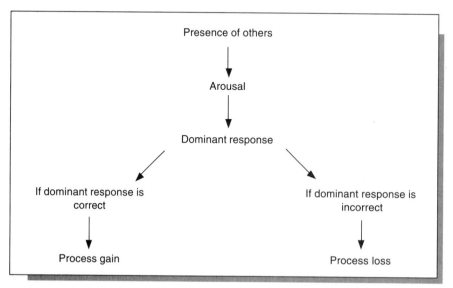

Drive Arousal: The excitement and energy that occur when other individuals are nearby.

FIGURE 9.2. The drive-arousal model of social facilitation. According to the social facilition model of Zajonc (1965), the mere presence of other produces arousal, which increases the probability that the dominant response will occur. If the dominant response is correct, process gains result, whereas if the dominant response is incorrect, process losses result.

are nearby. According to Zajonc's theory, the arousal that is produced by the presence of others, and the resulting effort put forward by the individual in these situations, increases the likelihood that the individual will perform the *dominant response*, where the dominant response is defined as the action that an individual is most likely to emit in a given situation.

The important aspect of Zajonc's theory was that the experience of arousal and the resulting increase in the performance of the dominant response could be used to predict whether the presence of others would either increase or decrease performance. Zajonc argued that when the task to be performed is relatively easy, or when the individual has learned to perform the task very well (tasks such as pedaling a bicycle, reeling in a fishing line, or tying one's shoes), the dominant response is likely to be the correct response, and the increase in drive caused by the presence of others would thus increase performance. On the other hand, when the task is difficult or not well learned (for instance, the ability to solve a complex problem or to tie a lab apron behind one's back), the dominant response is likely to be the incorrect one, and thus because the increase in arousal increases the occurrence of the (incorrect) dominant response, performance is hindered.

Zajonc's theory explained how the presence of others can both increase or decrease performance, depending on the nature of the task, and a great deal of experimental research has now confirmed his predictions. Indeed, one meta-analysis conducted to review the findings of over 200 studies using over 20,000 research participants found that the presence of others did significantly increase the rate of performing on simple tasks and decreased both the rate and the quality of performance on complex tasks (Bond & Titus, 1983).

One interesting aspect of Zajonc's theory is that, because it only requires the concepts of drive arousal and dominant response to explain task performance, it predicts that the effects of others on performance will not necessarily be confined to humans. Indeed, Zajonc reviewed evidence that dogs ran faster, chickens ate more feed, ants built bigger nests, and rats had more sex when other dogs, chickens, ants, and rats respectively were around! (Zajonc, 1965; Zajonc, Heingartner, & Herman, 1969). In fact, in one of the most unusual of all social psychology experiments, Zajonc et al. (1969) found that cockroaches ran faster when other cockroaches were observing them (from behind a plastic window) on straight runways, but that they also ran slower on a maze that involved making a more difficult turn in the presence of other roaches, presumably because running straight was the dominant response, whereas turning was not.

Mere Presence

One important aspect of this theory of social facilitation is that it predicts that the *mere presence* of others is sufficient to produce drive arousal and influence task performance, even in the absence of any competition, because the presence of others produces an increase in drive arousal. That is, performance should be influenced whenever others are around, regardless of whether they are even able to see or hear the performer. In one test of this prediction, Schmitt, Gilovich, Goore, and Joseph (1986) had participants type their names into a computer both in the normal way (a relatively easy task) as well as backward and with numbers interspersed among the letters (a more difficult task that the research participants were led to believe was required in order to provide a personal keycode). Furthermore, to create mere presence, in some conditions another person was in the room. However, this other person, who was supposedly participating in a sensory deprivation experiment being run by another experimenter, was blindfolded and was listening to earphones so that he or she could not see or hear the participant. Supporting the importance of mere presence, the participants typed their name in the easy way faster and in the more difficult way slower when the other person was there. Other experiments have also found that mere presence, even without any sort of competition or evaluation, can influence task performance (Haas & Roberts, 1975; Rajecki, Ickes, Corcoran, & Lenerz, 1977; Robinson-Staveley & Cooper, 1990).

Evaluation and Competition

Although the drive-arousal model proposed by Zajonc is perhaps the most elegant, other explanations have also been proposed to account for social facilitation (Guerin, 1983; Sanders, 1981a, b; Shaw, 1981). One difficulty with the arousal theory is that, although some research has shown that the mere presence of others appears sufficient to influence task performance, other studies have found small or no effects on performance if the others who are present cannot see the participants, if participants make their responses privately, or if the audience will not be evaluating their performance (Bond & Titus, 1983; Manstead & Semin, 1980; Martens & Landers, 1972). In fact, some research has found that being around others does not always even increase arousal (Moore & Baron, 1983).

One modification of drive-arousal theory argues that arousal primarily occurs in the presence of others when we perceive that others are able to provide us with rewards or punishments as a result of competition. Thus, this approach predicts that the influence of the presence of others will be greater when those others are perceived to be competing with us (Harkins & Szymanski, 1987). Competing with others increases our motivation to do well, and this motivation is successful on simple tasks, thus producing facilitation. However, on difficult tasks the arousal that accompanies the increased motivation disrupts successful performance of the task, resulting in poorer task performance.

Existing research suggests that expecting to be evaluated by the others who are observing us can increase both arousal and subsequent performance, above and beyond the mere presence of others (Geen, 1980; Weiss & Miller, 1971). For instance, Michael Strube and his colleagues (Strube et al., 1981) found that the presence of spectators only increased jogging speed when the spectators were facing the joggers, so that they could see them and assess their performance, but that the presence of others did not influence performance when they were facing in the other direction and thus could not see them. Taken together then, the evidence suggests that situations that produce perceptions of competition or evaluation may increase the influence of others on performance, above and beyond mere presence.

Distraction Caused by the Presence of Others

Still another approach to understanding social facilitation is based on the idea that, when others are around, we become more aware of the potential discrepancies between what we would like to be able to do and what we are actually accomplishing. When this discrepancy is perceived, we become distracted by the comparisons we are making and the presence of others then produces increased drive effects, which produce social facilitation (R. S. Baron, 1986; Sanders, Baron, & Moore, 1978). According to this *distraction-conflict model,* the resulting drive may increase performance on easy tasks (tests that we are well prepared for) because we concentrate harder in order to overcome the distraction. However, on hard tasks (those that we are not prepared for) our ability to try harder is not sufficient to overcome the distraction, and thus the presence of others produces poorer performance.

In some cases the presence of others who expect us to do well and who are thus likely to be particularly distracting can indeed have very negative outcomes on performance (Baumeister, 1984; Baumeister & Showers, 1986). For example, Baumeister and Steinhilber (1984) found that professional athletes frequently performed more poorly than would be expected in crucial games that were played in front of their own fans (such as the final baseball game of the World Series championship). Furthermore in a laboratory study designed to test this hypothesis experimentally, Baumeister, Hamilton, and Tice (1985) showed that participants performed more poorly when they thought that others expected them to do well on a complex task, in comparison to when they thought the others expected them to perform at an average level. Evidently, the high expectations led people to become distracted, which interfered with performance on these complicated tasks.

In summary, although there is now good agreement about when social facilitation occurs, there is still some disagreement about exactly why it happens. It is likely that each of the proposed underlying mechanisms has at least some influence on performance (C. F. Bond & Titus, 1983; Geen, 1980; Sanders, 1981a).

Coordination and Motivation Losses

As we have seen, process losses occur when the actual performance of the group is found to be less than would have been predicted given the abilities of the individual group members. Process losses occur regularly on maximizing tasks, and are caused by both the difficulty of coordinating the performance of the individuals and by the tendency of individuals to reduce their effort when they are in groups.

The Ringelmann Effect

In an important set of studies demonstrating process losses, Ringelmann (1913; reported in Kravitz & Martin, 1986) investigated the ability of individuals to reach their full potential when working together on tasks. In his best-known study, Ringelmann had men, individually and in groups of various sizes, pull as hard as they could on ropes while he measured the maximum amount that they were able to pull. Ringelmann assumed that rope pulling was an additive task, and thus that the total amount that could be pulled by the group should have been the sum of the contributions of the individuals. However, as shown in Figure 9.3, although he did find that adding individuals to the group increased the overall amount of pulling on the rope, he also found a substantial process loss. In fact, the loss was so large that groups of three men pulled at only 85 percent of their expected capability, whereas groups of eight pulled at only 37 percent of their expected capability!

Ringelmann Effect:
The tendency for group productivity to decrease as the size of the group increases.

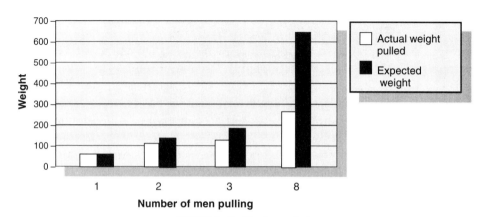

FIGURE 9.3. The Ringelmann effect.

This phenomenon, in which group productivity decreases as the size of the group increases, is known as the **Ringelmann effect**. The effect has been shown in many other experiments (Davis, 1969; G. W. Hill, 1982; Lorge, Fox, Davitz, & Brenner, 1958; Shepperd, 1993; Steiner, 1972; K. D. Williams & Karau, 1991) and has been found to occur on a wide variety of tasks, including pumping air (Kerr & Bruun, 1981; Kerr, 1983), clapping and cheering (Harkins, Latané, & Williams, 1980; Latané, Williams, & Harkins, 1979), folding papers (Zaccaro, 1984), swimming (K. D. Williams, Nida, Baca, & Latané, 1989), and evaluating a poem (Petty, Harkins, Williams, & Latané, 1977). Furthermore, these process losses have been observed in different cultures, including India, Japan, and Taiwan (Gabrenya, Wang, & Latané, 1985; Karau & Williams, 1993).

Coordination Losses

One of the causes of process losses, such as those observed by Ringelmann, is that the maximum group performance can only occur if all of the participants put forth their greatest effort at exactly the same time. Since, despite the best efforts of the group, it is difficult to perfectly coordinate the input of the group members, the likely result is a process loss such that the group performance is less than would be expected when calculated as the sum of the individual inputs. Thus, actual productivity in the group is reduced in part by *coordination losses*.

Coordination losses become more problematic as the size of the group increases, because coordinating the group members becomes correspondingly more difficult. For instance, Kelley, Condry, Dahlke, and Hill (1965) put individuals into separate booths and threatened them with electrical shocks. Each person could avoid the shock, however, by pressing a button in the booth for three seconds. But the situation was arranged in such a way that only one person in the group could press a button at any time, and so the group members needed to coordinate their actions. Kelley et al. found that larger groups had significantly more difficulty coordinating their actions to escape the shocks than did smaller groups.

Motivation Losses

In addition to being able to coordinate their activities, group members must also be motivated to put in individual effort on the task. *Motivation losses* are process losses that occur when the individuals do not work as hard in the group as they do when they are alone. The reduction in motivation and effort that occurs when individuals work together at a group task is sometimes referred to as **social loafing**, and it has been found in many experiments (a meta-analysis conducted by Karau & Williams, 1993, reported a moderate effect size of .44).

Social Loafing: The reduction in motivation and effort that occurs when individuals work together at a group task.

Latané, Williams, and Harkins (1979) conducted an experiment that allowed them to measure the extent to which groups suffered from process losses due to motivation and process losses due to coordination in the same experiment. Groups of two or six research participants were placed in a room with a microphone and instructed to shout as loud as they could when a signal was given. Furthermore, the participants were blindfolded and wore headsets that prevented them from either seeing or hearing the performance of the other group members. On some trials the participants were told (via the headsets) that they would be shouting alone, and on other trials they were told that they would be shouting with the other participants. However, although the individuals sometimes did shout in groups, in other cases (although they still thought that they were shouting in groups) they actually shouted alone. Thus Latané and his colleagues were able to measure the contribution of each individual, both when they thought they were shouting alone, and again when they thought they were shouting in a group of two or six people.

Latané et al.'s results are presented in Figure 9.4, which shows the amount of sound produced per person. The top line represents the potential productivity of the group, which was calculated as the average of the sound produced by the individuals as they performed alone. The middle line (white circles)

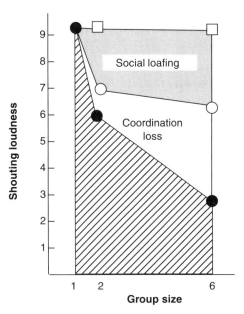

FIGURE 9.4. Motivation and coordination losses. Individuals who were asked to shout as loudly as they could shouted significantly less so when they were in larger groups, and this process loss was the result of both motivation and coordination losses. Data from Latané, B., Williams, K., & Harkins, S. (1979). Many hands make light the work: The causes and consequences of social loafing. *Journal of Personality and Social Psychology, 37,* 822–832.

represents the performance of nominal groups in which each person thought that they were shouting in a group of either two or six individuals, but where they were actually performing alone. Finally, the bottom line (black circles) represents the performance of real two-person and six-person groups who were actually shouting together.

The results of the study are very clear. First, as the number of people shouting increased (from one to two to six), each person's individual input got smaller, demonstrating the Ringelmann effect. Furthermore, the decrease for real groups (the lower line) is greater than the decrease for the nominal groups. Because performance in the nominal groups is a function of motivation, but not coordination, whereas the performance in real groups is a function of both motivation and coordination, Latané and his colleagues effectively showed how much of the process loss was due to each. Latané et al. also pointed out that the decrease in both motivation and coordination as a function of group size approximates a power function, similar to that found to describe the effects of others on social influence (see chapter 4).

Determinants of Social Loafing

A large number of studies have now investigated the determinants of social loafing, and the result is a good understanding of when it does and does not occur. Indeed, it has been found to be relatively easy to eliminate social loafing entirely, given the right conditions. We can divide the causes of social loafing into those that relate to the group process itself (group size and group norms), those that relate to the task being performed (task attractiveness and task significance), and those that relate to the individual's perception of his or her input to the group (deindividuation and free riding). Let us consider each of these variables.

Group Factors

As you can see by looking at Figure 9.4, one of the most important factors that contributes to social loafing is group size. As groups get bigger, they have more trouble coordinating their efforts, and as a result coordination losses increase. And increases in group size also produce more motivation losses, because individuals in larger groups are more likely to feel that their effort is not going to make a difference to the output of the group as a whole; they feel *dispensable* (Kerr & Bruun, 1981).

A second group factor that may either increase or decrease social loafing is the norms that the group has developed concerning appropriate effort. In some cases groups develop norms that prohibit members from working up to their full potential and thus encourage loafing. In a field study by Roethlisberger and Dickson (1939) at a Western Electric plant it was found that workers who worked too hard were ostracized by the other group members and labeled "rate busters." On the other hand, if the group has developed a strong group identity and the group members care about the ability of the group to do a good job (for instance, a cohesive sports or military team), the amount of social loafing is reduced (Brickner, Harkins, & Ostrom, 1986).

Task Attractiveness and Significance

The extent to which group members loaf has also been found to be influenced by the nature of the task itself. In general, tasks that are more rewarding and interesting to perform produce less loafing. Thus, it has been found that tasks that involve engaging in a number of different types of activities that make productive use of an individual's specific skills, and in which people feel that they have autonomy to work on the task at their own speed and using their own approaches, are less likely to produce loafing (Harkins & Petty, 1983; Shepperd & Wright, 1989; Zaccaro, 1984).

Social loafing is also reduced when the task is seen as personally important or involving, and when individuals feel that they are performing an important, whole, and visible piece of the work and thus are *not* dispensable (Brickner et al., 1986; Karau & Williams, 1993; Kerr & Bruun, 1983). Loafing can also be reduced when individuals are given a standard for performance, for instance, by being able to compare their own current performance with their past performance or with the performance of others.

Deindividuation

Social loafing occurs in part because individuals in groups become deindividuated, such that their own unique contribution to the group task is no longer identifiable. Williams, Harkins, and Latané (1981) found that when groups of individuals were asked to cheer as loudly as they could into a microphone placed in the center of the room, social loafing occurred. However, when each individual was given his or her own personal microphone, and thus believed that his or her own input could be measured, social loafing was virtually eliminated. Furthermore, in a second study, these researchers also found that when individuals thought their performance was identifiable, social loafing in groups was again eliminated. But they also found that when their performance was not identifiable, participants loafed even when they were working alone. Thus, if individual outcomes are observable, individuals do not loaf; but if outcomes are not identifiable, they do.

Evaluation Potential

Although the research reported in the previous section has clearly demonstrated that deindividuation increases social loafing, the procedures used in those experiments were also arranged so that the experimenters could have evaluated the performance of the individual. People may exert effort on tasks in part so that others will see that they are working hard. Harkins and Jackson (1985) tested this hypothesis by having groups of four participants work together on a task in which they were to generate uses for different common objects ("What can you do with a knife? What can you do with a brick?"). To identify individual performance, for half of the participants the lists that they had written were collected individually so that it was clear that the researcher would be able to judge the number and quality of their answers. The other half of the participants, who were in the low-identifiability condition, put their answers into a box along with the lists that had been created by other participants and believed that their answers would not be linked to them (in both conditions the experimenters were, in fact, able to determine who had contributed which list).

In addition to this manipulation of identifiability, Harkins and Jackson also manipulated whether all four participants were working on generating uses for the same object, or whether each participant was working on creating uses for a different object. The idea was that it would be possible to evaluate a person's performance, by comparing it to the performance of others, only if everyone was working on the same task. Thus the experiment had high and low levels of identifiability (whether or not your work could be identified as yours) and also had high and low levels of evaluation potential (whether or not your work could be compared to others who had worked on the same task).

Supporting prior research, the results clearly showed that social loafing could be reduced by making individuals identifiable. However, this only occurred in the conditions in which the participant's work could also be evaluated. In short, participants in these studies loafed in all conditions except those in which their work could be linked to them and the quality of their responses could be compared to others. Subsequent research has confirmed that the potential for evaluation is an important determinant of loafing, and it has also been found that evaluation that comes from the self, rather than others, can be important (Harkins, 1987; Szymanski & Harkins, 1987).

Free Riding

Social loafing may occur in part because individuals realize that other group members will do the work of the group and, therefore, that it is not necessary for them to contribute. **Free riding** refers to a type of social loafing that occurs

Free Riding: A type of social loafing that occurs when individuals rely on other group members to do the work for the group.

when individuals rely on other group members to do the group's work (Kerr & Bruun, 1983; Williams & Karau, 1991). For instance, imagine that you lived in a communal house with several roommates and that there was one roommate who was willing to wash the dishes every day. As long as this person continues to do the job, the other house members can free ride—they get the advantages of clean dishes without having to do any of the work.

To demonstrate the occurrence of free riding, Norbert Kerr (1983) had individuals work on a task that required pumping air into a tube by squeezing on a rubber bulb. The participants thought that they were working with another person, but they could not see him or her, and the performance of the other person was actually predetermined by the experimenter. The task was identifiable, in the sense that the participant could see his or her own performance as well as the performance of the "partner." Furthermore, the task was disjunctive, such that if either of the two partners succeeded on a trial (by pumping a certain amount of air within 30 seconds), the pair as a whole received a payment of 25 cents. The work took some effort, and people were therefore motivated to loaf.

The participants first completed four practice trials with their "partners." For some of the participants, this feedback indicated that the partner was able to perform the task (he or she succeed on three out of four of these trials). For other participants, feedback was given indicating that the participant had failed to pump the required amount of air (he or she succeeded on only one of the four practice trials). Then nine real air-pumping trials were conducted. As shown in the left two bars of Figure 9.5, over the course of the trials the individuals who thought their partners were able (because they had succeeded on the practice trials) began to free ride by working less hard on the task themselves (in comparison to individuals working alone), evidently because they figured that the partner could carry the performance of the pair.

Free riding occurs when group members monitor the behavior of other group members and learn that their own performance is dispensable—that is, the group performs just as well without them (Kerr, 1983). Furthermore, which individuals are most likely to perceive themselves as dispensable depends upon the type of task. In a disjunctive task in which performance depends on the ability of the best group member or members, members with low ability tend to free ride, relying upon the performance of other, better group members. However, on conjunctive tasks in which the performance of the worst group member determines the outcome, members with high ability tend to free ride (Kerr, 1983; Kerr & Bruun, 1983).

Although free riding is a type of social loafing, it seems to be determined more by one's perceived dispensability than on the basis of identifiability or the potential for evaluation. Individuals free ride when it seems that their

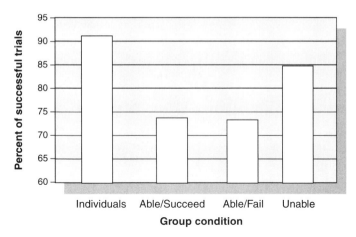

FIGURE 9.5. Free riding and the sucker effect. In comparison to individuals either alone or with another successful person who was not a partner (individual condition), participants who thought their partners were able and who succeeded on the following tasks (able-succeed) demonstrated free riding, whereas the individuals who thought their partners were able and who failed on the following tasks (able-fail) also slackened their efforts to avoid being a "sucker" to the free riding of the partner. When participants thought that their partners were unable to complete the task however (unable), they carried the incapable partner by performing well themselves. Data is from Kerr, N. L. (1983). Motivation losses in small groups: A social dilemma analysis. *Journal of Personality and Social Psychology, 45,* 819–828.

contribution doesn't matter, even if their performance is being monitored. Social loafing, on the other hand, occurs primarily when individuals slack off because their responses cannot be identified or evaluated.

The Sucker Effect

Both social loafing and free riding are determined in part by perceptions of appropriate group norms. In most cases, group norms indicate that individuals should contribute to reaching the group goals and that they should do so equitably: no member should work harder than another. When these norms are perceived to be broken, individuals may adjust their effort in the group to restore equity.

Kerr (1983) demonstrated this phenomenon in research in which partners worked on the air-pumping task. In another condition of his experiment (see Figure 9.5 again), he studied the behavior of participants who had been led to believe that their partner was capable of succeeding at the task, because they succeeded on the practice trials, but who did not perform up to his or her capability on the real trials (the able/fail condition). As expected, participants in this condition reduced their effort (again in comparison to individuals working alone) apparently to avoid being a "sucker" to the free riding of their partner. The **sucker effect** occurs when perceiving that one is contributing more to a task than others leads individuals to withhold effort as a means of

Sucker Effect: The tendency to withhold effort as a means of restoring equity and avoiding being taken advantage of that occurs when one perceives that he or she is contributing more to a task than others.

restoring equity and avoiding being taken advantage of. Although individuals may reduce effort when they think that others are free riding, in other cases equity norms may prevent loafing. For instance, when input is identifiable, people may attempt to avoid looking like they are taking advantage of others by increasing their efforts and working up to the group norm. Furthermore, as shown in the rightmost bar in Figure 9.5, if individuals perceive that other group members need help performing a task (in this case because they were unable to successfully pump the air), they will continue to contribute to the group effort, rather than slacking off.

Brainstorming

One technique that is frequently used to produce creative decisions in working groups is known as **brainstorming**. The technique was first developed by Osborn (1954) in an attempt to increase the effectiveness of group sessions at his advertising agency. Osborn had the idea that people might be able to effectively use their brains to "storm" a problem, by sharing ideas with each other in groups. Osborn felt that creative solutions would be increased when the group members generated a lot of ideas and when judgments about the quality of those ideas were initially deferred and only later evaluated. Thus brainstorming was based on the following rules:

- Each group member was to create as many ideas as possible, no matter how silly, unimportant, or unworkable they were thought to be.
- As many ideas as possible were to be generated by the group.
- No one was allowed to offer opinions about the quality of an idea (even one's own).
- The group members were encouraged and expected to modify and expand upon other's ideas.

Brainstorming: A technique used to produce creative decisions in working groups.

Researchers have devoted considerable effort to testing the effectiveness of brainstorming, and yet, despite the creativeness of the idea itself, there is very little evidence to suggest that it works (Diehl & Stroebe, 1987; Diehl & Stroebe, 1991; W. Stroebe & Diehl, 1994). In fact, virtually all individual studies, as well as meta-analyses of those studies find that, regardless of the exact instructions given to the group, brainstorming groups do not generate as many ideas as one would expect, and the ideas that they do generate are usually of lesser quality than those generated by nominal groups of equal size (Lamm & Trommsdorff, 1973; Mullen, Johnson, & Salas, 1991). Thus, brainstorming represents still another example of a case in which, despite the expectation of a process gain by the group, a process loss is instead observed.

Explanations for the Difficulties of Brainstorming

A number of explanations have been proposed for the failure of brainstorming to be effective, and many of these have been found to be important.

Social Loafing

Perhaps the most obvious potential detriment to effective brainstorming is social loafing by the group members. At least some research suggests that this does cause part of the problem. For instance, Paulus and Dzindolet (1993) found that social loafing in brainstorming groups occurred, in part, because individuals perceived that the other group members were not working very hard, and (to avoid being "suckers") they matched their own behavior to this perceived norm. Diehl and Stroebe (1987) compared face-to-face and nominal brainstorming groups and found that face-to-face groups generated fewer and less creative solutions than did an equal number of individuals working alone (the nominal groups). However, for some of the face-to-face groups the researchers set up a television camera to record the contributions of each of the participants, in order to make individual contributions to the discussion identifiable. As would be expected, identifiability reduced social loafing and increased the productivity of the individuals in the face-to-face groups; but the face-to-face groups still did not perform as well as the nominal groups.

Evaluation Apprehension

Even though individuals in brainstorming groups are told that no evaluation of the quality of the ideas is to be made, and thus that all ideas are good ones, individuals might nevertheless be unwilling to state some of their ideas in brainstorming groups because they are afraid that they will be negatively evaluated by the other group members. Indeed, research has suggested that this is the case, and thus that evaluation apprehension plays some role in reducing the effectiveness of interacting groups. For instance, when individuals are told that other group members are more expert than they are, they reduce their own contributions (Collaros & Anderson, 1969), and when they are convinced that they themselves are experts, their contributions increase (Diehl & Stroebe, 1987).

Production Blocking

Although social loafing and evaluation apprehension seem to cause some of the problem, the most important difficulty that reduces the effectiveness of brainstorming in face-to-face groups is that the mere fact of being with others hinders opportunities for idea production and expression. In a group, only one person can speak at a time, and this can cause people to forget their ideas because they are listening to others or to miss what others are saying because they are thinking of their own ideas. This problem is known as *production blocking*. Considered another way, production blocking occurs because, although individuals in nominal groups can spend the entire available time generating ideas, participants in face-to-face groups must perform other tasks as well, and this reduces their creativity.

Diehl and Stroebe (1987) demonstrated the importance of production blocking in another experiment that compared nominal and face-to-face groups. In this experiment, rather than changing things in the real group, they created production blocking in the nominal groups through a turn-taking procedure, such that the individuals, who were working in individual cubicles, had to express their ideas verbally into a microphone, but they were only able to speak when none of the other individuals were speaking. Having to coordinate in this way decreased the performance of nominal groups such that they were no longer better than the face-to-face groups.

Follow-up research (Diehl & Stroebe, 1991) showed that the main factor responsible for productivity loss in face-to-face brainstorming groups is that the group members are not able to make good use of their waiting time, in part because they forget their ideas and in part because they must concentrate on negotiating when it is going to be their turn to speak. In fact, even when the researchers gave the face-to-face groups extra time to perform the task (to make up for having to wait for others), they still did not reach the level of productivity of the nominal groups. Thus the necessity of monitoring the behavior of others and the delay that is involved in waiting to be able to express one's ideas reduce the ability to think creatively (Gallupe, Cooper, Grise, & Bastianutti, 1994).

The Illusion of Group Effectivity

Although research has demonstrated that brainstorming is not always effective, people who participate in brainstorming groups nevertheless think that they will be more productive than if they were to work alone (Paulus, Dzindolet, Poletes, & Camacho, 1993; Stroebe, Diehl, & Abakoumkin, 1992). Furthermore, those who have already participated in task-performing groups, such as brainstorming sessions, believe that the session was more effective than it really was (Larey & Paulus, 1995). In general, people also believe that their group was particularly effective, in comparison to other groups, and that they individually contributed more to the group goal than they really did (Paulus et al., 1993).

The tendency to overvalue the productivity of groups is known as the **illusion of group effectivity,** and it seems to occur for several reasons. For one, people tend to focus on the productivity of the group as a whole, which seems quite good, at least in comparison to the contributions of single individuals. In addition, people who work in brainstorming groups seem to think that the brainstorming rules are working; they think that they and the group are generating a lot of ideas, that their ideas were generated because they had heard the ideas expressed by others, and that their ideas are helping others develop good ideas, even though none of these things are usually true when assessed objectively.

The illusion of group effectivity poses a severe problem for effective group performance. For one thing, groups may continue to use and rely on brainstorming procedures even when those procedures are not actually effective. Furthermore, the feeling that the group is producing a lot of good ideas may lead the group to think that it is doing better than it really is. As a result, the group members may erroneously feel that they have been successful at the task and stop working earlier than they should.

Improving Brainstorming

One of the most important conclusions to be drawn from the literature that has studied brainstorming is that the technique is less effective than expected because group members are required to do other things in addition to being creative. However, this does not necessarily mean that brainstorming is not useful overall. Indeed, modifications of the original brainstorming procedures have been found to be quite effective in producing creative thinking in groups.

The Nominal Group Technique

One variation on the brainstorming idea is known as the **nominal group technique** (Fox, 1989; Delbecq, Van de Ven, & Gustafson, 1975). The nominal group technique capitalizes on the use of nominal groups to generate initial ideas and face-to-face groups to discuss and build on them. In this approach participants work alone to generate ideas, and write them down before the group discussion starts, and the group then records the ideas that are generated. Individuals then make their judgments individually and privately, and these judgments are then pooled. In addition, a round-robin procedure is used to make sure that each individual has a chance to communicate his or her ideas. Still another approach is the **stepladder technique** (Rogelberg, Barnes-Farrell, & Lowe, 1992) in which individuals join the group one at a time, and each entering member is instructed to think about the topics alone and come to a

Illusion of Group Effectivity: The tendency to overvalue the productivity of groups.

Nominal Group Technique: An approach to improving group decision making that uses nominal groups to generate initial ideas and face-to-face groups to discuss and build on them.

Stepladder Technique: A method of creative decision making in which individuals join the group and present their opinions one at a time.

conclusion before they enter the group discussion. Upon entering the group, the new member presents his or her ideas, ensuring that each person's ideas are fully heard by the group as a whole. Research on the effectiveness of the stepladder technique has shown that stepladder groups produce higher-quality decisions than conventional groups (Rogelberg et al., 1992). Other similar approaches include the *Delphi technique* (Hornsby, Smith, & Gupta, 1994: Reid, Pease, & Taylor, 1990) in which the judgments of individuals are pooled without any group meeting and *Synetics* (Stein, 1978; Wilson, Greer, & Johnson, 1973). How useful such techniques are in improving decision making is still a topic of research, but they are potentially effective because they have the ability to reduce production blocking by allowing initial individual thought, only later followed by group discussion.

Electronic Brainstorming

Contemporary advances in technology have given individuals the ability to work together on creativity tasks via computer. These computer systems, generally known as **group support systems (GSS),** are used in businesses and other organizations as well as in classroom settings. GSS are growing in number, and it has been estimated that several thousand that are now operational (Briggs, Adkins, Mittleman, Kruse, Miller, & Nunamaker, 1999). One use of GSS involves brainstorming on creativity tasks. Each individual in the group works at his or her own terminal on the problem. As he or she writes suggestions or ideas, they are passed to the other group members via the computer network so that each individual can see the suggestions of all of the group members, including one's own. A number of research programs have found that electronic brainstorming is more effective than face-to-face brainstorming (Collaros & Anderson, 1969; Dennis & Valacich, 1993; Gallupe et al., 1994; Siau, 1995).

Electronic brainstorming is effective because it reduces the production blocking that occurs in face-to-face groups. Each individual has the comments of all of the other group members handy and can read them when it is convenient. The individual can alternate between reading the comments of others and writing his or her own comments and so is not required to wait to express his or her ideas. In addition, electronic brainstorming can be effective because, particularly when the participants' contributions are anonymous, it reduces evaluation apprehension (Valacich, Dennis, & Nunamaker, 1991; Valacich, Jessup, Dennis, & Nunamaker, 1992).

Group Support Systems (GSS): Computer programs and networks designed to improve group decision making.

What Are the Benefits of Groups?

In summarizing the results of group performance on decision making and task performance, we could say, first, that groups influence performance primarily through their effects on the amount of effort that individuals put into the task and secondarily through effects on the ability of groups to coordinate their efforts. Our review of the literature concerning the relative performance of groups and individuals suggests that process losses are much more common than process gains. Individuals frequently withdraw effort when they are in groups, and this reduces task performance. Indeed, social loafing is so common that is has been referred to as a type of "social disease" that has "negative consequences for individuals, social institutions, and societies" (Latané et al., 1979, p. 831). Although these conclusions do seem to be warranted on the basis of the existing literature, we should not be led into the belief that groups are never useful and that people should always make their decisions alone. Of course, this is simply not true. Groups are a necessary and important part of successful task performance, and it is worth considering this fact more fully.

The Advantage of Numbers

In our prior discussion of group effectiveness, we have argued that groups are not generally more effective than we would expect them to be, in comparison to the expected performance of the same number of group members working alone. However, this is only one way of evaluating the effectiveness of group performance. In fact, because groups consist of many members, group performance is almost always better, and group decisions generally more accurate, than that of any individual acting alone. Presidents have advisors, and corporations have boards of directors precisely because groups have a real advantage over individuals—many heads *are* better than one, in terms of knowledge, memory, and ability more generally—and (even though group process can sometimes cause problems) this should always be kept in mind.

Evaluation Potential and Identifiability

As we have seen in our discussion of social facilitation, one type of process gain occurs when groups perform easy or well-learned tasks. These gains are particularly likely when the individuals in the situation are aware of each other's performance, and thus the performance is both identifiable and likely to be evaluated. On the other hand, process losses are more likely to be observed in tasks in which the individual's inputs are perceived as nonidentifiable or nonessential, because in these cases motivation to perform the task generally decreases. Overall, then, it is safe to say that groups are effective, but that they are particularly effective when the group members are also working as individuals—that is, when others are aware of and able to monitor each other's inputs.

Process Gains?

Drawing from the findings in the social facilitation literature, as well as from our understanding of group processes more generally, we might expect that process gains might be expected to occur primarily in groups that have a lot of experience working together and that are well trained for the task that they are performing. For these groups the presence of others should produce an increase in the dominant response—which in this case is the correct one—and these groups should also be well able to coordinate their efforts. The group from NASA that worked together to land a human on the moon, a rock band that is writing a new song together, or a surgical team in the middle of a complex operation may coordinate their efforts so well that is clear that the same outcome could never have occurred if the individuals had worked alone or in another group of less well suited individuals. In these cases the knowledge and skills of the individuals seem to work together to be effective, and the outcome of the group appears to be enhanced.

There is at least some, although limited, research evidence for process gains in groups. For instance, in one study Michaelsen, Watson, and Black (1989) had 222 groups of students, ranging in size from 3 to 6 and who had studied together as a group over the course of an academic semester, first take a multiple choice test alone and then work together in the groups to complete the same test. The average test score for individuals was 74.2 percent, the average score of the best member in each group was 82.6 percent, whereas the average score for groups was 89.9 percent. In fact, 97 percent of the groups scored better than their best member. On the basis of these data Michaelsen et al. argued that the groups showed a process gain, because on average they performed better than the best member in their group. Similarly, Sniezek and Henry (1989) found that the accuracy of groups was greater than the accuracy of the average of the group members on a compensatory task involving estimating the prevalence of various diseases in the U.S. population. And Liang, Moreland, and Argote (1995) found that groups that were trained together to perform a task subsequently performed better together in comparison to groups made up of members who had been trained individually. Thus, although these gains may not be as large as we might expect, under some limited conditions process gains may be possible (but see Tindale & Larson, 1992a, 1992b).

Other Outcomes

Finally, even if group performance is not as good as we might hope, in comparison to that of individuals, working in groups may still produce other positive outcomes. For one, the social identity that results from group membership may inspire individuals to make personal sacrifices that they might not have made had they not been part of the group. Indeed, Karau and Williams (1991) found that when individuals saw that other members of their groups were failing to meet group expectations, they rallied to help the group meet its goals, a phenomenon known as *social compensation*. The extraordinary performance of humans in wars, on sports teams, and in emergency situations are frequently driven in part by group membership and the social identity that group membership creates. As we have seen in chapter 3, groups also provide us with satisfaction, social support, and belongingness, and these outcomes are an important benefit for group members. People like working in groups, and this alone may be a reason for having them.

Finally, people prefer group decisions because they are perceived as being democratic and fair. We have more confidence in decisions made by groups rather than by individuals (Sniezek & Henry, 1989) because group decisions give people a "voice" or sense of ownership in the decision. As a result, collective decisions are more easily accepted by others and produce a greater commitment on the part of the group members to reach the relevant goals.

 ## Chapter Summary

Maximizing tasks are those in which the performance of the group is assessed in terms of the amount or quality of a product that is produced. This chapter has considered whether working in groups results in process gains or process losses on such tasks. Early research comparing the performance of individuals working alone versus in groups demonstrated process gains, and these gains became known as social facilitation. Social facilitation occurred on such tasks as bicycle riding or weight lifting, in which individuals tended to perform better when others were present than they did when they were alone. However, other research demonstrated that the presence of others might also produce process losses (social inhibition).

One approach to understanding the impact of working with others on task performance is drive-arousal theory. In this approach, working with others is assumed to produce arousal, which increases the dominant response. On easy or well-learned tasks the dominant response is the correct response, and thus working with others increases performance. On difficult or poorly learned tasks, on the other hand, the dominant response is the incorrect response, and thus working with others decreases performance. Although drive-arousal theory can explain much of the impact on performance of working in groups, group performance is also influenced by evaluation, competition, self-awareness, and distraction.

Process losses (such as the Ringelmann effect) occur both because individuals in groups have more trouble coordinating their responses and also because individuals in groups frequently withdraw their effort. This withdrawal is known as social loafing. The magnitude of process losses in groups is determined by the attractiveness and significance of the task for the individual, the identifiability of the individual as he or she performs the task, and whether the individual's performance will be evaluated. One type of social loafing in which individuals rely on others to do the work of the group is known as free riding. However, in contrast to social loafing, which is primarily determined by one's lack of identifiability, free riding is determined primarily by the perception that one's contribution is dispensable.

Brainstorming involves using groups to make decisions according to a set of rules that is designed to result in the generation of a large quantity of ideas, and which at the same time does not allow evaluation of those ideas. However, brainstorming has not always been found to be effective, in comparison to individuals working under the same instructions in nominal groups. This is in part because of the occurrence of social loafing and evaluation apprehension, but primarily because working in groups produces production blocking—the inability to think creatively and to remember one's ideas long enough to report them to the group. However, the illusion of group effectivity may lead individuals to think that brainstorming is effective even when it is not. Electronic brainstorming does, however, appear to be an effective method for developing creative ideas.

Although process gains are not common in groups, there are nevertheless some distinct advantages of working in groups. Groups do relatively better in situations in which identifiability and evaluation potential are high and when the members are well trained and have experience working together. Furthermore, people like working in groups, and because decisions made by groups are seen as fair they may be more easily accepted and implemented.

Review and Discussion Questions

1. What are the basic tenets of Zajonc's theory of social facilitation? What evidence favors the theory, and what alternatives to it have been proposed? Give examples from your own experience of social facilitation effects.
2. What variables influence the extent to which coordination loss and motivation loss influence group task performance?
3. What are social loafing and free riding? What is the difference between them, and under what conditions do they occur?
4. What is brainstorming? What factors keep it from being particularly effective in real groups? How can the effectiveness of brainstorming be improved?
5. Are "Two heads better than one" or do "Too many cooks spoil the broth"? Explain your answer.
6. Think of a time in which you worked in a group. Was the group effective, or did it suffer from process loss? If there was process loss, what caused it, and could it have been reduced?

Recommended Readings

On the difficulties of effective brainstorming:
Stroebe, W., & Diehl, M. (1994). Why groups are less effective than their members: On productivity losses in idea-generating groups. *European Review of Social Psychology, 5,* 271–303.

A meta-analysis of the effects of social loafing:
Karau, S. J., & Williams, K. D. (1993). Social Loafing: A meta-analytic review and theoretical integration. *Journal of Personality and Social Psychology, 65,* 681–706.

Zajonc's original development of social facilitation theory:
Zajonc, R. B. (1965). Social facilitation. *Science, 149,* 269–274.

Effective Working Groups

10

▶ *Contents at a Glance*

We have now reviewed the basic processes that occur in working groups, as well as their development and structure, and we have considered how and when groups make good decisions and efficiently perform tasks. With this basic knowledge in hand, it should be possible for a knowledgeable individual to help real working groups become more effective. A factory foreman should be able to develop an assembly line that has both a positive work attitude and is also highly productive, a counselor should be able to create a satisfactory and effective group therapy session, and a business manager should be able to create a harmonious work environment. Of course, these outcomes are not always easy to accomplish, but the goal of this chapter is to consider how they might be attained. In doing so we will apply some of the principles that we have discussed heretofore, but also discuss some other relevant research findings.

One approach to organizing our task is to work from the general, interactionist, model of group efficiency shown in Figure 10.1. This model is similar to those proposed by social scientists who have studied group effectiveness, including Hackman and Morris (1975), Fuller and Aldag (2001), and others. You can see that the important outcomes of the model are the quality of the group task performance or decision making, and that these are influenced by member characteristics, group characteristics, and group process—the activities that occur among the group members as they work. Furthermore, you can see that in this model the group outcomes are influenced by the satisfaction of the group members as they perform the task. You will also note that the relationships work in the other direction as well. Members of groups that have positive outcomes will experience more satisfaction, and this may lead to changes in member skills, group characteristics, and group process. In this chapter we will first review some of the relevant findings concerning how the different variables shown in Figure 10.1 combine to produce efficient groups and some methods of training and motivating groups. Then we will consider three examples of real groups in action—juries, teams, and electronic decision-making groups.

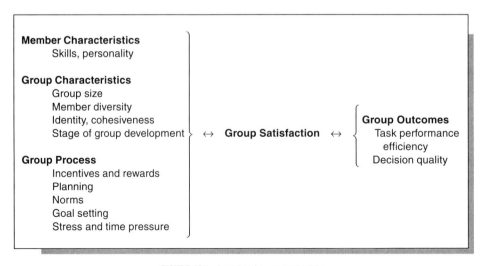

FIGURE 10.1. A model of group productivity.

Member Characteristics

Any efficient and productive group must begin with group members who have effective personalities and appropriate skills. However, the relationship between member characteristics and group performance is interactionist, in the sense that the skills and personalities must also be appropriate for the particular group under consideration and for the particular task it is performing (Bowers, Braun, & Morgan, 1997; Cannon-Bowers, Salas, Tannenbaum, & Mathieu, 1995; Widmeyer, 1990).

Member Skills

Groups such as sports teams, businesses, and political parties will naturally attempt to recruit the best people they can find to help them meet their goals. But the extent to which member skill influences group performance varies across different group tasks. On an automobile assembly line, performing the task requires only relatively minimal skills, and there is not a lot of coordination among the individuals involved. In this case it is primarily the number of individuals who are working on the task that influences the group outcome. In other cases, such as a surgical team or a large corporation, the group includes individuals with a wide variety of different skills, each working at very different tasks. In cases such as this, communication and coordination among the group members is essential, and thus group process will be very important. As an example of variation in the importance of member skills, M. B. Jones (1974) found that the skill of the individual players accounted for 99 percent of the team performance on baseball teams, but that individual skill counted for only 35 percent of the team performance on basketball teams.

Member Personality

In addition to having different skills, people also differ in their personality orientations. Some are motivated to become part of the important groups in their lives and hope to make positive contributions to those groups, whereas others are more wary of group membership and prefer to meet their goals working alone. Furthermore, when they are in groups, people may be expected to respond somewhat differently to group interactions, because they are each using the group to meet their individual social and personal goals.

Affiliation and Anxiety

Being a group member comes more easily to some than to others. Some individuals are naturally sociable, whereas for others interacting in groups is more difficult. Thus in some cases it may be useful to know about differences in the *need for affiliation* among the group members (McClelland, 1985; Smith, 1992). Research has found that people with high need for affiliation are more willing and interested in joining and working in groups and may accept other group members more quickly. They also report being happier when they are in groups than when they are alone. However, people with high needs for affiliation may also demand more of groups and may be more anxious or upset when the group doesn't perform up to their expectations.

On the other hand, some individuals have more difficulty fitting into groups, and may even suffer from *social anxiety* (Leary, 1995; Schlenker & Leary, 1982). These individuals also want to be accepted by others, and they try to create positive relationships with them, but they are hampered in their abilities to create positive relations because they feel awkward and tense in social settings. Because they feel that they cannot blend in with the group, they end up staying quiet and remain in the background.

Group Characteristics

Once a competent, and hopefully compatible, set of group members has been chosen, they are brought together and begin to do their job. Although it is to be expected that the member characteristics will have at least some influence on the effectiveness of this performance, the nature of the group itself will also be an important determinant of the group's success.

Group Size

In general, it might expected that larger working groups will be more efficient and productive than smaller groups because of the increased energy and expertise that larger numbers of individuals bring with them (Frank & Anderson, 1971; Haleblian & Finkelstein, 1993; Hill, 1982). Larger groups are also more able than smaller ones to diversify into specialized roles and activities, and this may make them efficient.

On the other hand, as we have seen in chapter 9, larger groups are also more likely to suffer from coordination problems, such as difficulties in communication and time management (Frank & Anderson, 1971; Latané, Williams, & Harkins, 1979; Steiner, 1966). Larger groups may also be more likely to suffer motivation losses, including social loafing and free riding, and may particularly suffer on conjunctive tasks in which the poor performance of some members may hold them back. There is also more likely to be conflict among the members of larger groups (Hare, 1981; O'Dell, 1968), and members of larger groups may also find it more difficult to cooperate (Brewer & Kramer, 1986; Hamburger, Guyer, & Fox, 1975).

Consistent with all of these suggestions, research has found that large groups may have problems that reduce their effectiveness. For instance, the amount of cheating and stealing is greater in larger groups (Diener, Fraser, Beaman, & Kelem, 1976; Erffmeyer, 1984), as is aggression and failure to help people in need (Latané, 1981; Mann, 1981). It is likely that these negative behaviors occur more frequently in larger groups because individuals feel less identifiable and more dispensable, because there is more diffusion of responsibility, and perhaps because identification with the group is lower.

In the end, due to the difficulties that accompany large groups, it turns out that the most effective working groups are of relatively small size—about four or five members. Research suggests that in addition to being more efficient, working in groups of about this size is also more enjoyable to the members, in comparison to being in larger groups. However, the optimal group size will be different for different types of tasks. Groups in which the members have high ability may benefit more from larger group size (Yetton & Bottger, 1983), and groups that have greater commitment or social identity may suffer less from motivational losses (Hardy & Latané, 1988).

Group Member Diversity

As we have seen, most groups tend to be made up of individuals who are, by and large, similar to each other. This isn't particularly surprising, because groups frequently come together as a result of common interests, values, and beliefs. Groups also tend to recruit new members who are similar to them, in the sense that they have personalities, beliefs, and goals that match those of the existing group members (Graves, 1995, 1988).

Advantages of Member Similarity

There are some potential advantages for groups in which the members share personalities, beliefs, and values. Similarity among group members will increase group cohesiveness, and as a result groups may be more quickly able to reach consensus on the best approaches to performing a task, and may be able to make decisions more quickly and effectively. Indeed, at least some research has found that groups that are similar in terms of their personality characteristics work better together, and have less conflict among the group members, probably at least in part because they are able to communicate well and to effectively coordinate their efforts (Evans & Dion, 1991; McLeod, Lobel, & Cox, 1996). Groups that are similar may also show better task performance

(Bond & Shiu, 1997). As we have seen in chapter 3, in some cases the group may even ostracize or expel members who are dissimilar, and this is particularly likely when it is important that the group make a decision or finish a task quickly and the dissimilarity prevents achieving these goals (Kruglanski & Webster, 1991; Schachter, 1951).

Advantages of Member Diversity

Although similarity among the group members may be useful in some cases, groups that are characterized by diversity among the members, for instance in terms of personalities, experiences, and abilities, might also have some potential advantages (S. Jackson, May, & Whitney, 1995; Magjuka & Baldwin, 1991; Maznevski, 1994; Pelz, 1956).

For one thing, diverse interests, opinions, and goals among the group members, assuming that people are willing to express them, may reduce tendencies toward conformity and groupthink by providing a wider range of opinions. Diverse groups may also be able to take advantage of the wider range of resources, ideas, and viewpoints that diversity provides, perhaps by increasing discussion of the issue, therefore improving creative thinking (Janis, 1972; Moreland, 1996). Such benefits may be particularly likely when the group has organized frameworks for understanding, accepting, and making use of diversity (Distefano & Maznevski, 2000). Supporting this expectation, Nemeth, Mosier, and Chiles (1992) found that groups that were believed to be made up of members with different opinions produced more creative solutions.

Also supporting the utility of diverse groups, Bantel and Jackson (1989) appraised the diversity of top management teams in 199 banks and found that the greater the diversity of the team, in terms of age, education, and length of time in the team, the greater the number of administrative innovations. Diversity has also been found to relate to positive attitudes among the group members (Gurin, Pena, Lopez, & Nagda, 1999).

Extreme levels of diversity, however, may be problematic for group process. One difficulty is that it may be harder for diverse groups to get past the formation stage and begin to work on the task, and once they get started it may take more time for them to make a decision. More diverse groups may also show more turnover over time (W. Wagner, Pfeffer, & O'Reilly, 1984), and group diversity may also produce increased conflict within the group (S. Jackson et al., 1995; Moreland, 1996).

Gender and Ethnic Diversity

One important type of diversity is the gender and ethnic membership of the group members (Hare, 1976; Shaw, 1981). In terms of potential benefits, men and women bring different orientations to the group, as do members of different ethnic groups, and this diversity in background and skills may help group performance. Wendy Wood (1987) found that there was at least some, although not statistically significant, evidence that groups composed of both men and women together tended to outperform same-sex groups (either all males or all females), at least in part because they brought different, complementary skills to the group. However, she also found that groups made up only of men performed well on tasks that involved task-oriented activities, whereas groups of women did better on tasks that involved social interaction. Thus, as expected by interactionist approaches, the congruency of members and tasks seems more important than the characteristics of the members or the group process alone.

However, although ethnic and gender diversity may have at least some benefits for groups, it also creates some potential costs. In a study of 151 work groups, Tsui, Egan, and O'Reilly (1992) found that groups consisting of individuals from diverse social categories had lower cohesion and lower social identity in comparison to groups that were more homogeneous. Furthermore, if there are differences in status between the members of the different ethnic or gender groups (such as when men have higher status than women), this may lead members of the group with lower status to feel that they are being treated unfairly and that they do not have equal opportunities for advancement, and this may produce intergroup conflict. Problems may also result if the number of individuals from one group is particularly small. When there are only a few (token) members of one group, these individuals may be seen and treated stereotypically by the members of the larger group (Eagly & Johnson, 1990; S. T. Fiske, 1993; Kanter, 1977). Taken together then, although diverse groups may have some advantages, the positive effects of group diversity seem to be small (Bowers, Pharmer, & Salas, 2000).

Group Process

Because group process is such an important determinant of group performance, increasing group productivity frequently involves teaching and motivating the group members to work together well and efficiently. The necessity of training is because group performance is not necessarily natural; groups need to learn how to go about their tasks most efficiently, and the group members need to learn how to get along with each other (C. G. Morris & Hackman, 1969; Swezey & Salas, 1992).

Incentives

Perhaps the most straightforward approach to increasing group performance is to provide incentives, either to the individual group members or to the group as a whole, for better performance. Individual rewards are perhaps most com-mon—corporations reward their employees with performance-based raises and bonuses, and players on sports teams are paid according to their successes on the field. Group incentives are also used, however—for instance, a bonus may be paid to every member of a sales team only if the group achieves its sales goals.

Individual Incentives

Although individual incentives may increase the effort of the individual group members, and thus enhance group performance, they also have some poten-tial disadvantages for group process. One potential problem is that the group members will compare their own rewards with those of others (remember our discussion of social comparison theory in chapter 4). It might be hoped that individuals would use their coworkers as models (upward comparison), which would inspire them to work harder. For instance, when corporations set up "employee of the week" programs, they are attempting to develop this type of positive comparison. On the other hand, if group members believe that others are being rewarded more than they are for what they perceive as the same work (downward comparison), they may change their behavior to attempt to restore equity. Perhaps they will attempt to work harder in order to receive greater rewards for themselves. But they may instead decide to reduce their effort to match what they perceive as a low level of current pay (Crosby, 1976; Baron & Pfeffer, 1994). It has been found, for instance, that job absenteeism is increased when employees make unfavorable comparisons between their own rewards and those of others (Geurts, Buunk, & Schaufeli, 1994).

Group Incentives

Group incentives are used in business and other organizations in which it is desired to create cohesive, cooperating groups (for instance, a sales or manu-facturing team). A recent review (Honeywell-Johnson & Dickinson, 1999) found that if the incentives are equally divided among the group members they are able to create and sustain high levels of productivity and employee satisfac-tion. Moreover, the effects of group incentives were comparable to those re-ported for individual incentives. Although some studies found that differentially divided group incentives resulted in higher performance than individual in-centives and equally divided group rewards, these procedures were perceived as less fair and satisfying, perhaps due to their competitive nature. Thus, group incentives may be useful, although they may create social loafing, free riding, and perceptions of unfairness. Perhaps the most useful type of incentive, and the one that is likely to have the most positive outcome on task performance, is to increase the group members' interest in the task itself. As we have seen in chapter 9, social loafing is reduced when the group members feel that they have autonomy to work on the task at their own speed and using their own approaches and when they feel that they are performing an important, whole, and visible piece of the work.

Planning

One phase of group decision making that is frequently overlooked, and which can have either positive or negative consequences for group performance, is that of initial planning or orienting. Newly formed groups, such as juries or business groups, frequently dive right into their task without first considering how they should go about it. In fact, group members may be so excited or interested in performing the task that they think they should not waste their time on what appears to be fruitless planning activity (Hackman & Morris, 1975).

Research suggests, however, that at least in some cases, spending some time in planning before beginning the task performance itself can have positive outcomes on decision making (Weingart, 1992; Wittenbaum, Vaughan, & Stasser, 1998). For instance, Hirokawa (1980) found that groups that planned ahead of time made more accurate decisions on the moon-landing task (see chapter 8). Furthermore, other research has found that when groups first discuss the procedures they are going to use, they later report being more satisfied with the outcomes and with the group process itself (Hackman & Morris, 1975; Vinokur, Burnstein, Sechrest, & Wortman, 1985).

However, planning is not always necessary or even useful. In one test of its importance, Richard Hackman (1974) convinced research participants in groups either to spend time thinking about a strategy before they began to work on the task or convinced them not to waste time on planning. Furthermore, in some groups the information given to the participants was shared, such that all participants had the same information, whereas in other cases the information was not shared. Hackman assumed that planning would be more useful where information is held only by some members. As shown in Figure 10.2, Hackman found that planning improved performance in the unshared information condition but harmed performance (presumably because it led to wasted time) in the shared information condition.

Breaking Inefficient Norms

One difficulty with many working groups is that, once they have developed a set of plans or strategies, these plans become established social norms, and it becomes very difficult for the group to later adopt new, alternative, and per-

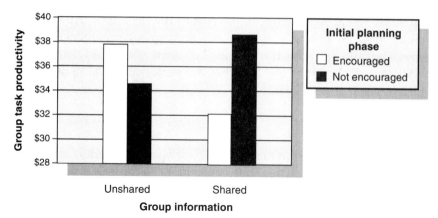

FIGURE 10.2. The costs and benefits of initial planning in groups. Groups that were encouraged to spend time planning their activities were more efficient when they needed to coordinate unshared information, but were less efficient when information was already shared and thus coordination was not necessary. Hackman, J., & Morris, C. (1975). Group tasks, group interaction processes, and group performance effectiveness: A review and proposed integration. In L. Berkowitz (Ed.), *Advances in experimental social psychology* (Vol. 8, pp. 45–99). New York: Academic Press.

haps better, strategies (recall, however, that most groups do change their course of action midway through their duration). As a result, even when the group is having difficulty performing effectively, it may nevertheless stick with its original methods.

The development of specific strategies that allow groups to break out of their existing patterns may in some cases be useful. Hackman and Morris (1975) suggest that having outside observers, particularly those who are experts in group process, provide feedback about relevant norms, and encouraging the groups to discuss them, can be helpful. *Process consultation* involves bringing in an outside expert who observes the group and potentially confronts the members about their strategies (Schmuck, 1995). In some cases the consultation may involve restructuring the group, for instance, by changing the status hierarchy or social norms, which may help reduce conflict and increase effective communication and coordination.

Goal Setting

One aspect of planning that has been found to be strongly related to positive group performance is the goals that the group uses to guide their work. Groups that set specific, difficult, and yet attainable goals (for instance, "improve sales by 10 percent over the next six months") are much more effective than groups that are given goals that are not very clear ("let's sell as much as we can!" Latham & Locke, 1991; Weldon & Weingart, 1993). Goals have been found to be as or more important in determining performance than are other incentives, including rewards such as praise and money.

Setting goals appears to be effective because it increases member effort and expectations of success, because it improves cooperation and communication among the members, and because it produces better planning and more accurate monitoring of the group's work. Specific goals may also result in increased commitment to the group (C. Lee, 1989; Locke & Latham, 1990; Weldon, Jehn, & Pradhan, 1991; Weldon & Weingart, 1993). When the goals are successfully attained, there is a resulting feeling of accomplishment, group identity, pride, a commitment to the task, and a motivation to set even higher goals. Moreover, there is at least some evidence that it may be useful to let the groups choose their own goals rather than assigning them to them. Groups tend to select more challenging goals, and, because they have set them themselves, they do not need to be convinced to accept them as appropriate. However, even assigned goals are effective as long as they are seen as legitimate and attainable (Latham, Winters, & Locke, 1994).

One potential problem associated with setting goals is that the goals may turn out to be too difficult. If the goals are set too high to be reached, or if the group perceives that they are too high even if they are not, the group may become demoralized and reduce its effort. Indeed, groups that are characterized by a sense of *collective efficacy*—the belief that they can accomplish the tasks given to them—have been found to perform better (Guzzo, Yost, Campbell, & Shea, 1993; Little & Madigan, 1997; Silver & Bufanio, 1996, 1997). Fortunately, over time, groups frequently adjust their goals to be attainable and yet difficult to achieve (Zander, 1971/1996).

Improving Communication

If groups are going to make effective decisions they will need to communicate effectively. Unfortunately, but perhaps not surprisingly, research suggests that this is not always the case.

Quantity and Quality of Discussion

In general, the more the group discusses and considers the issue at hand, the better the group's final decision will be. If the group does not have enough time to gather and consider all of the relevant information (for instance, when it is under pressure to make a decision quickly), this may result in a premature and potentially poor decision (Parks & Cowlin, 1995; Staw, Sandelands, & Dutton, 1981). However, even if the group does have sufficient time and resources, it may nevertheless fall victim to the illusion of group effectivity, decide that is has reached a good decision, and stop discussing the issue prematurely before it has fully considered all of the relevant information. In still other cases the amount of information available about the decision at hand may be overwhelming, and the group may become fatigued before it has finished organizing and discussing it. Another difficulty is that the group discussion may not always focus on the most important and relevant information, but may rather include irrelevant or trivial details. These findings suggest that one of the most important goals for successful leaders is to be aware of the amount and quality of information available to the group and to attempt to match these to the group's capabilities.

The Problem of Unshared Information

Although group discussion generally improves the quality of a group's decisions, this will only be true if the group discusses the information that is most useful to the decision that needs to be made. One difficulty is that groups tend to discuss some types of information more than others. As we have seen in our discussion of groupthink in chapter 8, for instance, the neglect of relevant information may sometimes be caused by conformity pressures that lead the group to consider only information that fits existing group norms or goals, and to avoid considering information that suggests that the group is not performing well.

In addition to motivational pressures to consider only some information, discussion is also influenced by the way the relevant information is originally shared among the group members. The problem is that group members tend to discuss information that they all have access to while ignoring equally important information that is available only to a few of the members. Groups tend to make poor decisions when the information is not adequately shared (Gigone & Hastie, 1997; Larson, Christensen, Abbott, & Franz, 1996; Larson, Foster-Fishman, & Keys, 1994; Stasser & Stewart, 1992; Stasser & Titus, 1985; D. D. Stewart & Stasser, 1995).

In one demonstration of the tendency for groups to preferentially discuss information that all of the group members know about, Stasser and Titus (1985) used an experimental design based on the *hidden profile task*, as shown in Figure 10.3. Students read descriptions of candidates for a hypothetical student body presidential election and then met in groups to discuss and pick

Group member	Information favoring Candidate A	Information favoring Candidate B
X	a1, a2	b1, b2, b3
Y	a1, a3	b1, b2, b3
Z	a1, a4	b1, b2, b3

FIGURE 10.3. Information sharing in groups. This is an example of the type of "hidden profile" that was used by Stasser and Titus (1985) to study information sharing in group discussion (their profiles were actually somewhat more complicated).

the best candidate. The information about the candidates was arranged such that one of the candidates (in this case, candidate A) had the more positive qualities, (a1, a2, a3, and a4), in comparison to the other candidate (in this case, candidate B with only three positive qualities: b1, b2, b3). Reflecting this superiority, in groups in which all of the members were given all of the information about the candidates, the members almost always chose the candidate with the most positive qualities after their discussion.

However, in some cases the experimenters made the task more difficult by creating a "hidden profile," in which each member of the group received only part of the information. Thus, although all of the information was potentially available, it was necessary that it be properly shared for the group members to make the correct choice. In the cases in which the information was unshared less than half of the groups chose the candidate with the most positive qualities, whereas the others chose the inferior candidate. This occurred because the information that was not originally shared among all of the group members was never discussed, although the group members had access to all of the positive information collectively. Furthermore, this bias occurred even in participants who were given explicit instructions to be sure to avoid expressing their initial preferences and to review all of the available facts (Stasser, Taylor, & Hanna, 1989). Subsequent research has shown that larger groups are more prone to difficulties in sharing information than are smaller groups (Stasser, Taylor, & Hanna, 1989).

Not only is unshared information less likely to be discussed, it is also frequently forgotten (N. K. Clark & Stephenson, 1989) and is not included in the group discussion because the group members return to discuss shared information more often than unshared information (Stasser, Taylor, & Hanna, 1989; Larson et al., 1996). Therefore, effective discussion requires not only being sure that the group members bring up the relevant information, but also being sure that they actively consider it and maintain focus on it.

Variables That Influence Information Sharing

Although the tendency to poorly share information seems to occur quite frequently, at least in experimentally created groups, it does not occur equally under all conditions. Groups have been found to better share information when the group members believe that there is a correct answer that can be found if there is sufficient discussion (Stasser & Stewart, 1992), and groups also are more likely to share information if they are forced to continue their discussion even after they believe that they have discussed all of the relevant information (Larson et al., 1994). These findings again suggest that an important job of the leader is to continue group discussion until he or she is convinced that all of the relevant information has been addressed.

The structure of the group may also influence information sharing. Groups in which the members are more physically separated and thus have difficulty communicating with each other may find that they need to reorganize themselves to improve communication. And the status of the group members can also be important. Group members with lower status may have less confidence and thus be unlikely to express their opinions (Stasser, Stewart, & Wittenbaum, 1995; Rashotte & Smith-Lovin, 1997). Wittenbaum (1998) found that group members with higher status were, indeed, more likely to share new information. However, those with higher status may dominate the discussion, even if the information that they have is not more valid or important. Because they have high status, leaders have the ability to solicit unshared information from the group members (Hollander, 1964; Larson et al., 1996), and they must be sure to do so, for instance, by making it clear that all members should feel free to present their unique information, that each member has important information to share, and that it is important to do so. Leaders may particularly need to solicit and support opinions from low-status or socially anxious group members.

Findings showing that groups neither share nor discuss originally unshared information have very disconcerting implications for group decision making, because they suggest that group discussion is likely to lead to very poor judgments. Not only is unshared information not brought to the table, but because the shared information is discussed repeatedly, it is likely to be seen as more valid and to have a greater influence on decisions as a result of its repeated expression (see chapter 8). It is not uncommon that individuals within a working group come to the discussion with different types of information, and thus this unshared information needs to be presented. For instance, in a meeting of a design team for a new building, the architects, the engineers, and the customer representatives will each have different, and potentially incompatible, information. Thus leaders of working groups must foster an open climate that encourages information sharing and discussion.

Implementing Decisions

Although our focus to this point has primarily been on how and when groups make good decisions, the group must also be able to implement the decision once it is made by getting the relevant people to accept the decision and to act upon it. The group members are more likely to accept the decision if they perceive that the process that led to the decision was fair and impartial. Allowing plenty of opportunity for group discussion is important in this regard, because it allows group members to express their opinions and increases the likelihood that they will perceive that the decision was fair and that their own opinions were considered. As a result, because they have been able to contribute to the decision, the group members may be happier with the group decision, and it may subsequently be easier for them to work toward group goals. It has been shown that decisions based on a unanimity decision scheme (rather than a majority rule, for instance) produce greater group satisfaction, particularly on matters that are of high importance to the group, once the decision has been made (Kaplan & Miller, 1987).

Member Satisfaction

As shown in Figure 10.1, one of the important determinants of group outcomes is the satisfaction of the group members with their experiences in the group. Although it may not seem as important as the product itself, it must always be kept in mind that individuals join groups and perform well in them at least in part as a result of the social rewards that come with group membership, and thus that the members of effective and productive working groups must find satisfaction as they work in the group.

Positive social interactions and relationships among the group members are important for effective group functioning (R. Kahn & Katz, 1953). For instance, Van Zelst (1952) found that carpenters and bricklayers both worked more productively and were more satisfied when they were able to work with partners that they liked. Group members also perform better when they feel that their input to the group is valued and that they have control over the planning of group processes. Furthermore, as we have seen in chapter 3, group members are also very sensitive to the fairness and legitimacy with which rewards are given to group members. If individuals experience relative deprivation within the group—for instance, by feeling that they are contributing more than their fair share or that they are undercompensated for their work—they are likely to become dissatisfied. This dissatisfaction may reduce their contributions to the group and may even lead them to attempt to sabotage the group performance (Dittrich & Carrell, 1979; Geurts, Buunk, & Schaufeli, 1994; Greenberg & Ornstein, 1983).

Although it is important for groups to feel positively about themselves and about each other, it is also possible for groups to become too sociable. Guzzo and Waters (1982) found that groups that expressed a lot of emotion early in their decision making made poorer decisions, potentially because the groups felt more cohesion and identity and were less willing to express conflicting ideas. It has also been found that the tendency to discuss shared rather than unshared information occurs in part because doing so makes people feel better about themselves and about other group members. Thus, groups that focus too much on task satisfaction may also neglect the task at hand, focusing instead on their feelings for each other.

Examples of Groups at Work

In the remainder of this chapter we will review examples of working groups, considering in each case the variables from Figure 10.1 that are important in determining their productivity and effectiveness. We will focus on three particular types of groups—juries, work teams, and electronic groups—although the processes that underlie these groups can also be found to operate in other groups that might be of interest, including, for instance, classrooms, families (Leik & Chalkley, 1997; Mishler & Waxler, 1968), and group therapy sessions.

Jury Decision Making

The jury is the foundation of the legal system in the United States and in many other countries. The notion of a "trial by one's peers" is based on the assumption that average individuals can make informed and fair decisions when they work together in groups. Because hundreds of jury trials are conducted every day, and the outcomes of such decisions have profound effects on those who are standing trial, it is perhaps not surprising that social scientists have spent much time studying jury decision making and have provided information to the federal and state governments about what they have learned (Hastie, 1993; Pennington & Hastie, 1990; Hastie, Penrod, & Pennington, 1983).

Because juries are usually made up of strangers who work together only for a short time, they are somewhat different than most working groups, which generally have longer tenures. Nevertheless, the principles that describe the functioning of working groups can and have been applied to understanding how juries go about their work. Because federal law prohibits the study of juries while their deliberations are in progress, social scientists frequently make use of *mock juries* to learn about the decision-making process used in juries. A mock jury is a group of individuals, such as college students, who hear information about fictitious or real court cases, and who then act as if they were a real jury, making decisions about the guilt or innocence of the defendant.

Member Characteristics

As a small working group, a jury has the potential to produce either a good or a poor decision, depending on many of the factors that we have discussed in the prior chapters. And one variable that influences the decision making of this group, at least to some degree, is the characteristics of the jurors. Indeed, during the voir dire (the questioning of potential jurors by lawyers to determine their competency to serve on the jury) the lawyers may attempt to select individuals that they feel will be sympathetic to their case and exclude individuals that they feel will not. Indeed, in American courts so many psychologists and other experts are used to help lawyers make decisions during voir dire that the selection process is frequently referred to as *scientific jury selection.*

There is some evidence that member characteristics do matter. For one thing, individuals who have already served on juries are more likely to be seen as experts, are more likely to be chosen to be the jury foreperson, and give more input during the jury's deliberation (Stasser, Kerr, & Bray, 1982). Not surprisingly, an individual's social status has also been shown to be important in determining the extent to which he or she influences the outcome of the jury's decision. Since the selection of the jury foreperson occurs early in the deliberation process, before the jury members know much about each other, and usually without much discussion, this decision is frequently based upon diffuse status characteristics. It has been found that jury members with higher status occupations and education, males rather than females, and those who talk first are more likely be chosen as the foreperson, and that these individuals also contribute more to the jury discussion (Stasser et al., 1982). In fact, as in other small groups, a minority generally dominates the jury discussion (Hastie, Penrod, & Pennington, 1983). As a result, relevant information or opinions may remain unshared because some individuals never or rarely participate in the discussion.

Perhaps the strongest evidence for the importance of member characteristics in the decision-making process concerns the selection of "death-qualified" juries in trials in which a potential sentence includes the death penalty. In order to be selected for such a jury, the potential members must indicate that they would, in principle, be willing to recommend the death penalty as a punishment. Potential jurors who indicate they are opposed to the death penalty cannot serve on these juries. However, this selection process creates a potential bias, because the individuals who say that they would not under any condition vote for the death penalty are also more likely to be rigid and punitive, and thus more likely to find a defendant guilty, a situation that increases the chances of a conviction of a defendant (Ellsworth, 1993).

Thus, although there are at least some member characteristics that have an influence upon jury decision making, as in the other cases that we have considered, the overall influence of member characteristics is generally small in comparison to the influence of group process. Indeed, despite the fact that the practice of scientific jury selection is used in some high-profile cases, most research indicates that member characteristics, including gender, race, and education, do not have a large impact upon jury decisions (Ellsworth, 1993; Hastie et al., 1983). It is simply not possible to predict how a given juror will respond, and the weight of the evidence is a more potent determinant of jurors' verdicts than are the characteristics of the jurors. Furthermore, although each jury member may be biased in his or her own way (for instance, by being prejudiced toward the social category to which the defendant belongs, by finding the defendant attractive, or by weighing the evidence unfairly), it appears that these individual biases are usually canceled out through the jury group discussion (Kerr & Huang, 1986).

Group Process

As in other working groups, group process plays a more important role in the outcome of jury decisions than do member characteristics. Like any group, juries develop their own group norms, and these norms can have a profound impact on how they reach their decision. Analysis of group process within juries shows that different juries take very different approaches to reaching a verdict. Some spend a lot of time in initial planning, whereas others immediately jump right into the deliberation. And some juries base their discussion around a review of the evidence, waiting to make a vote until it has all been considered, whereas other juries first determine which decision is preferred in the group by taking a poll, and then (if the first vote does not lead to a final verdict) organize their discussion around these opinions. These two approaches are used about equally often, but may in some cases lead to different decisions (Davis, Stasson, Ono, & Zimmerman, 1988; Hastie et al., 1983; Davis, Stasson, Parks, & Hulbert, 1993). The norms that develop in the jury can influence how much time it spends on each part of the deliberation process, and this can influence the decision it makes.

Eventually, as a result of the discussion, a group opinion will start to emerge. Not surprisingly, jury members who violate the social norms are likely to be seen negatively and perhaps even be ostracized by the others. Sanctions are particularly strong against jurors who hold a different opinion about the outcome under consideration and who are thus preventing the group from finishing its job. To reduce the time needed to reach a verdict, one or more jury members may well conform to the desires of the majority and change their vote, even when they do not personally believe that the rest of the members have the most accurate opinion. It is also possible that group polarization will operate in juries (Hastie et al., 1983).

When there is a greater number of jury members who hold the majority position, it becomes more and more certain that their opinion will prevail during the discussion (see, for instance, Figure 8.1 on page 178). This is not to say that minorities cannot ever be persuasive (and we have considered in chapter 4 the techniques that they might use), but it is very difficult for them. The strong influence of the majority is the result of both informational conformity (that is, that there are more arguments supporting the favored position) as well as normative conformity (the people on the majority side have more power to demand conformity).

Researchers studying juries have frequently used the decision-scheme approach to predict the outcome of the jury decision from knowledge about the jury members' initial opinions. One advantage in studying juries is that the decision scheme being used is often known, because it is presented to the jury by the judge. Some jury decisions require only a majority agreement, for instance, whereas others require it to be unanimous. As we have seen, knowing the decision scheme allows us to predict the jury's likely decision, given knowledge of the individual members' initial opinions. It has been found that this can be done quite accurately. The jury is more likely to be hung (unable to reach a verdict) when the decision scheme requires unanimous judgments. Unanimous decisions also take longer to reach, but they do not appear to be more lenient than are majority decisions.

The Leniency Bias

As we have seen in chapter 4, in addition to being influenced by both the initial opinions of the group members and the decision scheme, research has also found that juries that are evenly split (three to three or six to six) tend to vote toward acquittal more often than they vote toward guilt, all other factors being equal. This is in part because the juries are instructed to assume innocence unless there is sufficient evidence to confirm guilt—they must apply a burden of proof of guilt (for instance, "beyond a reasonable doubt"). This **leniency bias** in juries (MacCoun & Kerr, 1988) is particularly likely to occur when the potential penalty is more severe (Kerr, 1978). Indeed, the leniency bias is so strong that it may sometimes overwhelm an initial majority opinion favoring guilt.

Are Juries Effective?

Given what you now know about the potential difficulties that groups face in making good decisions, you might be worried that the verdicts rendered by juries may not be particularly effective, accurate, or fair. The evidence suggests that juries may not do as badly as we would expect. For one thing, the deliberation process does seem to cancel out many individual juror biases and focuses the jury members on considering the evidence itself. The deliberation also seems to be effective in preventing juries from using inadmissible evidence (Kerwin & Shaffer, 1994).

The good news on juries is, however, somewhat tempered by the fact that in the 1970s the U.S. Supreme Court ruled that in civil cases and in state criminal cases not potentially involving a death penalty, courts could use six-person rather than twelve-person juries. However, six-member juries have some problems in comparison to the more traditional twelve-member jury. First,

Leniency Bias: The tendency for juries to vote for acquittal more often than they vote for guilt, all other factors being equal.

simply because they are smaller, six-member juries will be less diverse in terms of the social category memberships as well as the values and beliefs of the participants, and this will likely reduce the representativeness of the jury in relation to the population. Second, in six-member juries a single individual who holds a contradictory belief is less likely to find support for that belief, which may reduce his or her ability to argue a contradictory opinion. Finally, because there are fewer group members, the amount of group discussion will be less in smaller juries. Taken together, then, we can say that it appears that the jury system is effective, but that twelve-member juries are probably more fair and accurate in their decisions.

Work Teams

Working groups in which the group members are highly interdependent, and which have specific and well-defined tasks to accomplish are known as **work teams** (Cannon-Bowers, Salas, & Converse, 1993; Guzzo & Dikson, 1996; Sundstrom, de Meuse, & Futrell, 1990; Swezey & Salas, 1992; Vogt & Griffith, 1988). Teams are used regularly in business, industry, government, and education settings, and a large proportion of the workforce spends at least some of its time working in a team. Frequently the members of the team are brought together because they have diverse knowledge, expertise, and experience, and so coordination and communication among the group members is particularly essential to reaching the goal. Teams are used to perform tasks, as in automobile factories, airline flight crews, sales groups, hospital teams (such as those operating in surgical and emergency rooms), emergency rescue crews, and sports teams. Teams are also used to make decisions, including managing, advising, negotiating, and reviewing policies. Because teams are ubiquitous, and their performance has important consequences, it is important to understand their effectiveness. Since the team represents a type of working group (one that is highly specialized and the members highly interdependent), the basic principles of group performance can be applied to understanding teams and improving their performance (Hackman & Morris, 1975).

Member Characteristics and Group Process

As with all working groups, the output of the team will be determined in large part by the group members that comprise it. Teams that have a wide range of skills and knowledge have been found to be more effective, unless the members are so diverse that they have difficulty communicating with each other. Specialized knowledge is particularly important for teams that are working with advanced technology.

Group process is also critical. In many teams there is not a well-defined

Work Team: A structured working group in which the group members are highly interdependent.

status hierarchy or leaders, and the organizational structural is lateral. However, in effective teams the role assignments of the members are made very clear, and each team member therefore knows what his or her role is, and is aware of the tasks that are being performed by the others. In teams where this is not the case, performance suffers (Cannon-Bowers et al., 1993; Cannon-Bowers, Salas, & Converse, 1990; Drinka & Streim, 1994; Peiro, Gonzalez-Roma, & Ramos, 1992). In some teams there is at least some status differential among the members (such as the relationship between the pilot and copilot of an airplane or a doctor and a nurse in a hospital). Conflict may result when the higher-status individuals are perceived as being unreceptive to contributions made by lower-status group members (Campbell-Heider & Pollock, 1987), and therefore teams often work to improve communication and cohesion.

In some cases teams are given latitude in their approaches to problem solving, for instance, by allowing team members to define their own roles and duties. This allows the team to be flexible and creative in its solutions to problems (Manz & Sims, 1987; G. L. Stewart & Manz, 1995). These *self-managing* teams can be effective, as long as they can get past the initial development stages in which problems with coordination are likely. These problems are particularly likely to occur if the team members are used to working in a more structured environment.

Training

A number of guidelines have been proposed for building effective teams, and these have been designed to work at both the individual and the group level (Swezey & Salas, 1992). Perhaps the best known and most successful of these approaches involves helping the group learn to set appropriate goals to serve as standards toward which they can work (Latham & Locke, 1991; Weldon & Weingart, 1993).

It is also suggested that team size be kept as small as is practical to allow effective communication. As with any other work group, as the group gets bigger communication and coordination become more difficult. Training in communication, such as by helping team members learn to listen and understand the opinions of other members, and by providing concise feedback to them, as well as changing social norms such that members are willing to express their views, may be effective in improving task performance (Skogstad, Dyregrov, & Hellesoy, 1995).

Team Effectiveness

Teams are frequently recommended for facilitating innovation (Kanter, 1988) as well as improving task performance (Walton & Hackman, 1986). However, the empirical research supporting the effectiveness of teams is mixed. In many cases the members of a team do display high group cohesion, identity, and satisfaction, but (as we have seen) this group feeling may not always transfer into effective performance (Sundstrom, de Meuse, & Futrell, 1990). In the end, we can conclude that work teams may be effective if appropriate conditions are met.

Electronic Groups

Traditionally, working groups could only communicate in a face-to-face setting. However, with the increased presence of technology, such as text messaging, cell phones, faxes, and e-mail, groups are more and more likely to communicate with each other across long distances and in situations in which the individuals are not able to have visual or direct contact. Such changes allow increased flexibility in work schedules and increase the ability of individuals from different locations to communicate and work together.

There is a substantial literature concerning the extent to which computer-based groups, which are used for decision making, idea generation, negotiation, management, training, education, and other group functions, follow the same or different processes as do face-to-face groups (Valacich, Dennis, & Nunamaker, 1991). It is clear that many of the phenomena that occur in face-to-face groups also occur in computer groups. For instance, just like face-to-face groups, computer groups also tend to preferentially discuss information that they have in common (Hightower & Sayeed, 1995) and display social loafing (Valacich, Jessup, Dennis, & Nunamaker, 1992). However, electronic groups also have some unique characteristics that make them different from face-to-face interactions.

Cues to Social Status

Because the individuals in electronic groups cannot see each other, they do not have the same access to cues that denote status differences, such as gender, ethnicity, and physical attractiveness, and it has been suggested that electronic groups will be therefore be more egalitarian (Dubrovsky, Kiesler, & Sethna, 1991; S. Kiesler, Siegel, & McGuire, 1984; Mantovani, 1994). As a result, in computer groups, it is expected that status is more likely to be earned—that is, determined by the number of messages delivered or by the quality of ideas proposed (Walther, 1992, 1993). There is at least some evidence that, because cues to social status are not as apparent in computer groups, there will be less hierarchy and more equal participation (Dubrovsky et al., 1991; Kiesler & Sproull, 1992; Siegel, Dubrovsky, Kiesler, & McGuire, 1986), although not all research has found this difference (Straus, 1996; Weisband, Schneider, & Connolly, 1995). For instance, it has been found that in electronic groups, just as in face-to-face groups, men tend to express more dominant behavior and contribute more ideas than women do.

Deindividuation

Because it is more difficult to monitor the behavior of members of computer groups, the norms may be less well articulated, and deindividuation may result. At least one study has found that normative conformity pressures are lessened in computer networks (Smilowitz, Compton, & Flint, 1988), and the lack of norms and the potential deindividuation that follows can even result in "flaming"—the making of inappropriate antisocial comments over the computer (Kiesler et al., 1984; Lea & Spears, 1991; Siegel et al., 1986; Spears, Lea, & Lee, 1990; Sproull & Kiesler, 1991). However, the occurrence of flaming seems limited (Matheson & Zanna, 1990; Walther, Anderson, & Park, 1994), at least in part because the fact that individuals are not identifiable in computer groups may actually increase identification with the group and therefore increase the tendency to conform to social norms. If the norm in the group is to be hostile, then computer groups may well increase these tendencies. On the other hand, if the norm of the group is to be fair, equitable, and productive, then computer groups may enhance these more positive tendencies. Supporting this hypothesis, Spears, Lea, and Lee (1990) found polarization toward the group norm when participants were deindividuated and group membership was made salient. In short, deindividuation seems to produce conformity to social norms, which may or may not promote flaming.

Satisfaction and Productivity

Although electronic communication seems to increase the productivity of brainstorming sessions in comparison to face-to-face groups (see chapter 9), it may not increase productivity overall (Levine & Moreland, 1990; Straus & McGrath, 1994). Siegel et al. (1986) compared groups that were attempting to reach consensus and which worked either face-to-face or through computer-mediated discussions. When groups were linked by computer, group members made fewer remarks and took longer to make their decisions.

Finally, a number of studies have found that individuals are less satisfied working in computer groups than in face-to-face interaction (Adrianson & Hjelmquist, 1991; Matheson & Zanna, 1990), perhaps because the task is more unfamiliar and because the opportunities for socioemotional relationships are more limited.

Chapter Summary

The effective performance of groups is dependent upon both member and task characteristics, as well as group process. An understanding of these basic principles will help groups be efficient. The skills and personalities of the group members, including ethnic and gender differences, constitute the member characteristics that must be considered. In terms of group process, group size is important—most effective groups are of a relatively small size. Group diversity has both positive and negative effects on group performance.

Groups must be trained and motivated to perform to their highest level of efficiency. One approach is to provide incentives, either to the groups or their members. Making the task interesting and challenging provides one important incentive. Whether the group engages in a planning session before it begins its task can influence the group outcome. Providing specific and attainable goals increases productivity.

Many groups do not effectively share the information that they have available to them, in part because they discuss information that is available to all of the group members, while tending to ignore information that is unique to only some group members. Leaders must work to ensure effective and complete communication. Groups also differ in terms of their ability to get their decisions implemented and in terms of member satisfaction.

Juries, teams, and electronic groups are three examples of particular working groups that can be understood in terms of the general principles of group decision making and task performance. For each, the member characteristics and group process determine their outcomes.

 Review and Discussion Questions

1. Consider the variables in Figure 10.1 and explain their relationships and implications for creating effective working groups.
2. What are the potential advantages and disadvantages of diversity in groups and organizations?
3. What are the factors that influence group productivity, and how can it be increased?
4. How is information shared in groups, and what factors may produce incomplete information sharing?
5. What aspects of jury decision making suggest that juries might make good decisions? What aspects suggest that they might make poor decisions?
6. What are the likely effects of excluding individuals who would not vote for

the death penalty from juries in capital cases? Do you think this policy should exist, or should it be changed?

7. What is a team? How does it differ from any other working group?
8. What are the advantages and disadvantages of working in electronic working groups?

Recommended Readings

Understanding jurors and juries:
Hastie, R. (1993). *Inside the Juror: The Psychology of Juror Decision Making.* New York: Cambridge University Press.

A summary of social interaction in computer groups:
Lea, M. (Ed.). (1992). *Contexts of Computer-mediated Communication.* Hemel Hempstead, UK: Harvester Wheatsheaf.

A classic model of small group performance:
Hackman, J., & Morris, C. (1975). Group tasks, group interaction processes, and group performance effectiveness: A review and proposed integration. In L. Berkowitz (Ed.), *Advances in Experimental Social Psychology* (Vol. 8, pp. 45–99). New York: Academic Press.

Cultures, Social Change, and Crowds 11

 Contents at a Glance

*O*ur focus in the last chapters has been on small groups that are working together to reach specific and usually well-defined goals. At this point we turn to study the social dynamics of larger social groups. Our discussion begins in this chapter with a consideration of the ways that our memberships in large social groups influence us, and the social processes that occur between and within such groups. We will focus particularly on one large social group—the *culture*—but will also consider to some extent a more temporary, but also relatively large group—the *crowd*. Then, in chapters 12 and 13 we will turn to the potential conflicts that may develop within and between individuals and groups and consider if and how such conflicts may be avoided.

Cultures

A **culture** is a large social group made up of individuals who are normally in geographic proximity with each other and who share a common set of descriptive and proscriptive norms, including important principles, such as religious and family values and other moral beliefs (Asch, 1952; A. Fiske, Kitayama, Markus, & Nisbett, 1998; Markus & Kitayama, 1991; Markus, Kitayama, & Heiman, 1996; McDougall, 1920; P. B. Smith & Bond, 1999; Triandis, 1995).

Unlike working groups, cultures are not formed for any particular goal or purpose, and individuals (unless they make a rather radical life change) do not generally choose to join, to leave, or to remain in them. Rather, cultures are generally determined by where and when we were born and live, and not through any choice on our own part, and we usually remain in the same culture throughout our lives. In contrast to working groups, cultures tend to be relatively unorganized, although there will likely be a status hierarchy that provides some members more status and power than others, and that designates some individuals as leaders. However, despite their large size, cultures may have a particular importance for us because they provide a fundamental part of our self-concept. We frequently develop strong identities with our cultures, and they have an important impact on many aspects of our thoughts and behavior.

Children learn cultural norms as they grow up, and it is not inappropriate to say that our culture defines our lives. Among other things, culture determines language, religion, and fundamental values. In the United States many of the fundamental beliefs that form the basis of our culture, such as beliefs in freedom, self-determination, and individual rights, are laid out in the Declaration of Independence, the Constitution, and the Bill of Rights, and they are found in similar oral and written documents in other countries. Although cultures can in some cases be the same as or similar to that defined by a nationality (for instance, the French culture), there is not generally a one-to-one relationship between nationality and culture. In some cases the culture crosses nations, such as the Arab culture in the Mideast or the Asian culture in the Far East. On the other hand, there may also be more than one culture within a single nation. In the United States there are distinct cultures that correspond to ethnic groupings—European-American, Japanese-American, Hispanic-American, and African-American cultures are examples.

It is important to be aware of cultures and cultural differences, at least in part because people with different cultural backgrounds are increasingly coming into contact with each other as a result of increased travel and immigration and the development of the Internet and other forms of communication. In the United States, for instance, there are many different ethnic groups, and

Culture: A large social group made up of individuals who are normally in geographic proximity with each other and who share a common set of social norms.

the proportion of the population that comes from minority (nonwhite) groups is increasing from year to year. Minorities will account for a much larger proportion of the total new entries into the U.S. workforce over the next decades (Judy & D'Amico, 1997). These changes will produce a great increase in cultural diversity in the United States, and although this will create the potential for useful cooperation and productive interaction, it may also produce unwanted social conflict. Being aware of cultural differences may help improve cross-cultural interactions and potentially prevent misunderstandings.

Independence and Interdependence

Cultures differ in terms of the particular norms that they find important and that guide the behavior of the group members, and many different attempts have been made to characterize basic differences among cultures. One cultural characteristic that has been extensively studied involves a fundamental difference between Western cultures (including the United States, Canada, Europe, Australia, and New Zealand) and East Asian cultures, including China, Japan, Taiwan, Korea, India, and Southeast Asia (A. Fiske et al., 1998; Markus et al., 1996; Triandis, 1995; Triandis, McCusker, & Hui, 1990).

Norms in Western cultures are primarily oriented toward *independence* and **individualism.** Children in Western cultures are taught to develop and to value a sense of their personal self and to see themselves as in large part separate from the other people around them. In Western culture people are oriented toward promoting their own individual success, frequently in comparison to (or even at the expense of) others. When asked to describe themselves, individuals in Western cultures generally tend to indicate that they like to "do their own thing," they prefer to live their lives independently, and they base their happiness and self-worth upon their own personal achievements.

Norms in the East Asian culture, on the other hand, indicate that people should be more fundamentally connected with others, and thus are oriented toward *interdependence* or **collectivism**. In these cultures children are taught to focus on developing harmonious social relationships with others, with particular importance placed upon the awareness of one's social roles. The predominant norms relate to group togetherness and connectedness and to duty and responsibility to one's family and other group memberships. The members of East Asian cultures, when asked to describe themselves, indicate that they are particularly concerned about the interests of others, including their close friends and their colleagues. They focus on maintaining positive relations with others, even at the cost of personal benefits (Cousins, 1989; Rhee, Uleman, Lee, & Roman, 1995), and may indicate a fear of being on one's own—separate or disconnected from the group. Children are taught to be obedient to their elders, and conformity is valued (Langfeldt, 1992; White & Levine, 1986).

Individualism: The tendency, common in Western cultures, to value the personal self and to see the self as in large part separate from other people.

Collectivism: The tendency, common in Eastern cultures, to focus on developing harmonious social relationships with others, with particular importance placed upon the awareness of one's social roles.

In short, we can say that in Western cultures the personal self is the relatively more important identity compared to the social identity, whereas in Eastern cultures the group or social identity is more important than the personal identity. Individuals from interdependent cultures tend to subordinate personal goals to group goals, show strong emotional attachment to the group, and are particularly concerned with other's opinions about them. For them conformity is a positive thing. On the other hand, in Western cultures the focus is on individualism, and conformity to group norms is frequently seen as compromising individual behavior.

One simple and yet powerful difference in cultures was demonstrated in research conducted by Kim and Markus (1999). In this research participants were contacted at the waiting area of the San Francisco airport and asked to fill out a short questionnaire for the researcher. The participants were selected so that about one-half of the participants subsequently indicated that they were European Americans with both parents born in the United States, whereas the other half indicated that they were Asian Americans, with both parents born in China, and who spoke Chinese at home. After completing the questionnaires (which were not used in the data analysis except to determine the cultural backgrounds), participants were asked if they would like to take a pen with them as a token of appreciation. The experimenter extended his or her hand, which contained five pens. However, it was arranged such that the pens handed to the participants had either three or four of one color, and either two or one of another color (the ink in the pens was always black). As shown in Figure 11.1, and consistent with the hypothesized preference for uniqueness in Western, but not Eastern cultures, results showed that the European Americans preferred to take a pen with the more uncommon color, whereas the Asian Americans preferred one with the more common color.

Outcomes of Independence and Interdependence

Because culture provides us with such important and fundamental norms, it has a profound influence on our self-concept and influences how we think about and relate to others. For instance, when describing themselves, East Asian students are more likely to make references to other people (such as "I try to make other people happy" and "I cook dinner with my sister") than do European-American students, and European Americans make more positive statements about themselves, whereas East Asians are more likely to make positive statements about others (Markus, Kitayama, & Heiman, 1996).

Culture also influences behavior through its influence on the self-concept. M. H. Bond, Wan, Leong, and Giacalone (1985) found that Chinese participants were less likely to deliver an insult to high-status members of the in-group in comparison to American students, suggesting that they had more

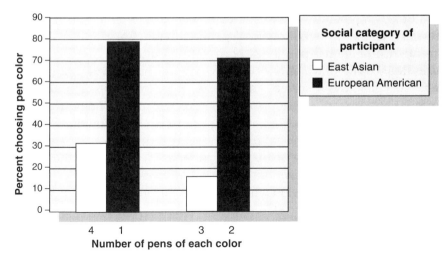

FIGURE 11.1. Independent and interdependent cultural orientations. In this study participants from either European-American or East Asian cultures were asked to choose a pen as a token of appreciation for completing a questionnaire. It was arranged such that there were either three or four pens of one color, and either one or two pens of another color. The figure shows that European Americans were significantly more likely to choose the more uncommon pen color in both cases. Data are from Kim, H., & Markus, H. (1999). Deviance or uniqueness, harmony or conformity: A cultural analysis. *Journal of Personality and Social Psychology, 77,* 785–800, Experiment 3.

stringent norms against such behaviors. Other research has found that individuals from Eastern cultures respond more cooperatively toward other ingroup members, in comparison to European American participants (Lobel & McLeod, 1991), for instance, by preferring to make reward allocations to themselves and their friends on the basis of equality rather than on the basis of equity (Leung & Bond, 1984). These patterns fit with the basic idea that the collectivistic orientation of East Asians leads them take into consideration the interests of others in order to maintain harmony and because they view reciprocity and fairness as an important social value in their interactions with ingroups (Gelfand & Christakopoulou, 1999; J. G. Miller & Bersoff, 1994).

Balancing the Two Orientations

Although our discussion of independence and interdependence to this point has made it sound as if all members of Western societies have independent orientations and all members of Eastern societies have interdependent orientations, this is, of course, not true. Individuals in Western cultures frequently join groups, develop strong identities with those groups, and use those groups to help them attain their goals. And individuals in East Asian cultures have well-developed self-concepts—indeed, those concepts are very sensitive to the opinions of others. Thus, within a culture both independence and interdependence are valued, but to different degrees and through different norms.

Although independence and interdependence refer to cultural values, their expression occurs through individuals, and individuals vary in terms of their independence or interdependence both within cultures as well as between cultures (Markus & Kitayama, 1991; Markus & Kitayama, 1994). Although the members of collectivistic societies differ on average from those in individualistic societies, most people in most societies have a mixture of both orientations, either of which can be displayed at any given time. For example, individuals who belong to more than one culture at the same time (such as Japanese living in the United States or Americans living in Japan) learn to activate both cultural orientations, and which cultural orientation is most likely to be used depends on the social context in which they are currently interacting (Gardner, Gabriel, & Lee, 1999; Hong & Chiu, 2001).

As we have seen in chapter 3, individuals prefer to maintain a balance between their individual and their social identities. This principle of *optimal distinctiveness* suggests that individuals in all cultures will prefer to maintain both their independent and their interdependent orientations, such that they consider themselves both in terms of their individual identity and also in terms of their relationships with others. Thus the difference among individualistic and collectivistic cultures is in terms of the relative the weight that individuals in the culture, on average, give to one versus the other of these two orientations.

Other Dimensions of Cultural Difference

Although it is independence versus interdependence that has been studied most fully, some other dimensions that differentiate cultures have also been found. Richard Nisbett and his colleagues (D. Cohen, Nisbett, Bosdle, & Schwarz, 1996) found that, within the United States, men from southern states responded more negatively, and with greater emotion, when they were insulted (in this case by being called an asshole) in comparison to individuals from northern states. They argued that there are general differences in culture between the north and the south, such that there is a strong *culture of honor* norm in the south that requires men to maintain their honor in the face of threats by actively defending it. The norm specifies that honor is based on courage, physical strength, and norms of reciprocity. Individuals who grew up in cultures that support the notion of honor find it difficult to tolerate insults, but such a norm is not so much a part of the culture in the north.

Other researchers have studied other cultural differences, such as those between urban and rural areas (Korte, 1980), and in orientations toward time, with some cultures being more concerned with arriving and departing according to a fixed schedule, whereas others consider time in a more flexible manner (J. M. Jones, 1996; R. V. Levine, 1997; R. V. Levine & Norenzayan, 1999). Robert Levine and colleagues (1999) found that the "pace of life," as assessed by average walking speed in downtown locations and the speed with which postal clerks completed a simple request, was fastest in Western countries (but also including Japan) and was slowest in economically undeveloped countries. Interestingly, the countries with faster paces also had higher rates of death from coronary heart disease, and higher smoking rates, but also had greater subjective well-being. It has also been argued that there are cultural differences in the extent and importance of cultural norms. Some cultures have many norms, accompanied by strong sanctions for violating those norms, whereas other cultures have fewer norms, low situational constraint, and are more tolerant of deviant behavior (Chan, Gelfand, Triandis, & Tzeng, 1996). There are also cultural differences in personal space, such as how close individuals stand to each other when talking, and in the communication styles they employ (Hall, 1966).

Organizations as Culture

One type of relatively large social group that has some characteristics in common with culture, and is sometimes considered a type of culture, is the *organization*. **Organizations** are large social groups that exist to produce products or to provide services and that are usually composed of smaller subgroups, such as divisions, branches, or sectors. It is not unreasonable to think of organizations as a type of culture, because they share many of the same social functions and structures and have similar influences on self-concept and behavior. An organization is made up of a network of connected individuals, and although they may not all be in frequent contact with each other, they nevertheless share important values and have a common social identity. Furthermore, the workers within the organization are interdependent in the sense that they train each other, provide rewards to each other for effective performance, and use each other to provide social comparison and social identity (Dunnette & Hough, 2001).

Organizational cultures also have a well-defined status hierarchy, in which some individuals receive more benefits (such as higher wages) than others, and in which directives and commands are given by those with higher status to those with lower status. Individuals in the organization frequently try to improve their status in the organization by contributing to meeting the organization's goals and through displays of power (Pfeffer, 1992). Organizations generally have strong pressures toward conformity, in part because higher-level workers attempt to get as much effort out of the lower-level workers as they can by developing high production norms (Coser, 1974; Kunda, 1992).

The members of organizations frequently develop a positive social identity, and the group members who develop the most positive social identity also express the most positive behaviors toward the organization as a whole

Organizations: Large social groups that exist to produce products or to provide services.

(Haslam, in press; Tyler & Blader, 2000). It is these highly identified individuals who go out of their way to help the group, perhaps by staying late when it is needed, by spending extra time training new employees, or by working at home over the weekend. The development of a positive social identity within the organization relates, in large part, to the individual's perceptions of his or her status and respect in the group. Individuals who feel that they are treated with respect and admired by the other group members have a more positive social identity; indeed, some employees (and particularly those who are the most successful) may gain their primary social identity from their membership in the organization. In one relevant study, Tyler, Degoey, and Smith (1996) found that the members of different social groups (ranging from families to employees at a large university) who reported feeling the most pride and respect for the group were also most likely to identify with the group and feel most committed to reaching the group's goals. The individuals who are the most highly identified with the organization are also those who work hardest (Tyler & Blader, 2000).

Organizations develop norms that determine appropriate behaviors and that reward or punish deviance from those norms. For example, organizations have norms about how people from different gender and ethnic groups are treated. In some organizations there are clear status differences between men and women and among the members of different ethnic groups, and these differences are maintained because of the cultural norms that support them. More effective organizations, on the other hand, learn to create an organizational culture that allows and values differences among individuals and that attempts to reduce hierarchies based upon social category memberships. In many cases they create training and educational programs to help them accomplish this goal.

As we have seen in other cases (for instance, in our discussions of group polarization and groupthink), having a well-established group structure, with strong norms and high group cohesion and social identification, may or may not result in a positive outcome for the group. Supporting this expectation in the real world, in a series of correlational and observational studies of existing corporations, Kotter and Heskett (1992) found that the organizational culture could either help or hinder the financial performance of a corporation, depending upon whether the current culture matched or mismatched the needs of the organization. They found that organizations with "strategically appropriate" cultures performed better than those for whom the culture was inappropriate. Furthermore, organizations in which the culture was too strongly entrenched found it difficult to adapt new strategies when the competitive climate changed.

If we consider organizations as cultures, then, it is possible to imagine what might happen when two organizations combine into one as the result of a takeover or friendly merger. In short, if the cultures in the two organizations are compatible or "fit" together well, then the merger should go smoothly, whereas if the two cultures have different underlying values, then problems are likely. Research on organizational mergers has confirmed these expectations (Y. Weber, 2000).

Social Representations

As we have seen, cultures are defined in large part by the common beliefs held by their members. But we have not yet been very specific about how those beliefs develop or what they really refer to. One way to think about the beliefs that hold a culture together is to consider them in terms of *social representations* (Moscovici, 1988). A **social representation** is a pattern of beliefs, values, norms, and practices that are shared by the members of a culture and that provide meaning for the culture. In, short, the social representation is the set of beliefs that are most important to the members of the culture—the ones that come to mind when symbols of the culture (such as flags, monuments, and photographs of important people) are presented to members of the culture.

The Development of Social Representations

Social representations are developed and maintained within a culture through social influence. As people within the culture converse with each other, and as the media reports on events and presents cultural information, these beliefs are shared and strengthened and become the important cultural norms. However, the principles of social influence might lead us to expect that, given enough time, the beliefs held by the members of a culture will become more and more homogeneous, and in the end there would be little variation in norms and beliefs among the individuals. For instance, we might expect that over time, within a nation such as the United States, the different cultures would become less pronounced, and the nation would become more culturally homogeneous. Yet a look at cultures and societies suggests otherwise. Even with the increased communication among people within cities, states, and nations, there are still a wide variety of subcultures, each with different values, opinions, and norms. Although these differences may slowly be decreasing, it is doubtful that they are going to entirely disappear any time soon.

Dynamic Social Impact Theory

The spread of social norms through a culture has been specified more fully by *dynamic social impact theory* (Latané, 1996; Nowak, Szamrej, & Latané, 1990).

Social Representation: A pattern of beliefs, values, norms, and practices that are shared by the members of a culture.

As we discussed in chapter 4, the theory of social impact (also developed by Latané) predicts that people develop their own opinions in large part through their interactions with others. Furthermore, beliefs are determined through the "force" or "impact" of others, where the force is itself a function of the *strength* (for instance, how persuasive an individual is), the *immediacy* (that is, how far away in space someone is), and the *number* of the others in the environment who hold the belief. **Dynamic social impact theory** applies this idea of social impact to understanding the development and sharing of beliefs within a large group of individuals, such as a culture.

Dynamic social impact assumes that relevant beliefs are spread throughout the culture because individuals communicate with other individuals (usually those who are in close physical contact with them). And, in line with predictions of social influence, it is expected that over time the size of the majority will increase and the size of the minority will decrease. However, in comparison to what would be expected in smaller groups, dynamic social impact theory does not predict that the large group will become completely homogeneous in their beliefs. Rather, because individuals share ideas with others who are nearby (their "neighbors"), it specifically predicts that clusters (or subcultures) of individuals who hold similar beliefs will develop within the larger culture, and thus that there will be cultural diversity. Furthermore, as a result of the frequent communication among their neighbors, the subclusters will develop sets of beliefs that they share with each other even if the culture as a whole holds different beliefs.

The predictions of dynamic social impact theory have been tested using computer simulations of influence among hypothetical people, as well as using actual human interactions. In the computer models (Nowak et al., 1990) a set of hypothetical individuals (say several hundred) are each given a random set of initial beliefs. In the example presented in Figure 11.2, the individuals have been given either belief ☺ or belief ☻. The hypothetical individuals are arranged in a matrix, and then assumed to "communicate" their original beliefs with those near them. Whether each individual maintains the original belief or changes to the other depends upon a mathematical rule based on the number of other people nearby having each belief. In short, if the individual's neighbors have the same belief, then the individual will not change, but if the neighbors primarily hold the other belief, social influence will result in belief change.

The computer model runs over a period of time, with the individuals "communicating" with each other and the beliefs changing as a result. Over time, the beliefs of the individuals do change (see the comparison between the left and the right panels in Figure 11.2). However, rather than becoming homogeneous, the social influence among a large group of hypothetical individuals results in smaller clusters of individuals who maintain minority posi-

Dynamic Social Impact Theory: A theory that predicts that relevant societal beliefs are spread throughout the society because individuals communicate with other individuals who are in contact with them.

A. Before communication

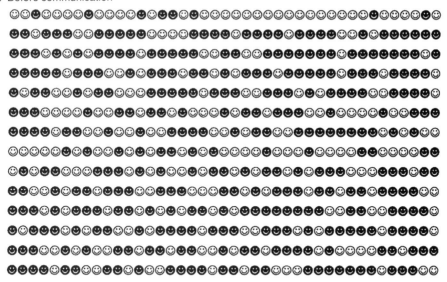

B. After communication

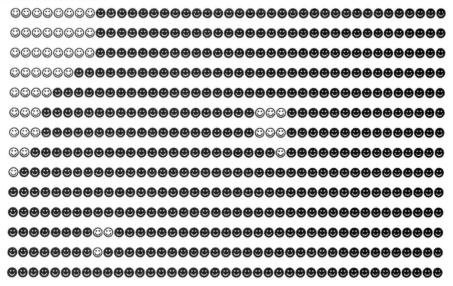

FIGURE 11.2. A computer simulation showing dynamic social impact. Based on Nowak, A., Szamrej, J., & Latané, B. (1990). From private attitude to public opinion: A dynamic theory of social impact. *Psychological Review, 97*, 362–376.

tions (the right side of Figure 11.2), even though the majority of the population maintains a different belief. In this way, although the minority clusters become smaller over time, and also become isolated from the rest of the culture—as "local minorities"—they are not wiped out. This occurs because, within the smaller clusters, the nearby "neighbors" support one anothers' opinions. Tests of real individuals acting over computer networks have also provided support for the predictions of dynamic social impact theory, showing that smaller subgroups of individuals with unique beliefs do persist within the larger group (Latané & L'Herrou, 1996).

Social Status and Social Change

Cultures develop norms that describe the appropriate behavior for their members and systems that specify social hierarchies among the group members. These status systems define the position of an individual within a group, and may also specify the position of a subculture within the larger culture (for instance, the relative status of African Americans and women in comparison to European Americans and men in the United States). Although the group norms and status systems within a culture are usually fairly stable over short periods of time, they are not completely fixed. Thus, an important issue for those interested in group behavior concerns the conditions under which groups and individuals will attempt to change the existing social relations within a nationality or culture. When and why do members of social groups either accept the existing social structure within the culture or, alternatively, work to change it?

It is natural to expect that individuals who are members of high-status groups will be content with their group membership, because it already provides them with status and positive social identity. These individuals value their own position in the society, and they realize that they are also valued by others. Membership in a low-status group, on the other hand, can have negative effects on the outcomes of individuals (B. B. Brown & Lohr, 1987; U. Wagner, Lampen, & Syllwasschy, 1986). Low-status groups are more frequently the targets of prejudice and discrimination, and thus should be motivated to improve the status of their groups in order to gain more positive rewards (Ellemers, Doosje, van Knippenberg, & Wilke, 1992; Ellemers, van Knippenberg, de Vries, & Wilke, 1988; H. J. Smith & Tyler, 1997).

Accepting or Rejecting the Existing Status Hierarchy

Whether or not individuals accept their low-status positions or attempt to change them depends upon the extent to which they see both a need and an opportunity to produce change. Furthermore, there are different possible approaches to attempting to make such changes, assuming doing so is seen as desirable and possible.

False Consciousness

In some cases people may be willing to live with the low status that their group provides, either because the costs of being in the low-status group do not seem that great or because they do not see a potential for being able to change the existing status system. In all societies some individuals have lower status than others, and the members of low-status groups may perceive that these differences, because they are an essential part of the social norms of the society, are acceptable. The acceptance of one's own low status as part of the proper and normal functioning of society is known as **false consciousness** (Jost & Banaji, 1994; Major, 1994; Sidanius & Pratto, 1999). Individuals who accept the existing status hierarchy, even if they are themselves in low-status groups, will not attempt to change things.

Individual Mobility

In cases in which the members of low-status groups do not accept their low status, they may attempt to improve their situation. One approach to changing social status is for the individual to attempt to leave the low-status group and move to a higher-status group—a strategy known as **individual mobility**. Individuals who attempt to work on their own to improve their social status by moving to a new, higher-status group begin by relinquishing their social identity with the original group and then increasingly direct their communication and behavior toward the higher-status groups in hopes of being able to join them (A. R. Cohen, 1958; Ellemers et al., 1988; Ellemers, Wilke, & Van Knippenberg, 1993; J. W. Mann, 1961; D. M. Taylor & McKirnan, 1984).

Although it represents the most direct method of change, the individual mobility strategy is not always desirable for the individual or effective if it is attempted. For one thing, if individuals are already highly identified with the low-status group, they may not wish to leave it despite the fact that it is low status. Doing so would sacrifice an important social identity, and it may be difficult to generate a new one with the new group (Ellemers, Spears, & Doosje, 1997; Spears, Doosje, & Ellemers, 1997). In addition, individual mobility is a likely response to low status only if the group member perceives that the existing group relationships are *permeable*, meaning that there is a chance for the individual to leave the group and potentially to move into a high-status group (Ellemers et al., 1993; Jackson, Sullivan, Harnish, & Hodge, 1996; Lalonde & Silverman, 1994). In some situations group memberships are constrained by physical appearance (such as when the low status is based on race) or cultural norms (such as in a caste system). There may also be individual constraints on the possibility of mobility—if individuals feel that they do not have the skills or ability to make the move, they will be unlikely to attempt to do so.

False Consciousness: The acceptance of one's own low group status as part of the proper and normal functioning of society.

Individual Mobility: Attempts on the part of individuals to leave a low-status group and move to a higher-status group.

Social Creativity

When group boundaries are not perceived as permeable, members of the low-status group may decide that they cannot leave the group. Instead, they may attempt to use a *social creativity* strategy. **Social creativity** refers to the use of strategies that allow members of low-status groups to perceive their group as better than other groups, at least on some dimensions, which allows them to gain some positive social identity (Blanz, Mummendey, Mielke, & Klink, 1998; Ellemers et al., 1997; Jackson et al., 1996). Social creativity frequently takes the form of finding alternative characteristics by which the group excels. For example, the students at a college that does not have a particularly good academic standing may look to the superior performance of their sports teams as a way of creating positive self-perceptions and social identity. Although the sports team's performance may be a less important dimension than academic performance overall, it does provide at least some positive feelings. Alternatively, the members of the low-status group might regain identity by perceiving their group as very cohesive, or homogeneous, thus emphasizing its positive characteristics. The outcome of this, as we have seen in chapter 5, is the perception of in-group homogeneity.

Collective Action

When individual mobility is not possible, group members may consider mobilizing the group into *collective action* (Gamson, 1992; A. Morris & Mueller, 1992; Simon, Loewy, Stuermer, Weber, Freytag, & Habig, 1998). **Collective action** refers to the attempts on the part of one group to change the social status hierarchy by improving the status of the in-group relative to others. This might occur either through peaceful methods, such as lobbying for new policies or laws requiring equal opportunity, or by resorting to violence. Collective action is more likely to occur when there is continual communication among the people in the low-status group; when there is available leadership to help define an ideology, organize the group, and formulate a program for action; and when the culture as a whole supports the attempts at change. Taking part in collective action, for instance, by joining feminist or civil rights movements in the United States or the Solidarity movement in Poland, is a method of maintaining and increasing one's group identity and attempting to change the current social structure.

Social Creativity: The use of strategies that allow members of low-status groups to perceive their group as better than other groups.

Collective Action: Attempts on the part of one group to change the social status hierarchy by improving the status of their own group relative to others.

Determinants of Attempts at Social Change

Now that we have considered the types of strategies that individuals and groups may use in their attempts to gain higher status, we can also consider the conditions under which they are more or less likely to take these actions (Ellemers, 1993; Tajfel, 1982; Taylor, Moghaddam, Gamble, & Zellerer, 1987). In short, we can say that we will be able to predict which actions members of low-status groups will take to improve their status when we understand how the individuals involved perceive the current group relations.

As we have discussed earlier, one factor that influences attempts to change the existing status hierarchy is perception of the permeability of the group boundaries. When the boundaries are seen as permeable, individual mobility is the most likely strategy. However, when individuals perceive the group boundaries as impermeable, and thus that individual mobility is not possible, they are more likely to prefer other strategies, such as social creativity and social mobility. Furthermore, the perception of group impermeability is particularly likely to produce the desire for social change when group identity is also high (Ellemers, 1993; Lalonde & Silverman, 1994; Simon et al., 1998).

A second and related variable that influences change attempts is the perceived *stability* of the group relationships. Stability refers to the possibility of change, but at the group, rather than the individual, level. If members of low-status groups perceive that the existing group differences are likely to change over time, they will be more motivated to attempt to change the status relationships through collective action than if they perceive that the group relations are stable and unlikely to change no matter what efforts are made (Ellemers, 1993). Again, these motivations for change may be particularly high when accompanied by high group identity.

Finally, the perceived *legitimacy* or *fairness* of the status differences among the groups is also a critical determinant of satisfaction with the existing group hierarchy as well as with one's position within the in-group (Lind & Tyler, 1988; T. Tyler, 1989; T. Tyler et al., 1996; Tyler & Lind, 1992). Group members who feel that the existing status relationships are fair and who perceive that the members of high-status groups are trustworthy and respectful are less likely to attempt to change this state of affairs than are those who feel that the existing relationship is unjust (D. M. Taylor & Moghaddam, 1994). The belief that those with higher status and power can be trusted to treat lower-status individuals fairly is known as **procedural justice** (Tyler, 1989, 1991).

The perception of illegitimacy is not based on the objective position of the group but, as would be expected on the basis of social comparison theory, the group's relative position. As we have seen in chapter 3, the perception that one's group has lower status than it deserves is called the perception of fraternalistic deprivation. For instance, African Americans in the United States may perceive that they have lower status than European Americans because they do not earn as much on average, receive poorer education, and often live in lower-class neighborhoods, even though they may be objectively better off than even the highest-status groups in other countries. Similarly, even members of high-status groups can feel threatened if they believe that their status is decreasing in comparison to other up-and-coming groups. Perceptions of

Procedural Justice: The belief that individuals with higher status and power can be trusted to treat lower-status individuals fairly.

fraternalistic deprivation, accompanied by strong social identity, increase the likelihood that individuals will resort to the use of collective action strategies of social change (Guimond & Dube-Simard, 1983; Gurin & Townsend, 1986; Lalonde & Silverman, 1994).

One example of a phenomenon that can be understood in terms of fraternal deprivation is the civil rights riots of the 1960s. They occurred after African Americans had made many gains in the United States, particularly in terms of new equal rights legislation. It has been argued that African Americans chose this time to engage in civil disobedience and violence because at this point they began to compare themselves to whites rather than to other blacks, and this upward comparison made their relatively lower status seem illegitimate (Gurr, 1970).

Summary

In short, we can say that, at least for individuals from Western cultures, people who view their low status as stable and legitimate and who see the group boundaries as permeable are likely to be content with the existing group relationships or, if they are not, to adopt an individual mobility strategy, attempting on their own to join a higher-status group. However, low-status groups that perceive the group boundaries as impermeable are more likely to adapt social creativity strategies, including changing group perceptions and collective action. Finally, those who see the group relationships as unstable are likely to engage in collective action, particularly when social identity is high.

Crowds

Crowd: A collection of a large number of individuals who come together in a common place for a common purpose.

Mob: A crowd in which some individuals are acting violently, harming the property of themselves and others, and potentially injuring other people.

Another large social group of interest is the **crowd,** defined as a collection of a large number of individuals who come together in a common place for a common purpose (R. W. Brown, 1965; Dunning, Murphy, & Williams, 1986; Le Bon, 1896/1960; Mullen, 1986; Reicher, 1987; Reicher, 1984a, 1984b; Reicher, Spears, & Postmes, 1995). In most cases crowds are harmless and even potentially productive groups, such as those made up of people who are shopping at a mall or watching a baseball game. However, in other cases an event occurs that changes the behavior of the group so that the behavior becomes more negative, and potentially even violent. As a result of the precipitating event, the crowd turns into a **mob.** A mob consists of a large number of individuals, some of whom are acting violently, harming the property of themselves and others, and potentially injuring other people as well. Mobs form frequently enough that they have been studied in some detail, and the causes and outcomes of mob behavior are beginning to be understood.

In some cases the mob behavior is the result of frustration. Riots have occurred over the inability to find enough food, the feelings that one's group is deprived of status within a society, the inability to get tickets to a rock concert, and losses by local sports teams (although, probably because of the presence of high arousal, mobs have also been known to form after the local team wins).

There are two primary explanations for when and why a crowd turns into a mob. One explanation assumes that in mobs the relevant social norms break down, creating deindividuation and leaving individuals to act on their own accord. In this approach it is assumed that the prior norms prevented individuals from engaging in violent behavior, and the loss of these restraining norms allows it to occur. The second approach assumes that norms of the crowd are still strong and important for the mob, but that they are different norms than those that were in place before the precipitating event occurred. In the following sections we will consider both of these possibilities.

Deindividuation

Perhaps the most common explanation for mob behavior is based on the notion of *deindividuation* (Diener, 1976, 1980; Festinger, Pepitone, & Newcomb, 1952; Zimbardo, 1969). As we have seen in chapter 1, deindividuation occurs when individuals in groups temporarily stop thinking of themselves as individuals, which may lead them to engage in unusual, extreme, or deviant behavior. According to this approach, in a mob the individuals in the group become anonymous; they no longer think of themselves as individuals and are not seen or paid attention to as individuals by others, and their individual behavior can no longer be identified. The result is that they behave in ways that they would not have behaved if they had been more focused on their individual selves rather than as members of a group. In these situations the social norms that normally prevent extreme behavior (which may be enforced by authority figures such as the police) have less of a restraining effect.

The theory of deindividuation is a descendant of Le Bon's concept of the group or collective mind, which argued that violent behavior started in one part of a crowd and then spread through it like a disease (Tarde, 1901/1969; Wheeler, 1966). The result of this "social contagion" of emotion within the group is that the individual group members lose their self-control and become capable of violating personal and social norms.

One basic prediction derived from the deindividuation approach is that, as the crowd becomes larger, each individual in the crowd will become relatively less likely to be identified as an individual, making him or her more likely to become deindividuated. Thus, larger crowds should produce more aggressive and harmful behaviors, because the resulting deindividuation increases the likelihood of breaking social norms that would normally prevent such behavior. Supporting this hypothesis, research has found that larger crowds are more likely to urge potential suicidal jumpers to jump (Mann, 1981), and larger crowds (of white men) also committed more violent lynchings of blacks (as reported in newspaper articles) from 1899 to 1946 (Mullen, 1986).

Norm Theories

Although individuals who are deindividuated are sometimes less likely to be influenced by the social norms that normally restrain deviant behavior, they are not entirely unaware of group norms. In one important experiment, R. D. Johnson and Downing (1979) created deindividuation in small groups of college students by having them wear a mask and overalls reminiscent of the Ku Klux Klan or by having them wear white nurse uniforms. Participants were then given an opportunity to administer shock to other individuals as part of a learning experiment. Although both groups of participants were deindividuated, and thus should have been free of social norms, the results showed that participants shocked significantly more when dressed in the Ku Klux Klan uniforms than they did when dressed as nurses. And Gergen, Gergen, and Barton (1973) found that when people were in the dark and thus deindividuated, they expressed more touching, caressing, and other affectionate behavior. Taken together, then, these results show that the deindividuated individual does not necessarily become more aggressive or antisocial, but may rather conform to what is perceived as the current social norm.

At least in part as a result of these findings, other explanations for mob behavior have been proposed that argue not that there is a loss of social norms in the mob but rather that new, often (but not always) more negative norms develop in the place of the existing ones (Reicher et al., 1995; Spears & Lea, 1992, 1994). The idea behind this approach is that deindividuation changes self-categorization from the individual level to the group level, and this transition from a personal to a social identity leads the individual to become less aware of personal norms and *more* conforming to group norms. Thus, in this approach individuals who are deindividuated also gain a stronger group identity rather than simply losing their personal identity. Supporting this explanation, a recent meta-analysis that reviewed the results of many studies of deindividuation found that conditions of deindividuation increased the extent to which the participants conformed to the situational norm, regardless of whether the norm was positive or negative (Postmes & Spears, 1998).

The norm-formation approach to understanding mob behavior also predicts that the tendency to adopt in-group norms will be greater when there is more than one group present in the situation and when each group therefore tries to distinguish itself from the other by adopting extreme norms. This explanation therefore seems well able to explain mob behavior that occurs between the fans of competing teams at sporting events and at demonstrations in which the demonstrators and the police constitute two distinct groups (Reicher, 1982, 1987; Reicher, 1984a, 1984b). In sum, then, there is at least some support for both the deindividuation and the norm-formation explanations of crowd behavior. Future research will certainly provide a better understanding of the behavior of crowds and mobs.

 Chapter Summary

A culture is a large social group made up of individuals who are normally in geographic proximity with each other and who share a common set of descriptive and proscriptive norms. Culture provides our fundamental values, beliefs, and social norms, and is becoming increasingly important to consider as societies become more diverse.

One cultural difference that has been extensively studied involves differences between the individualistic orientation found in Western cultures and the collectivistic orientation found in Far Eastern cultures. These cultural differences have important influences on both the self-concept of individuals and the norms and behavior in different cultures. People generally want to balance these two orientations and, according to the theory of optimal distinctiveness, prefer to perceive themselves both as individuals and as part of groups. There are other cultural differences that may also be important. One type of culture that has been studied extensively is the corporate or organizational culture. Organizations develop norms and values that have a broad impact on the satisfaction and productivity of their employees.

Social representations are the shared norms and values that define a culture and are developed through the exchange of ideas and values among the members of the culture. The outcome of this process, according to dynamic social impact theory, is a stable set of beliefs within the culture, but one in which there are both minority as well as majority opinions represented.

Individuals who have low social status within a society or culture may either accept their low position (false consciousness) or reject the existing status hierarchy and attempt to change the current state of affairs through individual mobility, social creativity, or collective action. Which of these approaches is taken depends on perceptions of the stability, permeability, and legitimacy of the social groups.

A crowd is a large collection of individuals who come together in a common place for a common purpose. In many cases the crowd is a harmless and even productive group. When a precipitating event occurs, however, the crowd may turn into a mob. Mob behavior has been explained both in terms of a loss of social norms (deindividuation) as well as in terms of an increase in conformity to group norms as a result of increased social identification.

Review and Discussion Questions

1. What is culture and how does it influence the beliefs and behaviors of individuals?
2. How do your perceptions of the beliefs of your important reference groups, such as collectives and cultures, influence your attitudes and behavior?
3. What are the characteristics of individualistic and collectivistic cultures? What is the importance of this distinction, and what are the outcomes of the difference? Do you consider yourself to be primarily individualistic or collectivistic? Explain why.
4. In Korea, a person's address might be listed as: Korea, Seoul, 814 Sunrise Street, Kim, John. What does such a listing indicate about the Korean culture in comparison, for instance, to U.S. culture?
5. What are social representations? What are the important social representations of the country in which you live? How does Latané's dynamic social influence model explain the spread of ideas through large social groups?
6. Review the individual-level and group-level processes that individuals may use to attempt to create positive social identity when they find themselves to be a member of a group that does not provide a positive social identity for them.
7. What is *deindividuation*, and how and when does it occur in large groups? What are the causes and outcomes of deindividuation on group behavior?
8. Discuss some group theories that might account for the prevalence of gang warfare in inner-city Los Angeles. Do you find these theories adequate to account for such behavior? Why or why not?

Recommended Readings

Understanding jurors and juries:
Hastie, R. (1993). *Inside the Juror: The Psychology of Juror Decision Making.* New York: Cambridge University Press.

A summary of social interaction in computer groups:
Lea, M. (Ed.). (1992). *Contexts of Computer-mediated Communication.* Hemel Hempstead, UK: Harvester Wheatsheaf.

A classic model of small group performance:
Hackman, J., & Morris, C. (1975). Group tasks, group interaction processes, and group performance effectiveness: A review and proposed integration. In L. Berkowitz (Ed.), *Advances in Experimental Social Psychology* (Vol. 8, pp. 45–99). New York: Academic Press.

Cooperation and Conflict Within Groups 12

*A*s we have discussed throughout this book, people join groups to obtain the benefits they provide. But because groups and group members are interdependent, gaining rewards frequently involves behavior that influences the rewards that can be gained by other people, both within and outside of the group. The goal of gaining rewards frequently leads to individual cooperation—

the reciprocal exchange of benefits with others—for instance, by working together to complete a project that no one person could accomplish alone. In other cases, however, cooperation breaks down and the group members turn to competition—as when an employee exaggerates his or her contributions to the project with the goal of getting a promotion over his or her coworkers, or when group members blame each other for the group's difficulties.

Groups may also themselves cooperate or compete with other groups. Two computer manufacturers may work together to create a new product or compete for market share for their own products. Similarly, two countries may engage in trade and cultural exchanges or go to war over disputed land. In still other cases the needs and goals of the individual may be in conflict with the needs of the group of which he or she is a member. This might occur, for instance, when individuals are asked to place their own needs (the desire to spend time with one's family) second to the needs of the group (the goal of finishing an important corporate report).

Chapters 12 and 13 consider group cooperation and conflict. In this chapter we will consider cooperation and conflict among the individuals within groups, and in chapter 13 we will turn to potential conflict between groups. In each case, in addition to discussing the potential causes of conflict we will also consider ways that this conflict might be avoided or reduced. These issues are important because they have real-world implications, such as understanding how best to negotiate solutions to international rivalries and hostilities, how to reduce prejudicial attitudes and discriminatory behaviors, and how to enhance the ability of people from different groups to come together to solve important social problems, such as conserving natural resources and providing needed community services.

Understanding Cooperation and Conflict

Fortunately, the relationships among individuals and among groups are almost always benign and favorable. Most people get along with others, enjoy working in groups, and generally work together in ways that allow the group members and the group as a whole to succeed. In these situations the interacting parties perceive that the gains made by others also improve their own chances of gaining rewards and that their goals are compatible. The parties engage in **cooperation** by acting in ways that they believe benefit both themselves and others (Deutsch, 1949, 1994). The players on a baseball team, for instance, cooperate with each other—the better any one of them does, the better the team as a whole does. In cooperative situations it may in some cases even be beneficial to accept some personal costs (such as bunting a player on first base to second base, even though it means an out for the self) in order to

Cooperation: Behaviors that occur when it is perceived that the goals of the self and others are compatible and in which individuals believe they are benefiting both themselves and others.

further the goals of the group (by placing the other player in scoring position).

Conflict, on the other hand, is a situation that occurs when it is perceived by the parties involved that gains made by others decrease their own chances of gaining rewards, and that their goals are thus incompatible (Deutsch, 1949, 1994; Kelley & Thibaut, 1969; Pruitt & Carnevale, 1993). The result of conflict is almost always **competition**—the attempts by each party to gain as many of the limited rewards as possible and to reduce the likelihood of success for the other parties.

Conflict is sometimes *realistic*, in the sense that the goals of the interacting parties really are incompatible. This would occur in a sporting event, for instance, when only one team can win, or when the members of one social category want to improve their status but a higher-status group attempts to prevent them from doing so. On the other hand, many conflicts are more *perceived* than realistic, because (although they may have a core of realistic conflict) they are based upon misperceptions of the intentions of others or the nature of the potential rewards. In some cases, although the situation is perceived as conflicting, the benefits gained for one party do not necessarily mean a loss for the other party. Both sides might work together to come to a compromise in which they both get, at least in part, what they want, and both parties are better off working together than working on their own. Regardless of whether the conflict is realistic or perceived, however, one of the biggest difficulties is that the perception of conflict tends to produce hostile behaviors, and the pattern frequently escalates, potentially resulting in hostility and even violence.

Outcomes of Cooperation and Conflict

In cooperative groups, individuals have trusting, friendly attitudes with the other group members, and they are interested in sharing information accurately and openly. Perhaps not surprisingly then, research has found that groups that have more cooperative atmospheres also end up being more productive. David Johnson and his colleagues (Johnson, Maruyama, Johnson, Nelson, & Skon, 1981; D. W. Johnson & Johnson, 1994; D. W. Johnson, Johnson, & Maruyama, 1983; see also Slavin, 1983) have conducted meta-analyses analyzing the results of hundreds of studies in educational and performance settings that compared groups that worked in cooperative and competitive atmospheres. They found that members of cooperative groups not only reported having more positive attitudes, but also produced more effective learning and better performance, in comparison to members of groups that were characterized by competitive environments.

Although conflict may make it more difficult for groups to be productive in the short run, the presence of low levels of conflict within a group does not

Conflict: A situation in which interacting parties perceive that gains made by others decrease their own chances of gaining rewards and that their goals are thus incompatible.

Competition: Attempts by interacting parties to gain rewards at the expense of the other party or parties.

necessarily produce negative outcomes in the long run. Conflict within groups can also produce innovation and creativity because it challenges existing norms and ways of making decisions (Coser, 1956; Coser, 1967; Tjosvold & Deemer, 1980). Groups can increase their productivity and make better decisions if they discuss important issues with each other, and this discussion is likely to produce at least some conflict. As we have seen in chapter 10, groups that are unwilling to experience conflict may not engage in enough discussion, and thus make poor decisions (groupthink!). Thus, conflict may be beneficial when it occurs in situations in which there are relatively positive relationships among the group members. The important question is whether the conflict in the group will take a destructive course, spiraling upward to create lasting hostilities among the group members, or whether the conflict will be more contained, constructive, and productive.

Public Goods and Social Dilemmas

Although there are many potential sources of conflict within groups, one type that has been studied extensively concerns situations in which individual members of large social groups are in potential conflict over the creation and use of **public goods**. Public goods are benefits that are shared by a community at large. Everyone in the group has access to them, regardless of whether or not they have personally contributed to the creation of the good (Issac, McCue, & Plott, 1982; Olson, 1965; V. L. Smith, 1979). Public goods include such things as the local school system or fire department, a public television or radio station, or the outcomes of research on cancer and heart disease.

In many cases the public good involves the responsible use of a resource that if used wisely by the group as a whole will remain intact but, if it is overused, will be destroyed. Consider for instance what Garrett Hardin (1968) called the *commons dilemma*. Hardin found that in many towns in Europe there was at one time a centrally located pasture, known as the commons, which was communally used by the inhabitants of the village to graze their livestock. But the commons was not always used wisely. The problem was that each individual who owned livestock wanted to be able to use the commons to graze his or her own animals. However, when each group member took full advantage of the commons by grazing many animals, the commons became overgrazed, the pasture died, and the commons was destroyed. Although Hardin initially focused on this particular example, he noted that the basic dilemma of individual needs versus the needs of the group could also be found in many contemporary public goods issues, including the use of limited water resources, harvesting of fish from the oceans, air pollution, land development, volunteering behavior, and the protection of animal species.

Public Goods:
Benefits that are shared by the members of a community, regardless of whether or not the members have personally contributed to the creation of the good.

Situations such as the commons dilemma, in which the goals of the individual conflict with the goals of the group are known as **social dilemmas** (Cross & Guyer, 1980; Lynn & Oldenquist, 1986; Komorita & Parks, 1994; Messick & Brewer, 1983; Orbell & Dawes, 1981). In social dilemmas the personally beneficial choice (such as using water during a water shortage or driving to work alone in one's own car) produces benefits for the individual, no matter what others do. And yet the paradox is that if everyone takes the personally selfish choice in an attempt to maximize their own rewards, the long-term result is poorer outcomes for every individual in the group (depletion of the water table, traffic jams). Each individual prefers to make use of the resources for himself or herself, whereas the best outcome for the group as a whole is to use the resources more slowly and wisely.

Harvesting and Contributions Dilemmas

There are two types of social dilemmas—*harvesting* and *contributions*, which involve the tendency of individuals to selfishly take public goods and the tendency to selfishly refuse to contribute to public goods, respectively. A **harvesting dilemma** is a situation in which individual group members are tempted to use the public goods to meet his or her own self-interest, but this behavior eventually leads to long-term loss either for the individual or for the group as a whole. The commons dilemma, discussed above, is an example of a harvesting dilemma. In large cities, as another example, many people prefer the convenience of driving his or her own car to work each day rather than taking public transportation. Yet the outcome of this behavior if everyone does it is that the roads become snarled and everyone ends up sitting in traffic. People are lured into the dilemma by short-term self-interest, seemingly without considering the potential long-term costs of the behavior, such as air pollution and the necessity of building even more highways.

Another type of harvesting dilemma occurs in crisis situations, as when a fire breaks out in a building. It has been observed that in many real situations there is frequently plenty of time for all of the individuals, if they can coordinate their efforts and work together, to escape the fire. However, because each person acts in their own self-interest, by attempting to be the first to leave the building and running into the stairwells and through the doors, disaster can result. Many harvesting dilemmas, such as overfishing in the oceans or the negative impact of global warming, work on a type of "time delay." The problem is that, because the long-term negative outcome (the extinction of fish species or dramatic changes in the climate) is far away in the future, it is difficult to avoid the dilemma.

A **contributions dilemma** occurs when the short-term costs of a behavior

Social Dilemma: A situation in which the goals of the individual conflict with the goals of the group.

Harvesting Dilemma: A social dilemma in which an individual group member is tempted to use public goods, but this behavior eventually leads to long-term loss either for the individual or for the group as a whole.

Contributions Dilemma: A social dilemma in which the short-term costs of a behavior lead individuals to avoid performing it, and this prevents the long-term benefits that would have occurred if the behaviors had been performed.

lead individuals to avoid performing it, and this may prevent the long-term benefits that would have occurred if the behaviors had been performed. An example of a contributions dilemma occurs when individuals have to determine whether or not to donate to the local public radio or television station. If most people do not contribute, the TV station may have lower-quality programming, or even go off the air entirely, thus producing a negative outcome for the group as a whole. However, if enough people do contribute, then it is not in anyone's own best interest to do so, because the others will pay for the programming for them. Contributions dilemmas thus represent a type of free riding in which the individual may rely on other group members to contribute for them, allowing them to reduce their own contribution (Kerr, 1983, 1986; Shepperd, 1993).

Although they may generally look out for their own interests, individuals do realize that there are both costs and benefits to making the selfish choice in social dilemmas (Blake & Mouton, 1961; Samuelson, Messick, Rutte, & Wilke, 1984). Although we might prefer to use as much gasoline as we want, and to buy a couple of new CDs rather than contribute to the local public radio station, at the same time we realize that doing so may have negative consequences for the group as a whole. Thus social dilemmas are a type of **mixed-motive decision**, in which there are simultaneous goals of cooperating and competing, and the individual must coordinate these goals in making a choice (Rubin, Pruitt, & Kim, 1994; Schelling, 1978).

Studying Cooperation and Conflict

One method of understanding how individuals and groups behave in social dilemmas is to create such situations in laboratory simulations. A number of different tasks have been used to simulate real-life encounters in the laboratory in order to study how people behave when they must make decisions that affect both their own and others' welfare (Kelley & Thibaut, 1969; Luce & Raiffa, 1957; Pruitt & Kimmel, 1977; Rapoport, 1973; Wrightsman, O'Connor, & Baker, 1972).

Matrix Games

Mixed-Motive Decision: A decision in which the individual must coordinate both cooperative and competitive goals in making a choice.

Perhaps the most common type of laboratory simulations are *matrix games* (Rapoport, 1973). Matrix games are based upon principles of social exchange theory (see chapter 3) and thus assume that individuals try to maximize their own rewards in their interactions with others. The outcomes of the decisions are expressed in the form of *payoff matrices* where numbers are used to express the potential outcomes for the individual, given the decisions made by the parties involved in the conflict. The outcomes are chosen beforehand by the experimenter on the basis of his or her perceptions of the characteristics of a given task. The payoff matrix allows us to predict the behavior of the individuals involved in the situation, if we assume that individuals attempt to maximize their own outcomes (Luce & Raiffa, 1957).

The Prisoner's Dilemma

The best-known matrix game is the **prisoner's dilemma** game (Luce & Raiffa, 1957; Pruitt & Kimmel, 1977; Rapoport, 1973; Schlenker & Bonoma, 1978). This game represents a simple social dilemma in which the goals of the individual compete with the goals of another individual, or with a group of individuals. In its original form, the prisoner's dilemma involves a situation in which two prisoners (we'll call them Frank and Malik) have been accused of committing a crime. The police have determined that the two worked together on the crime, but they have only been able to gather enough evidence to convict each of them of a more minor offense. In an attempt to gain more evidence, the police interrogate each of the prisoners individually, in hopes that one will confess to having been involved in the more major crime in return for a promise of a reduced sentence if he confesses first.

The incentives for either confessing or not confessing are expressed in the payoff matrix shown in Figure 12.1. The top of the matrix represents the two choices that Malik might make (either to confess that he did the crime or to not confess), and the side of the matrix represents the two choices that Frank might make (also to either confess or to not confess). The payoffs that each prisoner receives, given the choices of each of the two prisoners, are shown in each of the four squares.

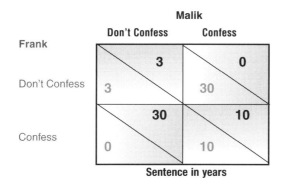

FIGURE 12.1. The prisoner's dilemma. In the prisoner's dilemma, two suspected criminals are interrogated separately. The matrix indicates the outcomes for each prisoner, measured as the number of years each is sentenced to prison, as a result of each combination of cooperative (don't confess) and competitive (confess) decisions. Outcomes for Malik are in black, and outcomes for Frank are in gray.

Prisoner's Dilemma: A social dilemma in which the goals of the individual compete with the goals of another individual or with a group of individuals.

If neither prisoner confesses (the situation represented in the upper left corner of the matrix), there will be a trial, the limited available information will be used to convict each prisoner, and they will each be sentenced to a short prison term of three years. However, if either of the prisoners confesses, turning "state's evidence," there will be enough information to convict the other prisoner of the larger crime, and that prisoner will receive a sentence of 30 years, whereas the prisoner who confesses will get off free. These outcomes are represented in the lower left and upper right corners of the matrix. Finally, it is possible that both players confess at the same time. In this case there is no need for a trial, and in return the prosecutors offer a somewhat reduced sentence (of ten years) to each of the prisoners.

The prisoner's dilemma represents a social dilemma in which the short-term interests of the individual conflict with the long-term gains for the group (or in this case, the "partnership" made up of the two prisoners) as a whole. Although initially specified in terms of the two prisoners, similar matrices have been used to predict behavior in many different types of dilemmas involving two or more parties, including choices between helping and not helping, working and loafing, and paying and not paying debts.

Characteristics of the Prisoner's Dilemma

The prisoner's dilemma has two interesting characteristics that make it a useful model of a social dilemma. For one thing, the prisoner's dilemma has **integrative outcomes**, which means that they are arranged so that a positive outcome for one player does not necessarily mean a negative outcome for the other player. If you consider again the matrix in Figure 12.1, you can see that if one player takes the cooperative choice (to not confess) and the other takes the competitive choice (to confess), then the prisoner who cooperates loses whereas the other prisoner wins. However, if both prisoners make the cooperative choice, neither gains more than the other, and both prisoners receive relatively light sentences. In this sense both players can win at the same time. Integrative situations are contrasted with *fixed-sum situations* in which the gain of one party always means a loss of the same amount for the other party.

Second, the prisoner's dilemma matrix is arranged such that each individual player is motivated to take the competitive choice, because this choice leads to a higher payoff regardless of what the other player does. Imagine for a moment that you are Malik, and you are trying to decide whether to cooperate (don't confess) or to compete (confess). And imagine that you are not really sure what Frank is going to do. Remember the goal of the individual is to maximize rewards. The values in the matrix make it clear that if you think that Frank is going to confess, you should confess yourself (to get 10 rather than 30

Integrative Outcome:
An outcome in which a positive outcome for one party does not necessarily mean a negative outcome for the other party.

years in prison). And, it is also clear that if you think Frank is not going to confess you should still confess (to get 0 rather than 3 year in prison). The matrix is arranged so that the "best" alternative for each player, at least in the sense of pure self-interest, is to make the competitive choice, even though in the end both players would prefer the combination in which both players co-operate to the one in which they both compete.

Variations on the Prisoner's Dilemma

Many studies have used the prisoner's dilemma to study cooperation and con-flict, making use of many different types of payoffs. And many variations on the basic procedure have also been developed. Frequently, the game is played over a series of trials in which players can modify their responses based on those given by their partners on previous trials. For instance, consider a ver-sion of a prisoner's dilemma game that models an arms race between two countries. Over a period of many trials, each "country" chooses whether to compete (by building missiles) or to cooperate (by building factories). Such long-term games frequently show heightened conflict in the early stages, but then more cooperation occurs on later trials as individuals experience the nega-tive outcomes of conflict and attempt to reduce them, for instance by opening lines of communication that can increase trust or by electing leaders (Messick, Wilke, Brewer, Kramer, Zemke, & Lui, 1983; Samuelson et al., 1984).

The prisoner's dilemma can also be expanded to be played by more than two players. The behavior of individuals leaving a crowded parking lot, for example, represents a type of prisoner's dilemma in which it is to each person's individual benefit to try to be the first to leave. However, if each person rushes to the exit without regard for others, a traffic jam is more likely to result, which slows down the process for everyone. If each individual takes the coop-erative choice—waiting until their turn—everyone wins.

Resource Dilemma Games

In addition to the prisoner's dilemma, social dilemmas have also been studied using games in which a group of individuals share a common pool of resources. In these *resource dilemma games* the participants may extract or harvest re-sources from the pool, and it is to their individual advantage to do so. Further-more, as the resources are used, the pool can replenish itself through a fixed schedule, which will allow the individuals to continue to harvest over long periods of time. Optimal use of the resource involves keeping the pool level up and harvesting only as much as will be replenished in the given time period. Overuse of the pool provides immediate gain for the individuals but has a long-term cost in the inability to make harvests at a later time (Brewer & Kramer,

1986; Dawes, 1980; Edney, 1980; Jorgenson & Papciak, 1981; Messick et al., 1983).

In one version of a resource dilemma game (Edney, 1979), the partici-pants sit around a bowl of metal nuts, and the goal is to get as many nuts as one can. The experimenter adds nuts to the bowl so that the number of nuts in the bowl doubles every ten seconds. However, the individual players are also motivated to harvest nuts for themselves. They are allowed to take out as many nuts as they like at any time. In Edney's research, rather than cooperat-ing and watching the pool grow, the participants almost immediately acted in their self-interest, grabbing the nuts from the bowl. In fact, Edley reported that 65 percent of the groups never got to the first ten-second replenishment!

The Trucking Game

Another example of a laboratory game that has been used to study conflict is the *trucking game*. In the original research (Deutsch & Krauss, 1960) pairs of women played the trucking game. Each woman was given $4.00 to begin with, and was asked to imagine herself as the owner of one of two trucking compa-nies (Acme or Bolt) that carried merchandise over the roads shown in Figure 12.2. Each time either player's truck reached the destination on the opposite

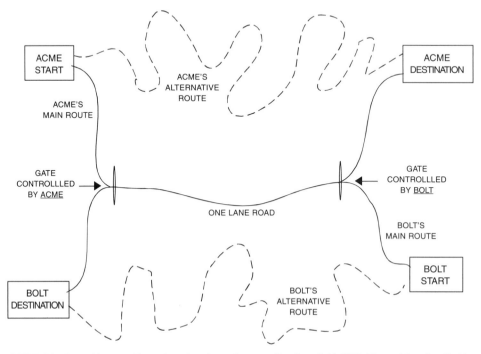

FIGURE 12.2. The trucking game. The road map from the trucking game. From Deutsch, M. (1973). *The resolution of conflict.* New Haven: Yale University Press, p. 219.

side of the board, she earned 60 cents, minus operating costs (1 cent for each second taken by the trip). However, the game was also arranged to create the potential for conflict. Each participant wanted to travel on the main road in order to get to the destination faster, but this road was arranged to be so narrow that only one truck could pass at a time. Whenever the two trucks met each other on this narrow road, one of them was eventually forced to back up. Thus, there are two choices to getting to the destination. The players had to either take the long winding roads, thus eliminating their profits (each player would lose 10 cents on each trip if she was forced to take the long road), or they could figure out a way to share the use of the one-lane road.

Deutsch and Krauss made the game even more interesting by creating experimental conditions in which either or both of the truck company owners had a gate that controlled access to the main road. In the *unilateral-threat* condition, only Acme had a gate. Thus if Bolt attempted to use the main road, Acme could close the gate, forcing Bolt to back up and enabling Acme to re-open the gate and proceed quickly to the destination. In the *bilateral-threat* condition both sides had gates, whereas in the third condition there were no gates.

As shown in Figure 12.3, participants without gates soon learned to share the one-lane road, and, on average, each made a profit. However, a threat in the form of a gate produced conflict and led to lower profits, although in many cases the participants learned to deal with these problems over time and improved their payoffs as the game went on (Lawler, Ford, & Blegen, 1988; Shomer, Davis, & Kelley, 1966). Participants lost the most money in the bilateral-threat condition in which both sides were given gates that they could control. In this situation, conflict immediately developed, and there were standoffs on the middle road that wasted time and prevented either truck from moving.

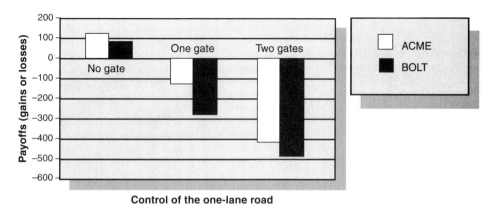

Control of the one-lane road

FIGURE 12.3. Outcomes of a trucking game study. The outcomes of the trucking game study in which the opponents had no gates, one of them had a gate, or both had gates. Data from Deutsch, M., & Krauss, R. M. (1960). The effect of threat upon interpersonal bargaining. *Journal of Abnormal and Social Psychology, 61,* 181–189.

Two results of this study are particularly surprising. First, in the unilateral-gate condition, both players (including Acme, who had control of the gate) lost money, in comparison to the no-gate condition (although it is true that in this condition Acme did lose less than Bolt). Thus being able to threaten the other was not successful for generating overall profits. Second, in the conditions in which both individuals had gates, *both individuals* actually did worse than they did when only one individual had a gate. Thus, when an opponent is able to threaten you, it may be to your benefit to not return with a threat of your own—the ability to counteract the threats of your partner may not always help you but may rather produce even more conflict and losses for both parties.

Critiques of Gaming Approaches

Although studying cooperation and conflict using laboratory games has been a very popular approach, the approach has also been criticized (Schlenker & Bonoma, 1978). One obvious question concerns potential difficulties in generalizing from the results found in the laboratory to likely behavior in everyday life. In the lab the situation may seem rather artificial, and the payoffs may not seem that large or important to the individuals. Despite these critiques, it is not clear that findings from laboratory games would not generalize to real-world behavior. If people take a competitive orientation under certain conditions in a resource dilemma game in the lab, it is logical to expect that they would take similar strategies in real-world applications in which the outcomes are even more important. Furthermore, laboratory games are effective to the extent that they simulate the important aspects of real-world behavior. They allow the researcher to create experimental manipulations and to study events that could not be examined in the real world.

Variables That Produce Cooperation and Conflict

By examining the many studies that have focused on cooperation and conflict, both in the real world and in the lab, it has been possible to draw conclusions about the specific characteristics that determine when and whether people cooperate or compete. These factors include the type of task, such as its rules and regulations, perceptions about the norms that are operating in the current situation, the characteristics of the individuals who are involved in the situation, and the information available to the individuals. We will consider these characteristics and their impact on cooperation and conflict in this section.

Task Characteristics

One factor that determines whether individuals cooperate or compete is the nature of the task or situation itself. The payoffs in some tasks are such that they result in primarily competitive responses, whereas others elicit more co-operation. In addition to determining whether cooperation is likely, these dif-ferences make it clear that, to the extent that it is possible to modify the task characteristics, doing so may promote more cooperation.

Rules and Regulations

Perhaps the most effective way to reduce conflict, when the approach is pos-sible, is to change the rules of the situation itself, for instance, by enacting and enforcing rules, laws, or other sanctions to encourage cooperation and to pre-vent free riding (McCusker & Carnevale, 1995; Tyler & Lind, 1992). As one example, taxes or dues may be assessed so that each person is required to contribute a fair share to support the public good. Indeed, people form gov-ernments in part to make sure that all individuals in the community contrib-ute to public goods by paying appropriate taxes. Similarly, the employees of a corporation may be required to join a labor union in order to maintain their jobs. Leaders may be elected by the group to enforce the rules, because the group members perceive that doing so will benefit the group as a whole (Samuelson et al., 1984; Samuelson & Messick, 1986). Rules can also be imple-mented that regulate the amount of the public good that can be taken by an individual at any one time. For instance, in a water crisis, rationing can be implemented in which individuals can only use a certain amount of water each month, thereby protecting the supply for all.

Incentives

When it is not possible to change the rules and regulations, it may still be possible to change behavior by altering the incentives to cooperate or compete through changes in the nature of the payoff matrix. The task outcomes influ-ence the likelihood of conflict in several ways. For one, when there are plenty of outcomes available, there is less need for competition, and thus it is less likely overall. When resources are scarce, however, competition will likely be greater. So providing more goods, if possible, should reduce conflict. And of course whether competition or cooperation occurs will depend in large part on the task outcomes. For example, a class in which the instructor has decided ahead of time that only 10 percent of the students can get As will be likely to produce a competitive orientation among the students. On the other hand, if the instructor says that he or she would be quite happy to assign each student an A, assuming each individual deserves one, a more cooperative orientation is likely to ensue. In general, cooperation will increase when it is rewarded, and competition will increase when it is rewarded (Caldwell, 1976).

Privatization

Another approach to increasing optimal use of resources is to privatize them; that is, to divide up the public good into smaller pieces so that each individual is responsible for a small share, rather than trusting the good to the group as a whole (Cass & Edney, 1978; Samuelson & Messick, 1986; Komorita & Lapworth, 1982). In a study by Messick and McClelland (1983) using a resource game, individuals who were given their own private pool of resources to manage maintained them for an average of 31 trials of the game before they ran out. However, individuals who were managing pools in groups maintained their pools for only about 10 trials, and therefore gained much lower outcomes. In other experimental games, the outcomes are arranged in such a way that the participants are working either for themselves or for the joint outcomes of the group (Deutsch, 1949). These studies have found that when individuals have control over their own outcomes, rather than sharing the resources with others, they tend to use them more efficiently. Of course, many public goods (such as air, water, and highways) cannot be privatized, and thus this does not represent a solution in all cases. However, an approach that does work in these situations is for the individuals to elect a group representative or leader who can be trusted to work toward the group goal and place decisions about appropriate behavior in his or her hands. For instance, a township or city might elect a board of supervisors to make decisions about zoning in the region. Although this approach is not particularly popular overall, it may be resorted to when the individuals involved feel that the management of the resource pool is difficult, and it will, in many cases, increase the group's outcomes (Cross & Guyer, 1980; Hardin, 1968; Messick et al., 1983).

Expectations of Others' Behavior

In addition to the task characteristics, decisions about whether to cooperate or compete will be influenced by expectations about the likely behavior of others (Rapoport, 1987). Stereotypes and prejudice may contribute to these perceptions (De Dreu, Yzerbyt, & Leyens, 1995). One factor that tends to produce conflict is that, overall, individuals expect others to take competitive, rather than cooperative orientations (Sattler & Kerr, 1991; DeBruin & Van Lange, 1999), and once they see the behavior of others, they are likely to interpret that behavior as being competitive, even if it is not. In one study (Maki,

Thorngate, & McClintock, 1979) individuals viewed the decisions that had supposedly been made by other individuals who had participated in a prisoner's dilemma task. Their task was to predict the choice that the partner had supposedly made from the payoff matrix. However, the choices had actually been preselected, on the basis of a computer program, to take either competitive or cooperative orientations. Overall, across all of the decisions, the participants were more accurate at making their predictions for partners who made competitive choices than for those who made cooperative choices, indicating that they expected the partners to be competitive, and as a result tended to interpret their behaviors as being competitive.

In addition to a general tendency to think that others will act in a competitive manner, the ability to predict and know what others are going to do also influences the tendency to cooperate or compete. When individuals have a good idea of what others are doing, they are likely to match their responses to those of others. When the others are seen as cooperating, the individual is likely to as well. In other cases, for instance, when the group is very large, it is difficult for the individual to be aware of or keep track of the behavior of others, and because there is less certainty about the behavior of others, taking the defensive (competitive) choice is more likely.

Social Norms and Entitlement

One particularly strong determinant of cooperation or competition is the prior norms of the individuals in the group (Pruitt, 1998; Pruitt & Kimmel, 1977). If the group norm favors cooperation, then cooperation is likely to ensue; but if the norm favors competition, then competition will probably result. Furthermore, groups create a substantial number of norms that are designed to reduce and channel conflict. These range from laws about the appropriate use of public goods to norms for resolving conflict once it occurs.

Societal norms generally specify who is entitled to what, and this knowledge, if agreed upon by all of the group members, can prevent competition and hostility. Of course, these norms also provide a relatively stable status and power hierarchy and do not generally specify that each person gets an equal amount. As a result, in almost every group some people get more than others. Yet, as we have seen in Chapter 11, the norms of the group may be so well established that most people, including those who are low in status or power, feel that the norms are appropriate and may accept their own lower outcomes without complaint or conflict. When social norms about the appropriate distribution of resources are weak, on the other hand, the potential for competition is higher.

In other cases the society may attempt to create or uphold social norms through appeals to appropriate social values. Lectures and sermons on "social responsibility" have been found to increase cooperation. Sattler and Kerr (1991) found that getting messages from others stressing the importance of cooperation can increase cooperative behavior, particularly for individuals who were already motivated to be cooperative and when the partner actually played cooperatively.

Group Size

There is a general tendency for cooperation to be less likely in larger groups than in smaller groups and for larger groups to make less efficient use of resources (Kerr & Bruun, 1983; Messick & McClelland, 1983). Again, the relationship between group size and cooperation is well defined by the principle of social impact, such that cooperation decreases as group size increases up to about four members, but adding new members beyond that point has little effect (Komorita & Parks, 1994). One explanation for the difficulties of larger groups is that as the number of group members increases, each person's contribution becomes less identifiable, which is likely to increase free riding. Furthermore, people feel that they can make less of a difference in the outcome of larger groups—that is, they feel dispensable—and so they are less likely to work toward the common group goals, even if their input is actually not less important or less likely to have an influence on the outcome (Kerr, 1989; Rapoport, 1988). Larger groups also lead people to feel more deindividuated, which may prevent them from conforming to group norms of cooperation. And in large groups there is likely to be more difficulty coordinating the efforts of the individuals, and this may reduce cooperation. For instance, in a study by Kelley, Condry, Dahlke, and Hill (1965) in which participants had to coordinate their efforts in a type of crisis situation in which only one person could "escape" from a situation at a time, larger groups had more difficulty coordinating their activities and tended to perform more poorly.

Communication

When communication between the parties involved in a conflict is nonexistent, or when it is hostile or negative in tone, disagreements frequently result in escalation of negative feelings and behaviors. In other cases, when communication is more open and positive, the parties in potential conflict are more likely to be able to deal with each other effectively, with a result that produces compromise and cooperation (Allison, Messick, & Samuelson, 1985; Brechner, 1977; Orbell, Van de Kragt, & Dawes, 1988).

Advantages of Communication

Communication has a number of benefits that improve the likelihood of cooperation. For one thing, communication allows individuals to tell others how they are planning to behave and what they are currently contributing to the group effort, which helps the group learn about the motives and behaviors of the others and to develop norms for cooperation (Bixentine, Levitte, & Wilson, 1966; Fox & Guyer, 1978). Communication has a positive effect because it increases the expectation that the others will act cooperatively and also reduces the potential of being a "sucker" to the free riding of others. Thus, communication allows the parties to develop a sense of *trust* (Messick & Brewer, 1983; Pruitt & Kimmel, 1977). Once cooperative norms are in place, they can improve the possibilities for long-term cooperation, because they produce a public commitment on the part of the parties to cooperate as well as an internalized obligation to honor those commitments. In fact, Norbert Kerr and his colleagues (Kerr, Garst, Lewandowski, & Harris, 1997; Kerr & Kaufman-Gilliland, 1994) have found that group discussion commits group members to act cooperatively to such an extent that it is not necessary to monitor their behavior—they will continue to cooperate because of a private, internalized commitment to it.

Communication can also allow planning and therefore help the group members better coordinate their efforts. For instance, in a resource dilemma game, discussion allows the group to monitor their withdrawals from the public good so that the pool is not depleted (Liebrand, 1984). And if only a certain number of individuals need to contribute in a contributions dilemma in order for the public good to be maintained, communication may allow the group members to set up a system that assures that this many, but not more, contribute in any given session.

Finally, communication may also help people realize the advantages, over the long term, of cooperating. If, as a result of communication, the individuals learn that the others are actually behaving cooperatively (something that might not have been apparent given prior misperceptions), this might increase one's own motivation to cooperate. Alternatively, learning that others are behaving competitively and thus threatening the resources may help make it clear to all of the parties that increased cooperation is essential (Jorgenson & Papciak, 1981; Messick & McClelland, 1983).

Communication is particularly effective in leading to integrative outcomes when the parties are able to discuss all of the relevant issues at the same time, rather than moving sequentially through them during the discussion. When all of the issues are put on the table at the beginning of the discussion it becomes more likely that each side will be able to see the relative importance of each issue for each side, leading to an increased likelihood of making deeper concessions on relatively unimportant issues (Weingart, Bennett, & Brett, 1993; Mannix, Thompson, & Bazerman, 2000).

Reducing Misperceptions

Perhaps the most important benefit of communication is the potential of learning that the goals of the parties involved in the conflict are not always incompatible (L. L. Thompson & Hrebec, 1996; L. L. Thompson, 1991). A major barrier to increasing cooperation is that individuals expect that situations are arranged so that they are fixed-sum and that other parties will act competitively to attempt to gain a greater share of the outcomes. Neither of these assumptions is necessarily true, however, and thus one potential benefit of communication is that the parties come to see the situation more accurately.

One example of a situation in which communication was successful is the meeting held at Camp David, Maryland, in 1978 between the delegates of Egypt and Israel. Both sides sat down together with President Jimmy Carter to attempt to reach an accord over the fate of the Sinai Peninsula, which Israel had occupied for many years. Initially, neither side would budge, and attempts to divide the land in half were opposed by both sides. It appeared that there was a fixed-sum situation in which land was the important factor, and neither wanted to give it up. In the course of the discussion, communication prevailed. It became clear that what Egypt really wanted out of the deal was sovereignty over lands that were perceived as historically part of Egypt. On the other hand, what Israel valued most was security. The outcome of the discussion was that Israel eventually agreed to return the land to Egypt in exchange for a demilitarized zone and the establishment of new air bases. Despite the initial perceptions, the situation turned out to be integrative, rather than fixed-sum, and both sides were able to get what they wanted.

Laboratory studies have also demonstrated the benefits of communication. In her research, Leigh Thompson (1991) found that groups in negotiation did not always effectively communicate, but those that did were better able to reach compromises that benefited both parties. Although the parties came to the interaction expecting a fixed-sum situation, communication allowed them to learn that the situation was actually integrative—the parties had different needs that allowed them to achieve a mutually beneficial solution. Interestingly, Thompson found that it did not matter whether both parties involved in the dispute were instructed to communicate or whether the communication came in the form of questions from only one of the two sides. In both cases the parties who communicated viewed the other's perspectives more accurately, and the result was better outcomes. Communication will not improve cooperation, however, if it is based on communicating hostility rather than working toward cooperation. In studies in which individuals played the trucking game, for instance, the communication was generally in the form of threats, and it did not reduce conflict (Deutsch, 1973; McClintock, Stech, & Keil, 1983).

Individual Differences

Although we have to this point focused on how group process variables influence the likelihood of cooperation, the characteristics of the individuals involved in the situation also play at least some role (De Dreu & McCusker, 1997). Two methods of characterizing individuals have been found to be useful in predicting their behavior—the social value orientation approach, and the dual-concerns approach.

Social Value Orientations

Paul Van Lange and his colleagues (De Dreu & Van Lange, 1995; Van Lange & Liebrand, 1991; Van Lange & Kuhlman, 1994) have found that it is possible to characterize individuals on the basis of their *social value orientations*—personality variables that lead them to tend to respond differently in social dilemmas. About half of the individuals they studied were classified as *prosocials*. Prosocials value cooperation and producing positive joint outcomes that maximize the gains of all parties, and thus they are likely to make cooperative choices. Another quarter were *individualists*, who tend to behave in a manner that enhances their own outcomes, whereas the last quarter were *competitors*, who are more mistrustful and act to gain a relative advantage over others by making competitive choices.

The Dual-Concern Approach

Although the social value orientation approach assumes that individuals vary in terms of their own desires to cooperate, a somewhat more complicated assumption is that individuals may vary both in terms of the extent of their concern for gaining their own individual interests and in terms of the extent of their concerns for meeting the goals of the other party or parties. The *dual-concern* model (Blake & Mouton, 1964; Pruitt & Rubin, 1986) is based on this approach, and the four resulting personality types are outlined in Figure 12.4. The dual-concern model suggests that individuals will relate to social dilemmas, or other forms of conflict, in different ways, depending upon their underlying personal orientations or as influenced by the characteristics of the situation that orient them toward a given concern. Individuals who are fo-

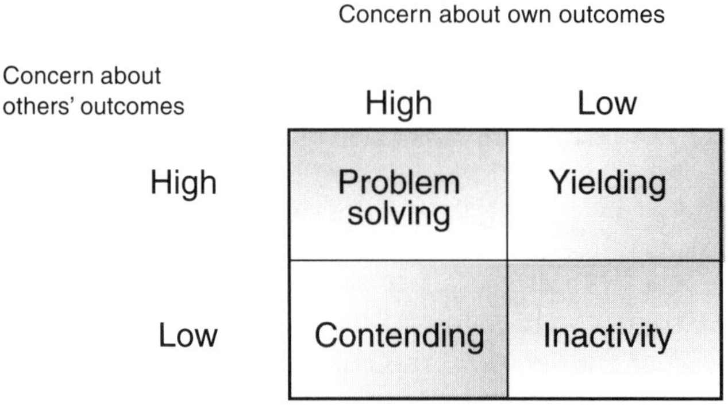

Concern about own outcomes

Concern about
others' outcomes

	High	Low
High	Problem solving	Yielding
Low	Contending	Inactivity

FIGURE 12.4. The dual-concern model. The dual-concern model of Pruitt and Rubin (1986) argues that each individual has one of four personality styles, and that these styles predict how they will relate to group conflict. Those who are *contending* focus on their own outcomes but do not care about the goals of others. Those who are *yielding* are focused primarily on others' outcomes. *Problem-solving* individuals take into consideration both their own goals and the goals of others, whereas *inactive* individuals are not concerned about the interests of either the self or others.

cused primarily on their own outcomes but who do not care about the goals of others are considered to be *contending* in orientation. These individuals are expected to try to take advantage of the other party, for instance, by withholding their contributions in social dilemmas. Those who are focused primarily on the others' outcomes, however, will be *yielding* and likely to make cooperative choices. Individuals who are not concerned about either the interests of the self or others are *inactive* and unlikely to care about the situation or to participate in solving it at all.

The interesting prediction of the dual-concern model is that being concerned with one's own outcomes is not necessarily harmful to the possibility of cooperation. Indeed, individuals who are focused on maximizing their own outcomes, but who are also concerned with the needs of the others, are expected to be as likely to cooperate as are those who are yielding. In fact, the dual-concern model suggests that these *problem-solving* individuals may be the most likely to succeed because they are most likely to go beyond the trap posed by the dilemma itself, searching for ways to produce new and creative solutions through integrative thinking, negotiation, and compromise (van Dijk & Wilke, 2000).

Strategies for Producing Cooperation

Individuals who are faced with situations in which conflict is occurring or has the potential to develop must create techniques to deal with it. There are a number of general responses that might be used, including withdrawing from the conflict entirely, direct competition (that is, attempting to impose one's preferred solution on the other party), or direct cooperation (lowering one's own aspirations, giving in, and settling for less than one hoped for). In most cases, however, the parties attempt to come to some sort of an agreeable compromise.

One difficulty that frequently occurs in conflict situations is that the parties involved each realize the potential costs of continuing to behave competitively, and yet they may not be sure about whether to cooperate or compete at any given time. A party that always competes will likely elicit competition from the other, whereas if he or she decides to cooperate, then the other side may take advantage of this behavior.

The Tit-for-Tat Strategy

In social dilemma games that are run over a number of trials, various strategies can be used by the parties involved. In games in which the decisions are binary—that is, the individual must either cooperate or compete—there is one simple strategy that seems to be the most successful, in the sense that it produces the most cooperative behavior by the parties taken together. The simple strategy that has been found to be effective in such situations is known as the **tit-for-tat strategy.** When using the tit-for-tat strategy the individual initially makes a cooperative choice and then waits for a given period of time to see what the other individual or individuals do. If it turns out that they also make a cooperative choice (or if most of them do), then the individual will again make a cooperative choice. On the other hand, if the other group members compete, then the individual again matches this behavior by competing. This process continues so that the individual always does what the others have done on the trial before.

Computers have been used to simulate the behavior of individuals who use the tit-for-tat strategy over a series of interactions, in comparison to other approaches for determining whether to cooperate or compete on each trial. The tit-for-tat strategy has been found to work better than straight cooperation or other types of strategies in producing cooperation among the parties (Komorita & Parks, 1994; Oskamp, 1971; Sheldon, 1999).

The tit-for-tat strategy seems to be so effective because, first, it is "nice" in the sense that the individual first cooperates and signals a willingness to cooperate. Second, the strategy seems to be successful because, since it is relatively simple and easy to understand, others can clearly see how the choices are being determined. Furthermore, the approach sends a clear message that competitive choices on the part of the other will not be tolerated and that cooperation will always be reciprocated. The other party cannot take advantage of a person who is using tit-for-tat on more than one trial because if they try to do

Tit-for-Tat Strategy: A method of responding in a social dilemma in which the party begins with a cooperative response and then matches his or her responses to those that are given by the other party.

so, the result will always be retaliation in the form of a competitive choice on the next trial. Indeed, it has been found that having people play against a partner who uses the tit-for-tat strategy can help them learn to be more cooperative (Sheldon, 1999), particularly once they become aware what the strategy is and how it is being used.

Despite the fact that it generally works better than most other strategies, tit-for-tat is not perfect. One problem that arises is that, because people are more likely to behave competitively than cooperatively, and so tit-for-tat is more likely to lead opponents to match competitive responses than to follow cooperation with cooperation. Thus tit-for-tat may in some cases produce a spiral of conflict (Kelley & Stahelski, 1970). This is particularly likely if the opposing party never makes a cooperative choice, and thus the party using tit-for-tat never gets a chance to play cooperatively after the first round. The same is true in cases in which there is some noise in the system and the responses given by the parties are not always perceived accurately. Variations of the tit-for-tat strategy in which the individual acts more cooperatively than demanded by the strategy (for instance, by giving some extra cooperative trials in the beginning or by being extra cooperative on other trials) have been found to be helpful in this regard, although they do allow the opponent to exploit the side who is playing tit-for-tat.

Negotiation

Negotiation is the process by which two or more parties attempt to resolve a perceived divergence of interest in order to avoid or reduce social conflict (Gelfand & Brett, 2003; Carnevale & Pruitt, 1992; Bazerman, Curhan, Moore, & Valley, 2000). The parties involved are often social groups, such as businesses or nations, although the groups may rely on one or a few representatives who actually do the negotiating. When negotiating, the parties who are in disagreement develop a formal set of communications in which they discuss their respective positions and attempt to develop a compromise agreement. To reach this agreement each side makes a series of offers, followed by counteroffers from the other side, each time hopefully moving closer to a position that they can each agree on (Pruitt & Carnevale, 1993; Thompson, 1990). Negotiation is successful if each of the parties finds that they have more to gain by remaining in the relationship or completing the transaction, even if they cannot get exactly what they want, than they would gain if they left the relationship entirely or continued the existing competitive state.

In some cases negotiation is a type of fixed-sum process in which each individual wants to get as much as they can of the same good or commodity. For instance, in the sale of a property, if the seller wants the highest price possible and the buyer wants the lowest price possible, the compromise will

Negotiation: A process in which two or more parties attempt to resolve a perceived divergence of interest in order to avoid or resolve social conflict.

involve some sacrifice for each, or else it will not occur at all (if the two parties cannot find a price on which they can agree). More often, the outcome of the negotiation is dependent upon the ability of the two parties to effectively communicate and to dispel negative misperceptions about the goals of the other party. When communication occurs and trust is obtained, the parties may find that the situation is not completely fixed sum but rather more integrative. The seller and buyer, for instance, may be able to find an acceptable solution that is based on other aspects of the deal, such as the time that the deal is made, the inclusion of a home warranty, or other costs and benefits involved. In fact, negotiators who maintain the assumption that the conflict is fixed-sum end up with lower individual and joint gain when compared to negotiators who change their perceptions to be more integrative (Thompson, 1991).

Negotiation is often accompanied by conflict, including threats and harassment of the other party or parties. In general, individuals who are firm in their positions will achieve more positive outcomes as a result of negotiation, unless both sides are too firm and no compromise can be reached. However, positive and cooperative communication is an important factor in improving negotiation. Individuals who truthfully represent their needs and goals with the other party will produce better outcomes for both parties, in part because they become more aware of each other's needs and are better able to empathize with them. Parties that are in negotiation should therefore be encouraged to communicate (Thompson, 1991).

Third-Party Intervention

In some serious cases of disagreement, the parties involved in the negotiation decide that they must bring in outside help, in the form of a third party, to help them reach an equitable solution or to prevent further conflict. The third party may be called upon by the parties who are in disagreement, their use may be required by laws, or in some cases a third party may rather spontaneously appear (as when a friend or coworker steps in to help solve a dispute). The goal of the third party is to help those who are in conflict to reach agreement without embarrassment to either party. In general, third-party intervention works better if it is implemented before the conflict is too great. If the level of conflict is already high, the attempts to help may increase hostility, and the disputants may not consent to third-party intervention.

Mediation

Mediation involves helping to create compromise by using third-party negotiation (Wall & Lynn, 1993). A mediator is a third party who is knowledgeable about the dispute and skilled at resolving conflict. During the mediation the

Mediation: An attempt to reach compromise by using third-party negotiation.

conflicting parties usually state the facts from their own perspective, which allows the mediator to determine each party's interests and positions.

Mediators have a number of potential tactics that they can use, and they choose those that seem best depending upon the current state of affairs (Carnevale, 1986; Pruitt, Whelton, Fry, McGillicuddy, Castrianno, & Zubeck, 1989). These tactics include attempting to help the parties have more trust in each other, conferring with each of the parties separately, and helping them to accept the necessity of compromise. Through these tactics the mediator may be able to reduce overt hostility and increase understanding of the others' positions, which may lead to more integrative solutions. If necessary, the mediator may attempt to force the parties to make concessions, especially if there is little common ground to begin with. Mediation works best when both parties believe that a compromise is possible and think that third-party intervention can help reach it. Mediators who have experience and training make better mediators (Deutsch, 1994).

Arbitration

Arbitration is a type of third-party intervention that avoids negotiation as well as the necessity of any meetings between the parties in conflict. In the most common type of arbitration—*binding arbitration*—both sides agree ahead of time to abide by the decision of the third party (the arbitrator). They then independently submit their offers or desires along with the basis for their claims, and the arbitrator chooses between them. Whichever offer is chosen becomes the outcome, and there is no negotiation (Heuer & Penrod, 1986; Pruitt & Carnevale, 1993). Arbitration is particularly useful when there is a single decision to be made under time constraints, whereas negotiation may be better if the parties have a long-term possibility for conflict and future discussion is necessary (Lewicki & Sheppard, 1985).

 Chapter Summary

Arbitration: A type of third-party intervention in which sides agree ahead of time to abide by the decision of the third party (the arbitrator).

One common outcome of relationships among individuals in groups is conflict over the rewards that the group provides—the group members must determine how to use and share the group benefits. In some cases the conflict involves the distribution of public goods, and these distributions frequently result in social dilemmas, in which the interests of the individual group members conflict with the interests of the group as a whole. Two types of social dilemmas are harvesting dilemmas and contributions dilemmas. Groups may respond to these dilemmas using either cooperation or competition.

The behavior of individuals in conflict situations has frequently been studied using laboratory games in which the conflict is simulated. In matrix games such as the the prisoner's dilemma the rewards to be gained for making a cooperative or a competitive choice are displayed in a payoff matrix. The matrix is arranged so that making a competitive choice is most beneficial for each individual considered alone and yet if the players each make a competitive choice, they will each lose. Other types of laboratory games include resource dilemma games and the trucking game.

Whether individuals cooperate or compete is determined by the characteristics of the task, including the rules and regulations, as well as the payoff or incentives. Privatizing the resource can often increase cooperation. The individual's perceptions of the task, the expectations about the likely behavior of the other parties, and the relevant social norms are also important in determining whether competition or cooperation will result. Cooperation is more likely when appropriate norms are available and the parties feel that the distributions are equitable. Communication generally improves the likelihood for cooperation because it reduces negative misperceptions and fosters trust as well as the ability to plan coordinated action.

Individual differences, including social value orientations and dual concerns, influence the likelihood of competition and cooperation. The tit-for-tat strategy is the most effective way to produce cooperation in games that require a series of choices. In some cases conflicts are resolved through negotiation or through the use of third-party mediators or arbitrators.

 Review and Discussion Questions

1. What are competition and cooperation, and how do they result in social dilemmas? Consider some groups that you have belonged to that were primarily cooperative or primarily competitive.
2. What are harvesting dilemmas and contributions dilemmas? Give an example of each, other than those mentioned in the chapter.
3. What laboratory games have been used to experimentally study conflict and cooperation between social groups? What are the advantages and disadvantages of gaming approaches?
4. Consider a social dilemma that you or another might be involved in and indicate how you might be able to promote cooperative rather than competitive behaviors within it.
5. Why does communication promote cooperation?
6. What are negotiation, mediation, and arbitration and how are they used to reduce conflict?

Recommended Readings

How to successfully use negotiation and meditaion:
Carnevale, P. J., & Pruitt, D. (1992). Negotiation and mediation. *Annual Review of Psychology, 43*, 531–582.

A recent review of the literature on cooperation and conflict among individuals and groups:
Pruitt, D. G. (1998). Social conflict. In D. Gilbert & S. T. Fiske & G. Lindzey (Eds.), *Handbook of Social Psychology* (4th ed., pp. 470–503). New York: McGraw-Hill.

A theory that helps explain when individuals feel that they are being treated fairly or unfairly in their groups:
Tyler, T., & Lind, E. (1992). A relational model of authority in groups. *Advances in Experimental Social Psychology, 25*, 115–191.

Cooperation and Conflict Between Groups 13

▷ *Contents at a Glance*

*I*n chapter 12 we considered the causes and outcomes of conflict among the individuals within groups as well as the potential conflict that can occur between individuals and the groups that they belong to. In this chapter we turn to the conflict that occurs between groups, with a particular focus on the potential conflicts among the members of different social categories. Although in many cases these issues involve relatively minor misunderstandings, in other cases the interactions are much more negative. Unfortunately, intergroup conflict is so frequently observed that it seems to be a basic part of the everyday life of social groups. As a result, it has been studied for many years by many researchers in many different fields (Brewer & Campbell, 1976; Deutsch, 1949;

Sedikides, Schopler, & Insko, 1998; Sherif, Harvey, White, Hood, & Sherif, 1961; Tajfel, 1982; D. M. Taylor & Moghaddam, 1987).

As we have seen in chapter 12, conflict occurs when there is more than one individual or more than one group attempting to reach incompatible goals and it is feared that not all parties will be able to realize their goal. Misperceptions about the characteristics and goals of the other individuals or groups intensify the tension and hostility of the situation and escalate the conflict. Thus, intergroup conflict results in part from the desires of groups and their members to gain positive outcomes for themselves, but is frequently reinforced by misperceptions about the characteristics and goals of the other group or groups. These misperceptions may take the form of stereotypes and prejudices, and the eventual outcome only too often is discrimination or even outright hostility or violence. The types of conflicts that can occur between groups range from disagreements about beliefs and values among the students from different cultures in a school to differential treatment of people from different ethnic groups in a business to wars between nations for land or natural resources and even to genocide, as practiced in Nazi Germany in the 1940s and in Yugoslavia in the 1990s in which the members of one group attempt to kill all of the members of another group. In extreme cases the individuals from one group may deindividuate members of the other group, such that they do not even consider them human beings (Bar-Tal, 1990; Staub, 1989). When such **dehumanization** occurs, the potential for hostility and violence is clear.

Objective and Perceived Conflict

Intergroup competition, conflict, and hostility occur in part because of real competition between groups, but they are also fueled through misperceptions of the true goals and characteristics of the other group or groups as well as through the desire, on the part of group members, to gain a positive social identity.

Realistic Conflict

Dehumanization: The tendency to deindividuate and devalue out-group members so that they are no longer seen as human beings.

One determinant of intergroup conflict is the desire on the part of group members to gain positive outcomes for themselves and for their group. Because relationships with other groups are (or are at least perceived as being) competitive, this goal is frequently combined with a secondary goal of preventing the other group from being able to gain the rewards for itself. When groups are in competition for objectively scarce resources, as when members of different ethnic groups are each attempting to find employment in the same factory in a city, or when two sports teams are vying for a league championship, we say that the situation involves **realistic group conflict** (Brewer & Campbell, 1976; R. A. Levine & Campbell, 1972). Conflict may result under such conditions because it is easy (and accurate) to blame the difficulties of one's own group on the competition produced by the other group or groups.

The Robber's Cave Study

In one of the best-known of all social psychological studies, Muzafer Sherif and his colleagues (1961) studied the group behavior of 11-year-old boys at a summer camp. Although the boys did not know it, the researchers carefully observed the behaviors of the children during the camp session with the goal of learning how group conflict developed and how it might be resolved among the children.

During the first week of the camp the boys were divided into two groups who camped at two different campsites. During this time friendly relationships developed among the boys within each of the two groups. Each group developed its own social norms and group structure and became quite cohesive, with a strong positive social identity. The two groups chose names for themselves (the Rattlers and the Eagles), and each made its own group flag and participated in separate camp activities.

At the end of this one-week baseline period, it was arranged that the two groups of boys would become aware of each other's presence. Furthermore, the researchers helped to create competition between the groups by arranging baseball games, a tug-of-war, and a treasure hunt and offered prizes for the group that won the competitions. Almost immediately, this competition between the two groups produced negative perceptions on the part of each group about the other group, and overt hostility quickly followed. By the end of the second week, the Eagles had snuck up to the Rattlers' cabin and stolen their flag. When the Rattlers discovered the theft, they in turn raided the Eagles' cabin, stealing things. There were food fights in the dining room, which was now shared by the groups, and the researchers documented a substantial increase in name-calling, prejudice, and stereotypes of the out-group. These feelings transferred into overt hostility—fistfights even erupted between some members of the different groups.

The heightened intergroup contact also changed the social structure within the groups. The two groups developed even greater cohesion and social identity, and the leadership structure was found to change within each of the groups. The children who were the most hostile to the out-group became the new leaders.

Realistic Group Conflict: The competition for objectively scarce resources that can occur between social groups.

Superordinate Goals

Eventually, the researchers had to intervene to prevent serious injuries to the campers. They began this third stage of the research by setting up a series of situations in which the boys had to work together to solve a problem. These situations were designed to present the boys with *superordinate goals*—goals that were both very important to them and yet required the cooperative efforts and resources of both the Eagles and the Rattlers to attain. These goals involved such things as the need to pool money across both groups in order to rent a movie that all of the campers wanted to view, or the need to pull together on ropes to get a food truck that had (supposedly) become stuck back onto the road. As the children worked together to meet these goals the negative perceptions of the group members gradually improved; there was at least some reduction of hostility between the groups and some emergence of more positive intergroup attitudes.

Perceived Conflict and Misperceptions

Although intergroup conflict such as that created in the summer camp frequently begins with some form of realistic conflict, the extent of competition and perceptions about the level of hostility desired by other group are frequently exaggerated. The initial conflict between the Rattlers and the Eagles was clearly the result of realistic competition for prizes and awards, but the campers also overreacted to the nature of the conflict. Their hostility was not in proportion to the magnitude of the actual conflict. It was a large camp, there was plenty of space and facilities, and it would have easily been possible for the two groups to share them cooperatively. There were also plenty of competitions offered to the groups, and thus each group could have won some prizes. Indeed, the prizes were only available because the presence of the other group allowed the competitions to occur. In short, in the summer camp the small perceptions of injustice or unfairness eventually escalated into larger ones, and once the negative perceptions of the out-group developed, it was very difficult to turn them back.

   Although misperceptions can occur between many different types of groups, they are perhaps most dangerous when they occur between nations, where a potential outcome is military action. The perennial Arab-Israeli conflict in the Mideast represents a classic example of this problem. At this point both sides perceive that the other side was the initial aggressor, and thus each side blames the other both for beginning the hostilities and also for perpetuating them. Thus there is a continuing tit-for-tat exchange in which both sides continue to reciprocate each other's aggressive behavior. Similar negative perceptions occurred between the Soviet Union and the United States during the years of the cold war.

Intergroup conflict is exaggerated in part as a result of in-group favoritism—the general tendency to favor our own group over others. As we have seen in chapter 5, when a member of the in-group performs a favorable behavior, this behavior is likely to be seen as representing stable, internal characteristics of the group as a whole. Similarly, negative behaviors on the part of the out-group are seen as caused by stable negative group characteristics. On the other hand, negative behaviors from the in-group and positive behaviors from the out-group are more likely to be seen as caused by temporary situational variables or by behaviors of specific individuals and are less likely to be attributed to the group. This general tendency, known as the **ultimate attribution error** results in the tendency for each of the competing groups to perceive the other extremely, and unrealistically, negatively (Hewstone, 1990; Pettigrew, 1979).

The Individual-Group Discontinuity

One of the most basic predictions about social groups (and particularly large groups) is that their members can become deindividuated, that deindividuation can result in the loss of adherence to social norms, and that this can result in negative group behaviors, including hostility and violence. Although we have seen in chapter 11 that deindividuation does not always produce negative behaviors on the part of group members, there is nevertheless substantial evidence that groups are more likely than individuals to perceive opponents as competitive and to behave competitively toward them (Insko, Pinkley, Hoyle, Dalton, Hong, Slim et al., 1987; Insko, Shopler, Hoyle, Dardis, & Graetz, 1990; Schopler, Insko, & Drigotas, 1993; Wildschut, Lodewijkx, & Insko, 2001). The tendency for groups to act more competitively than individuals is known as the **individual-group discontinuity**, and it has been found to occur for a wide variety of groups.

In one demonstration of this effect, Chester Insko and his colleagues (Insko et al., 1987) had research participants play 10 trials of a prisoner's dilemma game. The opponents sat in separate rooms to study the matrices and make their decisions, but then on each trial they went to meet each other in a common room where they indicated their cooperative or competitive choices. In one of the experimental conditions two individuals played against each other, whereas in another condition two groups of three individuals played against each other. Finally, in still another condition the players in the game were again two groups of three individuals, but the groups communicated their decisions by sending a single representative to play the game with a single representative from the other group. The representative reported back to the group about the outcomes of the game, and the group decided what to do on the next round.

Ultimate Attribution Error: The tendency to see positive behaviors of in-groups and negative behaviors of out-groups as representing stable internal characteristics of the group as a whole, while viewing positive behaviors of out-groups and negative behaviors of in-groups as caused by temporary, situational pressures or by behaviors of specific individuals.

Individual-Group Discontinuity: The tendency for groups to act more competitively than individuals.

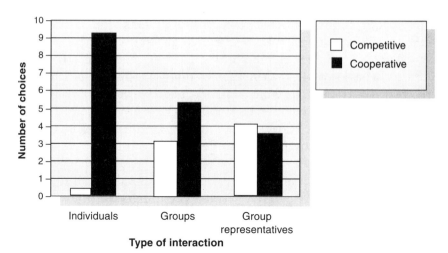

FIGURE 13.1. The individual-group discontinuity. Participants played a prisoner's dilemma game either as individuals, in groups, or in groups in which only one representative was sent to meet the other. Data is from Insko, C. A., Pinkley, R. L., Hoyle, R. H., Dalton, B., Hong, G., Slim, R. M., et al. (1987). Individual versus group discontinuity: The role of intergroup contact. *Journal of Experimental Social Psychology, 23,* 250–267.

As shown in Figure 13.1, the individual-group discontinuity occurred, such that although the individual players rarely chose to play competitively, the groups frequently did. And the groups also played more competitively than individuals even when the contact between the groups was only in the form of the individual representatives. In fact, although we might have expected that this latter situation would be more similar to the individual encounters, the condition in which the group representatives played for the groups actually produced the most competition. It appears that the group representatives felt pressure to uphold the competitive norms that the group had decided on in its prior deliberations (Pruitt & Lewis, 1975; Tjosvold & Deemer, 1980)

There are several reasons why groups tend to be more competitive than individuals. For one, people expect that groups will act competitively (Kramer & Messick, 1998; Hoyle, Pinkley, & Insko, 1989). As a result, when people know that they are competing against a group, they generally focus on the potential costs of cooperation, including their perceptions that the group will probably not cooperate in return, and the potential benefits of competition (that they may be able to take advantage of the other group). Furthermore, the individual group members are able to convince themselves that agreeing to act competitively is important because it demonstrates a positive in-group identity. There may also be a tendency for the group members to feel that they must behave competitively in order to prevent the other individual group members from being taken advantage of (an altruistic behavior, in a way), and competition may also occur at least in part as a result of deindividualization and diffusion of responsibility within the group.

Escalating Conflicts as a Result of Misperceptions

Although a common outcome of group hostility is the tit-for-tat exchange of aggressive behaviors, the situation can frequently be even worse, such that hostile behaviors on the part of one group are responded to with even more hostile responses on the part of the competing group. When the Rattlers stole the flag from the Eagle's cabin, the Eagles did not respond merely by stealing a flag in return, but rather replied with even more hostile and negative behaviors. It was as if "getting even" was not enough—an even greater retaliation was called for. In experimental research it has been found that although people tend to match their level of cooperation or competition to that of their partners, they are particularly concerned about matching any competition from the other with equal or greater levels of competition on their own part (Schlenker & Goldman, 1978; Mikolic, Parker, & Pruitt, 1997). Thus the magnitude of intergroup violence often increases over time. As the conflict continues, each group perceives the other group more negatively, and these perceptions make it more difficult for the escalating conflict to be reversed.

This escalation in negative perceptions between groups in conflict occurs in part because conflict makes the groups become even more cohesive and leads the group members to develop increasingly powerful social identities (Dion, 1973). These increases in identity are frequently accompanied by the development of even more hostile group norms, supported by the group members and their leaders, that sanction or encourage even more negative behaviors toward the out-group. Conflict also leads to the tendency to stereotype the out-group, increases perceptions of out-groups as homogeneous, and potentially even produces dehumanization of the out-group. The group conflict also reduces the amount of interaction among members of the competing groups, which makes it more difficult to change negative perceptions. The unfortunate outcome of such misperceptions is that initially small conflicts may become increasingly hostile until they get out of control. Duels to the death have been fought over small insults, and world wars have begun with relatively small encroachments.

Potential Benefits of Competition

Although intergroup relationships that involve hostility or violence are obviously to be avoided, it is worth pointing out again that not all intergroup competition or conflict is negative or problematic. Indeed, the Darwinian hypothesis, based on the idea of the "survival of the fittest," proposes that evolutionary progress occurs precisely because of the continued conflict among individuals within species and between different species as competing social groups. Over time, this competition, rather than being entirely harmful, increases diversity and the ability to adapt to changing environments. Competition between social groups may also lead to upward social comparison, which can lead both groups to set higher standards and motivate them to greater achievement. This might occur, for instance, when one corporation attempts to gain market share over another corporation or a sports team practices to improve so that it can beat a better team.

Also, conflict can sometimes have positive outcomes for each individual group. Conflict produces increases in cohesion and social identity within each of the competing groups (Dion, 1973; R. A. Levine & Campbell, 1972; Wilson & Miller, 1961; Worchel, Lind, & Kaufman, 1975). For instance, in the summer camp study, Sherif noted that the members of the Rattlers and the Eagles each developed greater liking for each other and greater group identity as the competition between the two groups increased. In situations in which a group is facing the threat of war from another group, the resulting group cohesion can be useful in combating the threat by mobilizing the group members to work effectively together and to make sacrifices for the group. However, extreme threat to the group may have the opposite effect—leading the individuals to look toward their own interests rather than those of the group—if it does not seem that group action is going to be successful.

Persistence and Change of Negative Attitudes

As we have seen in chapter 5, one of the reasons that it is so difficult to change negative perceptions of other social groups is that stereotypes and prejudice operate so strongly to maintain themselves. People tend to seek out and remember information that supports their stereotypes, and self-fulfilling prophecies operate in a way that actually makes negative beliefs come true. Because these negative beliefs fuel intergroup conflict, this presents a potential problem for improving intergroup relations. However, although some research has confirmed the tendency for group relations to remain stable over time in the real world, other findings suggest that these negative beliefs can and do change.

In one study documenting the persistence of negative beliefs, Mark Schaller and his colleagues (2002) found that the correlation between the ratings in 1922 and the ratings in 1998 of the stereotypes of a number of ethnic groups was over .80, indicating that there was virtually no change in these perceptions over these years. However, according to the principles of realistic group conflict, intergroup perceptions should change if the threat posed by the competing group or groups also changes (Brewer & Campbell, 1976; R. A. Levine & Campbell, 1972). Supporting this idea, Karlins, Coffman, and Walters

(1969) found that the most common stereotypes of Japanese held by Americans changed from "intelligent" in 1933 (before World War II) to "industrious" in 1967, at which time the Japanese were perceived as creating an economic threat to the United States. These changes in stereotype content seem to match the type of threat posed by the group, as one would expect according to realistic group conflict theory.

Current research in the United States has also found some changes in stereotyping and prejudice over time, even though these changes are frequently slow moving. In general, attitudes are changing to be more positive, tolerant, and accepting. Negative stereotyping of blacks and Latinos by whites has declined, and whites' acceptance of minority group members across a range of social settings is at an all-time high (J. Davis & Smith, 1996; Schuman, Steeh, Bobo, & Krysan, 1997). In 1958 most U.S. whites said they would *not* be willing to vote for a well-qualified black candidate for president, but in 1994 over 90 percent said they would (J. Davis & Smith, 1996). On the other hand, there are still large gaps between blacks and whites in social, economic, and personal well-being. Minorities are increasingly underrepresented in industry, education, and governmental jobs in terms of status, power, and financial rewards (J. M. Jones, 1996).

Reducing Intergroup Conflict

Taken together, then, intergroup conflict and negative intergroup perceptions remain relatively stable over time, and are therefore difficult, but not impossible, to change. This is because social categorization is a basic human process, and the result of categorization is often negative intergroup perceptions. These factors make it clear that it will be difficult to prevent conflicts between groups from occurring and to change their course once they get started. However, a number of techniques for making negative intergroup attitudes more positive and for reducing intergroup conflict have been proposed, and at least some of them have been found to be effective.

Individuating Others

Perhaps the most straightforward approach to reducing intergroup conflict is to get people to consider each other more as individuals and less as members of social categories (Brewer & Miller, 1984; S. T. Fiske & Neuberg, 1990). If we could treat people as unique individuals (for instance, treating me as Charles Stangor) and ignore their social category memberships (that I'm a male, older than 50, and a college professor), then our judgments of others would be more fair. Individuating others should be fairer than categorizing them, not only because the stereotypes that are held about the other group may be inaccurate, but also because individuating others reduces our reliance on stereotypes even if they are in some sense accurate. That is, even if a stereotype is in fact true of many of the group members, it may not be true of the individual under consideration (Stangor, 1995). Individuation is successful because it changes group perception to a more personal level.

Decreasing Out-Group Homogeneity

In addition to preventing unfair judgments of others, individuating rather than categorizing also has the benefit that it is likely to reduce the utility of the category for the individual. When people get to know category members as individuals, they will see that there is a great deal of variability among the group members and that the global and undifferentiating group stereotypes are actually not that informative (Rothbart & John, 1985). In short, individuation tends to reduce the perception of out-group homogeneity.

Still another advantage of attempting to improve intergroup relations by increasing individuation is that it does not require that we change people's stereotypes or reduce their prejudices—something that is very difficult to accomplish. If this approach were successful, at least some negative beliefs about the category might remain intact, but people would use them less often because they would consider the individual's own personal characteristics as more valid information—in essence, getting beyond their prejudices and stereotypes.

Individuation and Interdependence

Individuation is most likely to be effective in situations in which the individuals have enough time and motivation to get to know each other very well (Bettencourt, Brewer, Croak, & Miller, 1992; Marcus-Newhall, Miller, Holtz, & Brewer, 1993; Miller, Brewer, & Edwards, 1985), and particularly when they are dependent on them. For instance, teachers and students who get to know each other personally over the course of a semester or a year probably will end up thinking about each other more as individuals than as category members. And in working groups the interdependence required to meet task goals may increase individuation and reduce social categorization. For example, it has been found that expecting to interact with the others in the future reduces competition in the prisoner's dilemma game (Danheiser & Graziano, 1982), probably because it leads people to individuate the competitors (Orbell, Van de Kragt, & Dawes, 1988).

The Difficulty of Ignoring Categories

Although ignoring, or at least getting beyond, the social categories of others is an admirable goal, in reality it is generally difficult to avoid categorization entirely, and it may even be impossible. Social categories are important parts of our individual self-concepts as well as our cultural beliefs, and we use them almost habitually to make judgments about others. As a result, social categorization occurs frequently and quickly, and categorical judgments follow. Social categories may also play an important role for the person being stereotyped, because they provide individuals with a social identity; ignoring them in social interaction deprives people of this important source of self-worth. Therefore, although members of groups that may be the targets of stereotyping and prejudice do not want to be discriminated against, they may nevertheless not want their category memberships to be ignored entirely. Because of the importance of social categorization, for both the categorizer and the categorized, it has been argued that it is not possible, or perhaps even desirable, to ignore social categories entirely (Schofield, 1986).

Changing Stereotypes and Prejudice through Intergroup Contact

If it is not possible to get completely beyond the category memberships of others, then stereotypes and prejudice are likely to come into play in our social interactions. But this suggests that a second potentially useful approach to improving intergroup relations is to change beliefs about the groups and the group members, for instance, by increasing the number of positive beliefs or reducing the number of negative beliefs held about the group.

The Contact Hypothesis

According to the **contact hypothesis**, allowing individuals from different social categories to come into contact with each other will reduce negative attitudes and stereotypes about the groups that are contacted, as long as the groups are not in conflict with each other. Contact is expected to be effective for a number of reasons. For one, intergroup contact provides information that dispels stereotypes and prejudice because it makes people see the similarities between themselves and members of the out-group, and leads them to realize that their negative beliefs are untrue and overgeneralized (G. W. Allport, 1954; Cook, 1984; Wilder & Thompson, 1980). Contact may also decrease the anxiety that people might have about interacting with members of other groups, making it more likely that they will be willing to interact with them in the future and making the interactions that they do have less negative. In addi-

Contact Hypothesis: The expectation that contact between individuals from different social categories will reduce negative attitudes and stereotypes about the groups that are contacted, as long as the groups are not in conflict with each other.

tion, contact may change social norms in the groups such that expressing negative beliefs is no longer seen as appropriate.

There is substantial support for the effectiveness of intergroup contact in producing changes in group attitudes, both in naturally occurring situations such as the military forces and public housing, and in school systems (Pettigrew, 1998b; Stephan, 1999). Pettigrew and Tropp (2000) conducted a meta-analysis in which they reviewed 203 studies that had investigated the effects of contact on group attitudes. They found that there was a moderate effect size of about .40 across all of the studies such that contact did reduce prejudice. Furthermore, positive effects of contact were found on many types of measures, including emotional responses, attitudes, and stereotypes, for many types of people and many types of contacted groups, and in a variety of different social settings, including organizational, travel, and school settings.

Desegregating U.S. Schools

One important example of the potential for contact to influence attitudes comes from the U.S. Supreme Court case *Brown v. Board of Education* (1954). In this case the Court agreed, based in large part on the testimony of psychologists, that racial segregation in schools was unconstitutional. One result of this decision was that other courts mandated the practice of busing black children to schools attended primarily by white children (and vice versa) with the expectation that this would produce positive social outcomes on intergroup attitudes, not only because it provided black children with access to better schools, but also because the resulting intergroup contact would reduce negative attitudes between black and white children.

A number of studies regarding the effectiveness of desegregating schools have now been conducted. These have shown, first, that the policy was effective in changing school makeup—the number of segregated schools decreased dramatically during the 1960s after the busing policies were begun (Stephan, 1999). And this desegregation has also had at least some positive influence on the educational and occupational achievement of blacks, and was also found to have increased the desire of blacks to interact with whites, for instance, by forming cross-race friendships (Stephan, 1986; Stephan, 1999). Overall, then, the case for desegregating schools in the U.S. supports the expectation that intergroup contact, at least in the long run, can be successful in changing attitudes. Nevertheless, at least in part because the observed changes were very slow, the policy of desegregating schools via busing was not continued past the 1990s.

Experimental Evidence

One difficulty with much field research on the effects of group contact (including that studying the effects of busing) is that it is correlational, making it is difficult to determine whether contact causes more positive group attitudes or whether people who initially have positive attitudes toward a group are more likely to engage in intergroup contact. However, experimental research has also shown that intergroup interaction can increase positive attitudes.

In one interesting experiment, Desforges, Lord, Ramsey, Mason, van Leeuwen, West, and Lepper (1991) found that cooperative intergroup contact can make attitudes more positive, not only toward the individuals who are contacted, but also toward the social group as a whole. In the research, participants participated in an experiment on "learning strategies" in which they interacted with a confederate who indicated that she had formerly been a mental patient. The particular social category was chosen because prior testing had showed that the students in this population had negative attitudes about mental patients. During the interaction, the partners either worked alone to learn information from a book passage or worked together cooperatively. As shown in Figure 13.2, the participants who worked with the confederate on the learning task subsequently showed more positive attitudes toward her, and also showed more positive attitudes toward former mental patients, as a social category, in comparison to the individuals who worked alone. Thus, at

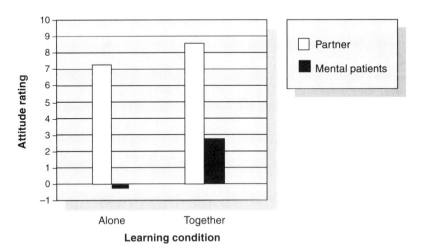

FIGURE 13.2. Improving attitudes through cooperative contact. Participants in this research studied in a room along with a partner who they thought was a former mental patient. In the Together condition, the two partners studied cooperatively, whereas in the Alone condition, they studied the material separately. Participants' attitudes toward both the partner and toward the social category of former mental patients became more positive for those who worked together. Data are from Desforges, D. M., Lord, C. G., Ramsey, S. L., Mason, J. A., Van Leeuwen, M. D., West, S. C., et al. (1991). Effects of structured cooperative contact on changing negative attitudes toward stigmatized social groups. *Journal of Personality and Social Psychology, 60*, 531–544.

least in some cases, cooperative interaction can produce changes in group beliefs, at both the individual and the group levels.

Conditions That Foster Change through Contact

Although the laboratory research by Lord and his colleagues demonstrated that positive attitude change as a function of contact is possible, it is by no means assured. For instance, in the study by Sherif and his colleagues, contact between the two groups of campers made attitudes more negative and increased intergroup conflict. Taken together, research testing the ability of contact to improve intergroup attitudes has shown that, although contact can be effective in reducing prejudice and negative stereotypes, it only works under certain specific conditions. We can summarize these conditions as follows:

1. The norms of the situation must promote *equal status* among the groups that are in contact. If the groups are treated unequally, for instance, by a teacher who is himself prejudiced and who therefore treats children from the different groups differently, there will be no benefit.
2. The situation must create the possibility for the original negative beliefs to be disconfirmed through exposure to positive perceptions of the other group. This condition is particularly likely to be met when the contact situation is accompanied by cooperative rather than competitive relations. If the situation is one in which the groups are acting in a competitive manner, the perceptions are likely to be negative and contact may backfire, leading to even more negative attitudes.
3. The situations should involve interdependence, such that the members of the groups have to work together to solve a problem or meet a goal.
4. It is important that the broader culture, particularly including those who are in authority, such as teachers and other leaders, provide and support appropriate norms concerning the acceptance of intergroup contact and positive intergroup beliefs and relations.
5. Finally, it is important that enough time be allowed for the changes to take effect. In the case of busing in the United States, for instance, the positive effects of contact seemed to have been occurring, but they were not happening particularly fast.

The Generalization Problem

One of the major difficulties of producing more positive intergroup beliefs through intergroup contact is that, although beliefs about the specific individuals who are contacted frequently become more positive, attitudes toward other members of the group, or the group as a whole, may not change. For instance, in his seminal research on the effects of contact on attitudes of European-American participants toward African Americans, Stuart Cook (1978, 1984) had white and black participants work together in a simulated work setting over a period of several weeks. Cook found that although the research participants developed very positive feelings toward each other over the course of the study—indeed, they frequently reported that they had become good friends—there was little change in the attitudes of the individuals in terms of their stereotypes and prejudices about the social categories (blacks or whites) as a group. Thus, although intergroup contact may be effective at improving interactions at the individual level, it may fail to produce real change at the group level because the individuals who are encountered are perceived as exceptions and not typical of the group as a whole.

Although producing generalization from the contacted individuals to the group as a whole is difficult, it is increased under certain conditions. Most importantly, generalization is more likely when the individual contacted is considered a member of the group, rather than a unique individual. This is more likely when the person "fits" our perceptions of what the group is like on most characteristics, even though he or she does not fit the stereotype on other dimensions (Desforges et al., 1991; Rothbart & John, 1985).

In one experimental demonstration of this effect, Scarberry, Ratcliff, Lord, Lanicek, and Desforges (1997) had college students interact with another person (actually an experimental confederate) who they were led to believe was a homosexual. During the interaction the confederate expressed information about himself that made him appear as a very likable person. However, in one of the experimental conditions this information was presented in a very personal way, including primarily information about himself, whereas in the other condition the information was more general. Results showed that, although the confederate was perceived equally positively in both conditions, the participants in the personal information condition nevertheless continued to perceive homosexuals, *as a group*, negatively, in comparison to the participants in the impersonal information condition who became more positive in their attitudes. It appears that providing personal information individuated the confederate so that he did not seem as representative of the group, and thus although the positive information that he provided made him seem likable this information did not generalize to the group as a whole.

What this research suggests, then, is that the effects of contact may be limited. A basic difficulty with producing change through contact is that the individuals with whom people are most likely to have contact may also be those who are least typical of the other group as a whole. However, although these results suggest that contact would be expected to change attitudes at an individual level more easily than it does at a group level, the meta-analysis by Pettigrew and Tropp (2002) found that contact produced significant change on both types of measures.

Changing Social Norms

Although intergroup beliefs may well change as a result of positive intergroup contact (at least in some cases), this cannot be the only way that these changes occur. For one thing, research has found that people have very strong beliefs and prejudices about groups with which they have had very little direct contact (Hartley, 1946), and people have been found to express very different behaviors in different social contexts. For example, Minard (1952) found that white and black coal miners in West Virginia were integrated belowground but almost completely segregated aboveground. While at work, the workers held attitudes that were egalitarian, and there was little racial conflict. However, when the workers returned to their homes and communities, there was almost no interaction between the two groups in their social lives, and attitudes and behavior were more negative. These results suggest that, at least in part, the extent to which individuals hold stereotypes and prejudice, and even the extent to which they engage in discrimination, is determined not only by their personal experiences with members of the relevant groups, but also by their perceptions of social norms about the appropriateness of expressing either positive or negative beliefs and behaviors.

According to this latter approach, stereotypes and prejudice are seen not so much as individual beliefs developed through personal experience, but more as cultural norms regarding both the categorization systems that are important, as well as perceptions regarding the appropriate treatment of members of out-groups (Stangor & Crandall, 2000; Stangor & Schaller, 1996). Of course, individuals vary in the extent to which they hold stereotypes and prejudicial attitudes, and in terms of their propensity to engage in discriminatory behavior, but these beliefs are determined in large part by the individual's perceptions of appropriate social norms (Sidanius, Pratto, Martin, & Stallworth, 1991).

Experimental research has demonstrated the importance of social norms in the development and change of stereotypes and prejudice (Jetten, Spears, & Manstead, 1996; Pettigrew, 1959). In one relevant study, Jetten, Spears, and Manstead (1997) manipulated whether individuals thought that the other members of their university favored equal treatment of others or believed that others thought it was appropriate to favor the in-group. They found that perceptions of what the other group members believed had an important influence on the beliefs of the individuals themselves—individuals were more likely to show in-group favoritism when they believed that the norm of their in-group was to do so, and this tendency was increased for individuals who had high social identification with the in-group.

In another example of the importance of social norms, Sechrist and Stangor (2001) selected white college students who were either high or low in expressed prejudice toward blacks, and then provided them with information indicating that their beliefs were either shared or not shared by other members of a reference group (students at their university). Then the students were asked to take a seat in a hallway to wait for the next part of the experiment. An African-American confederate was sitting in one seat at the end of the row, and the dependent measure was how far away the students sat from her.

As shown in Figure 13.3, students who were initially high in prejudice sat farther away from the confederate in comparison to low prejudice students overall. Furthermore, and supporting the importance of perceived social norms, high prejudice students who believed their beliefs were shared sat farther away from the confederate than did high prejudice individuals who believed their beliefs were not shared. But students who were initially low in prejudice and who believed these views were shared sat closer, in comparison to low prejudice individuals who were led to believe that their beliefs were not shared. These results suggest that, in addition to creating beliefs, social norms can also strengthen or weaken individuals' tendency to engage in discriminatory behaviors.

Taken together, these results are quite consistent with the expectation that long-lasting changes in group beliefs will only occur if they are supported

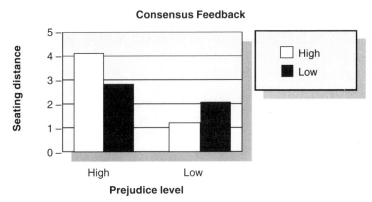

FIGURE 13.3. The role of norms in intergroup behavior. In this research white college students were selected for either high or low prejudice toward African Americans. Those who had been told that their beliefs were shared with other group members at their university expressed their positive (or negative) attitudes more strongly by how close they sat to an African-American confederate. Data are from Sechrist, G., & Stangor, C. (2001). Perceived consensus influences intergroup behavior and stereotype accessibility. *Journal of Personality and Social Psychology, 80,* 645–654.

by changes in social norms. In short, prejudice thrives in environments in which it is perceived to be supported, but dies when the existing social norms do not allow it. Thus, these results suggest that a potential approach to changing stereotypes and prejudice is through education and appropriate leadership that provides people with information that disconfirms their stereotypes or that convinces them that their perceptions of existing norms justifying negative group beliefs and behaviors are not accurate or appropriate (Rothbart & John, 1985). Indeed, education does matter. Meta-analyses by Stephan and Stephan (1989) and by McGregor (1993) both showed that programs designed to educate students about the real differences between and similarities among social groups were effective in breaking down stereotypes and prejudice.

Changing Categorizations

To this point we have considered two major methods of improving intergroup attitudes and preventing intergroup conflict—preventing categorization from occurring at all, and changing negative beliefs in case it does. However, a third approach to improving intergroup relations is based on the assumption that, even if we cannot prevent categorization itself, and even if we cannot completely eradicate the negative beliefs about social categories, we may nevertheless be able to change the categorizations that are used in social judgment. Most basically, the idea is that if we could lead people to view out-group members as more similar to themselves, then conflict and negative beliefs might be reduced. This can be accomplished by changing the categorization process—individuals who originally see themselves as members of two distinct groups (for instance, as blacks versus whites) might be likely to be in conflict, but this would be less likely if they categorized themselves as members of a common group (for instance, that they are all students at the same university).

Creating a Common In-Group Identity

You will recall that Sherif and his colleagues were able to reduce intergroup hostility between the two groups of campers by creating situations in which they were led to cooperate with each other to reach superordinate goals. This strategy was effective because it led the campers to perceive both the in-group and the out-group as one large group ("we"), rather than as two separate groups ("us" and "them"). As differentiation between the in-group and the out-group decreases, so should in-group favoritism, prejudice, and conflict. In this case differences between the original categories are still present, but they are potentially counteracted by similarities on the second superordinate category. This basic idea is known as the goal of creating a *common in-group identity* (Gaertner, Dovidio, Anastasio, Bachman, & Rust, 1993; Gaertner, Mann,

Dovidio, Murrell, & Pomare, 1990), and we can diagram the relationship as follows:

Cooperation → Common In-Group Identity → Favorable Intergroup Attitudes

Research has supported the predictions of the common in-group identity model (Dovidio, Gaertner, Validzic, Matoka et al., 1997; Gaertner, Mann, Murrell, & Dovidio, 1989). For instance, Samuel Gaertner and his colleagues (1989) tested the hypothesis that intergroup cooperation reduces negative beliefs about an out-group because it leads people to see the out-group members as part of the in-group (by creating a common identity). In this research college students were first assigned to teams of three members and given a chance to create a group identity. Then two groups of three students were brought into a single room to work on a problem. In one condition the two groups worked together as a larger six-member team to solve the problem, whereas in the other condition the two groups worked separately.

Consistent with the expected positive results of creating a common group identity, the interdependence created in the cooperative work condition increased the tendency of the group members to see themselves as members of a single, larger group, and this in turn reduced the tendency for each group to show in-group favoritism. Many other research projects have confirmed this basic finding—individuals are less likely to hold stereotypes and prejudice about out-groups, and are less likely to discriminate against their members, when they perceive that the in-group and the out-group members share one or more category memberships (Commins & Lockwood, 1978; Dovidio, Gaertner, Isen, & Lowrance, 1995; Gaertner, Dovidio, & Bachman, 1996; Gaertner, Rust, Dovidio, Bachman et al., 1994; Hewstone, Islam, & Judd, 1993; Kramer & Brewer, 1984; Marcus-Newhall et al., 1993; Vanbeselaere, 1987).

In a field study demonstrating the effectiveness of creating a common in-group identity, Neir, Gaertner, Dovidio, Banker, Ward, and Rust (2001) had black and white interviewers approach white students of the same sex who were attending a football game and ask them to help out by completing a questionnaire. However, the interviewers also wore hats representing one or the other of the two universities who were playing in the game. As shown in Figure 13.4, the data were analyzed both by whether the request was from a white (in-group) or black (out-group) interviewer, and also in terms of whether the individual who was approached wore a hat from the same university that experimenter wore or a hat from the other university. As expected from the common in-group identity approach, the white students were significantly more likely to help the black interviewers when he or she wore a hat of the same university as that worn by the interviewee. However, whether the indi-

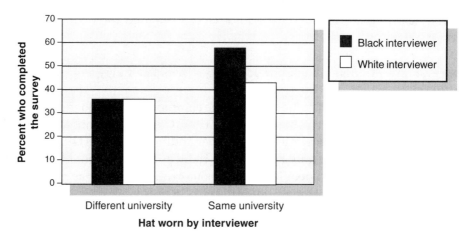

FIGURE 13.4. Recategorization and helping behavior. In this field study, white interviewers asked white (in-group) and black (out-group) students attending a football game to help them by completing a questionnaire. The data were analyzed both by whether the request was to a white (in-group) or black (out-group) student, and also in terms of whether the individual whose help was sought wore a hat from the same university that the interviewer did or a hat from a different university. Results supported the common in-group identity model. Helping was much greater for out-group members when hats were the same. Data are from Neir, J. A., Gaertner, S. L., Dovidio, J. F., Banker, B. S., Ward, C. M., & Rust, C. R. (2001). Changing interracial evaluations and behavior: The effects of a common group identity. *Group Processes & Intergroup Relations, 4,* 299–316.

viduals shared university affiliation did not significantly influence helping the white interviewers, presumably because they were already a member of a relevant in-group (the participants were also white).

The Extended-Contact Hypothesis

Although the contact hypothesis proposes that direct intergroup contact may produce more positive attitudes between members of different social groups, recent evidence suggests that prejudice can also be reduced for people who have friends who are friends with members of the out-group, even if the individual does not have direct contact with the out-group members himself or herself. This hypothesis is known as the **extended-contact hypothesis**. Supporting this prediction, Wright, Aron, McLaughlin-Volpe, and Ropp (1997) found in two correlational studies that college students who reported that their own friends had friends who were from another ethnic group also reported more positive attitudes toward that out-group, even controlling for the participants' own out-group friendships.

Furthermore, Wright et al. (1997) also tested the extended-contact hypothesis experimentally by creating a laboratory replication of the Sherif summer camp study. Participants were 4 groups of 14 students, each of which spent a whole day in the lab. On arrival, 7 participants were assigned to the "green" group, and 7 to the "blue" group, supposedly on the basis of similar

Extended-Contact Hypothesis: The expectation that people who have friends who are friends with members of an out-group will have more positive attitudes toward that out-group, even if they do not have direct contact with the out-group members themselves.

interests. To create in-group cohesion and to foster out-group competition the group members wore blue and green T-shirts and engaged in a series of competitive tasks (the experimenters even rigged out-group feedback about the in-group's task performance to be very negative). Participants then expressed their thoughts and feelings about the out-group and its members.

Then, supposedly as part of an entirely different study, one participant was randomly selected from each group, and the two were taken to a separate room in which they engaged in a task that has been shown to quickly create feelings of friendship between two strangers through a series of gradually escalating mutual self-disclosure and relationship-building tasks. The two members from each team were then reunited with their original groups, where they were encouraged to describe their experience with the other group member in the friendship-building task.

In the final phase, the groups then engaged in another competitive task, and participants rated their thoughts and feelings about the out-group and its members again. Supporting the extended-contact hypothesis, results showed that the participants (including those who did *not* participate in closeness task) were more positive toward the out-group after than before the team members had met.

Cooperation in the Classroom

In short, it appears that negative intergroup beliefs are most likely to be reduced in situations that allow positive intergroup contact, supported by the relevant authorities, and in which social norms about tolerance and egalitarianism prevail. Because these outcomes are particularly likely to occur when the situation involves positive intergroup cooperation among individuals from the different social groups, it is no surprise that techniques to create intergroup cooperation have been developed and used to change intergroup beliefs in the real world.

The most widespread use of cooperative techniques has been in educational settings, where it has frequently been found that cooperative experiences among students from different social groups can be effective in reducing negative stereotyping and prejudice (Johnson, Maruyama, Johnson, Nelson, & Skon, 1981; Johnson & Johnson, 1992). Consistent with prior theorizing about contact, these situations are arranged to promote equal status among the children from the different groups and involve acceptance of tolerance by the teachers. Furthermore, these situations are usually arranged so that they do not ignore group differences, but rather allow students to make use of them, as long as this does not occur in a negative way.

One example of the use of cooperative learning techniques is known as the *jigsaw classroom* (Aronson, Blaney, Stephan, Sikes, & Snapp, 1978). In this approach, the assigned material to be learned is divided into as many parts as there are students in the group. Each student then learns his or her own part of the material and presents this piece of the puzzle to the other members of the group. The students in each group are therefore interdependent when learning all of the material. A wide variety of techniques, based on principles of the jigsaw classroom, are in use in many schools around the United States, and research has found that these approaches are, by and large, successful in improving intergroup attitudes (Stephan, 1999). The jigsaw classroom is effective in improving the intergroup attitudes of school children for a variety of reasons (Stephan, 1999). For one, cooperation provides a sense of group cohesiveness and identity which contributes to pride in accomplishment. When the cooperating groups succeed, children gain a good deal of positive social identity. And as, we have seen in chapter 5, interdependence also leads the children to be more likely to individuate, rather than categorize, each other. It is, however, important that teachers attempts to maintain equal-status relationships among the group members. If some children perform at a higher level than others, and therefore receive higher individual grades, the perceived status differences may limit the effectiveness of the cooperating groups.

 ## *Chapter Summary*

One common outcome of group behavior in everyday life is intergroup conflict and hostility. In some cases the conflict is based upon realistic competition for scarce resources. However, realistic conflict is frequently amplified by misperceptions about the goals and desires of the other group. In extreme cases, the out-group may be extremely deindividuated or dehumanized.

As demonstrated in the Robber's Cave studies of Sherif and his colleagues, intergroup conflict frequently results in a series of tit-for-tat exchanges of negative behaviors, and may in some cases spiral upward as the behaviors become increasingly negative and hostile. Intergroup conflicts are enhanced though the ultimate attribution error—the tendency to see positive behaviors of in-groups and negative behaviors of out-groups as representing characteristics of the group as a whole and to view positive behaviors of out-groups and negative behaviors of in-groups at the individual level. These factors make negative intergroup beliefs, once they get started, very persistent and resistant to change. It has also been found that groups act more competitively than individuals, an effect known as the individual-group discontinuity.

Despite this difficulty, it is possible to change intergroup beliefs under some circumstances. One approach is to attempt to get people to individuate, rather than categorize, each other. This is more fair, and reduces out-group homogeneity. Because it is virtually impossible for people to ignore social categories entirely, however, another approach is to attempt to change beliefs, and this is frequently accomplished through intergroup contact.

As predicted by the contact hypothesis, intergroup contact has been found to be an effective means of changing beliefs, given certain conditions: the norms of the situation must promote equal status among the groups who are in contact; the situation must create the possibility for the original negative beliefs to be disconfirmed; the situations must involve interdependence and cooperation; and the broader context must support appropriate norms concerning the acceptance of intergroup contact and positive intergroup beliefs and relations. It is also important that enough time be allowed for the changes to take effect. Nevertheless, changes in beliefs frequently do not generalize to the group as a whole. Intergroup attitudes can also be changed by changing social norms and by recategorization of groups into a common in-group identity. These approaches have been used in real-world programs, particularly those designed to produce intergroup cooperation in classrooms.

 Review and Discussion Questions

1. Review the findings of Sherif's Robber's Cave experiments. What caused intergroup hostility in this research, and what decreased it?
2. What is realistic group conflict theory and how does it explain intergroup hostility?
3. What is the "individual-group discontinuity," and why does it occur?
4. What approaches have been used to improve negative intergroup attitudes, and what are the potential problems with each approach?
5. In what situations is contact between social groups likely to increase or decrease negative group perceptions and intergroup conflict?
6. If you were given the task of reducing negative group beliefs and behaviors among the students and faculty at your university, what approaches do you think would be most successful, and why?

Recommended Readings

Can schools help reduce prejudice?
Stephan, W. (1999). *Reducing prejudice and stereotyping in schools*. New York: Teacher's College Press.

Why it may not be possible to be truly "colorblind":
Schofield, J. (1986). Causes and consequences of the colorblind perspective. In J. F. Dovidio & S. L. Gaertner (Eds.), *Prejudice, Discrimination, and Racism* (pp. 231–253). San Diego, CA: Academic Press.

A recent summary of the effectiveness of intergroup contact in changing group beliefs:
Pettigrew, T. F. (1998). Intergroup contact theory. *Annual Review of Psychology, 49,* 65–85.

Glossary

acceptance See private acceptance.

additive task A task in which the inputs of each of the group members are added together to create the group performance.

applied research Research designed to investigate issues that have implications for everyday life and to provide solutions to problems.

arbitration A type of third-party intervention in which sides agree ahead of time to abide by the decision of the third party (the arbiter).

attachment style A description of the different types of relationships that people may have with other individuals, and particularly with one's parents.

basic research Research designed to answer fundamental questions about behavior, without a particular concern for how that knowledge will be used.

behavioral measures Measures in which participants' behavior is recorded.

brainstorming A technique used to produce creative decisions in working groups.

coercive power Power based on the ability to punish others.

cohesion See group cohesion.

collective action Attempts on the part of one group to change the social status hierarchy by improving the status of their own group relative to others.

collectivism The tendency, common in Eastern cultures, to focus on developing harmonious social relationships with others, with particular importance placed upon the awareness of one's social roles.

compensatory task A task in which the group input is combined in such a way that the performance of the individuals is averaged.

competition Attempts by interacting parties to gain rewards at the expense of the other party or parties.

compliance See public compliance.

conflict A situation in which interacting parties perceive that gains made by others decrease their own chances of gaining rewards and that their goals are thus incompatible.

conformity The change in opinion or behavior that is the result of social influence.

conjunctive task A task in which a group's performance is determined by its worst member.

contact hypothesis The expectation that contact between individuals from different social categories will reduce negative attitudes and stereotypes about the groups that are contacted, as long as the groups are not in conflict with each other.

contingency model of leadership effectiveness A theory of leadership effectiveness based on the interaction between individual's leadership style and the group's task demands.

contributions dilemma A social dilemma in which the short-term costs of a behavior lead individuals to avoid performing it, and this prevents the long-term benefits that would have occurred if the behaviors had been performed.

cooperation Behaviors that occur when it is perceived that the goals of the self and others are compatible and in which individuals believe they are benefiting both themselves and others.

correlational research design A research design in which the goal is to search for and describe the relationships among two or more variables.

criterion tasks Tasks in which there is a clearly correct answer to the problem that is being posed.

crowd A temporary collection of a large number of individuals who come together in a common place for a common purpose.

culture A large social group made up of individuals who are normally in geographic proximity with each other and who share a common set of social norms.

decision scheme A rule that predicts how groups will combine their opinions together to reach consensus.

dchumanization The tendency to deindividuate and devalue out-group members so that they are no longer seen as human beings.

deindividuation A state that occurs when the normal restraints on behavior are loosened and people behave in an impulsive or deviant manner.

diffuse status The status that one accrues as a result of one's social category memberships.

discrimination Unjustified negative behaviors toward members of out-groups that are based on their group membership.

disjunctive task A task in which the group's performance is determined by its best group member.

divisible task A task in which the work can be divided up among individuals.

drive arousal The excitement and energy that occur when other individuals are nearby.

dyad Two individuals who are in a close relationship, as in a strong friendship or a marriage.

dynamic social impact theory A theory that predicts that relevant societal beliefs are spread throughout the society because individuals communicate with other individuals who are in contact with them.

ecological validity The extent to which research is conducted in situations that are similar to the everyday life experiences of the participants.

effect size A statistic that indicates the strength of a relationship between or among variables. Zero indicates that there is no relationship between the variables, and larger effect sizes indicate stronger relationships.

empirical. Based upon systematic collection of data.

entitativity The feeling or perception that a collection of individuals is a social group.

equity The perception that things are fair, in the sense that people are receiving rewards that are proportionate to the contributions they make to the group.

evolutionary psychology A theoretical approach based on the assumption that the behavior of all living things is determined by attempts to meet the goals of survival and reproduction.

experimental research design A research design in which the independent variable is created by the experimenter through the experimental manipulation, and the research hypothesis is that the manipulated independent variable causes changes in the measured dependent variable.

expert power Power that is based on expertise.

extended-contact hypothesis The expectation that people who have friends who are friends with members of an out-group will have more positive attitudes toward that out-group, even if they do not have direct contact with the out-group members themselves.

external validity The extent to which relationships observed in research can be expected to hold up when they are tested again in different ways.

factorial experimental design An experiment that has more than one independent variable.

false consciousness The acceptance of one's own low group status as part of the proper and normal functioning of society.

field experiment An experiment that is conducted in an everyday setting, such as in a school or organization.

fraternalistic deprivation The perception that one's in-group has lower status than it deserves.

free riding A type of social loafing that occurs when individuals rely on other group members to do the work for the group.

group cohesion The emotional attachment that group members have with the other members of the group.

group dynamics An approach to studying social groups, developed by the social psychologist Kurt Lewin, that is based upon the principle of interactionism.

group-level approach An approach to studying groups in which the focus is upon the groups themselves rather than on the individuals who make up the groups.

group mind A collection of interacting individual minds.

group polarization A tendency for group member's opinions to become more extreme as a result of group discussion.

group process The events that occur while the group is working together on the task.

group structure The rules that define group norms, roles, and status.

group support systems (GSS) Computer programs and networks designed to improve group decision making.

groupthink A process that occurs when a group makes poor decisions as a result of flawed group process and strong conformity pressures.

harvesting dilemma A social dilemma in which an individual group member is tempted to use public goods, but this behavior eventually leads to long-term loss either for the individual or for the group as a whole.

illusion of group effectivity The tendency to overvalue the productivity of groups.

individual-group discontinuity The tendency for groups to act more competitively than individuals.

individualism The tendency, common in Western cultures, to value the personal self and to see the self as in large part separate from other people.

individual-level approach An approach to studying groups in which the focus is upon the individuals who make up the groups.

individual mobility Attempts on the part of individuals to leave a low-status group and move to a higher-status group.

in-group A group to which one belongs.

in-group favoritism Expressing more positive attitudes or behaving more positively toward in-group members than toward out-group members.

integrative outcome An outcome in which a positive outcome for one party does not necessarily mean a negative outcome for the other party.

intellective task Tasks that involve the ability of the group to make a decision or a judgment.

interaction Communication among group members.

interactionism The assumption that social behavior is determined in part by the individual and in part by the relationship between the individual and the group.

interdependence The extent to which the group members are mutually dependent upon each other to reach a goal.

internal validity The ability to draw the conclusion that the independent variable caused the dependent variable.

judgmental tasks Tasks in which there is no clearly correct answer to the problem that is being posed.

leadership The process of influencing others to effectively obtain group goals.

legitimate power Power that is successful because members of the group accept it as appropriate.

leniency bias The tendency for juries to vote for acquittal more often than they vote for guilt, all other factors being equal.

majority influence Influence that occurs when a larger subgroup produces change in a smaller subgroup.

maximizing task A task that involves performance that is measured by how rapidly the group works or by how much of a product they are able to make.

mediation An attempt to reach compromise by using third-party negotiation.

member characteristics The traits, skills, or abilities of the individual group members.

meta-analysis A type of data analysis in which the data are drawn from the results of existing studies and combined to determine what conclusions can be drawn on the basis of all of the studies taken together.

minimal intergroup effect In-group favoritism that occurs in groups that are not very meaningful.

minority influence Influence that occurs when a smaller subgroup produces change in a larger subgroup.

mixed-motive decision A decision in which the individual must coordinate both co-operative and competitive goals in making a choice.

mob A crowd in which some individuals are acting violently, harming the property of themselves and others, and potentially injuring other people.

negotiation A process in which two or more parties attempt to resolve a perceived divergence of interest in order to avoid or resolve social conflict.

network analysis A method of assessing group structure in which the relationships or feelings (usually assessed in terms of liking or time spent together) of each group member about each other group member are assessed.

nominal group A group of individuals who work as individuals but who are considered a group by the researchers.

nominal group technique An approach to improving group decision making that uses nominal groups to generate initial ideas and face-to-face groups to discuss and build on them.

norm See social norm.

observational research Research in which observations are made of behavior, and those observations are recorded in an objective manner.

operational definition The method used to measure a variable of interest.

optimal distinctiveness The tendency of individuals to prefer to maintain both their independent as well as their interdependent cultural orientations.

organizations Large social groups that exist to produce products or to provide services.

out-group A group to which one does not belong.

out-group homogeneity The tendency to view members of out-groups as extremely similar to each other.

perceptual accentuation The tendency to amplify perceived between-group differences and within-group similarities.

prejudice An unjustifiable negative attitude toward an out-group or toward members of that out-group.

prisoner's dilemma A social dilemma in which the goals of the individual compete with the goals of another individual or with a group of individuals.

private acceptance Conformity that involves real change in opinions on the part of the individual being influenced.

procedural justice The belief that individuals with higher status and power can be trusted to treat lower-status individuals fairly.

process gain When the outcome of the group performance is more than would be expected on the basis of the member characteristics.

process loss When the outcome of the group performance is less than would be expected on the basis of the member characteristics.

psychological reactance A reaction to conformity pressures that results from a desire to restore threatened freedom.

public compliance A change in behavior (including the public expression of opinions) that is not accompanied by an actual change in one's private opinion.

public goods Benefits that are shared by the members of a community, regardless of whether or not the members have personally contributed to the creation of the good.

realistic group conflict The competition for objectively scarce resources that can occur between social groups.

reference group A group of individuals that we look up to and identify with because we admire and want to be like those who belong to it.

referent power Power that comes from identification with the power-holder.

relative deprivation The perception that we (or our in-group) do not compare as positively as we might like with a relevant other or other group.

research hypothesis A specific prediction regarding the relationship between two or more variables.

reward power The ability of one person to influence others by providing them with positive outcomes.

Ringelmann effect The tendency for group productivity to decrease as the size of the group increases.

role See social role.

role ambiguity A situation in which goals and objectives of one's role are not clear to the person, and he or she is unsure of what is demanded.

role conflict A situation in which the individual is expected to fulfill more than one conflicting role or when it is difficult to fulfill one's role because the demands from one set of people compete with those of another set of people.

self-categorization The social categorization of oneself as a member of a social group.

self-categorization theory A theory that proposes that when we are interacting with other people we sometimes act as individuals and sometimes as members of a social group.

self-fulfilling prophecy The outcome of behaving in accordance with one's expectations so that those expectations come true.

self-report measures Measures in which participants are asked to respond to questions posed by an interviewer or on a questionnaire.

social aggregate A group of people who are in the same location, but who are not meaningfully related to each other, and thus who do not have entitatively.

social categorization The process of thinking about someone as a member of a meaningful social group.

social category A large and relatively permanent social group, such as people who share a gender, a religion, a nationality, or a physical disability.

social comparison The process of learning about our own abilities and opinions by comparing them with the abilities and opinions of others.

social creativity The use of strategies that allow members of low-status groups to perceive their group as better than other groups.

social dilemma A situation in which the goals of the individual conflict with the goals of the group.

social exchange The sharing of social rewards and social costs among people.

social facilitation Process gains on the performance of maximizing tasks that are caused by the influence of others.

social group A collection of three or more individuals who are perceived, by themselves or others, to be a group.

social identity The part of the self-concept that results from our membership in social groups.

social inhibition Process losses on the performance of maximizing tasks that are caused by the influence of others.

social impact The increase in the amount of conformity that is produced by each new member added to a group.

social influence The processes through which individuals or groups change the thoughts, feelings, and behaviors of others.

social loafing The reduction in motivation and effort that occurs when individuals work together at a group task.

social network A set of individuals within a group who are connected through social relationships, such as friendship, and social influence and thus who communicate frequently with one another.

social norm A way of thinking, feeling, or behaving that is perceived by group members as appropriate or normal.

social perception The process of thinking about others with the goal of understanding and learning about them.

social power The ability of one individual to create behavioral or opinion changes in another person, even when the person being influenced may attempt to resist those changes.

social representation A pattern of beliefs, values, norms, and practices that are shared by the members of a culture.

social role A group norm that specifies the behaviors expected to be performed by individual group members.

social sciences Approaches to understanding human behavior that are based upon careful scientific analysis.

social support The approval, assistance, advice, comfort, and other aid that we receive from those with whom we have developed stable positive relationships.

sociogram A visual display of a social network.

specific status Status that is gained through effective and competent performance on group tasks.

spurious relation A relation between two variables that is caused by a third, but usually unmeasured, variable.

statistical significance A method of testing the likelihood that the observed relationships between or among variables is due to chance.

status The amount of authority, prestige, or reputation that a group member has in the group.

stepladder technique A method of creative decision making in which indivudals join the group and present their opinions one at a time.

stereotype A belief about the characteristics of a social group or the members of a social group.

subtyping In the process of social categorization, recategorizing an individual into a lower-level group membership.

sucker effect The tendency to withhold effort as a means of restoring equity and avoiding being taken advantage of that occurs when one perceives that he or she is contributing more to a task than others.

SYMLOG (System of Multiple Level of Observation of Groups) A system of collecting data that involves observing the behaviors of a working group, and coding the observed interactions into a limited number of types of activities.

team See work team.

theory An integrated set of principles that explains and predicts observed relationships within a given domain of inquiry.

tit-for-tat strategy A method of responding in a social dilemma in which the party begins with a cooperative response and then matches his or her responses to those that are given by the other party.

ultimate attribution error The tendency to see positive behaviors of in-groups and negative behaviors of out-groups as representing stable internal characteristics of the group as a whole, while viewing positive behaviors of out-groups and negative behaviors of in-groups as caused by temporary, situational pressures or by behaviors of specific individuals.

unitary task A task in which the work cannot be divided up among individuals.

variable Anything that varies, for instance among individuals or among groups.

work team A highly structured working group in which the group members are highly interdependent.

working group A group consisting of between about 3 and 12 individuals who are actively attempting to meet a specific goal.

References

Abelson, R. P., Dasgupta, N., Park, J., & Banaji, M. R. (1998). Perceptions of the collective other. *Personality and Social Psychology Review, 2*, 243–250.

Aboud, F. E., & Doyle, A.-B. (1996). Parental and peer influences on children's racial attitudes. *International Journal of Intercultural Relations Special Issue: Prejudice, Discrimination and Conflict, 20*(3–4)(Sum-Fal 1996), 371–383.

Abrams, D., Wetherell, M., Cochrane, S., & Hogg, M. (1990). Knowing what to think by knowing who you are: Self-categorization and the nature of norm formation, conformity, and group polarization. *British Journal of Social Psychology, 29*, 97–119.

Adams, J. (1965). Inequity in social exchange. In L. Berkowitz (Ed.), *Advances in experimental social psychology* (Vol. 2, pp. 267–299). New York: Academic Press.

Adrianson, L., & Hjelmquist, E. (1991). Group processes in face-to-face and computer-mediated communication. *Behaviour and Information Technology, 10*(4), 281–296.

Ainsworth, M. S. (1989). Attachments beyond infancy. *American Psychologist, 44*(4), 709–716.

Alexander, R. (1987). *The biology of moral systems.* New York: A. de Gruyter.

Allen, V. L. (1965). Situational factors in conformity. In L. Berkowitz (Ed.), *Advances in experimental social psychology* (Vol. 2). New York: Academic Press.

Allen, V. L. (1975). Social support for nonconformity. In L. Berkowitz (Ed.), *Advances in experimental social psychology* (Vol. 8). New York: Academic Press.

Allen, V. L., & Wilder, D. A. (1980). Impact of group consensus and social support on stimulus meaning: Mediation of conformity by cognitive restructuring. *Journal of Personality and Social Psychology, 39*, 1116–1124.

Allison, S. T., Messick, D. M., & Samuelson, C. D. (1985). Effects of soliciting opinions on contributions to a public good. *Journal of Applied Social Psychology, 15*, 201–206.

Allport, F. H. (1924). *Social psychology.* New York: Houghton Mifflin.

Allport, F. H. (1962). A structuronomic conception of behavior: Individual and collective. I. Structural theory and the master problem of social psychology. *Journal of Abnormal and Social Psychology, 64*, 3–30.

Allport, G. W. (1954). *The nature of prejudice.* Reading, MA: Addison-Wesley.

Ancona, D. G., & Caldwell, D. F. (1992). Demography and design: Predictors of new product team performance. *Organization Science, 3*, 321–341.

Anderson, C. M., & Martin, M. M. (1995). The effects of communication motives, interaction, involvement, and loneliness on satisfaction: A model of small groups. *Small Group Research, 26*, 118–137.

Anderson, L. R., & Blanchard, P. N. (1982). Sex differences in task and social-emotional behavior. *Basic and Applied Social Psycholgy, 3*, 109–139.

Andreoli, V. A., & Folger, R. (1977). Intergroup cooperation and intergroup attraction: The effect of previous interaction and outcome of combined effort. *Journal of Experimental Social Psychology, 13*(2), 131–140.

Arbuthnot, J., & Wayner, M. (1982). Minority influence: Effects of size, conversion, and sex. *Journal of Psychology, 111*(2), 285–295.

Arcuri, L. (1982). Three patterns of social categorization in attribution memory. *European Journal of Social Psychology, 12*, 271–282.

Argyle, M. (1987). *The psychology of happiness.* London: Methuen.

Arkin, R. M., & Burger, J. M. (1980). Effects of unit relation tendencies on interpersonal attraction. *Social Psychology Quarterly, 43*, 380–391.

Aronson, E., Blaney, N., Stephan, C., Sikes, J., & Snapp, M. (1978). *The jig-saw classroom.* London: Sage.

Aronson, E., Ellsworth, P. C., Carlsmith, J. M., & Gonzales, M. H. (1990). *Methods of research in social psychology.* New York: McGraw-Hill.

Aronson, E., & Mills, J. (1959). The effect of severity of initiation on liking for a group. *Journal of Abnormal and Social Psychology, 59*, 171–181.

Arrow, H. (1997). Stability, bistability, and instability in small group influence patterns. *Journal of Personality and Social Psychology, 72*, 75–85.

Asch, S. E. (1955). Opinions and social pressure. *Scientific American, 11*, 32.

Asch, S. E. (1952). *Social psychology.* Englewood Cliffs, NJ: Prentice-Hall.

Aspinwall, L. G., & Taylor, S. E. (1993). Effects of social comparison direction, threat, and self-esteem on affect, self-evaluation, and expected success. *Journal of Personality and Social Psychology, 64*, 708–722.

Ayman, R., Chemers, M. M., & Fiedler, F. (1995). The contingency model of leadership effectiveness: Its level of analysis. *Leadership Quarterly, 6*(2), 147–167.

Bach, P. B., Cramer, L. D., Warren, J. L., & Begg, C. B. (1999). Racial differences in the treatment of early-stage lung cancer. *New England Journal of Medicine, 341*(16), 1198–1205.

Back, K. W. (1951). Influence through social communication. *Journal of Abnormal and Social Psychology, 46*, 9–23.

Baker, W. E. (1992). The network organization in theory and practice. In N. Nohria & R. G. Eccles (Eds.), *Networks and organizations.* Boston: Harvard Business School Press.

Bales, R. F. (1950). *Interaction process analysis: A method for the study of small groups.* Chicago: University of Chicago Press.

Bales, R. F. (1970). *Personality and interpersonal behavior.* New York: Holt, Rinehart & Winston.

Bales, R. F. (1999). *Social interaction systems.* New Brunswick, NJ: Transaction.

Bales, R. F., Strodtbeck, F. L., Mills, T. M., & Roseborough, M. E. (1951). Channels of communication in small groups. *American Sociological Review, 16*, 461–468.

Balka, E. (1993). "Women's access to on-line discussions about feminism."*Electronic Journal of Communication 3*(1). http://www.cios.org/

Banas, P. A. (1988). Employee involvement: A sustained labor/management initiative at the Ford Motor Company. In J. P. Campbell & R. J. Campbell & Assoc. (Eds.), *Productivity in organizations: New perspectives from industrial and organizational psychology* (pp. 388–416). San Francisco: Jossey-Bass.

Bantel, K. A., & Jackson, S. E. (1989). Top management and innovations in banking: Does the composition of the top team make a difference? *Strategy Management Journal.*

Barash, D. P. (1982). The fitness of categories and vice versa. *Neuroscience and Biobehavioral Reviews, 6*(1), 95–104.

Barker, I. V. L., & Patterson, P. W. (1996). Top management team tenure and top manager causal attributions at declining firms attempting turnarounds. *Group and Organization Management, 21*(3), 304–336.

Baron, J., & Pfeffer, J. (1994). The social psychology of organizations and inequality. *Social Psychology Quarterly, 57*(3), 190–209.

Baron, R. S. (1986). Distraction/conflict theory: Progress and problems. In L. Berkowitz (Ed.), *Advances in experimental social psychology* (Vol. 19). New York: Academic Press.

Baron, R. S., Kerr, N. L., & Miller, N. (1992). *Group process, group decision, group action.* Pacific Grove, CA: Brooks-Cole.

Baron, R. S., Moore, D., & Sanders, G. S. (1978). Distraction as a source of drive in social facilitation research. *Journal of Personality and Social Psychology, 36,* 816–824.

Baron, R. S., Roper, G., & Baron, P. H. (1974). Group discussion and the stingy shift. *Journal of Personality and Social Psychology, 30,* 538–545.

Baron, R. S., Vandello, J. A., & Brunsman, B. (1996). The forgotten variable in conformity research: Impact of task importance on social influence. *Journal of Personality and Social Psychology, 71*(5), 915–927.

Barrera, M., & Ainlay, S. L. (1983). The structure of social support: A conceptual and empirical analysis. *Journal of Community Psychology, 11,* 133–143.

Barrera, M., Jr. (1986). Distinctions between social support concepts, measures, and models. *Academy of Management Review, 2,* 231–351.

Bar-Tal, D. (1990). *Group Beliefs.* New York: Springer Verlag.

Bar-Tal, D. (2000). *Shared beliefs in a society: Social psychological analysis.* Thousand Oaks, CA: Sage.

Bartlett, F. C. (1932). *Remembering.* Cambridge: Cambridge University Press.

Bartol, K. M., & Martin, D. C. (1986). Women and men in task groups. In A. F. K. R. D. Del Boca (Ed.), *The social psychology of female-male relations.* New York: Academic Press.

Bass, B. M. (1985). *Leadership and performance beyond expectations.* New York: Free Press.

Bass, B. M. (1999). Current developments in transformational leadership: Research and applications. *Psychologist-Manager Journal, 3,* 5–21.

Bass, B. M., & Norton, F. T. M. (1951). Group size and leaderless discussion. *Journal of Applied Psychology, 35,* 397–400.

Baumeister, R. F. (1984). Choking under pressure: Self-consciousness and paradoxical effects of incentives on skillful performance. *Journal of Personality and Social Psychology, 46,* 610–620.

Baumeister, R. F., Hamilton, J. C., & Tice, D. M. (1985). Public versus private expectancy of success: Confidence booster or performance pressure? *Journal of Personality and Social Psychology, 48*(6), 1447–1457.

Baumeister, R. F., & Leary, M. (1995). The need to belong: Desire for interpersonal attachments as a fundamental human motivation. *Psychological Bulletin, 117,* 497–529.

Baumeister, R. F., & Showers, C. J. (1986). A review of paradoxical performance effects: Choking under pressure in sports and mental tests. *European Journal of Social Psychology, 16*(4), 361–383.

Baumeister, R. F., & Steinhilber, A. (1984). Paradoxical effects of supportive audiences on performance under pressure: The home-field disadvantage in sports championships. *Journal of Personality and Social Psychology, 47*(1), 85–93.

Baumeister, R. F., & Tice, D. M. (1990). Anxiety and social exclusion. *Journal of Social and Clinical Psychology, 9,* 165–195.

Bazerman, M. H., Curhan, J. R., Moore, D. A., & Valley, K. L. (2000). Negotiation. *Annual Review of Psychology, 51,* 279–314.

Bell, P. R., & Jamieson, B. D. (1970). Publicity of initial decisions and the risky shift phenomenon. *Journal of Experimental Social Psychology, 6,* 329–345.

Bem, S. L. (1981). Gender schema theory: A cognitive account of sex typing. *Psychological Review, 88,* 354–364.

Benne, K. D., & Sheats, P. (1948). Functional roles of group members. *Journal of Social Issues, 4*(2), 41–49.

Berkowitz, L. (1954). Group standards, cohesiveness, and productivity. *Human Relations, 7,* 509–519.

Berkowitz, L. (1954). Studies in Group Norms: The Perception of Group Attitudes as Related to Criteria of Group Effectiveness. *USAF Personnel & Training Research Center Research Bulletin* (AFPTRC-TR-54-62), iv, 20.

Berkowitz, S. D. (1982). *An introduction to structural analysis.* Toronto: Butterworths.

Berscheid, E., & Reis, H. T. (1998). Attraction and close relationships. In D. T. Gilbert & S. T. Fiske, & G. Lindzey (Eds.), *The handbook of social psychology* (pp. 193–281). New York: McGraw-Hill.

Bernthal, P. R., & Insko, C. A. (1993). Cohesiveness without groupthink: The interactive effects of social and task cohesion. *Group and Organizational Management, 18,* 66–87.

Bettencourt, B. A., Brewer, M. B., Croak, M. R., & Miller, N. (1992). Cooperation and the reduction of intergroup bias: The role of reward structure and social orientation. *Journal of Experimental Social Psychology, 28*(4), 301–319.

Beyer, J. M. (1999). Taming and promoting charisma to change organizations. *Leadership Quarterly, 10*(2), 307–330.

Biddle, B. J. (1986). Recent developments in role theory. *Annual Review of Sociology, 12,* 67–92.

Billig, M., & Tajfel, H. (1973). Social categorization and similarity in intergroup behavior. *European Journal of Social Psychology, 3,* 27–52.

Bixentine, V. E., Levitte, C. A., & Wilson, K. V. (1966). Collaboration among six persons in a prisoner's dilemma game. *Journal of Conflict Resolution, 10,* 488–496.

Blake, R. R., & Mouton, J. S. (1961). Reactions to intergroup competition under win-lose conditions. *Management Science, 7,* 420–435.

Blake, R. R., & Mouton, J. S. (1964). *The managerial grid.* Houston: Gulf.

Blanz, M., Mummendey, A., Mielke, R., & Klink, A. (1998). Responding to negative social identity: A taxonomy of identity management strategies. *European Journal of Social Psychology, 28*(5), 697–729.

Blau, P. (1964). *Exchange and power in social life.* New York: Wiley.

Bodenhausen, G. V. (1990). Stereotypes as judgmental heuristics: Evidence of circadian variations in discrimination. *Psychological Science, 1,* 319–322.

Bodenhausen, G. V., & Lichtenstein, M. (1987). Social stereotypes and information processing strategies: The impact of task complexity. *Journal of Personality and Social Psychology, 52,* 871–880.

Bodenhausen, G. V., Schwarz, N., Bless, H., & Wanke, M. (1995). Effects of atypical exemplars on racial beliefs: Enlightened racism or generalized appraisals? *Journal of Experimental Social Psychology, 31,* 48–63.

Bonacich, P., Shure, G. H., Kahan, J. P., & Meeker, R. J. (1976). Cooperation and group size in the n-person prisoners' dilemma. *Journal of Conflict Resolution, 20,* 687–706.

Bond, C. F., & Titus, L. J. (1983). Social facilitation: A meta-analysis of 241 studies. *Psychological Bulletin, 94*(2), 265–292.

Bond, M. A., & Keys, C. B. (1993). Empowerment, diversity, and collaboration: Promoting synergy on community boards. *American Journal of Community Psychology, 21,* 37–57.

Bond, M. H., & Shiu, W. Y.-F. (1997). The relationship between a group's personality resources and the two dimensions of its group process. *Small Group Research, 28*(2), 194–217.

Bond, M. H., Wan, K.-c., Leong, K., & Giacalone, R. A. (1985). How are responses to verbal insult related to cultural collectivism and power distance? *Journal of Cross-Cultural Psychology, 16*(1), 111–127.

Borgatta, E. F., & Bales, R. (1953). Task and accumulation of experience as factors in the interacting of small groups. *Sociometry, 26,* 239–252.

Borgatta, E. F., Cottrell, L. S., Jr., & Meyer, H. J. (1956). On the dimensions of group behavior. *Sociometry, 19,* 223–240.

Bornstein, R. F. (1992). The dependent personality: Developmental, social, and clinical perspectives. *Psychological Bulletin, 112*(1), 3–23.

Boster, F. J., Hunter, J. E., & Hale, J. L. (1991). An information-processing model of jury decision making. *Communication Research, 18,* 524–547.

Bottger, P. C., & Yetton, P. W. (1987). Improving group performance by training in individual problem solving. *Journal of Applied Psychology, 72*(4), 651–657.

Bourhis, R. Y., Giles, H., Leyens, J. P., & Tajfel, H. (1979). Psycholinguistic distinctiveness: Language divergence in Belgium. In H. Giles & R. S. Clair (Eds.), *Language and social psychology* (pp. 158–185). Oxford: Blackwell.

Bowers, C. A., Braun, C. C., & Morgan, B. B., Jr. (1997). Team workload: Its meaning and measurement. In M. T. Brannick & E. Salas (Eds.), *Team performance assessment and measurement: Theory, methods, and applications* (pp. 85–108). Mahwah, NJ: Erlbaum.

Bowers, C. A., Pharmer, J., & Salas, E. (2000). When member homogeneity is needed in work teams: A meta-analysis. *Small Group Research, 31,* 305–327.

Bowlby, J. (1969). Disruption of affectional bonds and its effects on behavior. *Canada's Mental Health Supplement, 59,* 12.

Bowlby, J. (1979). On knowing what you are not supposed to know and feeling what you are not supposed to feel. *Canadian Journal of Psychiatry, 24*(5), 403–408.

Boyanowsky, E. O., & Allen, V. L. (1973). In-group norms and self-identity as determinants of discriminatory behavior. *Journal of Personality and Social Psychology, 25,* 408–418.

Branscombe, N. R., Schmitt, M. T., & Harvey, R. D. (1999). Perceiving pervasive discrimination among African Americans: Implications for group identification and well-being. *Journal of Personality and Social Psychology, 77*(1), 135–149.

Branscombe, N. R., Wann, D. L., Noel, J. G., & Coleman, J. (1993). In-group or out-group extremity: Importance of the threatened social identity. *Personality and Social Psychology Bulletin, 19,* 381–388.

Brass, D. J. (1984). Being in the right place: A structural analysis of individual influence in an organization. *Administrative Science Quarterly, 29*(4), 518–539.

Brauer, M., & Judd, C. M. (1996). Group polarization and repeated attitude expressions: A new take on an old topic. *European Review of Social Psychology, 7,* 173–207.

Braver, S. L., & Barnett, B. (1976). Effects of modeling on cooperation in a prisoner's dilemma game. *Journal of Personality and Social Psychology, 33,* 161–169.

Brawley, L. R., Carron, A. V., & Widmeyer, W. N. (1987). Assessing the cohesion of teams: Validity of the Group Environment Questionnaire. *Journal of Sport Psychology, 9*(3), 275–294.

Bray, R. M., Kerr, N. L., & Atkin, R. S. (1978). Effects of group size, problem difficulty, and sex on group performance and member reactions. *Journal of Personality and Social Psychology, 36,* 1224–1240.

Breakwell, G. M. (1993). Integrating paradigms, methodological implications. In G. M. Breakwell & D. V. Canter (Eds.), *Empirical approaches to social representations* (pp. 180–201). Oxford: Clarendon Press.

Brechner, K. C. (1977). An experimental analysis of social traps. *Journal of Experimental Social Psychology, 13,* 552–564.

Brehm, J. (1966). *A theory of psychological reactance.* New York: Academic Press.

Brewer, M. B. (1979). In-group bias in the minimal intergroup situation: A cognitive-motivational analysis. *Psychological Bulletin, 86,* 307–324.

Brewer, M. B. (1988). A dual process model of impression formation. In T. K. Srull & R. S. Wyer (Eds.), *Advances in social cognition* (Vol. 1, pp. 1–36). Hillsdale, NJ: Erlbaum.

Brewer, M. B. (1991). The social self: On being the same and different at the same time. *Personality and Social Psychology Bulletin, 17,* 475–482.

Brewer, M. B. (1996). When stereotypes lead to stereotyping: The use of stereotypes in person perception. In C. N. Macrae, C. Stangor, & M. Hewstone (Eds.), *Stereotypes and stereotyping* (pp. 254–275). New York: Guilford Press.

Brewer, M. B., & Campbell, D. T. (1976). *Ethnocentrism and intergroup attitudes: East African evidence.* New York: Sage.

Brewer, M. B., Dull, L., & Lui, L. (1981). Perceptions of the elderly: Stereotypes as prototypes. *Journal of Personality and Social Psychology, 41,* 656–670.

Brewer, M. B., & Kramer, R. M. (1986). Choice behavior in social dilemmas: Effects of social identity, group size, and decision framing. *Journal of Personality and Social Psychology, 50,* 543–547.

Brewer, M. B., & Miller, N. (1984). Beyond the contact hypothesis: Theoretical perspectives on desegregation. In N. Miller & M. Brewer (Eds.), *Groups in contact: The psychology of desegregation* (pp. 281–302). Orlando: Academic Press.

Brewer, M. B., Weber, J. G., & Carini, B. (1995). Person memory in intergroup contexts: Categorization versus individuation. *Journal of Personality and Social Psychology, 69*(1), 29–40.

Brickner, M. A., Harkins, S. G., & Ostrom, T. M. (1986). Effects of personal involvement: Thought-provoking implications for social loafing. *Journal of Personality and Social Psychology, 51*(4), 763–770.

Brief, A. P., Aldag, R. J., Russell, C. J., & Rude, D. E. (1981). Leader behavior in a police organization revisited. *Human Relations, 34*(12), 1037–1051.

Briggs, R., Adkins, M., Mittleman, D. D., Kruse, J., Miller, S., & Nunamaker, J. F. (1999). A technology transition model derived from field investigation of GSS use aboard the U.S.S. CORONADO. *Journal of Management Information Systems, 15,* 151–196.

Brodt, S. E., & Ross, L. D. (1998). The role of stereotyping in overconfident social prediction. *Social Cognition, 16,* 225–252.

Brown, B. B., & Lohr, M. J. (1987). Peer-group affiliation and adolescent self-esteem: An integration of ego-identity and symbolic-interaction theories. *Journal of Personality and Social Psychology, 52,* 47–55.

Brown, R. (1986). *Social psychology—The second edition.* New York: Free Press.

Brown, R. (1995). *Prejudice: Its social psychology.* Cambridge, MA: Blackwell.

Brown, R. (2000). *Group processes: Dynamics within and between groups* (2nd ed.). Oxford: Basil-Blackwell.

Brown, R. (1965). *Social psychology.* New York: Free Press.

Bruner, J. S. (1957). On perceptual readiness. *Psychological Review, 64,* 123–152.

Burns, J. M. (1978). *Leadership.* New York: Harper & Row.

Burt, R. S. (1982). *Toward a structural theory of action.* New York: Academic Press.

Buss, D., & Kenrick, D. (1998). Evolutionary social psychology. In D. T. Gilbert, S. T. Fiske, & G. Lindzey (Eds.), *Handbook of social psychology* (4 ed., Vol. 2, pp. 982–1026). Boston: McGraw Hill.

Buunk, B. P., & Gibbons, F. X. (Eds.). (1997). *Health, coping, and well-being: Perspectives from social comparison theory.* Mahwah, NJ: Erlbaum.

Buys, B. J. (1978). Humans would do better without groups. *Personality and Social Psychology Bulletin, 4,* 123–125.

Byrne, D. (1969). Attitudes and attraction. In L. Berkowitz (Ed.), *Advances in experimental social psychology* (Vol. 4). New York: Academic Press.

Cadinu, M. R., & Rothbart, M. (1996). Self-anchoring and differentiation processes in the minimal group setting. *Journal of Personality and Social Psychology, 70*, 661–677.

Cairns, R., Cairns, D., Necerman, J., Gest, S., & Gariépy, J.-L. (1988). Social networks and aggressive behavior: Peer support or peer rejection? *Developmental Psychology, 24*, 815–823.

Caldwell, M. D. (1976). Communication and sex effects in a five-person prisoner's dilemma game. *Journal of Personality and Social Psychology, 33*, 273–280.

Callaway, M. R., & Esser, J. K. (1984). Groupthink: Effects of cohesiveness and problem-solving procedures on group decision making. *Social Behavior and Personality, 12*, 157–164.

Campbell, D. T. (1958). Common fate, similarity, and other indices of the status of aggregate persons as social entities. *Behavioral Science, 3*, 14–25.

Campbell-Heider, N., & Pollock, D. (1987). Barriers to physician nurse collegiality: An anthropological perspective. *Social Science and Medicine, 25*, 421–425.

Cannon-Bowers, J. A., Salas, E., & Converse, S. (1993). Shared mental models in expert team decision making. In N. J. Castellan, , Jr. (Ed.), *Individual and group decision making: Current issues* (pp. 221–246). Hillsdale, NJ: Erlbaum.

Cannon-Bowers, J. A., Salas, E., & Converse, S. A. (1990). Cognitive psychology and team training: Shared mental models in complex systems. *Human Factors Bulletin, 33*, 1–4.

Cannon-Bowers, J. A., Salas, E., Tannenbaum, S. I., & Mathieu, J. E. (1995). Toward theoretically based principles of training effectiveness: A model and initial empirical investigation. *Military Psychology, 7*(3), 141–164.

Cantor, N., & Harlow, R. E. (1994). Social intelligence and personality: Flexible life task pursuit. In R. J. Sternberg & P. Ruzqis (Eds.), *Personality and intelligence* (pp. 137–168). New York: Cambridge University Press.

Cantor, N., & Mischel, W. (1977). Traits as prototypes: Effects on recognition memory. *Journal of Personality and Social Psychology, 35*, 38–48.

Caporael, L. R. B., M. B. (1991). The quest for human nature: Social and scientific issues in evolutionary psychology. *Journal of Social Issues, 47*(3), 1–10.

Carnevale, P. J. (1986). Strategic choice in mediation. *Negotiation Journal, 2*, 41–56.

Carnevale, P. J., & Pruitt, D. (1992). Negotiation and mediation. *Annual Review of Psychology, 43*, 531–582.

Carnevale, P. J., Pruitt, D. G., & Seilheimer, S. D. (1981). Looking and competing: Accountability and visual access in integrative bargaining. *Journal of Personality and Social Psychology, 40*(1), 111–120.

Carron, A. B. (1980). *Social psychology of sport.* Ithaca, NY: Mouvement Publications.

Cartwright, D., & Zander, A. (Eds.). (1968). *Group dynamics: Research and theory* (3 ed.). New York: Harper & Row.

Carver, C. S., & Scheier, M. F. (1981). *Attention and self-regulation: A control-theory approach to human behavior.* New York: Springer Verlag.

Cass, R. C., & Edney, J. J. (1978). The commons dilemma: A simulation testing resource visibility and territorial division. *Human Ecology, 6*, 371–386.

Cassidy, J., & Shaver, P. (Eds.). (1999). *Handbook of attachment: Theory, research, and clinical applications.* New York: Guilford Press.

Cattell, R. B. (1951). New concepts for measuring leadership in terms of group syntality. *Human Relations, 4*, 161–184.

Chaiken, S., & Stangor, C. (1987). Attitudes and attitude change. In M. R. Rosenzweig, L. W. Porter, et al. (Eds.), *Annual review of psychology, Vol. 38. Annual review of psychology* (pp. 575–630). Palo Alto, CA: Annual.

Chan, D. K. S., Gelfand, M. J., Triandis, H. C., & Tzeng, O. (1996). Tightness-looseness revisited: Some preliminary analyses in Japan and the United States. *International Journal of Psychology, 31*, 1–12.

Chemers, M. M., Hays, R. B., Rhodewalt, F., & Wysocki, J. (1985). A person-environment analysis of job stress: A contingency model explanation. *Journal of Personality and Social Psychology, 49*(3), 628–635.

Choi, J. N., & Kim, M. U. (1999). The organizational application of groupthink and its limitations in organizations. *Journal of Applied Psychology, 84*(2), 297–306.

Cialdini, R. B. (1993). *Influence: Science and practice* (4 ed.). Boston: Allyn & Bacon.

Cialdini, R. B., Borden, R. J., Thorne, A., Walker, M. R., Freeman, S., & Sloan, L. R. (1976). Basking in reflected glory: Three (football) field studies. *Journal of Personality and Social Psychology, 34*, 366–374.

Cialdini, R. B., Kallgren, C. A., & Reno, R. R. (1991). A focus theory of normative conduct. *Advances in Experimental Social Psychology, 24*, 201–234.

Clark, K., & Clark, M. (1947). Racial identification and preference in Negro children. In E. Maccoby, T. Newcomb, & E. Hartley (Eds.), *Readings in social psychology* (pp. 602–611). New York: Holt, Rinehart & Winston.

Clark, M. S., & Reis, H. T. (1988). Interpersonal processes in close relationships. In M. R. P. Rosenzweig & W. Lyman (Eds.), *Annual review of psychology, Vol. 39* (pp. 609–672). Palo Alto, CA: Annual Reviews.

Clark, N. K., & Stephenson, G. M. (1989). Group remembering. In P. B. Paulus (Ed.), *Psychology of group influence* (Vol. 2, pp. 357–391). Hillsdale, NJ: Erlbaum.

Clark, R. D., Crockett, W. H., & Archer, R. L. (1971). Risk-as-value hypothesis: The relationship between perception of self, others, and the risky shift. *Journal of Personality and Social Psychology, 20*, 425–429.

Cohen, A. R. (1958). Upward communication in experimentally created hierarchies. *Human Relations, 11*, 41–53.

Cohen, D., Nisbett, R. E., Bosdle, B., & Schwarz, N. (1996). Insult, aggression, and the southern culture of honor: An "experimental ethnography." *Journal of Personality and Social Psychology, 70*, 945–960.

Cohen, E. G. (1982). Expectation states and interracial interaction in school settings. *Annual Review of Sociology, 8*, 209–235.

Cohen, J. (1992). A power primer. *Psychological Bulletin, 112*, 155–159.

Cohen, S., Sherrod, D., & Clark, M. (1986). Social skills and the stress-protective role of social support. *Journal of Personality and Social Psychology, 50*(5), 963–973.

Cohen, S., Tyrrell, D. A., & Smith, A. P. (1991). Psychological stress and susceptibility to the common cold. *New England Journal of Medicine, 325*(9), 606–612.

Cohen, S., & Wills, T. (1985). Stress, social support, and the buffering hypothesis. *Psychological Bulletin, 98*, 310–357.

Collaros, P. A., & Anderson, I. R. (1969). Effect of perceived expertness upon creativity of members of brainstorming groups. *Journal of Applied Psychology, 53*, 159–163.

Commins, B., & Lockwood, J. (1978). The effects on intergroup relations of mixing Roman Catholics and Protestants: An experimental investigation. *European Journal of Social Psychology, 8*, 383–386.

Computing: Social and policy issues. (Special issue). *Social Science Computer Review, 8*(1), 1–12.

Conger, J. A., & Kanungo, R. N. (1998). *Charismatic leadership in organizations.* Thousand Oaks, CA: Sage.

Connolly, T., Routhieaux, R. L., & Schneider, S. K. (1993). On the effectiveness of group brainstorming: Test of one underlying cognitive mechanism. *Small Group Research, 24*(4), 490–503.

Cook, S. W. (1978). Interpersonal and attitudinal outcomes in cooperating interracial groups. *Journal of Research in Developmental Education, 12,* 97–113.

Cook, S. W. (1984). Cooperative interaction in multiethnic contexts. In N. Miller & M. B. Brewer (Eds.), *Groups in contact.* New York: Academic Press.

Cooley, C. H. (1902). *Human nature and social order.* New York: Scribner.

Cooley, C. H. (1909). *Social organization.* New York: Scribner.

Corning, P. (1986). *Winning with synergy.* New York: Harper & Row.

Coser, L. A. (1956). *The functions of social conflict.* Glencoe, IL: Free Press.

Coser, L. A. (1967). *Continuities in the study of social conflict.* New York: Free Press.

Coser, L. A. (1974). *Greedy institutions: Patterns of undivided commitment.* New York: Free Press.

Cota, A. A., & Dion, K. L. (1986). Salience of gender and sex composition of ad hoc groups: An experimental test of distinctiveness theory. *Journal of Personality and Social Psychology, 50*(4), 770–776.

Cota, A. A., Evans, C. R., Dion, K. L., Kilik, L., et al. (1995). The structure of group cohesion. *Personality and Social Psychology Bulletin, 21,* 572–580.

Cottrell, N. (1968). Performance in the presence of other human beings: Mere presence, audience, and affiliation effects. In E. Simmel, R. Hoppe, & G. Milton (Eds.), *Social facilitation and imitative behavior.* Boston: Allyn & Bacon.

Cousins, S. D. (1989). Culture and self-perception in Japan and the United States. *Journal of Personality and Social Psychology, 56,* 124–131.

Coyne, J. C., & Downey, G. (1991). Social factors and psychopathology: Stress, social support, and coping processes. *Annual Review of Psychology, 42,* 401–425.

Crandall, C. S. (1988). Social contagion of binge eating. *Journal of Personality and Social Psychology, 55*(4), 588–598.

Crano, W. D., & Chen, X. (1998). The leniency contract and persistence of majority and minority influence. *Journal of Personality and Social Psychology, 74,* 1437–1450.

Cratty, B. J. (1981). *Social psychology in athletics.* Englewood Cliffs, NJ: Prentice-Hall.

Crawford, M. T., Sherman, S. J., & Hamilton, D. L. (2002). Perceived entitativity stereotype formation, and the interchangeability of group members. *Journal of Personality and Social Psychology, 83,* 1076–1094.

Crocker, J., & Luhtanen, R. (1990). Collective self-esteem and in-group bias. *Journal of Personality and Social Psychology, 58,* 60–67.

Cronshaw, S. F., & Lord, R. G. (1987). Effects of categorization, attribution, and encoding processes on leadership perceptions. *Journal of Applied Psychology, 72*(1), 97–106.

Crosbie, P. V. (1979). Effects of status inconsistency: Negative evidence from small groups. *Social Psychology Quarterly, 83,* 85–113.

Crosby, F. (1976). A model of egoistical relative deprivation. *Psychological Review, 83,* 85–113.

Cross, J. G., & Guyer, M. J. (1980). *Social traps.* Ann Arbor: University of Michigan Press.

Crott, H. W., & Werner, J. (1994). The Norm-Information-Distance model: A stochastic approach to preference change in group interaction. *Journal of Experimental Social Psychology, 30*(1), 68–95.

Crutchfield, R. S. (1955). Conformity and character. *American Psychologist, 10,* 191–198.

Cutrona, C. (1989). Ratings of social support by adolescents and adult informants: Degree of correspondence and prediction of depressive symptoms. *Journal of Personality and Social Psychology, 57,* 723–730.

Dabbs Jr., J. M., & Ruback, R. B. (1987). Dimensions of group process: Amount and structure of vocal interaction. In L. Berkowitz (Ed.), *Advances in experimental social psychology* (Vol. 20, pp. 123–169). San Diego: Academic Press.

Danheiser, P. R., & Graziano, W. G. (1982). Self-monitoring and cooperation as a self-presentational strategy. *Journal of Personality and Social Psychology, 42*(3), 497–505.

Darley, J. M., & Fazio, R. H. (1980). Expectancy confirmation processes arising in the social interaction sequence. *American Psychologist, 35*, 867–881.

Dasgupta, N., Banaji, M., & Abelson, R. (1999). Group entativity and group perception: Associations between physical features and psychological judgment. *Journal of Personality and Social Psychology, 77*, 991–1003.

Dashiell, J. F. (1930). An experimental analysis of some group effects. *Journal of Abnormal and Social Psychology, 25*, 190–199.

Davis, J. H. (1969a). *Group performance*. New York: Addison-Wesley.

Davis, J. H. (1969b). Individual-group problem solving, subject preference, and problem type. *Journal of Personality and Social Psychology, 13*, 362–374.

Davis, J. H. (1973). Group decision and social interaction: A theory of social decision schemes. *Psychological Review, 80*, 97–125.

Davis, J. H. (1975). The decision processes of 6- and 12-person mock juries assigned unanimous and two-thirds majority rules. *Journal of Personality and Social Psychology, 32*(1), 1–14.

Davis, J. H., Stasson, M. F., Ono, K., & Zimmerman, S. (1988). Effects of straw polls on group decision making: Sequential voting pattern, timing, and local majorities. *Journal of Personality and Social Psychology, 55*(6), 918–926.

Davis, J. H., Stasson, M. F., Parks, C. D., Hulbert, L., et al. (1993). Quantitative decisions by groups and individuals: Voting procedures and monetary awards by mock civil juries. *Journal of Experimental Social Psychology, 29*(4), 326–346.

Davis, J., & Smith, T. (1996). *General Social Surveys, 1972–1996*. National Opinion Research Center. Available: www.icpsr.umich.edu/GSS99.

Dawes, R. M. (1980). Social dilemmas. *Annual Review of Psychology, 31*, 169–193.

De Bruin, E. N. M., & Van Lange, P. A. M. (1999). Impression formation and cooperative behavior. *European Journal of Social Psychology, 29*, 305–328.

De Dreu, C. K. W., & McCusker, C. (1997). Gain-loss frames and cooperation in two-person social dilemmas: A transformational analysis. *Journal of Personality and Social Psychology, 72*(5), 1093–1106.

De Dreu, C. K. W., & Van Lange, P. A. M. (1995). The impact of social value orientations on negotiator cognition and behavior. *Personality and Social Psychology Bulletin, 21*(11), 1178–1188.

De Dreu, C. K. W., Yzerbyt, V. Y., & Leyens, J.-P. (1995). Dilution of stereotype-based cooperation in mixed-motive interdependence. *Journal of Experimental Social Psychology, 31*, 575–593.

Deaux, K. (1996). Social identification. In E. T. Higgins & A. W. Kruglanski (Eds.), *Social psychology: Handbook of basic principles* (pp. 777–798). New York: Guilford Press.

Deaux, K., & Lewis, L. (1984). The structure of gender stereotypes: Interrelationships among components and gender label. *Journal of Personality and Social Psychology, 46*, 991–1004.

Deaux, K., Reid, A., Mizrahi, K., & Ethier, K. A. (1995). Parameters of social identity. *Journal of Personality and Social Psychology, 68*(2), 280–291.

DeLamater, J. A. (1974). A definition of "group." *Small Group Behavior, 5*, 30–44.

Delbecq, A. L., Van de Ven, A. H., & Gustafson, D. H. (1975). *Group techniques for program planning: A guide to nominal group and delphi processes*. Glenview, IL: Scott, Foresman.

Dennis, A. R., & Valacich, J. S. (1993). Computer brainstorms: More heads are better than one. *Journal of Applied Psychology, 78*, 531–537.

Desforges, D. M., Lord, C. G., Ramsey, S. L., Mason, J. A., Van Leeuwen, M. D., West, S. C., et al. (1991). Effects of structured cooperative contact on changing negative attitudes toward stigmatized social groups. *Journal of Personality and Social Psychology, 60*(4), 531–544.

Deutsch, M. (1949a). A theory of cooperation and competition. *Human Relations, 2*, 129–152.

Deutsch, M. (1949b). An experimental study of the effects of cooperation and competition upon group processes. *Human Relations, 2*, 199–231.

Deutsch, M. (1973). *The resolution of conflict.* New Haven: Yale University Press.

Deutsch, M. (1994). Constuctive conflict resolution: Principles, training, and research. *Journal of Social Issues, 1*, 13-32.

Deutsch, M., & Collins, M. E. (1968). *Interracial housing: A psychological evaluation of a social experiment.* New York: Russell & Russell.

Deutsch, M., & Gerard, H. B. (1955). A study of normative and informational social influences upon individual judgment. *Journal of Abnormal and Social Psychology, 51*, 629–636.

Deutsch, M., & Krauss, R. M. (1960). The effect of threat upon interpersonal bargaining. *Journal of Abnormal and Social Psychology, 61*, 181–189.

Devine, P. G. (1989). Stereotypes and prejudice: Their automatic and controlled components. *Journal of Personality and Social Psychology, 56*, 5–18.

Devine, P. G., & Baker, S. M. (1991). Measurement of racial stereotype subtyping. *Personality and Social Psychology Bulletin, 17*, 44–50.

Devine, P. G., & Elliot, A. J. (1995). Are racial stereotypes really fading? The Princeton trilogy revisited. *Personality and Social Psychology Bulletin, 21*, 1139–1150.

Diehl, M. (1989). Justice and discrimination between minimal groups: The limits of equity. *British Journal of Social Psychology, 28*(3), 227–238.

Diehl, M., & Stroebe, W. (1987). Productivity loss in brainstorming groups: Toward the solution of a riddle. *Journal of Personality and Social Psychology, 53*, 497–509.

Diehl, M., & Stroebe, W. (1991). Productivity loss in idea-generating groups: Tracking down the blocking effect. *Journal of Personality and Social Psychology, 61*(3), 392–403.

Diener, E. (1976). Effects of prior destructive behavior, anonymity, and group presence on deindividuation and aggression. *Journal of Personality and Social Psychology, 33*, 497–507.

Diener, E. (1980). Deindividuation: The absence of self-awareness and self-regulation in group members. In P. Paulus (Ed.), *The psychology of group influence.* Hillsdale, NJ: Erlbaum.

Diener, E., Fraser, S. C., Beaman, A. L., & Kelem, R. T. (1976). Effects of deindividuation variables on stealing among stealing Halloween trick-or-treaters. *Journal of Personality and Social Psychology, 33*, 178–183.

Dion, K. L. (1973). Cohesiveness as a determinant of in-group-out-group bias. *Journal of Personality and Social Psychology, 28*, 163–171.

Dion, K. L. (1979a). Intergroup conflict and intergroup cohesiveness. In W. G. Austin & S. Worchel (Eds.), *The social psychology of intergroup relations.* Monterey, CA: Brooks-Cole.

Dion, K. L. (1979b). Status equity, sex composition of group, and intergroup bias. *Personality and Social Psychology Bulletin, 5*(2), 240–244.

Dion, K. L. (1986). Responses to perceived discrimination and relative deprivation. In J. M. Olson, C. P. Herman, & M. P. Zanna (Eds.), *Relative deprivation and social comparison: The Ontario symposium* (Vol. 5, pp. 159–179). Hillsdale, NJ: Erlbaum.

Dion, K. L., & Evans, C. R. (1992). On cohesiveness: Reply to Keyton and other critics of the construct. *Small Group Research, 23*, 242–250.

Distefano, J. J., & Manznevski, M. L. (2000). Creating value with diverse teams in global management. *Organizational Dynamics, 29*, 45–62.

DiTommaso, E., & Spinner, B. (1997). Social and emotional loneliness: A re-examination of Weiss's typology of loneliness. *Personality and Individual Differences, 22*, 242–250.

Dittrich, J., & Carrell, M. (1979). Organization equity perceptions, employee job satisfaction, and departmental absence and turnover rates. *Organizational Behavior and Human Performance, 24*, 29–40.

Doosje, B., Ellemers, N., & Spears, R. (1995). Perceived intragroup variability as a function of group status and identification. *Journal of Experimental Social Psychology, 31*(5), 410–436.

Dovidio, J. F., Brigham, J. C., Johnson, B. T., & Gaertner, S. L. (1996). Stereotyping, prejudice, and discrimination: Another look. In C. N. Macrae, C. Stangor, & M. Hewstone (Eds.), *Stereotypes and stereotyping* (pp. 276–322). New York: Guilford Press.

Dovidio, J. F., Brown, C. E., Heltman, K., Ellyson, S. L., & Keation, C. F. (1988). Power displays between women and men in discussions of gender linked tasks: A multichannel study. *Journal of Personality and Social Psychology, 55*, 580–587.

Dovidio, J., Evans, N., & Tyler, R. (1986). Racial stereotypes: The contents of their cognitive representations. *Journal of Experimental Social Psychology, 22*, 22–37.

Dovidio, J. F., Gaertner, S. L., Isen, A. M., & Lowrance, R. (1995). Group representations and intergroup bias: Positive affect, similarity, and group size. *Personality and Social Psychology Bulletin, 21*(8), 856–865.

Dovidio, J. F., Gaertner, S. L., Validzic, A., Matoka, K., et al. (1997). Extending the benefits of recategorization: Evaluations, self-disclosure, and helping. *Journal of Experimental Social Psychology, 33*(4), 401–420.

Drinka, T. J. K., & Streim, J. E. (1994). Case studies from purgatory: Maladaptive behavior within geriatrics health care teams. *Gerontologist, 34*(4), 541–547.

Driskell, J. E., Hogan, R., & Salas, E. (1987). Personality and group performance. In C. Hendrick (Ed.), *Group processes and intergroup relations* (pp. 91–112). Newbury Park, CA: Sage.

Driskell, J. E., & Mullen, B. (1990). Status, expectations, and behavior: A meta-analytic review and test of the theory. *Personality and Social Psychology Bulletin, 16*, 541–553.

Dubrovsky, V. J., Kiesler, S., & Sethna, B. N. (1991). The equalization phenomenon: Status effects in computer-mediated and face-to-face decision-making groups. *Human-Computer Interaction, 6*, 119–146.

Duncan, B. L. (1976). Differential social perception and attribution of intergroup violence: Testing the lower limits of stereotyping of blacks. *Journal of Personality and Social Psychology, 34*, 590–598.

Dunnette, M. D., & Hough, L. M. (Eds.). (2001). *Handbook of industrial and organizational psychology*. Palo Alto, CA: Consulting Psychology.

Dunning, E., Murphy, P., & Williams, J. (1986). Spectator violence at football matches: Towards a sociological explanation. *British Journal of Sociology, 37*(2), 221–244.

Durkheim, E. (1938/1982). *The rules of sociological method*. New York: Free Press.

Durkheim, E. (1951). *Suicide*. Glencoe, IL: Free Press.

Durkheim, E., & Mauss, M. (1903). *Primitive classification*. London.

Duval, S., & Wicklund, R. A. (1972). *A theory of objective self-awareness*. New York: Academic Press.

Eagly, A. H. (1978). Sex differences in influenceability. *Psychological Bulletin, 85*(1), 86–116.

Eagly, A. H. (1983). Gender and social influence: A social psychological analysis. *American Psychologist, 38*(9), 971–981.

Eagly, A. H. (1987). *Sex differences in social behavior: A social-role interpretation*. Hillsdale, NJ: Erlbaum.

Eagly, A. H., & Carli, L. L. (1981). Sex of researchers and sex-typed communications as determinants of sex differences in influenceability: A meta-analysis of social influence studies. *Psychological Bulletin, 90*, 1–20.

Eagly, A. H., & Chaiken, S. (1978). Causal inferences about communicators and their effect on opinion change. *Journal of Personality and Social Psychology, 36*, 424–435.

Eagly, A. H., & Chaiken, S. (1993). *The psychology of attitudes*. Fort Worth, TX: Harcourt Brace Jovanovich.

Eagly, A. H., & Chrvala, C. (1986). Sex differences in conformity: Status and gender-role interpretations. *Psychology of Women Quarterly, 10,* 203–220.

Eagly, A. H., & Johnson, B. T. (1990). Gender and leadership style: A meta-analysis. *Psychological Bulletin, 108,* 233–256.

Eagly, A. H., Karau, S. J., & Makhijani, M. G. (1995). Gender and the effectiveness of leaders: A meta-analysis. *Psychological Bulletin, 117*(1), 125–145.

Eagly, A. H., Makhijani, M. G., & Klonsky, B. G. (1992). Gender and evaluation of leaders: A meta-analysis. *Psychological Bulletin, 111,* 3–22.

Eagly, A. H., & Steffen, V. J. (1984). Gender stereotypes stem from the distribution of women and men into social roles. *Journal of Personality and Social Psychology, 46,* 735–754.

Eagly, A. H., & Wood, W. (1982). Inferred sex differences in status as a determinant of gender stereotypes about social influence. *Journal of Personality and Social Psychology, 43,* 915–928.

Ebbesen, E. B., & Bowers, R. J. (1974). Proportion of risky to conservative arguments in a group discussion and choice shifts. *Journal of Personality and Social Psychology, 29,* 316–327.

Edney, J. J. (1979). The nuts game: A concise commons dilemma analog. *Environmental Psychology and Nonverbal Behavior, 3*(4), 252–254.

Edney, J. J. (1980). The commons problem: Alternative perspectives. *American Psychologist, 35,* 131–150.

Einhorn, H. J., Hogarth, R. M., & Klempner, E. (1977). Quality of group judgment. *Psychological Bulletin, 84*(1), 158–172.

Eisenberg, E. M., Monge, P. R., & Miller, K. I. (1983). Involvement in communication networks as a predictor of organizational commitment. *Communication Research, 10,* 179–201.

Eiser, R. J., & Stroebe, W. (1972). *Categorization and social judgment.* New York: Academic Press.

Ellemers, N. (1993). The influence of socio-structural variables on identity management strategies. *European Review of Social Psychology, 4,* 22–57.

Ellemers, N., Doosje, B., Van Knippenberg, A., & Wilke, H. (1992). Status protection in high status minority groups. *European Journal of Social Psychology, 22,* 123–140.

Ellemers, N., Spears, R., & Doosje, B. (1997). Sticking together or falling apart: In-group identification as a psychological determinant of group commitment versus individual mobility. *Journal of Personality and Social Psychology, 72,* 617–626.

Ellemers, N., Van Knippenberg, A., de Vries, N., & Wilke, H. (1988). Social identification and permeability of group boundaries. *European Journal of Social Psychology, 18,* 497–513.

Ellemers, N., Van Knippenberg, A., & Wilke, H. A. (1990). The influence of permeability of group boundaries and stability of group status on strategies of individual mobility and social change. *British Journal of Social Psychology, 29*(3), 233–246.

Ellemers, N., Wilke, H., & Van Knippenberg, A. (1993). Effects of the legitimacy of low group or individual status on individual and collective status-enhancement strategies. *Journal of Personality and Social Psychology, 64,* 766–778.

Ellsworth, P. C. (1993). Some steps between attitudes and verdicts. In R. Hastie (Ed.), *Inside the juror: The psychology of juror decision making.* New York: Cambridge University Press.

Emler, N., & Hopkins, N. (1990). Reputation, social identity and the self. In D. Abrams & M. Hogg (Eds.), *Social identity theory: Constructive and critical advances.* New York: Springer Verlag.

Ennett, S. T., & Bauman, K. E. (1994). The contribution of influence and selection to adolescent peer group homogeneity: The case of adolescent cigarette smoking. *Journal of Personality and Social Psychology, 67,* 653–663.

Epley, S., & Cottrell, N. (1977). Effect of presence of a companion on speed of escape from electric shock. *Psychological Reports, 40*(3, pt 2), 1299–1308.

Erffmeyer, E. S. (1984). Rule violation on the golf course. *Perceptual and Motor Skills, 59*, 591–596.

Ethier, K. A., & Deaux, K. (1994). Negotiating social identity when contexts change: Maintaining identification and responding to threat. *Journal of Personality and Social Psychology, 67*, 243–251.

Evans, C. R., & Dion, K. L. (1991). Group cohesion and performance: A meta-analysis. *Small Group Research, 22*, 175–186.

Evans, M. G. (1970). The effects of supervisory behavior on the path-goal relationship. *Organizational Behavior and Human Decision Processes, 5*, 277–298.

Fairhurst, G. T. (1993). The leader-member exchange patterns of women leaders in industry: A discourse analysis. *Communication Monographs, 60*(4), 321–351.

Fazio, R., Jackson, J., Dunton, B., & Williams, C. (1995). Variability in automatic activation as an unobtrusive measure of racial attitudes: A bona fide pipeline? *Journal of Personality and Social Psychology, 69*, 1013–1027.

Fein, S., & Spencer, S. J. (1997). Prejudice as self-image maintenance: Affirming the self through derogating others. *Journal of Personality and Social Psychology, 73*, 31–44.

Feldbaum, C. L., Christenson, T. E., & O'Neal, E. C. (1980). An observational study of the assimilation of the newcomer to the preschool. *Child Development, 51*, 497–507.

Feldman, D. C. (1984). The development and enforcement of group norms. *Academy of Management Review, 9*(1), 47–53.

Festinger, L. (1950). Informal social communication. *Psychological Review, 57*, 271–282.

Festinger, L. (1954). A theory of social comparison processes. *Human Relations, 7*, 117–140.

Festinger, L., Pepitone, A., & Newcomb, T. (1952). Some consequences of deindividuation in a group. *Journal of Abnormal and Social Psychology, 47*, 382–389.

Festinger, L., Riecken, H. W., & Schachter, S. (1956). *When prophecy fails: A social and psychological study of a modern group that predicted the destruction of the world.* Minneapolis: University of Minnesota Press.

Festinger, L., Schachter, S., & Back, K. (1950). *Social pressures in informal groups.* New York: Harper.

Fielding, K. S., & Hogg, M. A. (1997). Social identity, self-categorization, and leadership: A field study of small interactive groups. *Group Dynamics, 1*, 39–51.

Fiedler, F. E. (1967). *A theory of leadership effectiveness.* New York: McGraw-Hill.

Fiedler, F. E., & Garcia, J. E. (1987). *New approaches to effective leadership: Cognitive resources and organizational performance.* New York: Wiley.

Finch, J. F., Barrera, M. J., Okun, M. A., Bryant, W. H., Pool, G. J., & Snow-Turek, A. L. (1997). The factor structure of received social support: Dimensionality and the prediction of depression and life satisfaction. *Journal of Social and Clinical Psychology, 16*, 323–342.

Fisek, M. H., Berger, J., & Norman, R. Z. (1991). Participation in heterogeneous and homogeneous groups: A theoretical integration. *American Journal of Sociology, 97*(1), 114–142.

Fiske, A. P., & Haslam, N. (1996). Social cognition is thinking about relationships. *Current Directions in Psychological Science, 5*(5), 137–142.

Fiske, A. P., Haslam, N., & Fiske, S. T. (1991). Confusing one person with another: What errors reveal about the elementary forms of social relations. *Journal of Personality and Social Psychology, 60*, 656–674.

Fiske, A. P., Kitayama, S., Markus, H., & Nisbett, R. (1998). The cultural matrix of social psychology. In D. Gilbert, S. Fiske, & G. Lindzey (Eds.), *The handbook of social psychology* (4th ed., pp. 915–981). New York: McGraw-Hill.

Fiske, S. T. (1982). Social cognition and affect. In J. Harvey (Ed.), *Cognition, social behavior and the environment.* Hillsdale, NJ: Erlbaum.

Fiske, S. T. (1989). Examining the role of intent: Toward understanding its role in stereotyping and prejudice. In J. S. Uleman & J. A. Bargh (Eds.), *Unintended thought* (pp. 253–286). New York: Guilford.

Fiske, S. T. (1993). Controlling other people: The impact of power on stereotyping. *American Psychologist, 48*, 621–628.

Fiske, S. T. (1998). Stereotyping, prejudice and discrimination. In D. T. Gilbert, S. T. Fiske, & G. Lindzey (Eds.), *Handbook of social psychology* (4th ed., Vol. 2, pp. 357–414). New York: McGraw-Hill.

Fiske, S. T., Bersoff, D. N., Borgida, E., Deaux, K., & Heilman, M. E. (1991). Social science research on trial: The use of sex stereotyping research in Price Waterhouse vs. Hopkins. *American Psychologist, 46*, 1049–1060.

Fiske, S. T., & Neuberg, S. L. (1990). A continuum of impression formation, from category based to individuating processes: Influences of information and motivation on attention and interpretation. In M. P. Zanna (Ed.), *Advances in experimental social psychology* (Vol. 23, pp. 1–74). New York: Academic Press.

Fiske, S. T., & Taylor, S. E. (1991). *Social cognition* (2nd ed.). New York: McGraw-Hill.

Flaherty, T. B., Dahlstrom, R., & Skinner, S. J. (1999). Organizational values and role stress as determinants of customer-oriented selling performance. *Journal of Personal Selling and Sales Management, 19*(2), 1–18.

Flowers, M. L. (1977). A laboratory test of some implications of Janis's groupthink hypothesis. *Journal of Personality and Social Psychology, 35*, 888–896.

Foels, R., Driskell, J., Mullen, B., & Salas, E. (2000). The effects of democratic leadership on group member satisfaction: An integration. *Small Group Research, 31*, 676–701.

Folkman, S., & Lazarus, R. S. (1980). An analysis of coping in a middle-aged community sample. *Journal of Health & Social Behavior, 21*(3), 219–239.

Ford, T. E., & Stangor, C. (1992). The role of diagnosticity in stereotype formation: Perceiving group means and variances. *Journal of Personality and Social Psychology, 63*(3), 356–367.

Forsyth, D. (1999). *Group dynamics* (3rd ed.). Belmont, CA: Brooks-Cole.

Foschi, M. (1996). Double standards in the evaluation of men and women. *Social Psychology Quarterly, 48*, 237–254.

Fox, J., & Guyer, M. (1978). "Public" choice and cooperation in n-person prisoner's dilemma. *Journal of Conflict Resolution, 22*, 469–481.

Fox, W. M. (1989). The improved Nominal Group Technique (NGT). *Journal of Management Development, 8*, 20–27.

Fraley, R. C. (2002). Attachment stability from infancy to adulthood: Meta-analysis and dynamic modeling of developmental mechanisms. *Personality and Social Psychology Review, 6*, 123–151.

Frank, F., & Anderson, L. R. (1971). Effects of task and group size upon group productivity and member satisfaction. *Sociometry, 34*, 135–149.

Fraser, C., Gouge, C., & Billig, M. (1971). Risky shifts, cautious shifts, and group polarization. *European Journal of Social Psychology, 1*, 7–30.

Freedman, J. L., & Doob, A. N. (1968). *Deviancy: The psychology of being different*. New York: Academic Press.

French, J. R. P., & Raven, B. H. (1959). The bases of social power. In D. Cartwright (Ed.), *Studies in social power* (pp. 150–167). Ann Arbor, MI: Institute for Social Research.

Freud, S. (1922). *Group psychology and the analysis of the ego*. London: Hogarth.

Fry, L. W., & Slocum, J. W. (1984). Technology, structure and workgroup effectiveness. *Academy of Management Journal, 27*, 221–246.

Fuller, S. R., & Aldag, R. J. (2001). The GGPS Model: Broadening the perspective on group problem solving. In M. E. Turner (Ed.), *Groups at work: Theory and research* (pp. 3–24). Mahwah, NJ: Erlbaum.

Fyock, J., & Stangor, C. (1994). The role of memory biases in stereotype maintenance. *British Journal of Social Psychology, 33*(3), 331–343.

Gabrenya, W. K., Wang, Y.-e., & Latané, B. (1985). Social loafing on an optimizing task: Cross-cultural differences among Chinese and Americans. *Journal of Cross-Cultural Psychology, 16*(2), 223–242.

Gaertner, S. L., & Schopler, J. (1998). Perceived ingroup entitativity and intergroup bias: An interconnection of self and others. *European Journal of Social Psychology, 28*, 963–980.

Gaertner, S. L., Dovidio, J. F., Anastasio, P. A., Bachman, B. A., & Rust, M. C. (1993). The common ingroup identity model: Recategorization and the reduction of intergroup bias. In W. Stroebe & M. Hewstone (Eds.), *European review of social psychology* (Vol. 4, pp. 1–26). Chichester, UK: Wiley.

Gaertner, S. L., Dovidio, J. F., & Bachman, B. A. (1996). Revisiting the contact hypothesis: The induction of a common ingroup identity. *International Journal of Intercultural Relations, 20*(2 & 4), 1–290. Special issue: International Congress on Prejudice, Discrimination and Conflict, Jerusalem, Israel.

Gaertner, S. L., Mann, J. A., Dovidio, J. F., Murrell, A. J., & Pomare, M. (1990). How does cooperation reduce intergroup bias? *Journal of Personality and Social Psychology, 59*(4), 692–704.

Gaertner, S. L., Mann, J., Murrell, A., & Dovidio, J. F. (1989). Reducing intergroup bias: The benefits of recategorization. *Journal of Personality and Social Psychology, 57*(2), 239–249.

Gaertner, S. L., Rust, M. C., Dovidio, J. F., Bachman, B. A., et al. (1994). The contact hypothesis: The role of a common in-group identity on reducing intergroup bias. *Small Group Research, 25*(2), 224–249.

Gal, R. (1986). Unit morale: From a theoretical puzzle to an empirical illustration: An Israeli example. *Journal of Applied Social Psychology, 16*(6), 549–564.

Gallupe, R. B., Cooper, W. H., Grise, M.-L., & Bastianutti, L. M. (1994). Blocking electronic brainstorms. *Journal of Applied Psychology, 79*(1), 77–86.

Gamson, W. A. (1992). The social psychology of collective action. In A. D. Morris & C. M. Mueller (Eds.), *Frontiers in social movement theory* (pp. 53–76). New Haven, CT: Yale University Press.

Gardner, R. C. (1994). Stereotypes as consensual beliefs. In M. P. Zanna & J. M. Olson (Eds.), *The psychology of prejudice: The Ontario symposium* (Vol. 7, pp. 1–31). Hillsdale, NJ: Erlbaum.

Gardner, W. L., Gabriel, S., & Lee, A. Y. (1999). "I" value freedom, but "we" value relationships: Self-construal priming mirrors cultural differences in judgment. *Psychological Science, 10*, 321–326.

Geen, R. G. (1980). The effects of being observed on performance. In P. B. Paulus (Ed.), *Psychology of group influence*. Hillsdale, NJ: Erlbaum.

Geen, R. G. (1989). Alternative conceptions of social facilitation. In P. Paulus (Ed.), *Psychology of group influence* (2nd ed., pp. 15–51). Hillsdale, NJ: Erlbaum.

Geis, F. L., Boston, M. B., & Hoffman, N. (1985). Sex of authority role models and achievement by men and women: Leadership performance and recognition. *Journal of Personality and Social Psychology, 49*, 636–653.

Gelfand, M., & Brett, J. M. (Eds.). (2003). *Culture and negotiation: Integrative approaches to theory and research*. Stanford, CA: Stanford University Press.

Gelfand, M., & Christakopoulou, S. (1999). Culture and negotiator cognition: Judgment accuracy and negotiation processes in individualistic and collectivistic cultures. *Organizational Behavior and Human Decision Processes, 79*, 248–269.

George, C., Kaplan, N., & Main, M. (1985). The Berkeley Adult Attachment Interview. Unpublished manuscript, University of California at Berkeley.

Gerard, H. B. (1963). Emotional uncertainty and social comparison. *Journal of Abnormal and Social Psychology, 66*, 568–573.

Gerard, H. B., & Matthewson, G. C. (1966). The effects of severity of initiation on liking for a group: A replication. *Journal of Experimental Social Psychology, 2*, 278–287.

Gerard, H. B., & Rabbie, J. (1961). Fear and social comparison. *Journal of Abnormal and Social Psychology, 62*, 586–592.

Gergen, K. J., Gergen, M. M., & Barton, W. H. (1973). Deviance in the dark. *Psychology Today, 7*, 129–133.

Gersick, C. J. (1989). Marking time: Predictable transitions in task groups. *Academy of Management Journal, 32*, 274–309.

Gersick, C. J. (1988). Time and transition in work teams: Toward a new model of group development. *Academy of Management Journal, 31*(1), 9–41.

Gerth, H., & Mills, C. W. (1953). *Character and social structure*. New York: Harcourt Brace.

Gerwirtz, J., & Baer, D. (1958). The effect of brief social deprivation on behaviors for a social reinforcer. *Journal of Abnormal and Social Psychology, 56*, 49–56.

Geurts, S. A., Buunk, B. P., & Schaufeli, W. B. (1994). Social comparisons and absenteeism: A structural modeling approach. *Journal of Applied Social Psychology, 24*(21), 1871–1890.

Geurts, S. A., Buunk, B. P., & Schaufeli, W. B. (1994). Social comparisons and absenteeism: A structural modeling approach. *Journal of Applied Social Psychology, 24*(21), 1871–1890.

Gibbons, F. X. (1985). Social stigma perception: Social comparison among mentally retarded persons. *American Journal of Mental Deficiency, 90*, 98–106.

Gibbons, F. X., Gerrard, M., Lando, H., & McGovern, P. (1991). Social comparison and smoking cessation: The role of the "typical smoker." *Journal of Experimental Social Psychology, 27*, 239–258.

Gigone, D., & Hastie, R. (1997). The impact of information on small group choice. *Journal of Personality and Social Psychology, 72*, 132–140.

Glick, P., Zion, C., & Nelson, C. (1988). What mediates sex discrimination in hiring decisions? *Journal of Personality and Social Psychology, 55*(2), 178–186.

Goethals, G. R., & Darley, J. M. (1977). Social comparison theory: An attributional approach. In J. S. R. L. Miller (Ed.), *Social comparison processes: Theoretical and empirical perspectives*. Washington: Hemisphere.

Goldstein, I. L., & Gilliam, P. (1990). Training system issues in the year 2000. *American Psychologist, 45*, 134–143.

Goodman, P., & Leyden, D. (1991). Familiarity and group productivity. *Journal of Applied Psychology, 76*, 578–586.

Gottman, J., & Krokoff, L. (1989). Marital interaction and satisfaction: A longitudinal view. *Journal of Consulting and Clinical Psychology, 57*(1), 47–52.

Gottman, J., & Levenson, R. (1992). Marital processes predictive of later dissolution: Behavior, physiology, and health. *Journal of Personality and Social Psychology, 63*(2), 221–233.

Graen, G. B., & Uhl-Bien, M. (1998). Relationship-based approach to leadership: Development of Leader-Member Exchange (LMX) theory of leadership over 25 years: Applying a multi-level multi-domain perspective. In F. Dansereau & F. J. Yammarino (Eds.), *Leadership: The multiple-level approaches: Contemporary and alternative* (pp. 103–155). Stamford, CT: JAI Press.

Graves, L. M., & Powell, G. N. (1995). The effect of sex similarity on recruiters' evaluations of actual applicants: A test of the similarity-attraction paradigm. *Personnel Psychology, 48*, 85–98.

Graves, L. M., & Powell, G. N. (1988). An investigation of sex discrimination in recuriters' evaluations of actual applicants. *Journal of Applied Psychology, 73,* 20–29.

Greenberg, J., & Ornstein, S. (1983). High status job title compensation for underpayment: A test of equity theory. *Journal of Applied Psychology, 68*(2), 285–297.

Greenwald, A. G., McGhee, D. E., & Schwartz, J. L. K. (1998). Measuring individual differences in implicit cognition: The Implicit Association Test. *Journal of Personality and Social Psychology, 74,* 1464–1480.

Griffitt, W. B. (1966). Interpersonal attraction as a function of self-concept and personality similarity-dissimilarity. *Journal of Personality and Social Psychology, 4*(5), 581–584.

Guerin, B. (1983). Social facilitation and social monitoring: A test of three models. *British Journal of Social Psychology, 22*(3), 203–214.

Guetzkow, H., & Simon, H. A. (1955). The impact of certain communication nets upon organization and performance in certain task oriented groups. *Management Science, 1*(Apr.–July), 233–250.

Guimond, S., & Dube-Simard, L. (1983). Relative deprivation theory and the Quebec nationalist movement: The cognition-emotion distinction and the personal-group deprivation issue. *Journal of Personality and Social Psychology, 44*(3), 526–535.

Gurin, P., Penn, T., Lopez, G., & Nagda, B. A. (1999). Context, identity, and intergroup relations. In D. A. Prentice & D. T. Miller (Eds.), *Cultural divides: Understanding and overcoming group conflict* (pp. 133–170). New York: Russell Sage Foundation.

Gurin, P., & Townsend, A. (1986). Properties of gender identity and their implications for gender consciousness. *British Journal of Social Psychology, 25,* 139–148.

Gurr, T. (1970). *Why men rebel.* Princeton, NJ. Princeton University Press.

Guzzo, R. A., & Waters, J. A. (1982). The expression of affect and the performance of decision-making groups. *Journal of Applied Psychology, 67*(1), 67–74.

Guzzo, R. A., Yost, P. R., Campbell, R. J., & Shea, G. P. (1993). Potency in groups: Articulating a construct. *British Journal of Social Psychology, 32*(1), 87–106.

Guzzo, R. A., & Dikson, M. (1996). Teams in organizations: Recent research on performace and effectiveness. *Annual Review of Psychology, 47,* 307–338.

Haas, J., & Roberts, G. C. (1975). Effect of evaluative others upon learning and performance of a complex motor task. *Journal of Motor Behavior, 7*(2), 81–90.

Hackman, J., & Morris, C. (1975). Group tasks, group interaction processes, and group performance effectiveness: A review and proposed integration. In L. Berkowitz (Ed.), *Advances in experimental social psychology* (Vol. 8, pp. 45–99). New York: Academic Press.

Hackman, R. (1976). Group influences on individuals. In M. Dunnette (Ed.), *Handbook of industrial and organizational psychology.* Chicago: Rand McNally.

Hains, S. C., Hogg, M. A., & Duck, J. M. (1997). Self-categorization and leadership: Effects of group prototypicality and leader stereotypicality. *Personality and Social Psychology Bulletin, 23*(10), 1087–1099.

Haleblian, J., & Finkelstein, S. (1993). Top management team size, CEO dominance, and firm performance: The moderating roles of enviornmental turbulence and discretion. *Academy of Management Journal, 36,* 844–863.

Hall, E. (1966). *The hidden dimension.* Garden City, NY: Doubleday.

Hall, J., & Williams, M. S. (1970). Group dynamics training and improved decision making. *Journal of Applied Behavioral Science, 6,* 27–32.

Hamburger, H., Guyer, M., & Fox, J. (1975). Group size and cooperation. *Journal of Conflict Resolution, 19,* 503–531.

Hamilton, D. L., & Rose, T. L. (1980). Illusory correlation and the maintenance of stereotypic beliefs. *Journal of Personality and Social Psychology, 39,* 832–845.

Hamilton, D. L., & Sherman, J. W. (1994). Stereotypes. In R. S. Wyer & T. K. Srull (Eds.),

Handbook of social cognition (Vol. 2, pp. 1–68). Hillsdale, NJ: Erlbaum.

Hamilton, D. L., & Sherman, S. J. (1996). Perceiving persons and groups. *Psychological Review, 103*(2), 336–355.

Haney, C., Banks, C., & Zimbardo, P. (1973). Interpersonal dynamics in a simulated prison. *International Journal of Criminology and Penology, 1,* 69–87.

Harasty, A. S. (1997). The interpersonal nature of social stereotypes: Differential discussion patterns about in-groups and out-groups. *Personality and Social Psychology Bulletin, 23,* 270–284.

Hardin, C., & Higgins, E. T. (1996). Shared reality: How social verification makes the subjective objective. In R. M. Sorrentino & E. T. Higgins (Eds.), *Handbook of motivation and cognition: Foundations of social behavior* (Vol. 3, pp. 28–84). New York: Guilford.

Hardin, G. (1968). The tragedy of the commons. *Science, 162,* 1243–1248.

Hardy, C. J., & Latané, B. (1988). Social loafing in cheerleaders: Effects of team membership and competition. *Journal of Sport and Exercise Psychology, 10*(1), 109–114.

Hardy, C. J., Richman, J. M., & Rosenfeld, L. B. (1991). The role of social support in the life stress/injury relationship. *The Sports Psychologist, 5,* 128–139.

Hare, A. P. (1976). *Handbook of small group research* (2nd ed.). New York: Free Press.

Hare, A. P. (1981). Group size. *American Behavioral Scientist, 24,* 695–708.

Hare, A. P., Borgatta, E. F., & Bales, R. F. (1965). *Small groups: Studies in social interaction.* New York: Knopf.

Harkins, S. G. (1987). Social loafing and social facilitation. *Journal of Experimental Social Psychology, 23*(1), 1–18.

Harkins, S. G., & Jackson, J. M. (1985). The role of evaluation in eliminating social loafing. *Personality and Social Psychology Bulletin, 11*(4), 457–465.

Harkins, S. G., Latané, B., & Williams, K. (1980). Social loafing: Allocating effort or taking it easy? *Journal of Experimental Social Psychology, 16*(5), 457–465.

Harkins, S. G., & Petty, R. E. (1982). Effects of task difficulty and task uniqueness on social loafing. *Journal of Personality and Social Psychology, 43*(6), 1214–1229.

Harkins, S. G., & Petty, R. E. (1987). Information utility and the multiple source effect. *Journal of Personality and Social Psychology, 52*(2), 260–268.

Harkins, S. G., & Szymanski, K. (1987). Social loafing and social facilitation: New wine in old bottles. In C. Hendrick (Ed.), *Group processes and intergroup relations* (pp. 167–188). Thousand Oaks, CA: Sage.

Harkins, S. G., & Szymanski, K. (1988). Social loafing and self-evaluation with an objective standard. *Journal of Experimental Social Psychology, 24,* 354–365.

Harlow, R. E., & Cantor, N. (1994). Social pursuits of academics: Side effects and spillover of strategic resassurance seeking. *Journal of Personality and Social Psychology, 66,* 386–397.

Harlow, R., & Cantor, N. (1996). Still participating after all these years: A study of life task participation in later life. *Journal of Personality and Social Psychology, 71,* 1235–1249.

Harper, R. G. (1985). Power, dominance, and nonverbal behavior: An overview. In S. L. Ellyson & J. F. Dovidio (Eds.), *Power, dominance, and nonverbal behavior* (pp. 29–48). New York: Springer Verlag.

Hartley, E. L. (1946). *Problems in prejudice.* New York: King's Crown Press.

Hartup, W. W., & Stevens, N. (1997). Friendships and adaptation in the life course. *Psychological Bulletin, 121,* 355–370.

Haslam, S. A. (in press). *Psychology in organizations: The social identity approach.* Thousand Oaks, CA: Sage.

Haslam, S. A., Oakes, P. J., & Turner, J. C. (1996). Social identity, self-categorization, and the perceived homogeneity of ingroups and outgroups: The interaction between social motivation and cognition. In R. M. Sorrentino & E. T. Higgins (Eds.), *Handbook of motivation and cognition, Vol. 3: The interpersonal context* (pp. 182–222). New York: Guilford Press.

Hastie, R. (1986). Experimental evidence on group accuracy. In B. Grofman & G. Owen (Eds.), *Decision research* (Vol. 2, pp. 129–157). Greenwich, CT: JAI.

Hastie, R. (1993). *Inside the jurror: The psychology of juror decision making.* New York: Cambridge University Press.

Hastie, R., Penrod, S. D., & Pennington, N. (1983). *Inside the jury.* Cambridge, Mass: Harvard University Press.

Haythorn, W., Couch, A. S., Hafner, D., Langham, P., & Carter, L. F. (1956). The effects of varying combinations of authoritarian and equalitarian leaders and followers. *Journal of Abnormal and Social Psychology, 53,* 201–219.

Heider, F. (1958). *The psychology of interpersonal relations.* Hillsdale, NJ: Erlbaum.

Heilman, M. E., Block, C. J., & Martell, R. F. (1995). Sex stereotypes: Do they influence perceptions of managers? *Journal of Social Behavior and Personality, 10*(6), 237–252.

Hembroff, L. A. (1982). Resolving status inconsistency: An expectation states thory and test. *Social Forces, 61,* 183–205.

Herbert, T., & Cohen, S. (1993). Stress and immunity in humans: A meta-analytic review. *Psychosomatic Medicine, 55,* 364–379.

Herring, S. (2000). "Gender differences in CMC: Findings and implications." Computer Professionals for Social Responsibility Newsletter, Winter 2000.

Heuer, L. B., & Penrod, S. (1986). Procedural preference as a function of conflict intensity. *Journal of Personality and Social Psychology, 51*(4), 700–710.

Hewstone, M. (1990). The "ultimate attribution error"? A review of the literature on intergroup causal attribution. *European Journal of Social Psychology, 20*(4), 311–335.

Hewstone, M., Islam, M. R., & Judd, C. M. (1993). Models of crossed categorization and intergroup relations. *Journal of Personality and Social Psychology, 64,* 779–793.

Hightower, R., & Sayeed, L. (1995). The impact of computer-mediated communication systems on biased group discussion. *Computers in Human Behavior, 11*(1), 33-44.

Hill, G. W. (1982). Group versus individual performance: Are N+1 heads better than one? *Psychological Bulletin, 91,* 517–539.

Hill, T. E., & Schmitt, N. (1977). Individual differences in leadership decision making. *Organizational Behavior and Human Decision Processes, 19*(2), 353–367.

Hilton, J. L., & Darley, J. M. (1985). Constructing other persons: A limit on the effect. *Journal of Experimental Social Psychology, 21,* 1–18.

Hilton, J. L., & von Hippel, W. (1990). The role of consistency in the judgment of stereotype-relevant behaviors. *Personality and Social Psychology Bulletin, 16,* 430–448.

Hinkle, S., & Brown, R. (1990). Intergroup comparisons and social identity: Some links and lacunae. In D. Abrams & M. A. Hogg (Eds.), *Social identity theory: Constructs and critical advances* (pp. 48–70). New York: Harverster Wheatsheaf.

Hinsz, V. B. (1990). Cognitive and consensus processes in group recognition memory performance. *Journal of Personality and Social Psychology, 59*(4), 705–718.

Hinsz, V. B. (1995). Goal setting by groups performing an additive task: A comparison with individual goal setting. *Journal of Applied Social Psychology, 25*(11), 965–990.

Hinsz, V. B. (1999). Group decision making with responses of a quantitative nature: The theory of social decision schemes for quantities. *Organizational Behavior and Human Decision Processes, 80*(1), 28–49.

Hirokawa, R. Y. (1980). A comparative analysis of communication patterns within effective and ineffective decision-making groups. *Communication Monographs, 47,* 312–321.

Hobfoll, S., & London, P. (1986). The relationship of self-concept and social support to emotional distress among women during war. *Journal of Social and Clinical Psychology, 4*(2), 189–203.

Hogan, R., Curphy, G. J., & Hogan, J. (1994). What we know about leadership: Effectiveness and pesonality. *American Psychologist, 49,* 493–504.

Hogg, M. A. (1992). *The social psychology of group cohesiveness: From attraction to social identity.* New York: New York University Press.

Hogg, M. A., & Abrams, D. (1988). *Social identifications: A social psychology of intergroup relations and group processes.* London: Routledge.

Hogg, M. A., Hardie, E. A., & Reynolds, K. J. (1995). Prototypical similarity, self-categorization, and depersonalized attraction: A perspective on group cohesiveness. *European Journal of Social Psychology, 25,* 159–177.

Hogg, M. A., & McGarty, C. (1990). Self-categorization and social identity. In D. Abrams & M. A. Hogg (Eds.), *Social identity theory: Constructive and critical advances* (pp. 10–27). London and New York: Harvester Wheatsheaf and Springer Verlag.

Hogg, M. A., Turner, J. C., & Davidson, B. (1990). Polarized norms and social frames of reference: A test of the self-categorization theory of group polarization. *Basic and Applied Social Psychology, 11*(1), 77–100.

Hollander, E. P. (1958). Conformity, status, and idiosyncracy credit. *Psychological Review, 65,* 117–127.

Hollander, E. P. (1964). *Leaders, groups, and influence.* New York: Oxford University Press.

Hollander, E. P. (1960). Competence and conformity in the acceptance of influence. *Journal of Abnormal and Social Psychology, 61,* 365–369.

Hollander, E. P., & Julian, J. W. (1970). Studies in leader legitimacy, influence, and innovation. In L. Berkowitz (Ed.), *Advances in experimental social psychology* (Vol. 5). New York: Academic Press.

Homans, G. C. (1950). *The human group.* Harcourt, Brace & World.

Homans, G. C. (1961). *Social behavior: Its elementary forms.* New York: Harcourt, Brace, World.

Honeywell-Johnson, J. A., & Dickinson, A. M. (1999). Small group incentives: A review of the literature. *Journal of Organizational Behavior Management, 19,* 89–120.

Hong, Y.Y., Chiu, C.Y., & Kung, T. M. (1997). Bringing culture out in front: Effects of cultural meaning system activation on social cognition. In K. Leung, Y. Kashima, U. Kim, & S. Yamaguchi (Eds.), *Progress in Asian social psychology* (Vol. 1, pp. 135–146). Singapore: Wiley.

Hong, Y.-y., & Chiu, C.-y. (2001). Toward a paradigm shift: From cross-cultural differences in social cognition to social-cognitive mediation of cultural differences. *Social Cognition, 19,* 181–196.

Hornsby, J. S., Smith, B. N., & Gupta, J. N. D. (1994). The impact of decision-making methodology on job evaluation outcomes: A look at three consensus approaches. *Group and Organization Management, 19,* 112–128.

House, R. J., Filley, A. C., & Gujarati, D. N. (1971). Leadership style, hierarchical influence, and the satisfaction of subordinate role expectations: A test of Likert's influence proposition. *Journal of Applied Psychology, 55,* 422–432.

House, R. J., & Mitchell, T. R. (1974, Fall). Path-goal theory of leadership. *Contemporary Business, 3,* 81–98.

Howard, J. A., Blumstein, P., & Schwartz, P. (1986). Sex, power, and influence tactics in intimate relationships. *Journal of Personality and Social Psychology, 51*(1), 102–109.

Howard, J. W., & Rothbart, M. (1980). Social categorization and memory for in-group and out-group behavior. *Journal of Personality and Social Psychology, 38,* 310.

Hoyle, R. H., Pinkley, R. L., & Insko, C. A. (1989). Perceptions of social behavior: Evidence of differing expectations for interpersonal and intergroup interaction. *Personality and Social Psychology Bulletin, 15*(3), 365–376.

Hyman, H. (1942). The psychology of status. *Archives of Psychology, 38,* 269.

Ibarra, H. (1993). Personal networks of women and minorities in management: A conceptual framework. *Academy of Management Review, 18*(1), 56–87.

Insko, C. A. (1982). Seniority in the generational transition of laboratory groups: The effects of social familiarity and task experience. *Journal of Experimental Social Psychology, 18,* 557–580.

Insko, C. A., Pinkley, R. L., Hoyle, R. H., Dalton, B., Hong, G., Slim, R. M., et al. (1987). Individual versus group discontinuity: The role of intergroup contact. *Journal of Experimental Social Psychology, 23,* 250–267.

Insko, C. A., Shopler, J., Hoyle, R. H., Dardis, D. J., & Graetz, K. A. (1990). Individual-group discontinuity as a function of fear and greed. *Journal of Personality and Social Psychology, 58,* 68–79.

Isenberg, D. J. (1986). Group polarization: A critical review and meta-analysis. *Journal of Personality and Social Psychology, 50*(6), 1141–1151.

Israel, J. (1956). *Self-evaluation and rejection in groups: Three experimental studies and a conceptual outline.* Uppsala, Sweden: Almqvist & Wiksell.

Issac, R. M., McCue, R. F., & Plott, C. R. (1982). *Public goods provision in an experimental environment.* Pasadena, CA: California Institute of Technology.

Jackson, J. M., & Williams, K. D. (1985). Social loafing on difficult tasks: Working collectively can improve performance. *Journal of Personality and Social Psychology, 49*(4), 937–942.

Jackson, L., Sullivan, L., Harnish, R., & Hodge, C. (1996). Achieving positive social identity: Social mobility, social creativity, and permeability of group boundaries. *Journal of Personality and Social Psychology, 70,* 241–254.

Jackson, S. E., & Ruderman, M. N. (Eds.). (1995). *Diversity in work teams: Research paradigms for a changing workplace.* Washington, DC: American Psychological Association.

Jackson, S. E., May, K., & Whitney, K. (1995). Understanding the dynamics of diversity in decision-making teams. In R. Guzzo & E. Salas (Eds.) *Team effectiveness and decision making in organizations.* San Francisco: Jossey Bass.

Jacobs, R. C., & Campbell, D. T. (1961). The perpetuation of an arbitrary tradition through several generations of a laboratory microculture. *Journal of Abnormal and Social Psychology, 62,* 649–658.

Jaffe, Y., & Yinon, Y. (1979). Retaliatory aggression in individuals and groups. *European Journal of Social Psychology, 9,* 177–186.

Jago, A. G., & Vroom, V. H. (1980). An evaluation of two alternatives to the Vroom/Yetton normative model. *Academy of Management Journal, 23*(2), 347–355.

James, W. (1890). *The principles of psychology.* New York: Dover.

Janis, I. L. (1972). *Victims of groupthink: A psychological study of foreign policy decisions and fiascos.* Boston: Houghton-Mifflin.

Janis, I. L. (1982). *Groupthink* (2nd ed.). Boston: Houghton-Mifflin.

Jellison, J. M., & Riskind, J. (1970). A social comparison of abilities interpretation of risk-taking behavior.

Jetten, J., Branscombe, N. R., Schmitt, M. T., & Spears, R. (2001). Rebels with a cause: Group identification as a response to perceived discrimination from the mainstream. *Personality and Social Psychology Bulletin, 27,* 1204–1213.

Jetten, J., Spears, R., & Manstead, A. S. R. (1996). Intergroup norms and intergroup discrimination: Distinctive self-categorization and social identity effects. *Journal of Personality and Social Psychology, 71,* 1222–1233.

Jetten, J., Spears, R., & Manstead, A. S. R. (1997a). Distinctiveness threat and prototypicality:

Combined effects on intergroup discrimination and collective self-esteem. *European Journal of Social Psychology, 27,* 635–657.

Jetten, J., Spears, R., & Manstead, A. S. R. (1997b). Strength of identification and intergroup differentiation: The influence of group norms. *European Journal of Social Psychology, 27*(5), 603–609.

Johnson, D. W., & Johnson, F. P. (1994). *Joining together: Group theory and group skills* (5th ed.). Englewood, NJ: Prentice-Hall.

Johnson, D. W., & Johnson, R. (1992). Positive interdependence: Key to effective cooperation. In R. Hertz-Lazarowitz & N. Miller (Eds.), *Interaction in cooperative groups* (pp. 174–199). New York: Cambridge University Press.

Johnson, D. W., & Johnson, R. T. (1989). *Cooperation and competition: Theory and research.* Edina, MN: Interaction Book Company.

Johnson, D. W., Johnson, R. T., & Maruyama, G. (1983). Interdependence and interpersonal attraction among heterogeneous and homogeneous individuals: A theoretical formulation and a meta-analysis of the research. *Review of Educational Research, 53*(1), 5–54.

Johnson, D. W., Maruyama, G., Johnson, R. T., Nelson, D., & Skon, L. (1981). Effects of cooperative, competitive and individualistic goal structures on achievement: A meta-analysis. *Psychological Bulletin, 89,* 47–62.

Johnson, M. H., Dziurawiec, S., Ellis, H., & Morton, J. (1991). Newborns' preferential tracking of facelike stimuli and its subsequent decline. *Cognition, 40*(1–2), 1–19.

Johnson, R. D., & Downing, L. L. (1979). Deindividuation and valence of cues: Effects on prosocial and antisocial behavior. *Journal of Personality and Social Psychology, 37,* 1532–1538.

Johnston, L., & Macrae, C. N. (1994). Changing social stereotypes: The case of the information seeker. *European Journal of Social Psychology, 24,* 581–592.

Jones, E. E., Wood, G. C., & Quattrone, G. A. (1981). Perceived variability of personal characteristics in in-groups and out-groups: The role of knowledge and evaluation. *Personality and Social Psychology Bulletin, 7,* 523–528.

Jones, J. M. (1996). *Prejudice and racism.* Boston: McGraw-Hill.

Jones, M. B. (1974). Regressing group on individual effectiveness. *Organizational Behavior and Human Decision Processes,* (3), 426–451.

Jorgenson, D. O., & Papciak, A., S. (1981). The effects of communication, resource feedback, and identifiability on behavior in a simulated commons. *Journal of Experimental Social Psychology, 17,* 373–385.

Jost, J. T., & Banaji, M. R. (1994). The role of stereotyping in system-justification and the production of false consciousness. *British Journal of Social Psychology, 33,* 1–27.

Judge, T. A., & Bono, J. E. (2000). Five-factor model of personality and transformational leadership. *Journal of Applied Psychology, 85*(5), 751–765.

Judge, T. A., Bono, J. E., Ilies, R., & Gerhardt, M. W. (2002). Personality and leadership: A qualitative and quantitative review. *Journal of Applied Psychology, 87*(4), 765–780.

Judy, R., & D'Amico, C. (1997). *Work force 2020: Work and workers in the 21st century.* Indianapolis: Hudson Institute.

Jussim, L. (1989). Teacher expectations: Self-fulfilling prophecies, perceptual biases, and accuracy. *Journal of Personality and Social Psychology, 57,* 469–480.

Jussim, L. (1991). Social perception and social reality: A reflection-construction model. *Psychological Review, 98,* 54–73.

Jussim, L., & Fleming, C. (1996). Self-fulfilling prophecies and the maintenance of social stereotypes: The role of dyadic interactions and social forces. In C. N. Macrae, C. Stangor, & M. Hewstone (Eds.), *Stereotypes and stereotyping* (pp. 161–192). New York: Guilford Press.

Kahn, A., & Ryen, A. H. (1972). Factors influencing the bias towards one's own group. *International Journal of Group Tensions, 2*, 33–50.

Kahn, R., & Katz, D. (1953). Leadership practices in relation to productivity and morale. In D. Cartwright & A. Zander (Eds.), *Group dynamics: Research and theory*. Evanston, IL: Row, Peterson.

Kanter, R. M. (1977). Some effects of proportions on group life: Skewed sex ratios and responses to token women. *American Journal of Sociology, 82*, 965–990.

Kanter, R. M. (1988). When a thousand flowers bloom: Structural, collective, and social conditions for innovation in organization. In B. M. Staw & L. L. Cummings (Eds.), *Research in organizational behavior* (Vol. 10, pp. 169–211). Greenwich, CT: JAI.

Kaplan, M. F. (1977). Discussion polarization effects in a modified jury decision paradigm: Informational influences. *Sociometry, 40*, 262–271.

Kaplan, M. F., & Miller, C. E. (1983). Group discussion and judgment. In P. B. Paulus (Ed.), *Basic group processes* (pp. 65–94). New York: Springer Verlag.

Kaplan, M. F., & Miller, C. E. (1987). Group decision making and normative versus informational influence: Effects of type of issue and assigned decision rule. *Journal of Personality and Social Psychology, 53*(2), 306–313.

Karau, S. J., & Williams, K. D. (1993). Social loafing: A meta-analytic review and theoretical integration. *Journal of Personality and Social Psychology, 65*, 681–706.

Karlins, M., Coffman, T., & Walters, G. (1969). On the fading of social stereotypes: Studies in three generations of college students. *Journal of Personality and Social Psychology, 13*, 1–16.

Kashy, D. A., & Kenny, D. A. (2000). The analysis of data from dyads and groups. In H. T. Reis & C. M. Judd (Eds.), *Handbook of research methods in social and personality psychology* (pp. 451–477). New York: Cambridge University Press.

Katz, D., & Braly, K. W. (1933). Racial stereotypes of one hundred college students. *Journal of Abnormal and Social Psychology, 28*, 280–290.

Kelley, H. H. (1952). Two functions of reference groups. In G. Swans, T. Newcomb, & E. Hartley (Eds.), *Readings in social psychology* (pp. 410–414). New York: Holt, Rinehart, & Winston.

Kelley, H. H. (1967). Attribution theory in social psychology. In D. Levine (Ed.), *Nebraska symposium on motivation* (Vol. 15, pp. 192–240). Lincoln: University of Nebraska Press.

Kelley, H. H., Condry, Jr, J. C., Dahlke, A. E., & Hill, A. H. (1965). Collective behavior in a simulated panic situation. *Journal of Experimental Social Psychology, 1*, 19–54.

Kelley, H. H., & Stahelski, A. J. (1970). Social interaction basis of cooperators' and competitors' beliefs about others. *Journal of Personality and Social Psychology, 16*, 66–91.

Kelley, II. H., & Thibaut, J. W. (1969). Group problem solving. In G. Lindzey & E. Aronson (Eds.), *The handbook of social psychology* (2nd ed., pp. 1–101). Reading, MA: Addison-Wesley.

Kelman, H. (1961). Processes of opinion change. *Public Opinion Quarterly, 25*, 57–78.

Kenny, D. A., & la Voie, L. (1985). Separating individual and group effects. *Journal of Personality and Social Psychology, 48*(2), 339–348.

Kenny, D. A., & Zaccaro, S. J. (1983). An estimate of variance due to traits in leadership. *Journal of Applied Psychology, 68*(4), 678–685.

Kerr, N. L. (1989). Illusions of efficacy: The effects of group size on perceived efficacy in social dilemmas. *Journal of Experimental Social Psychology, 25*, 287–313.

Kerr, N. L. (1995). Norms in social dilemmas. In D. Schroeder (Ed.), *Social dilemmas: Perspectives on individuals and groups* (pp. 31–47). Westport, CT: Praeger.

Kerr, N. L. (1978). Severity of prescribed penalty and mock jurors' verdicts. *Journal of Personality and Social Psychology, 36*(12), 1431–1442.

Kerr, N. L. (1983). Motivation losses in small groups: A social dilemma analysis. *Journal of Personality and Social Psychology, 45*(4), 819–828.

Kerr, N. L., & Huang, J. Y. (1986). Jury verdicts: How much difference does one juror make? *Personality and Social Psychology Bulletin, 12*(3), 325–343.

Kerr, N. L., & Bruun, S. (1981). Ringelmann revisited: Alternative explanations for the social loafing effect. *Personality and Social Psychology Bulletin, 7*, 224–231.

Kerr, N. L., & Bruun, S. E. (1983). Dispensability of member effort and group motivation losses: Free-rider effects. *Journal of Personality and Social Psychology, 44*(1), 78–94.

Kerr, N. L., Davis, J. H., Meek, D., & Rissman, A. K. (1975). Group position as a function of member attitudes: Choice shift effects from the perspective of social decision scheme theory. *Journal of Personality and Social Psychology, 31*(3), 574–593.

Kerr, N. L., Garst, J., Lewandowski, D. A., & Harris, S. E. (1997). That still, small voice: Commitment to cooperate as an internalized versus a social norm. *Personality and Social Psychology Bulletin, 23*(12), 1300–1311.

Kerr, N. L., & Kaufman-Gilliland, C. M. (1994). Communication, commitment, and cooperation in social dilemma. *Journal of Personality and Social Psychology, 66*(3), 513–529.

Kerr, N. L., & MacCoun, R. J. (1985). The effects of jury size and polling method on the process and product of jury deliberation. *Journal of Personality and Social Psychology, 48*(2), 349–363.

Kerr, S., Schreisheim, C. A., Murphy, C. J., & Stogdill, R. M. (1974). Toward a contingency theory of leadership based upon the consideration and initiating structure literature. *Organizational Behavior and Human Decision Processes, 12*(1), 62–82.

Kerwin, J., & Shaffer, D. R. (1994). Mock jurors versus mock juries: The role of deliberations in reactions to inadmissible testimony. *Personality and Social Psychology Bulletin, 20*(2), 153–162.

Kiesler, C. A., & Kiesler, S. B. (1969). *Conformity*. Reading, MA: Addison-Wesley.

Kiesler, S., Siegel, J., & McGuire, T. (1984). Social psychological aspects of computer-mediated communication. *American Psychologist, 39*, 1123–1134.

Kiesler, S., & Sproull, L. (1992). Group decision making and communication technology. *Organizational Behavior and Human Decision Processes, 52*(1), 96–123.

Kim, H., & Markus, H. (1999). Deviance or uniqueness, harmony or conformity: A cultural analysis. *Journal of Personality and Social Psychology, 77*, 785–800.

Kindermann, T. A. (1993). Natural peer groups as contexts for individual development: The case of children's motivation in school. *Developmental Psychology, 29*, 970–977.

Kipnes, D. (1972). Does power corrupt? *Journal of Personality and Social Psychology, 24*, 33–41.

Kipnis, D. (1984). The use of power in organizations and in interpersonal settings. *Applied Social Psychology Annual, 5*, 179–201.

Kirchmeyer, C. (1993). Multicultural task groups: An account of the low contribution level of minorities. *Small Group Research, 24*(1), 127–148.

Klimoski, R., & Mohammed, S. (1994). Team mental model: Construct or metaphor? *Journal of Management, 20*(2), 403–437.

Kogan, N., & Wallach, M. A. (1967). Risky-shift phenomenon in small decision-making groups: A test of the information-exchange hypothesis. *Journal of Experimental Social Psychology, 3*, 75–84.

Komorita, S. S., & Lapworth, C. W. (1982). Cooperative choice among individuals versus groups in an N-person dilemma situation. *Journal of Personality and Social Psychology, 42*, 487–496.

Komorita, S. S., & Parks, C. D. (1994). *Social dilemmas*. Dubuque, IA: Brown & Benchmark.

Korte, C. (1980). Urban-nonurban differences in social behavior and social psychological models of urban impact. *Journal of Social Issues, 36*(3), 29–51.

Kotter, J. P., & Heskett, J. L. (1992). *Corporate culture and performance*. New York: Free Press.

Kram, K., & Isabella, L. (1985). Monitoring alternatives: The role of peer relationships in career development. *Academy of Management Journal, 28*, 110–132.

Kramer, R. M., & Brewer, M. B. (1984). Effects of group identity on resource use in a simulated commons dilemma. *Journal of Personality and Social Psychology, 46*, 1044–1057.

Kramer, R. M., & Messick, D. M. (1998). Getting by with a little help from our enemies: Collective paranoia and its role in intergroup relations. In C. Sedikides, J. Shopler, & C. A. Insko (Eds.), *Intergroup cognition and intergroup behavior* (pp. 233–255). Mahwah, NJ: Erlbaum.

Kraus, L. A., Bazzini, D., Davis, M., Church, M., & Kirchman, C. M. (1993). Personal and social influences on loneliness: The mediating effect of social provisions. *Social Psychology Quarterly, 56*(1), 37–53.

Krauss, R., & Fussell, S. (1991). Perspective-taking in communication: Representations of others' knowledge in reference. *Social Cognition, 9*(1), 2–24.

Kraut, R., Patterson, M., Lundmark, V., Kiesler, S., Mukophadhyay, T., & Scherlis, W. (1998). Internet paradox: A social technology that reduces social involvement and psychological well-being? *American Psychologist, 53*(9), 1017–1031.

Kravitz, D. A., & Martin, B. (1986). Ringelmann rediscovered: The original article. *Journal of Personality and Social Psychology, 50*, 936–941.

Kretch, D., & Crutchfield, R. S. (1958). *Elements of psychology.* New York: Knopf.

Krueger, J. (1998). Enhancement bias in descriptions of self and others. *Personality and Social Psychology Bulletin, 24*(5), 505–516.

Kruglanski, A. W., & Freund, T. (1983). The freezing and unfreezing of lay inferences: Effects on impressional primacy, ethnic stereotyping, and numerical anchoring. *Journal of Experimental Social Psychology, 19*, 448–468.

Kruglanski, A. W., & Mackie, D. M. (1990). Majority and minority influence: A judgmental process analysis. *European Review of Social Psychology, 1*, 230–261.

Kruglanski, A. W., & Webster, D. M. (1991). Group members' reactions to opinion deviates and conformists at varying degrees of proximity to decision deadline and of environmental noise. *Journal of Personality and Social Psychology, 61*, 212–225.

Kuhn, M. H., & McPartland, T. S. (1954). An empirical investigation of self attitudes. *American Sociological Review, 19*, 68–76.

Kunda, G. (1992). *Engineering culture: Control and commitment in a high-tech corporation.* Philadelphia: Temple University Press.

Kuypers, B. C., Davies, D., & Hazewinkel, A. (1986). Developmental patterns in self-analytic groups. *Human Relations, 39*(9), 793–815.

Lalonde, R., & Silverman, R. (1994). Behavioral preferences in response to social injustice: The effects of group permeability and social identity salience. *Journal of Personality and Social Psychology, 66*, 78–85.

Lamm, H., & Myers, D. G. (1978). Group-induced polarization of attitudes and behavior. In L. Berkowitz (Ed.), *Advances in experimental social psychology* (Vol. 2, pp. 147–195). New York: Academic Press.

Lamm, H., & Trommsdorff, G. (1973). Group versus individual performance on tasks requiring ideational proficiency (brainstorming): A review. *European Journal of Social Psychology, 3*, 361–388.

Langfeldt, H. (1992). Teachers' perceptions of problem behaviour: A cross-cultural study between Germany and South Korea. *British Journal of Educational Psychology, 62*, 217–224.

Larey, T. S., & Paulus, P. B. (1995). Social comparison goal setting in brainstorming groups. *Journal of Applied Social Psychology, 26*(18), 1579–1596.

Larson, J. R., & Christensen, C. (1993). Groups as problem-solving units: Toward a new meaning of social cognition. *British Journal of Social Psychology, 32*, 5–30.

Larson, J. R. J., Christensen, C., Abbott, A. S., & Franz, T. M. (1996). Diagnosing groups: Charting the flow of information in medical decision-making teams. *Journal of Personaliy and Social Psychology, 71*, 315–370.

Larson, J. R. J., Foster-Fishman, P. G., & Keys, C. B. (1994). The discussion of shared and unshared information in decision-making groups. *Journal of Personality and Social Psychology, 67*, 446–461.

Latané, B. (1981). The psychology of social impact. *American Psychologist, 36*, 343–356.

Latané, B. (1996). Strength from weakness: The fate of opinion minorities in spatially distributed groups. In E. Witte & J. Davis (Eds.), *Understanding group behavior: Consensual action by small groups* (Vol. 1, pp. 193–219). Mahwah, NJ: Erlbaum.

Latané, B., & L'Herrou, T. (1996). Spatial clustering in the conformity game: Dynamic social impact in electronic groups. *Journal of Personality and Social Psychology, 70*(6), 1218–1230.

Latané, B., Williams, K., & Harkins, S. (1979). Many hands make light the work: The causes and consequences of social loafing. *Journal of Personality and Social Psychology, 37*(6), 822–832.

Latham, G. P., & Locke, E. A. (1991). Self-regulation through goal setting. *Organizational Behavior and Human Decision Processes, 50*(2), 212–247.

Latham, G. P., Winters, D. C., & Locke, E. A. (1994). Cognitive and motivational effects of participation: A mediator study. *Journal of Organizational Behavior, 15*(1), 49–63.

Laughlin, P. R. (1996). Group decision making and collective induction. In E. H. Witte & J. H. Davis (Eds.), *Understanding group behavior, Vol. 1: Consensual action by small groups* (pp. 61–80). Mahwah, NJ: Erlbaum.

Laughlin, P. R. (1999). Collective induction: Twelve postulates. *Organizational Behavior and Human Decision Processes, 80*(1), 50–69.

Laughlin, P. R., & Adamopoulos, J. (1980). Social combination processes and individual learning for six-person cooperative groups on an intellective task. *Journal of Personality and Social Psychology, 38*(6), 941–947.

Laughlin, P. R., Bonner, B., & Altermatt, T. (1998). Collective versus individual induction with single versus multiple hypotheses. *Journal of Personality and Social Psychology, 75*, 1481–1489.

Laughlin, P. R., & Bitz, D. S. (1975). Individual versus dyadic performance on a disjunctive task as a function of initial ability level. *Journal of Personality and Social Psychology, 31*, 487–496.

Laughlin, P. R., & Earley, P. C. (1982). Social combination models, persuasive arguments theory, social comparison theory, and choice shift. *Journal of Personality and Social Psychology, 42*(2), 273–280.

Laughlin, P. R., & Ellis, A. L. (1986). Demonstrability and social combination processes on mathematical intellective tasks. *Journal of Experimental Social Psychology, 22*(3), 177–189.

Laughlin, P. R., Kerr, N. L., Munch, M. M., & Haggarty, C. A. (1976). Social decision schemes of the same four-person groups on two different intellective tasks. *Journal of Personality and Social Psychology, 33*, 80–88.

Laughlin, P. R., & Shippy, T. A. (1983). Collective induction. *Journal of Personality and Social Psychology, 45*(1), 94–100.

Lawler, E. J., Ford, R. S., & Blegen, M. A. (1988). Coercive capability in conflict: A test of bilateral deterrence versus conflict spiral theory. *Social Psychology Quarterly, 51*(2), 93–107.

Lazarus, R., & Folkman, S. (1984). *Stress, appraisal and coping.* New York: Springer Verlag.

Le Bon, G. (1896, 1960). *Psychology of crowds* (R.K Merton, trans). New York: Viking Press.

Lea, M., & Spears, R. (1991). Computer-mediated communications, deindividuation and group decision making. In S. Greenberg (Ed.), *Computer-supported cooperative work and groupware* (pp. 155–174). New York: Harcourt Brace Jovanovich.

Leana, C. R. (1985). A partial test of Janis's groupthink model: Effects of group cohesiveness and leader behavior on defective decision making. *Journal of Management, 11*(1), 5–17.

Leary, M. R., & Forsyth, D. R. (1987). Attributions of responsibility for collective endeavors. *Review of Personality and Social Psychology, 8,* 167–188.

Leary, M. R., & Kowalski, R. M. (1995). *Social anxiety.* New York: Guilford Press.

Leary, M. R., Tambor, E. S., Terdal, S. K., & Downs, D. L. (1995). Self-esteem as an interpersonal monitor: The sociometer hypothesis. *Journal of Personality and Social Psychology, 68,* 518–530.

Leavitt, H. J. (1951). Some effects of certain communication patterns on group performance. *Journal of Abnormal and Social Psychology, 38*–50.

Lee, C. (1989). The relationship between goal-setting, self-efficacy, and female field hockey team performance. *International Journal of Sport Psychology, 202*(2), 147–161.

Lee, M. T., & Ofshe, R. (1981). The impact of behavioral style and status characteristics on social influence: A test of two competing theories. *Social Psychology Quarterly, 44*(2), 73–82.

Lee, R. M., & Robbins, S. B. (1995). Measuring belongingness: The social connectedness and the social assurance scales. *Journal of Counseling Psychology, 42,* 232–241.

Lee, Y. T., Jussim, L. J., & McCauley, C. R. (1995). *Stereotype accuracy: Toward appreciating group differences.* Washington, DC: American Psychological Association.

Leik, R. K., & Chalkley, M. A. (1997). On the stability of network relations under stress. *Social Networks, 19*(1), 63–74.

Lemyre, L., & Smith, P. M. (1985). Intergroup discrimination and self-esteem in the minimal group paradigm. *Journal of Personality and Social Psychology, 49,* 660–670.

Lepore, L., & Brown, R. (1997). Category and stereotype activation: Is prejudice inevitable? *Journal of Personality and Social Psychology, 72,* 275–287.

Leung, K., & Bond, M. H. (1984). The impact of cultural collectivism on reward allocation. *Journal of Personality and Social Psychology, 47,* 793–804.

Levine, J. M. (1980). Reaction to opinion deviance in small groups. In P. B. Paulus (Ed.), *Psychology of group influence* (pp. 375–429). Hillsdale, NJ: Erlbaum.

Levine, J. M., & Moreland, R. (1990). Progress in small group research. In M. Rosenzweig & L. Porter (Eds.), *Annual review of psychology* (Vol. 41, pp. 585–634). Palo Alto, CA: Annual Reviews, Inc.

Levine, J. M., & Moreland, R. (1994). Group socialization: Theory and research. In W. Stroebe & M. Hewstone (Eds.), *European review of social psychology* (Vol. 5, pp. 305–336). Chichester UK: Wiley.

Levine, J. M., & Moreland, R. L. (1998). Small groups. In *The handbook of social psychology* (4th ed., Vol. 2, pp. 415–469). New York: McGraw-Hill.

Levine, J. M., & Russo, E. M. (1987). Majority and minority influence. In C. Hendrick (Ed.), *Group processes* (pp. 13–54). Newbury Park, CA: Sage.

Levine, R. A., & Campbell, D. T. (1972). *Ethnocentrism.* New York: Wiley.

Levine, R. V. (1997). *A geography of time: The temporal misadventures of a social psychologist, or how every culture keeps time just a little bit differently.* New York: Basic.

Levine, R. V., & Norenzayan, A. (1999). The pace of life in 31 countries. *Journal of Cross-Cultural Psychology, 30*(2), 178–205.

Lewicki, R. J., & Sheppard, B. H. (1985). Choosing how to intervene: Factors affecting the use of process and outcome control in third party dispute resolution. *Journal of Occupational Behaviour, 6*(1), 49–64.

Lewin, K. (1948/1951/1997). *Resolving social conflicts; and, Field theory in social science.* Washington, DC: American Psychological Association.

Lewin, K., & Gold, M. (1999). *The complete social scientist: A Kurt Lewin reader.* Washington, DC: American Psychological Association.

Lewin, K., Lippitt, R., & White, R. (1939). Patterns of aggressive behavior in experimentally created "social climates." *Journal of Social Psychology, 10,* 271–279.

Liang, D. W., Moreland, R., & Argote, L. (1995). Group versus individual training and group performance: The mediating factor of transactive memory. *Personality and Social Psychology Bulletin, 21*(4), 384–393.

Lickel, B., Hamilton, D. L., Wieczorkowska, G., Lewis, A., Sherman, S. J., & Uhles, A. N. (2000). Varieties of groups and the perception of group entitativity. *Journal of Personality and Social Psychology, 78*(2), 223–246.

Liden, R. C., & Graen, G. (1980). Generalizability of the vertical dyad linkage model of leadership. *Academy of Management Journal, 23*(3), 451–465.

Liebrand, W. B. (1984). The effect of social motives, communication and group size on behaviour in an N-person multistage mixed-motive game. *European Journal of Social Psychology, 14*(3), 239–264.

Lincoln, J. R. (1982). Intra (and inter-) organizational networks. In S. B. Bacharach (Ed.), *Research in the sociology of organizations* (Vol. 1). Greenwich, CT: JAI Press.

Lind, E., & Tyler, T. (1988). *The social psychology of procedural justice.* New York: Plenum.

Lindt, H., & Pennal, H. (1962). On the defensive quality of groups: A commentary on the use of the group as a tool of control reality. *International Journal of Group Psychotherapy, 12*(2), 171–179.

Linehan, M. (2001). Networking for female managers' career development: Empirical evidence. *Journal of Management Development, 20*(10), 823–829.

Linville, P. W., & Jones, E. E. (1980). Polarized appraisals of out-group members. *Journal of Personality and Social Psychology, 38,* 689–703.

Linville, P. W., Salovey, P., & Fischer, G. W. (1986). Stereotyping and perceived distributions of social characteristics: An application to in-group–out-group perception. In J. F. Dovidio & S. L. Gaertner (Eds.), *Prejudice, discrimination and racism.* Orlando: Academic Press.

Lippmann, W. (1922). *Public opinion.* New York: Harcourt Brace.

Little, B. L., & Madigan, R. M. (1997). The relationship between collective efficacy and performance in manufacturing work teams. *Small Group Research, 28*(4), 517–534.

Lobel, S. A., & McLeod, P. L. (1991). Effects of ethnic group cultural differences on cooperative and competitive behavior on a group task. *Academy of Management Journal, 34*(4), 827–847.

Locke, E. A. (1976). The nature and causes of job satisfaction. In M. D. Dunnette (Ed.), *Handbook of industrial and organizational psychology.* Chicago: Rand McNally.

Locke, E. A., & Latham, G. P. (1990). *A theory of goal setting and task performance.* Englewood Cliffs, NJ: Prentice-Hall.

Locksley, A., Borgida, E., Brekke, N., & Hepburn, C. (1980). Sex stereotypes and judgments of individuals. *Journal of Personality and Social Psychology, 39,* 821–831.

Locksley, A., Ortiz, V., & Hepburn, C. (1980). Social categorization and discriminatory behavior: Extinguishing the minimal intergroup discrimination effect. *Journal of Personality and Social Psychology, 39,* 773–783.

Lockwood, P., & Kunda, Z. (1997). Superstars and me: Predicting the impact of role models on the self. *Journal of Personality and Social Psychology, 73,* 91–103.

Lord, C. G., Lepper, M. R., & Mackie, D. (1984). Attitude prototypes as determinants of attitude-behavior consistency. *Journal of Personality and Social Psychology, 46,* 1254–1266.

Lord, R. G. (1977). Functional leadership behavior: Measurement and relation to social power and leadership perceptions. *Administrative Science Quarterly, 22*(1), 114–133.

Lord, R. G., de Vader, C. L., & Alliger, G. M. (1986). A meta-analysis of the relation between personality traits and leadership perceptions: An application of validity generalization procedures. *Journal of Applied Psychology, 71*(3), 402–410.

Lorge, I., Fox, D., Davitz, J., & Brenner, M. (1958). A survey of studies contrasting the quality of group performance and individual performance. *Psychological Bulletin, 55,* 337–372.

Lorge, I., & Solomon, H. (1955). Two models of group behavior in the solution of Eureka-type problems. *Psychometrica, 20*(2).

Lott, A. J., & Lott, B. E. (1961). Group cohesiveness, communication level, and conformity. *Journal of Abnormal and Social Psychology, 62,* 408–412.

Lott, A. J., & Lott, B. E. (1965). Group cohesiveness as interpersonal attraction: A review of relationships with antecedent and consequent variables. *Psychological Bulletin, 64,* 259–309.

Lovaglia, J. J., & Houser, J. A. (1996). Emotional reactions and status in groups. *American Sociological Review, 61,* 867–883.

Luce, R. D., & Raiffa, H. (1957). *Games and decisions.* New York: Wiley.

Luhtanen, R., & Crocker, J. (1992). A collective self-esteem scale: Self-evaluation of one's social identity. *Personality and Social Psychology Bulletin, 18,* 302–318.

Lynn, M., & Oldenquist, A. (1986). Egoistic and nonegoistic motives in social dilemmas. *American Psychologist, 41,* 529–534.

Maass, A., & Arcuri, L. (1996). Language and stereotyping. In C. N. Macrae, C. Stangor, & M. Hewstone (Eds.), *Stereotypes and stereotyping* (pp. 193–226). New York: Guilford Press.

Maass, A., Ceccarielli, R., & Rudin, S. (1996). Linguistic intergroup bias: Evidence for ingroup–protective motivation. *Journal of Personality and Social Psychology, 71*(3), 512–526.

Maass, A., & Clark, R. D. (1983). Internalization versus compliance: Differential processes underlying minority influence and conformity. *European Journal of Social Psychology, 13,* 197–215.

Maass, A., & Clark, R. D. (1986). Conversion theory and simultaneous majority/minority influence: Can reactance offer an alternative explanation? *European Journal of Social Psychology, 16,* 305–309.

Maass, A., & Clark, R. D. (1984). Hidden impact of minorities: Fifteen years of minority influence research. *Psychological Bulletin, 95,* 428–450.

MacCoun, R. J., & Kerr, N. L. (1988). Asymmetric influence in mock jury deliberation: Jurors' bias for leniency. *Journal of Personality and Social Psychology, 54*(1), 21–33.

Mackie, D. M. (1986). Social identification effects in group polarization. *Journal of Personality and Social Psychology, 50*(4), 720–728.

Mackie, D. M., & Cooper, J. (1984). Attitude polarization: Effects of group membership. *Journal of Personality and Social Psychology, 46,* 575–585.

Mackie, D. M., & Goethals, G. R. (1987). Individual and group goals. In C. Hendrick et al. (Eds.), *Group processes: Review of personality and social psychology* (Vol. 8, pp. 144–166). Newbury Park, CA: Sage.

MacNeil, M. K., & Sherif, M. (1976). Norm change over subject generations as a function of arbitrariness of prescribed norms. *Journal of Personality and Social Psychology, 34*(5), 762–773.

Macrae, C. N., Hewstone, M., & Griffiths, R. J. (1993). Processing load and memory for stereotype-based information. *European Journal of Social Psychology, 23,* 77–87.

Macrae, C. N., Milne, A. B., & Bodenhausen, G. V. (1994). Stereotypes as energy-saving devices: A peek inside the cognitive toolbox. *Journal of Personality and Social Psychology, 66,* 37–47.

Madon, S., Jussim, L., Keiper, S., Eccles, J., Smith, A., & Palumbo, P. (1998). The accuracy and power of sex, social class, and ethnic stereotypes: A naturalistic study in person perception. *Personality and Social Psychology Bulletin, 24*(12), 1304–1318.

Magjuka, R., & Baldwin, T. (1991). Team-based employee involvement programs: Effects of design and administration. *Person Psychology, 44,* 793–812.

Major, B. (1994). From social inequality to personal entitlement: The role of social comparisons, legitimacy appraisals, and group membership. *Advances in Experimental Social Psychology, 26,* 293–348.

Major, B., Sciacchitano, A., & Crocker, J. (1993). In-group versus out-group comparisons and self-esteem. *Personality and Social Psychology Bulletin, 19,* 711–721.

Maki, J. E., Thorngate, W. B., & McClintock, C. G. (1979). Prediction and perception of social motives. *Journal of Personality and Social Psychology, 37*(2), 203–220.

Mann, J. W. (1961). Group relations in hierarchies. *Journal of Social Psychology, 54,* 283–314.

Mann, L. (1980). Cross-cultural studies of small groups. In H. C. Triandis (Ed.), *Handbook of cross-cultural psychology: Social psychology* (Vol. 5). Boston: Allyn & Bacon.

Mann, L. (1981). The baiting crowd in episodes of threatened suicide. *Journal of Personality and Social Psychology, 41,* 703–709.

Mannix, E. A., Thompson, L. L., & Bazerman, M. H. (1989). Negotiation in small groups. *Journal of Applied Psychology, 74*(3), 508–517.

Manstead, A. S., & Semin, G. R. (1980). Social facilitation effects: Mere enhancement of dominant responses? *British Journal of Social and Clinical Psychology, 19*(2), 119–136.

Mantovani, G. (1994). Is computer-mediated communication intrinsically apt to enhance democracy in organizations? *Human Relations, 47*(1), 45–62.

Manz, C. C., & Sims, H. P. (1987). Leading workers to lead themselves: The external leadership of self-managing work teams. *Administrative Science Quarterly, 32*(1), 106–129.

Marchand, B. (1970). Auswirkung einer emotional wertrollen und einer emotional neutralen klassifikation auf die Schatzung einer Stimulus-Serie. *Zeitschrift fur Soziale Psychologie, 1,* 264–274.

Marcus-Newhall, A., Miller, N., Holtz, R., & Brewer, M. B. (1993). Cross-cutting category membership with role assignment: A means of reducing intergroup bias. *British Journal of Social Psychology, 32*(2), 125–146.

Markus, H. R. (1978). The effect of mere presence on social facilitation: An unobtrusive test. *Journal of Experimental Social Psychology, 14,* 389–397.

Markus, H. R., & Kitayama, S. (1991). Culture and the self: Implications for cognition, emotion, and motivation. *Psychological Review, 2,* 224–253.

Markus, H. R., & Kitayama, S. (1994). A collective fear of the collective: Implications for selves and theories of selves. *Personality and Social Psychology Bulletin, 20,* 568–579.

Markus, H. R., Kitayama, S., & Heiman, R. J. (1996). Culture and "basic" psychological principles. In E. T. Higgins & A. W. Kruglanski (Eds.), *Social psychology: Handbook of basic principles* (pp. 857–913). New York: Guilford Press.

Marques, J. M., Robalo, E. M., & Rocha, S. A. (1992). In-group bias and the "black sheep" effect: Assessing the impact of social identification and perceived variablity on group judgments. *European Journal of Social Psychology, 22*(4), 331–352.

Marques, J. M., & Yzerbyt, V. Y. (1988). The black sheep effect: Judgmental extremity towards in-group members in inter- and intra-group situations. *European Journal of Social Psychology, 18*(3), 287–292.

Marques, J. M., Yzerbyt, V. Y., & Leyens, J.-P. (1988). The "black sheep effect": Extremity of judgments towards ingroup members as a function of group identification. *European Journal of Social Psychology, 18*(1), 1–16.

Martens, R., & Landers, D. M. (1972). Evaluation potential as a determinant of coaction effects. *Journal of Experimental Social Psychology, 4,* 347–359.

Martin, C. L. (1987). A ratio measure of sex stereotyping. *Journal of Personality and Social Psychology, 52,* 489–499.

Matheson, K., & Zanna, M. P. (1990). Computer-mediated communications: The focus is on me. *Social Science Computer Review, 8,* 1–12.

Maznevski, M. L. (1994). Understanding our differences: Performance in decision-making groups with diverse members. *Human Relations, 47*(5), 531–552.

Mazur, A. (1985). A biosocial model of status in face-to-face groups. *Social Forces, 64,* 377–402.

McCauley, C. (1989). The nature of social influence in groupthink: Compliance and internalization. *Journal of Personality and Social Psychology, 57*(2), 250–260.

McCauley, C. (Ed.). (1991). *Terrorism research and public policy.* London: F. Cass.

McCauley, C. R., & Segel, M. E. (1989). Terrorist individuals and terrorist groups: The normal psychology of extreme behavior. In J. Giroebel & J. H. Goldstein (Eds.), *Terrorism: Psychological perspectives.* Series of psychobiology (pp. 39–64). Sevilla, Spain: Publicaciones de la Universidad deSevilla.

McClelland, D. C. (1985). How motives, skills, and values determine what people do. *American Psychologist, 40*(7), 812–825.

McClelland, D. C., Atkinson, J., Clark, R., & Lowell, E. (1953). *The achievement motive.* New York: Appleton-Century-Crofts.

McClintock, C. G., Stech, F. J. & Keil, L. J. (1983). The influence of communication on bargaining. In P. B. Paulus (Ed.), *Basic group processes* (pp. 205–233). New York: Springer Verlag.

McCranie, E. W., & Kimberley, J. C. (1973). Rank inconsistency, conflicting expectations, and injustice. *Sociometry, 36,* 152–176.

McCusker, C., & Carnevale, P. J. (1995). Framing in resource dilemmas: Loss aversion and the moderating effects of sanctions. *Organizational Behavior and Human Decision Processes, 61*(2), 190–201.

McDougall, W. (1920). *The group mind.* Cambridge: Cambridge University Press.

McGlynn, R. P., Gibbs, M. E., & Roberts, S. J. (1982). Effects of cooperative versus competitive set and coaction on creative responding. *Journal of Social Psychology, 118*(2), 281–282.

McGrath, J. E. (1984). *Groups: Interaction and performance.* Englewood Cliffs, NJ: Prentice-Hall.

McGrath, J. E., & Gruenfeld, D. H. (1993). Toward a dynamic and systemic theory of groups: An integration of six temporally enriched perspectives. In M. M. Chemers & R. Ayman (Eds.), *Leadership theory and research: Perspectives and directions* (pp. 217–243). San Diego, CA: Academic Press.

McGregor, J. (1993). Effectiveness of role-playing and antiracist teaching in reducing student prejudice. *Journal of Educational Research, 86,* 215–226.

McGuire, W. J., McGuire, C. V., Child, P., & Fujioka, T. (1978). Salience of ethnicity in the spontaneous self-concept as a function of one's ethnic distinctiveness in the social environment. *Journal of Personality and Social Psychology, 36,* 511 520.

McKenna, K. Y. A., & Bargh, J. A. (1998). Coming out in the age of the Internet: Identity "demarginalization" through virtual group participation. *Journal of Personality and Social Psychology, 75*(3), 681–694.

McKenna, K. Y. A., & Bargh, J. A. (2000). Plan 9 from cyberspace: The implications of the Internet for personality and social psychology. *Personality and Social Psychology Review, 4*(1), 57–75.

McLeod, P. L., Lobel, S. A., & Cox, T. H. (1996). Ethnic diversity and creativity in small groups. *Small Group Research, 27*(2), 248–264.

Mead, G. H. (1934). *On social psychology.* Chicago: University of Chicago Press.

Meeker, B. F., & Turner, R. H. (1990). Expectation states and interpersonal behavior. In M. T. Rosenberg (Ed.), *Social psychology: Sociological perspectives* (pp. 290–319). New Brunswick, NJ: Transaction.

Megargee, E. I. (1969). Influence of sex roles on the manifestation of leadership. *Journal of Applied Psychology, 53*(5), 377–382.

Merton, R. K. (1948). The self-fulfilling prophecy. *Antioch Review, 8,* 193–210.

Merton, R. K. (1957). *Social theory and social structure*. New York: Free Press.

Messé, L. A., & Sivacek, J. M. (1979). Predictions of others' responses in a mixed-motive game: Self-justification or false consensus? *Journal of Personality and Social Psychology, 37*(4), 602–607.

Messick, D. M., & Brewer, M. B. (1983). Solving social dilemmas: A review. In L. Wheeler & P. Shaver (Eds.), *Review of personality and social psychology* (Vol. 4, pp. 11–44). Beverly Hills, CA: Sage.

Messick, D. M., & McClelland, C. L. (1983). Social traps and temporal traps. *Personality and Social Psychology Bulletin, 9*, 105–110.

Messick, D. M., Wilke, H., Brewer, M. B., Kramer, R. M., Zemke, P. E., & Lui, L. (1983). Individual adaptations and structural change as solutions to social dilemmas. *Journal of Personality and Social Psychology, 44*, 294–309.

Michaelsen, L. K., Watson, W. E., & Black, R. H. (1989). A realistic test of individual versus group consensus decision making. *Journal of Applied Psychology, 74*(5), 834–839.

Mikolic, J. M., Parker, J. C., & Pruitt, D. G. (1997). Escalation in response to persistent annoyance: Groups versus individuals and gender effects. *Journal of Personality and Social Psychology, 72*(1), 151–163.

Milgram, S. (1974). *Obedience to authority: An experimental view*. New York: Harper & Row.

Milgram, S., Bickman, L., & Berkowitz, L. (1969). Note on the drawing power of crowds of different size. *Journal of Personality and Social Psychology, 13*, 79–82.

Miller, C. E. (1989). The social psychological effects of group decision rules. In P. B. Paulus (Ed.), *Psychology of group influence* (2nd ed.). Hillsdale, NJ: Erlbaum.

Miller, D. T., & Prentice, D. A. (1996). The construction of social norms and standards. In E. T. Higgins & A. W. Kruglanski (Eds.), *Social psychology: Handbook of basic principles* (pp. 799–829). New York: Guilford.

Miller, D. T., & Turnbull, W. (1986). Expectancies and interpersonal processes. *Annual Review of Psychology, 37*, 233–256.

Miller, J. G., & Bersoff, D. (1994). Cultural influences on the moral status of reciprocity and the discounting of endogenous motivation. *Personality and Social Psychology Bulletin, 20*, 592–602.

Miller, N., Brewer, M. B., & Edwards, K. (1985). Cooperative interaction in desegregated settings: A laboratory analogue. *Journal of Social Issues, 41*(3), 63–79.

Miller, N., & Davidson-Podgorny, G. (1987). *Theoretical models of intergroup relations and the use of cooperative teams as an intervention for desegregated settings in Review of Personality and Social Psychology*. Newbury Park: Sage.

Minard, R. D. (1952). Race relationships in the Pocohontas coal field. *Journal of Social Issues, 8*, 29–44.

Mishler, E. G., & Waxler, N. E. (1968). *Interaction in families: An experimental study of family processes and schizophrenia*. New York: Wiley.

Molm, L. D. (1986). Gender, power, and legitimation: A test of three theories. *American Journal of Sociology, 91*, 1156–1186.

Molm, L. D. (1997). *Coercive power in social exchange*. New York: Cambridge University Press.

Monteith, M. J. (1993). Self-regulation of prejudiced responses: Implications for progress in prejudice-reduction efforts. *Journal of Personality and Social Psychology, 65*, 469–485.

Monteith, M. J., Sherman, J. W., & Devine, P. G. (1998). Suppression as a stereotype control strategy. *Personality and Social Psychology Review, 2*, 63–82.

Monteith, M. J., Ashburn-Nardo, L., Voils, C. I., & Czopp, A. M. (2002). Putting the brakes on prejudice: On the development and operation of cues for control. *Journal of Personality and Social Psychology, 83*(5), 1029–1050.

Moore, D., & Baron, R. S. (1983). Social facilitation: A psychophysiological analysis. In J. T.

Cacioppo & R. E. Petty (Eds.), *Social psychophysiology: A sourcebook* (pp. 434–466). New York: Guilford.

Moorhead, G. (1982). Groupthink: Hypothesis in need of testing. *Group and Organization Studies, 7*(4), 429–444.

Moorhead, G., & Montanari, J. R. (1986). An empirical investigation of the groupthink phenomenon. *Human Relations, 39*(5), 399–410.

Moreland, R. L. (1985). Social categorization and the assimilation of "new" group members. *Journal of Personality and Social Psychology, 48*(5), 1173–1190.

Moreland, R. L. (1987). The formation of small groups. In C. Hendrick (Ed.), *Group processes. Review of personality and social psychology* (Vol. 8, pp. 80–110). Newbury Park, CA: Sage.

Moreland, R. L. (1996). Creating the ideal group: Composition effects at work. In E. H. Witte & J. H. Davis (Eds.), *Understanding group behavior, Vol. 2: Small group processes and interpersonal relations* (pp. 11–35). Hillsdale, NJ: Erlbaum.

Moreland, R. L., Hogg, M. A., & Hains, S. C. (1994). Back to the future: Social psychological research on groups. *Journal of Experimental Social Psychology, 30*(6), 527–555.

Moreland, R. L., & Levine, J. M. (1982). Socialization in small groups: Temporal changes in individal-group relations. In L. Berkowitz (Ed.), *Advances in experimental social psychology* (Vol. 15). New York: Academic Press.

Moreland, R. L., Levine, J., & Cini, M. (1993). Group socialization: The role of commitment. In M. A. Hogg & D. Abrams (Eds.), *Group motivation: Social psychological perspectives.* New York: Harvester Wheatsheaf.

Morris, A., & Mueller, C. (1992). *Frontiers in social movement theory.* New Haven: Yale University Press.

Morris, C. G., & Hackman, J. R. (1969). Behavioral correlates of perceived leadership. *Journal of Peronality and Social Psychology, 13,* 350–361.

Morse, S., & Gergen, K. (1970). Social comparison, self-consistency, and the concept of self. *Journal of Personality and Social Psychology, 16*(1), 148–156.

Moscovici, S. (1980). Toward a theory of conversion behavior. In L. Berkowitz (Ed.), *Advances in experimental social psychology* (Vol. 13, pp. 209–239). New York: Academic Press.

Moscovici, S. (1988). Notes towards a description of social representations. *European Journal of Social Psychology, 18,* 211–250.

Moscovici, S., & Lage, E. (1976). Studies in social influence: III. Majority versus minority influence in a group. *European Journal of Social Psychology, 6*(2), 149–174.

Moscovici, S., Lage, E., & Naffrechoux, M. (1969). Influence of a consistent minority on the responses of a majority in a colour perception task. *Sociometry, 32,* 365–380.

Moscovici, S., Mucchi-Faina, A., & Maass, A. (Eds.). (1994). *Minority influence.* Chicago: Nelson-Hall.

Moscovici, S., Mugny, G., & Van Avermaet, E. (1985). *Perspectives on minority influence.* New York: Cambridge University Press.

Moscovici, S., & Personnaz, B. (1980). Studies in social influence: V. Minority influence and conversion behavior in a perceptual task. *Journal of Experimental Social Psychology, 16*(3), 270–282.

Moscovici, S., & Personnaz, B. (1986). Studies on latent influence by the spectrometer method: I. The impact of psychologization in the case of conversion by a minority or a majority. *European Journal of Social Psychology, 16*(4), 345–360.

Moscovici, S., & Personnaz, B. (1991). Studies in social influence: VI. Is Lenin orange or red? Imagery and social influence. *European Journal of Social Psychology, 21*(2), 101–118.

Moscovici, S., & Zavalloni, M. (1969). The group as a polarizer of attitudes. *Journal of Personality and Social Psychology, 12,* 125–135.

Moskowitz, G. B., Wasel, W., Schaal, B., & Gollwitzer, P. M. (1999). Preconscious control of stereotype activation through chronic egalitarian goals. *Journal of Personality and Social Psychology, 77*, 167–184.

Mudrack, P. E. (1989). Defining group cohesiveness: A legacy of confusion? *Small Group Behaivor, 26*, 542–571.

Mugny, G. (1982). *The power of minorities.* London: Academic Press.

Mullen, B. (1983). Operationalizing the effect of the group on the individual: A self-attention perspective. *Journal of Experimental Social Psychology, 19*, 295–322.

Mullen, B. (1986). Atrocity as a function of lynch mob composition: A self-attention perspective. *Personality and Social Psychology Bulletin, 12*(2), 187–197.

Mullen, B. (1987a). Introduction: The study of group behavior. In B. Mullen & G. R. Goethals (Eds.), *Theories of group behavior* (pp. 125–146). New York: Springer Verlag.

Mullen, B. (1987b). Self-attention theory: The effects of group composition on the individual. In B. Mullen & G. R. Goethals (Eds.), *Theories of group behavior.* New York: Springer Verlag.

Mullen, B., & Baumeister, R. F. (1987). Group effects on self-attention and performance: Social loafing, social facilitation, and social impairment. In C. Hendrick (Ed.), *Group processes and intergroup relations* (pp. 189–206). Thousand Oaks, CA: Sage.

Mullen, B., Brown, R., & Smith, C. (1992). Ingroup bias as a function of salience, relevance, and status: An integration. *European Journal of Social Psychology, 22*, 103-122.

Mullen, B., & Copper, C. (1994). The relation between group cohesiveness and performance: An integration. *Psychological Bulletin, 115*(2), 210–227.

Mullen, B., & Goethals, G. R. (Eds.). (1987). *Theories of group behavior.* New York: Springer Verlag.

Mullen, B., Johnson, C., & Salas, E. (1991). Productivity loss in brainstorming groups: A meta-analytic integration. *Basic and Applied Social Psychology, 12*(1), 3–23.

Mullen, B., Salas, E., & Driskell, J. E. (1989). Salience, motivation, and artifact as contributions to the relation between participation rate and leadership. *Journal of Experimental Social Psychology, 25*(6), 545–559.

Mullen, B., Symons, C., Hu, L.-t., & Salas, E. (1989). Group size, leadership behavior, and subordinate satisfaction. *Journal of General Psychology, 116*(2), 155–170.

Myers, D. G. (1982). Polarizing effects of social interaction. In H. Brandstatter, J. H. Davis, & G. Stocher-Kreichgauer (Eds.), *Contemporary problems in group decision making.* New York: Academic Press.

Myers, D. G., & Bishop, G. D. (1970). Discussion effects on racial attitudes. *Science, 3947*, 788–799.

Myers, D. G., & Kaplan, M. F. (1976). Group-induced polarization in simulated juries. *Personality and Social Psychology Bulletin, 2*(1), 63–66.

Myers, D. G., & Lamm, H. (1976). The group polarization phenomenon. *Psychological Bulletin, 83*, 602–627.

Neir, J. A., Gaertner, S. L., Dovidio, J. F., Banker, B. S., Ward, C. M., & Rust, C. R. (2001). Changing interracial evaluations and behavior: The effects of a common group identity. *Group Processes and Intergroup Relations, 4*, 299–316.

Nemeroff, P. M., & King, D. C. (1975). Group decision-mkaing performance as influenced by consensus and self-orientation. *Human Relations, 28*, 1–21.

Nemeroff, P. M., Passmore, W. A., & Ford, D. L. (1976). The effects of two normative structural interventions on established and ad hoc groups: Implications for improving decision-making effectiveness. *Decision Sciences, 7*, 841–855.

Nemeth, C. J., & Kwan, J. L. (1987). Minority influence, divergent thinking and the detection of correct solutions. *Journal of Applied Social Psychology, 17*, 788–799.

Nemeth, C. J., Mosier, K., & Chiles, C. (1992). When convergent thought improves performance: Majority versus minority influence. *Personality and Social Psychology Bulletin, 18*, 139–144.

Nemeth, C. J., & Wachtler, J. (1974). Creating the perceptions of consistency and confidence: A necessary condition for minority influence. *Sociometry, 37*(4), 529–540.

Nemeth, C. J., & Wachtler, J. (1983). Creative problem solving as a result of majority vs minority influence. *European Journal of Social Psychology, 13*(1), 45–55.

Nemeth, C. J., Wachter, J., & Endicott, J. (1977). Increasing the size of the minority: Some gains and some losses. *European Journal of Social Psychology, 7*(1), 15–27.

Neuberg, S. L., & Fiske, S. T. (1987). Motivational influences on impression formation: Outcome dependency, accuracy-driven attention, and individuating processes. *Journal of Personality and Social Psychology, 53*, 431–444.

Newcomb, T. M. (1943). *Personality and social change: Attitude formation in a student community.* New York: Dryden Press.

Newcomb, T. M. (1956). The prediction of interpersonal attraction. *American Psychologist, 11*, 575–586.

Newcomb, T. M. (1961). *The acquaintance process.* New York: Holt, Rinehart & Winston.

Newcomb, T. M. (1963). Persistence and regression of changed attitudes: Long range studies. *Journal of Social Issues, 19*, 3–14.

Newcomb, T. M. (1965). Attitude development as a function of reference groups: The Bennington study. In B. S. H. Proshansky (Ed.), *Basic studies in social psychology.* New York: Holt, Reinhart and Winston.

Newcomb, T. M., & Charters, W. W., Jr. (1950). *Social psychology.* New York: Dryden Press.

Newcomb, T. M., Koening, K. E., Flacks, R., & Warwick, D. P. (1967). *Persistence and change: Bennington College and its students after 25 years.* New York: Wiley.

Newman, G. A., Edwards, J. E., & Raju, N. S. (1989). Organizational development interventions: A meta-analysis of their effects. *Personnel Psychology, 42*, 461–489.

Norris, F., & Murrell, S. (1990). Social support, life events, and stress as modifiers of adjustment to bereavement by older adults. *Psychology and Aging, 5*(3), 429–436.

Nowak, A., Szamrej, J., & Latané, B. (1990). From private attitude to public opinion: A dynamic theory of social impact. *Psychological Review, 97*(3), 362–376.

Nye, J. L., & Forsyth, D. R. (1991). The effects of prototype-based biases on leadership appraisals: A test of leadership categorization theory. *Small Group Research, 22*, 360–379.

Nyquist, L. V., & Spence, J. T. (1986). Effects of dispositional dominance and sex role expectations on leadership behaviors. *Journal of Personality and Social Psychology, 50*(1), 87–93.

O'Dell, J. W. (1968). Group size and emotional interaction. *Journal of Personality and Social Psychology, 8*, 75–78.

Oakes, P. J., Haslam, S. A., & Turner, J. C. (1994). *Stereotyping and social reality.* Oxford: Blackwell.

Oakes, P. J., & Turner, J. (1980). Social categorization and intergroup behaviour: Does minimal intergroup discrimination make social identity more positive. *European Journal of Social Psychology, 10*, 295–301.

Oakes, P. J., & Turner, J. (1990). Is limited information processing capacity the cause of social stereotyping? *European Review of Social Psychology, 1*, 111–135.

Oakes, P. J., Turner, J. C., & Haslam, S. A. (1991). Perceiving people as group members: The role of fit in the salience of social categorizations. *British Journal of Social Psychology, 30*, 125–144.

Oldham, G. R., Kulik, C. T., Stepina, L. P., & Ambrose, M. L. (1986). Relations between job facet comparisons and employee reactions. *Organizational Behavior and Human Decision Processes, 38*(1), 28–47.

Olson, M. (1965). *The logic of collective action: Public goods and the theory of groups.* Cambridge: Harvard University Press.

Orbell, J. M., & Dawes, R. M. (1981). Social dilemmas. In G. Stephenson & J. M. Davis (Eds.), *Progress in applied social psychology* (Vol. 1, pp. 37–65). New York: Wiley.

Orbell, J. M., Van de Kragt, A. J., & Dawes, R. M. (1988). Explaining discussion-induced cooperation. *Journal of Personality and Social Psychology, 54,* 811–819.

Orcutt, J. D. (1973). Societal reaction and the response to deviation in small groups. *Social Forces, 52,* 259–267.

Organizational psychology. (Special issue). *American Psychologist, 45*(2), 134–143.

Orive, R. (1988). Social projection and social comparison of opinions. *Journal of Personality and Social Psychology, 54,* 953–964.

Osborn, A. F. (1954). *Applied imagination.* New York: Scribner.

Oskamp, S. (1971). Effects of programmed strategies on cooperation in the prisoner's dilemma and other mixed-motive games. *Journal of Conflict Resolution, 15,* 225–259.

Ostrom, T. M., & Sedikides, C. (1992). Out-group homogeneity effects in natural and minimal groups. *Psychological Bulletin, 112*(3), 536–552.

Park, B., & Rothbart, M. (1982). Perception of out-group homogeneity and levels of social categorization: Memory for the subordinate attributes of in-group and out-group members. *Journal of Personality and Social Psychology, 42,* 1051–1068.

Parks, C. D., & Cowlin, R. (1995). Group discussion as affected by number of alternatives and by a time limit. *Organizational Behavior and Human Decision Processes, 62*(3), 267–275.

Parks, C. D., & Cowlin, R. (1996). Acceptance of uncommon information into group discussion when that information is or is not demonstable. *Organizational Behavior and Human Decision Processes, 66*(3), 307–315.

Parsons, T. (1951). *The social system.* New York: Free Press.

Paulus, P. B., & Dzindolet, M. T. (1993). Social influence processes in group brainstorming. *Journal of Personality and Social Psychology, 64*(4), 575–586.

Paulus, P. B., Dzindolet, M. T., Poletes, G., & Camacho, L. M. (1993). Perception of performance in group brainstorming: The illusion of group productivity. *Personality and Social Psychology Bulletin, 19*(1), 78–89.

Peiro, J. M., Gonzalez-Roma, V., & Ramos, J. (1992). The influence of work-team climate on role stress, tension, satisfaction and leadership perceptions. *European Review of Applied Psychology, 42,* 49–58.

Pelz, D. C. (1956). Some social factors related to performance in a research organization. *Administrative Science Quarterly, 1,* 310–325.

Pennebaker, J. W., & Sanders, D. Y. (1976). American graffiti: Effects of authority and reactance arousal. *Personality and Social Psychology Bulletin, 2*(3), 264–267.

Pennington, N., & Hastie, R. (1990). Practical implications of psychological research on juror and jury decision making. *Personality and Social Psychology Bulletin, 16*(1), 90–105.

Pepitone, A., & Reichling, G. (1955). Group cohesiveness and the expression of hostility. *Human Relations, 8,* 327–337.

Peters, L. H., Hartke, D. D., & Pohlmann, J. T. (1985). Fiedler's contingency theory of leadership: An application of the meta-analysis procedures of Schmidt and Hunter. *Psychological Bulletin, 97*(2), 274–285.

Pettigrew, T. F. (1959). Regional differences in anti-Negro prejudice. *Journal of Abnormal and Social Psychology, 59,* 28–36.

Pettigrew, T. F. (1979). The ultimate attribution error: Extending Allport's cognitive analysis of prejudice. *Personality and Social Psychology Bulletin, 5*(4), 461–476.

Pettigrew, T. F. (1998a). Reactions toward the new minorities of Western Europe. *Annual Review of Sociology, 24,* 77–103.

Pettigrew, T. F. (1998b). Intergroup contact theory. *Annual Review of Psychology, 49,* 65–85.

Pettigrew, T. F., & Tropp, L. R. (2000). Does intergroup contact reduce prejudice: Recent meta-analytic findings. In S. Oskamp (Ed.), *Reducing prejudice and discrimination* (pp. 93–135). Mahwah, NJ: Erlbaum.

Petty, R. E., Harkins, S. G., & Williams, K. D. (1980). The effects of diffusion of cognitive effort on attitudes: An information processing view. *Journal of Personality and Social Psychology, 38,* 81–92.

Petty, R. E., Harkins, S. G., Williams, K. D., & Latané, B. (1977). The effects of group size on cognitive effort and evaluation. *Personality and Social Psychology Bulletin, 3*(4), 579–582.

Pew Research Center. (2000, May 10). Tracking online life: How women use the Internet to cultivate relationships with family and friends. *Pew Internet and American Life Project,* p. 410.

Pfeffer, J. (1992). *Managing with power.* Cambridge: Cambridge University Press.

Phinney, J. S., Cantu, C. L., & Kurtz, D. A. (1997). Ethnic and American identity as predictors of self-esteem among African-Americans, Latino, and white adolescents. *Journal of Youth and Adolescence, 26,* 165–195.

Piaget, J. (1942). *Classes, relations et nombres: essai sur les "grouements" de la logistique et la reversibilitié del la pensée.* Paris: Vrin.

Pickett, C. L. (2001). The effects of entitativity beliefs on implicit comparisons between group members. *Personality and Social Psychology Bulletin, 27,* 515–525.

Pilkington, C., Tesser, A., & Stephens, D. (1991). Complementarity in romantic relationships: A self-evaluation maintenance perspective. *Journal of Social and Personal Relationships, 8,* 481–504.

Pinel, E. (1999). Stigma-consciousness: The psychological legacy of social stereotypes. *Journal of Personality and Social Psychology, 76,* 114–128.

Platow, M. J., Harley, K., Hunter, J. A., Hanning, P., et al. (1997). Interpreting in-group–favouring allocations in the minimal group paradigm. *British Journal of Social Psychology, 36*(1), 107–117.

Platow, M. J., Howard, M. L., & Stringer, M. (1996). Social identity and intergroup evaluative bias: Realistic categories and domain specific self-esteem in a conflict setting. *European Journal of Social Psychology, 26*(4), 631–647.

Platow, M. J., O'Connell, A., Shave, R., & Hanning, P. (1995). Social evaluations of fair and unfair allocators in interpersonal and intergroup situations. *British Journal of Social Psychology, 34*(4), 363–381.

Platt, J. (1973). Social traps. *American Psychologist, 28,* 641–651.

Podsakoff, P. M., MacKenzie, S. B., Ahearne, M., & Bommer, W. H. (1995). Searching for a needle in a haystack: Trying to identify the illusive moderators of leadership behaviors. *Journal of Management, 21,* 423–470.

Podsakoff, P. M., MacKenzie, S. B., Moorman, R. H., & Fetter, R. (1990). Transformational leader behaviors and their effects on followers' trust in leader, satisfaction, and organizational citizenship behaviors. *Leadership Quarterly, 1*(2), 107–142.

Porter, N., Geis, F. L., Cooper, E., & Newman, E. (1985). Androgyny and leadership in mixed-sex groups. *Journal of Personality and Social Psychology, 49*(3), 808–823.

Postmes, T., Branscombe, N. R., Spears, R., & Young, H. (1999). Comparative processes in personal and group judgments: Resolving the discrepancy. *Journal of Personality and Social Psychology, 76*(2), 320–338.

Postmes, T., & Spears, R. (1998). Deindividuation and antinormative behavior: A meta-analysis. *Psychological Bulletin, 123,* 238–259.

Prejudice, discrimination, and conflict. (Special issue). *International Journal of Intercultural Relations, 20*(3-4), 271–290.

Prentice, D. A., Miller, D. T., & Lightdale, J. R. (1994). Asymmetries in attachments to groups and to their members: Distinguishing between common-identity and common-bond groups. *Personality and Social Psychology Bulletin, 20*(5), 484–493.

Prentice-Dunn, S., & Rogers, R. W. (1983). Deindividuation and aggression. In R. G. Geen & E. I. Donnerstein (Eds.), *Aggression: Theoretical and empirical reviews* (Vol. 1). New York: Academic Press.

Pruitt, D. G. (1998). Social conflict. In D. Gilbert, S. T. Fiske, & G. Lindzey (Eds.), *Handbook of social psychology* (4th ed., pp. 470–503). New York: McGraw-Hill.

Pruitt, D. G., & Carnevale, P. J. (1993). *Negotiation in social conflict*. Pacific Grove, CA: Brooks-Cole.

Pruitt, D. G., & Kimmel, M. J. (1977). Twenty years of experimental gaming: Critique, synthesis, and suggestions for the future. *Annual Review of Psychology, 28*(36), 3–392.

Pruitt, D. G., & Lewis, S. A. (1975). Development of integrative solutions in bilateral negotiation. *Journal of Personality and Social Psychology, 31*(4), 621–633.

Pruitt, D. G., & Rubin, J. Z. (1986). *Social conflict: Escalation, stalemate, and settlement*. New York: McGraw-Hill.

Pruitt, D. G., Welton, G. L., Fry, W. R., McGillicuddy, N. B., Castrianno, L., & Zubek, J. M. (1989). The process of mediation: Caucusing, control, and problem solving. In M. A. Rahim (Ed.), *Managing conflict: An interdisciplinary approach*. New York: Praeger.

Pugh, M. D. & Wahrman, R. (1983). Neutralizing sexism in mixed-sex groups: Do women have to be better than men? *American Journal of Sociology, 88*, 746–762.

Putallaz, M., & Gottman, J. M. (1981). An interactional model of children's entry into peer groups. *Child Development, 52*, 986–994.

Rabbie, J. M. (1963). Differential preference for companionship under threat. *Journal of Abnormal and Social Psychology, 67*(6), 643–648.

Rabbie, J. M., & Horwitz, M. (1969). Arousal of in-group out-group bias by a chance win or loss. *Journal of Personality and Social Psychology, 3*, 269–277.

Rajecki, D. W., Ickes, W., Corcoran, C., & Lenerz, K. (1977). Social facilitation of human performance: Mere presence effects. *Journal of Social Psychology, 102*(2), 297–310.

Rapoport, A. (1973). *Experimental games and their uses in psychology*. Morristown, NJ: General Learning Press.

Rapoport, A. (1987). Research paradigms and expected utility models for the provision of step-level public goods. *Psychological Review, 94*(1), 74–83.

Rapoport, A. (1988). Provision of step-level public goods: Effects of inequality in resources. *Journal of Personality and Social Psychology, 54*(3), 432–440.

Rapoport, A., Bornstein, G., & Erev, I. (1989). Intergroup competition for public goods: Effects of unequal resources and relative group size. *Journal of Personality and Social Psychology, 56*(5), 748–756.

Rashotte, L. S., & Smith-Lovin, L. (1997). Who benefits from being bold: The interactive effects of task cues and status characteristics on influence in mock jury groups. *Advances in group processes* (Vol. 14). Stamford, CT: JAI Press.

Raven, B. H. (1992). A power/interaction model of interpersonal influence: French and Raven thirty years later. *Journal of Social Behavior and Personality, 7*(2), 217–244.

Reagans, R., & Zuckerman, E. W. (2001). Networks, diversity, and productivity: The social captial of corporate R&D teams. *Organization Science, 12*, 502–517.

Reckman, R. F., & Goethals, G. R. (1973). Deviancy and group orientation as determinants of group composition preferences. *Sociometry, 36*, 419–423.

Reicher, S. D. (1982). The determination of collective behavior. In H. Tajfel (Ed.), *Social identity and intergroup relations* (pp. 41–83). Cambridge: Cambridge University Press.

Reicher, S. D. (1987). Crowd behavior as social action. In J. C. Turner, M. A. Hogg, P. J. Oakes, S. D. Reicher, & M. S. Wetherell (Eds.), *Rediscovering the social group: A self-categorization theory*. Oxford & New York: Blackwell.

Reicher, S. D. (1984a). Social influence in the crowd: Attitudinal and behavioural effects of deindividuation in conditions of high and low group salience. *British Journal of Social Psychology, 23*, 341–350.

Reicher, S. D. (1984b). The St. Paul's riot: An explanation of the limits of a crowd action in terms of a social identity model. *European Journal of Social Psychology, 14*, 1–21.

Reicher, S. D., Spears, R., & Postmes, T. (1995). A social identity model of deindividuation phenomena. *European Review of Social Psychology, 6*, 161–198.

Reid, W. M., Pease, J., & Taylor, R. G. (1990). The Delphi Technique as an aid to organization development activities. *Organizational Development Journal, 8*, 37–42.

Reis, H. T. (1990). The role of intimacy in interpersonal relations. *Journal of Social and Clinical Psychology, 9*(1), 15–30.

Reno, R. R., Cialdini, R. B., & Kallgren, C. A. (1993). The transsituational influence of social norms. *Journal of Personality and Social Psychology, 64*, 104–112.

Rhee, E., Uleman, J. S., Lee, H. K., & Roman, R. J. (1995). Spontaneous self-descriptions and ethnic identities in individualistic and collectivistic cultures. *Journal of Personality and Social Psychology, 69*(1), 142–152.

Ridgeway, C. L., & Balkwell, J. W. (1997). Group processes and the diffusion of status beliefs. *Social Psychology Quarterly, 60*, 14–31.

Riordan, C. (1983). Sex as a general status characteristic. *Social Psychology Quarterly, 46*(3), 261–267.

Robinson-Staveley, K., & Cooper, J. (1990). Mere presence, gender, and reactions to computers: Studying human-computer interaction in the social context. *Journal of Experimental Social Psychology, 26*(2), 168–183.

Roethlisberger, F. J., & Dickson, W. J. (1939). *Management and the worker*. Cambridge: Cambridge University Press.

Rofe, Y. (1984). Stress and affiliation: A utility theory. *Psychological Review, 91*(2), 235–250.

Rogelberg, S. G., Barnes-Farrell, J. L., & Lowe, C. A. (1992). The stepladder technique: An alternative group structure facilitating effective group decision making. *Journal of Applied Psychology, 77*, 730–737.

Rohrer, J. H., Baron, S. H., Hoffman, E. L., & Swander, D. V. (1954). The stability of autokinetic judgments. *American Journal of Psychology, 67*, 143–146.

Rojahn, K., & Willemsen, T. M. (1994). The evaluation of effectiveness and likability of gender-role congruent and gender-role incongruent leaders. *Sex Roles, 30*(1–2), 109–119.

Rokeach, M. (1960). *The open and closed mind*. New York: Basic Books.

Rook, K. (1984). The negative side of social interaction: Impact on psychological well-being. *Journal of Personality and Social Psychology, 46*, 1097–1108.

Rosenberg, M. (1979). *Conceiving the self*. New York: Basic Books.

Rosenthal, R., & Jacobson, L. (1966). Teachers' expectancies: Determinants of pupils IQ gains. *Psychological Reports, 19*, 115–118.

Rossi, P. H., & Freeman, H. E. (1993). *Evaluation: A systematic approach*. Newbury Park, CA: Sage Publications.

Rothbart, M., & John, O. P. (1985). Social categorization and behavioral episodes: A cognitive analysis of the effects of intergroup contact. *Journal of Social Issues, 41*, 81–104.

Rothbart, M., & John, O. P. (1993). Intergroup relations and stereotype change: A social-cognitive analysis and some longitudinal findings. In P. M. Sniderman & P. E. Tetlock (Eds.),

Prejudice, politics, and the American dilemma (pp. 32–59). Stanford, CA: Stanford University Press.

Rothberg, J., & Jones, F. (1987). Suicide in the U.S. Army: Epidemiological and periodic aspects. *Suicide and Life-Threatening Behavior, 17*(2), 119–132.

Roy, D. F. (1953). Work satisfaction and social reward in quota achievement. *American Sociological Review, 18*, 507–514.

Roy, D. F. (1959). Banana time. *Human Organization, 18*, 158–168.

Rubenstein, C., & Shaver, P. (1982). The experience of loneliness. In L. Peplau & D. Perlman (Eds.), *Loneliness: A sourcebook of current theory, research, and therapy.* New York: Wiley-Interscience.

Rubin, J. Z., Pruitt, D. G., & Kim, S. H. (1994). *Social conflict: Escalation, stalemate, and settlement* (2nd ed.). New York: McGraw-Hill.

Rubin, M., & Hewstone, M. (1998). Social identity theory's self-esteem hypothesis: A review and some suggestions for clarification. *Personality and Social Psychology Review, 2*, 40–62.

Ruble, D. N., & Ruble, T. L. (1982). Sex stereotypes. In A. G. Miller (Ed.), *In the eye of the beholder: Contemporary issues in stereotyping.* New York: Praeger.

Rudman, L. A., & Glick, P. (1999). Feminized management and backlash toward agentic women: The hidden costs to women of a kinder, gentler image of middle managers. *Journal of Personality and Social Psychology, 77*(5), 1004–1010.

Runciman, W. (1966). *Relative deprivation and social justice.* London: Routledge & Kegan Paul.

Rusbult, C., Verette, J., Whitney, G., Slovik, L., et al. (1991). Accommodation processes in close relationships: Theory and preliminary empirical evidence. *Journal of Personality and Social Psychology., 60*(1), 53–78.

Rusbult, C. E. (1980). Commitment and satisfaction in romantic associations: A test of the investment model. *Journal of Experimental Social Psychology, 16*(2), 172–186.

Rusbult, C. E., Zembrodt, I. M., & Gunn, L. K. (1982). Exit, voice, loyalty, and neglect: Responses to dissatisfaction in romantic involvements. *Journal of Personality and Social Psychology, 43*(6), 1230–1242.

Ruscher, J. B. (2001). *Prejudiced communication: A social psychological perspective.* New York: Guilford.

Ruscher, J. B., & Duval, L. L. (1998). Multiple communicators with unique target information transmit less stereotypical impressions. *Journal of Personality and Social Psychology, 74*(2), 329–344.

Russell, D., Curtona, C. E., Rose, J., & Yurko, K. (1984). Social and emotional loneliness: An examination of Weiss's topology of loneliness. *Journal of Personality and Social Psychology, 46*, 1313–1321.

Sachdev, I., & Bourhis, R. (1990). Bilinguality and multilinguality. In H. R. Giles & W. Peter, (Eds.), *Handbook of language and social psychology* (pp. 293–308). Chichester, UK: Wiley.

Sachdev, I., & Bourhis, R. Y. (1985). Social categorization and power differentials in group relations. *European Journal of Social Psychology, 15*, 415–434.

Sachdev, I., & Bourhis, R. Y. (1987). Status differentials and intergroup behavior. *European Journal of Social Psychology, 17*, 277–293.

Sachdev, I., & Bourhis, R. Y. (1991). Power and status differentials in minority and majority group relations. *European Journal of Social Psychology, 21*(1), 1–24.

Sagar, H. A., & Schofield, J. W. (1980). Racial and behavioral cues in black and white children's perception of ambiguously aggressive acts. *Journal of Personality and Social Psychology, 39*, 590–598.

Sampson, R., & Laub, J. (1993). *Crime in the making: Pathways and turning points through life.* Cambridge, MA: Harvard University Press.

Samuelson, C. D., & Messick, D. M. (1986). Alternative structural solutions to resource dilemmas. *Organizational Behavior and Human Decision Processes, 37*(1), 139–155.

Samuelson, C. D., Messick, D. M., Rutte, C. G., & Wilke, H. (1984). Individual and structural solutions to resource dilemmas in two cultures. *Journal of Personality and Social Psychology, 47,* 94–104.

Sanders, G. S. (1981a). Driven by distraction: An integrative review of social facilitation theory and research. *Journal of Experimental Social Psychology, 17,* 227–251.

Sanders, G. S. (1981b). The interactive effect of social comparison and objective information on the decision to see a doctor. *Journal of Applied Social Psychology, 11,* 390–400.

Sanders, G. S., & Baron, R. S. (1977). Is social comparison irrelevant for producing choice shifts? *Journal of Experimental Social Psychology, 13*(4), 303–314.

Sanders, G. S., Baron, R. S., & Moore, D. L. (1978). Distraction and social comparison as mediators of social facilitation effects. *Journal of Experimental Social Psychology, 14*(3), 291–303.

Sanna, L. J., & Parks, C. D. (1997). Group research trends in social and organizational psychology: Whatever happened to intragroup research? *Psychological Science, 8,* 261–267.

Sasfy, J., & Okun, M. (1974). Form of evaluation and audience expertness as joint determinants of audience effects. *Journal of Experimental Social Psychology, 10*(5), 461–467.

Sattler, D. N., & Kerr, N. L. (1991). Might versus morality explored: Motivational and cognitive bases for social motives. *Journal of Personality and Social Psychology, 60*(5), 756–765.

Scarberry, N. C., Ratcliff, C. D., Lord, C. G., Lanicek, D. L., & Desforges, D. M. (1997). Effects of individuating information on the generalization part of Allport's contact hypothesis. *Personality and Social Psychology Bulletin, 23*(12), 1291–1299.

Schachter, S. (1951). Deviation, rejection, and communication. *Journal of Abnormal and Social Psychology, 46,* 190–207.

Schachter, S. (1959). *The psychology of affiliation.* Stanford, CA: Stanford University Press.

Schacter, S., Ellertson, N., McBride, D., & Gregory, D. (1951). An experimental study of cohesiveness and productivity. *Human Relations, 4,* 229–238.

Schaller, M., & Conway, G. (1999). Influence of impression-management goals on the emerging content of group stereotypes: Support for a social-evolutionary perspective. *Personality and Social Psychology Bulletin, 25,* 819–833.

Schaller, M., & Conway, L. I. (2000). The origins of stereotypes that really matter. In G. Moscowitz (Ed.), *Cognitive social psychology: On the tenure and future of social cognition.* Hillsdale, NJ: Erlbaum.

Schaller, M., Conway, L. G., & Tanchuk, T. L. (2002). Selective pressures on the once and future contents of ethnic stereotypes: Effects of the communicability of traits. *Journal of Personality and Social Psychology, 82,* 861–877.

Schaller, M., & Latané, B. (1996). Dynamic social impact and the evolution of social representations: A natural history of stereotypes. *Journal of Communication, 46,* 64–77.

Schelling, T. C. (1978). *Micromotives and macrobehavior.* New York: Norton.

Schemo, D. (2000). Virginity pledges by teenagers can be highly effective, federal study finds. *New York Times.*

Schlenker, B. R., & Bonoma, T. V. (1978). Fun and games: The validity of games for the study of conflict. *Journal of Conflict Resolution, 22,* 393–410.

Schlenker, B. R., & Forsyth, D. R. (1977). On the ethics of psychological research. *Journal of Experimental Social Psychology, 13,* 369–396.

Schlenker, B. R., & Goldman, H. J. (1978). Cooperators and competitors in conflict: A test of the "triangle model." *Journal of Conflict Resolution, 22*(3), 393–410.

Schlenker, B. R., & Leary, M. R. (1982). Social anxiety and self presentation: A conceptualization and model. *Psychological Bulletin, 92*, 641–669.

Schmidt, N., & Sermat, V. (1983). Measuring loneliness in different relationships. *Journal of Personality and Social Psychology, 44*, 1038–1047.

Schmitt, B. H., Gilovich, T., Goore, N., & Joseph, L. (1986). Mere presence and social facilitation: One more time. *Journal of Experimental Social Psychology, 22*, 242–248.

Schmitt, M. T., Silvia, P. J., & Branscombe, N. R. (2000). The intersection of self-evaluation maintenance and social identity theories: Intragroup judgment in interpersonal and intergroup contexts. *Personality and Social Psychology Bulletin, 26*(12), 1598–1606.

Schmuck, R. A. (1995). Process consultation and organization development. *Journal of Educational and Psychological Consultation, 6*, 199–205.

Schofield, J. (1986). Causes and consequences of the colorblind perspective. In J. F. Dovidio & S. L. Gaertner (Eds.), *Prejudice, discrimination, and racism* (pp. 231–253). San Diego, CA: Academic Press.

Schopler, J., Insko, C. A., & Drigotas, S. M. (1993). Individual-group discontinuity: Further evidence for mediation by fear and greed. *Personality and Social Psychology Bulletin, 19*, 419–431.

Schriesheim, C. A., Tepper, B. J., & Tetrault, L. A. (1994). Least preferred coworker score, situational control, and leadership effectiveness: A meta-analysis of contingency model performance predictions. *Journal of Applied Psychology, 79*(4), 561–573.

Schuman, H., Steeh, C., Bobo, L., & Krysan, M. (1997). *Racial attitudes in America: Trends and interpretations.* Cambridge, MA: Harvard University Press.

Schutz, W. C. (1958). *FIRO: A three-dimensional theory of interpersonal behavior.* New York: Rinehart.

Schwenk, C. R. (1983). Laboratory research on ill-structured decision aids: The case of dialectical inquiry. *Decision Sciences, 14*, 140–144.

Seashore, S. E. (1954). *Group cohesiveness in the industrial work group.* Ann Arbor, MI: Institute for Social Research.

Sechrist, G., & Stangor, C. (2001). Perceived consensus influences intergroup behavior and stereotype accessibility. *Journal of Personality and Social Psychology, 80*, 645–654.

Secord, P. F., Bevan, W., & Katz, B. (1956). The Negro stereotype and perceptual accentuation. *Journal of Abnormal and Social Psychology, 53*, 78–83.

Sedikides, C., Schopler, J., & Insko, C. A. (Eds.). (1998). *Intergroup cognition and intergroup behavior.* Mahwah, NJ: Erlbaum.

Seta, C., Seta, J. J., & Donaldson, S. (1992). Observers and participants in an intergroup setting. *Journal of Personality and Social Psychology, 63*(4), 629–643.

Seta, J. J., & Seta, C. E. (1996). Big fish in small ponds: A social hierarchy analysis of intergroup bias. *Journal of Personality and Social Psychology, 71*(6), 1210–1221.

Shackelford, S., Wood, W., & Worchel, S. (1996). Behavioral styles and the influence of women in mixed-sex groups. *Social Psychology Quarterly, 59*(3), 284–293.

Shah, J. Y., Kruglanski, A. W., & Thompson, E. P. (1998). Membership has its (epistemic) rewards: Need for closure effects on intergroup favoritism. *Journal of Personality and Social Psychology, 75*, 383–393.

Shaver, P., & Buhrmester, D. (1983). Loneliness, sex-role orientation and group life: A social needs perspective. In P. B. Paulus (Ed.), *Basic group processes* (pp. 259–288). New York: Springer Verlag.

Shaw, M. E. (1932). A comparison of individuals and small groups in the rational solution of complex problems. *American Journal of Psychology, 44*, 491–504.

Shaw, M. E. (1964). Communication networks. *Advances in Experimental Social Psychology, 1*, 111–147.

Shaw, M. E. (1981). *Group dynamics: The psychology of small group behavior*. New York: McGraw-Hill.

Sheldon, K. M. (1999). Learning the lessons of tit-for-tat: Even competitors can get the message. *Journal of Personality and Social Psychology, 77*(6), 1245–1253.

Shepperd, J. A. (1993). Productivity loss in performance groups: A motivation analysis. *Psychological Bulletin, 113*, 67–81.

Shepperd, J. A., & Wright, R. A. (1989). Individual contributions to a collective effort: An incentive analysis. *Personality and Social Psychology Bulletin, 15*, 141–149.

Sherif, M. (1935). A study of some social factors in perception. *Archives of Psychology, 187*.

Sherif, M. (1936). *The psychology of social norms*. New York: Harper & Row.

Sherif, M., Harvey, O. J., White, B. J., Hood, W. R., & Sherif, C. (1961). *Intergroup conflict and cooperation: The robbers' cave experiment*. Norman: University of Oklahoma Press.

Sherif, M., & Sherif, C. W. (1953). *Groups in harmony and tension*. New York: Harper & Row.

Sherif, M., & Sherif, C. W. (1956). *An outline of social psychology*. New York: Harper.

Sherif, M., & Sherif, C. W. (1967). *Social psychology*. New York: Harper & Row.

Shomer, R. W., Davis, A. H., & Kelley, H. H. (1966). Threats and the development of coordination: Further studies of the Deutsch and Krauss trucking game. *Journal of Personality and Social Psychology, 4*, 119–126.

Siau, K. L. (1995). Group creativity and technology. *Psychosomatics, 31*, 301–312.

Sidanius, J., & Pratto, F. (1999). *Social dominance: An intergroup theory of social hierarchy and oppression*. New York: Cambridge University Press.

Sidanius, J., Pratto, F., Martin, M., & Stallworth, L. M. (1991). Consensual racism and career track: Some implications of social dominance theory. *Political Psychology, 12*, 691–721.

Siegel, J., Dubrovsky, V., Kiesler, S., & McGuire, T. W. (1986). Group processes in computer-mediated communication. *Organizational Behavior and Human Decision Processes, 37*(2), 157–187.

Silver, W. S., & Bufanio, K. M. (1996). The impact of group efficacy and group goals on group task performance. *Small Group Research, 27*(3), 347–359.

Silver, W. S., & Bufanio, K. M. (1997). Reciprocal relationships, causal influences, and group efficacy: A reply to Kaplan. *Small Group Research, 28*(4), 559–562.

Simmel, G. (1920). Zur Philosophie des Schauspielers. *Logos, 1*, 339–362.

Simmel, G. (1955). *Conflict*. New York: Free Press.

Simon, B., & Brown, R. J. (1987). Perceived intragroup homogeneity in minority-majority contexts. *Journal of Personality and Social Psychology, 53*, 703–711.

Simon, B., & Hamilton, D. L. (1994). Self-stereotyping and social context: The effects of relative in-group size and in-group status. *Journal of Personality and Social Psychology, 66*(4), 699–711.

Simon, B., Pantaleo, G., & Mummendey, A. (1995). Unique individual or interchangeable group member? The accentuation of intragroup differences versus similarities as an indicator of the individual self versus the collective self. *Journal of Personality and Social Psychology, 69*(1), 106–119.

Simon, B., & Pettigrew, T. F. (1990). Social identity and perceived group homogeneity: Evidence for the in-group homogeneity effect. *European Journal of Social Psychology, 20*, 269–286.

Simon, B., Loewy, M., Stuermer, S., Weber, U., Freytag, P., Habig, C., Kampmeier, C., & Spahlinger, P. (1998). Collective identification and social movement participation. *Journal of Personality and Social Psychology, 74*(3), 646–658.

Simonton, D. K. (1986). Presidential personality: Biographical use of the Gough Adjective Check List. *Journal of Personality and Social Psychology, 51*, 149–160.

Simonton, D. K. (1987). *Why presidents succeed: A political psychology of leadership.* New Haven, CT: Yale University Press.

Simonton, D. K. (1988). Presidential style: Personality, biography, and performance. *Journal of Personality and Social Psychology, 55,* 928–936.

Simonton, D. K. (1994). *Greatness: Who makes history and why.* New York: Guilford.

Simonton, D. K. (1995). Personality and intellectual predictors of leadership. In D. H. Saklofske & M. Zeidner (Eds.), *International handbook of personality and intelligence. Perspectives on individual differences* (pp. 739–757). New York: Plenum.

Simpson, J. A., & Harris, B. A. (1994). Interpersonal attraction. In A. L. Weber & J. H. Harvey (Eds.), *Perspectives on close relationships* (pp. 45–66). Boston: Allyn & Bacon.

Simpson, J. A., Rholes, W. S., & Phillips, D. (1996). Conflict in close relationships: An attachment perspective. *Journal of Personality and Social Psychology, 71*(5), 899–914.

Singer, J. E., Brush, C. A., & Lublin, S. C. (1965). Some aspects of deindividuation: Identification and conformity. *Journal of Experimental Social Psychology, 1,* 365–378.

Skogstad, A., Dyregrov, A., & Hellesoy, O. H. (1995). Cockpit cabin crew interaction: Satisfaction with communication and information exchange. *Aviation, Space, and Environmental Medicine, 66*(9), 841–848.

Slater, P. E. (1958). Contrasting correlates of group size. *Sociometry, 21,* 129–139.

Slavin, R. E. (1983). When does cooperative learning increase student achievement? *Psychological Bulletin, 94*(3), 429–445.

Smilowitz, M., Compton, D. C., & Flint, L. (1988). The effects of computer mediated communication on an individual's judgment: A study based on the methods of Asch's social influence experiment. *Computers in Human Behavior, 4,* 311–321.

Smith, C. (1992). *Motivation and personality: Handbook of thematic content anaylsis.* New York: Cambridge University Press.

Smith, E. R., & Henry, S. (1996). An in-group becomes part of the self: Response time evidence. *Personality and Social Psychology Bulletin, 22*(6), 635–642.

Smith, E. R., & Zarate, M. A. (1990). Exemplar and prototype use in social categorization. *Social Cognition, 8*(3), 243–262.

Smith, H. J., Spears, R., & Oyen, M. (1994). "People like us": The influence of personal deprivation and group membership salience on justice evaluations. *Journal of Experimental Social Psychology, 30*(3), 277–299.

Smith, H. J., & Tyler, T. R. (1997). Choosing the right pond: The impact of group membership on self-esteem and group-oriented behavior. *Journal of Experimental Social Psychology, 33*(2), 146–170.

Smith, P. B., & Bond, M. H. (1999). *Social psychology across cultures: Analysis and perspectives.* Boston: Allyn & Bacon.

Smith, V. L. (1979). Incentive-compatible experimental processes for the provision of public goods. In V. L. Smith (Ed.), *Research in experimental economics.* Greenwich, CT: JAI Press.

Sniezek, J., & Henry, R. (1989). Accuracy and confidence in group judgment. *Organizational Behavior and Human Decision Making Processes, 43,* 1–28.

Snyder, C. R., Cheavens, J., & Sympson, S. (1997). Hope: An individual motive for social commerce. *Group Dynamics: Theory, Research, and Practice, 1,* 107–118.

Snyder, C. R., Lassegard, M., & Ford, C. E. (1986). Distancing after group success and failure: Basking in reflected glory and cutting off reflected failure. *Journal of Personality and Social Psychology, 51,* 382–388.

Snyder, M. (1981). On the self-perpetuating nature of social stereotypes. In D. L. Hamilton (Ed.), *Cognitive processes in stereotyping and intergroup behavior* (pp. 183–212). Hillsdale, NJ: Erlbaum.

Snyder, M., & Ickes, W. (1985). Personality and social behavior. In G. Lindzey & E. Aronson (Eds.), *Handbook of social psychology* (3rd ed.). New York: Random House.

Snyder, M., Tanke, E. D., & Berscheid, E. (1977). Social perception and interpersonal behavior: On the self-fulfilling nature of social stereotypes. *Journal of Personality and Social Psychology, 35*(9), 656–666.

Snyder, M., & Uranowitz, S. W. (1978). Reconstructing the past, some cognitive consequences of person perception. *Journal of Personality and Social Psychology, 36*, 941–950.

Solomon, Z., Waysman, M., & Mikulincer, M. (1990). Family functioning, perceived societal support, and combat-related psychopathology: The moderating role of loneliness. *Journal of Social and Clinical Psychology, 9*(4), 456–472.

Sommer, R. (1969). *Personal space*. Englewood Cliffs, NJ: Prentice-Hall.

Sorrentino, R. M., & Boutillier, R. G. (1975). The effect of quantity and quality of verbal interaction on ratings of leadership ability. *Journal of Experimental Social Psychology, 11*(5), 403–411.

Sorrentino, R. M., & Field, N. (1986). Emergent leadership over time: The functional value of positive motivation. *Journal of Personality and Social Psychology, 50*(6), 1091–1099.

Sorrentino, R. M., King, G., & Leo, G. (1980). The influence of the minority of perception: A note on a possible alternative explanation. *Journal of Experimental Social Psychology, 16*, 293–301.

Sours, J. (1974). The anorexia nervosa syndrome. *International Journal of Psycho-Analysis, 55*(4), 567–576.

Spears, R., Doosje, B., & Ellemers, N. (1997). Self-stereotyping in the face of threats to group status and distinctiveness: The role of group identification. *Personality and Social Psychology Bulletin, 23*, 538–553.

Spears, R., & Haslam, S. A. (1997). Stereotyping and the burden of cognitive load. In R. Spears, P. J. Oakes, N. Ellemers, & S. Haslam (Eds.), *The social psychology of stereotyping and group life* (pp. 171–207). Oxford, UK: Blackwell.

Spears, R., & Lea, M. (1992). Social influence and the influence of the "social" in computer-mediated communication. In M. Lea (Ed.), *Contexts of computer-mediated communication* (pp. 30–65). Hemel Hempstead, UK: Harvester Wheatsheaf.

Spears, R., & Lea, M. (1994). Panacea or panopticon? The hidden power in computer-mediated communication. *Communication Research, 21*, 427–459.

Spears, R., Lea, M., & Lee, S. (1990). De-individuation and group polarization in computer-mediated communication. *British Journal of Social Psychology, 29*, 121–134.

Spears, R., & Manstead, A. S. R. (1997). Distinctiveness threat and prototypicality: Combined effects on intergroup discrimination and collective self-esteem. *European Journal of Social Psychology, 27*(6), 635–657.

Sproull, L., & Kiesler, S. B. (1991). Connections: New ways of working in the networked organization. *Administrative Science Quarterly, 27*, 548–570.

Strange, J. M., & Mumford, M. D. (2002). The origins of vision: Charismatic versus ideological leadership. *Leadership Quarterly, 13*, 334–377.

Stangor, C. (1995). Content and application inaccuracy in social stereotyping. In Y. T. Lee, L. J. Jussim, & C. R. McCauley (Eds.), *Stereotype accuracy: Toward appreciating group differences* (pp. 275–292). Washington, DC: American Psychological Association.

Stangor, C., & Crandall, C. (2000). Threat and the social construction of stigma. In T. Heatherton, R. Kleck, M. Hebl, & J. Hull (Eds.), *The social psychology of stigma* (pp. 62–87). New York: Guilford.

Stangor, C., & Lange, J. (1994). Mental representations of social groups: Advances in conceptualizing stereotypes and stereotyping. *Advances in Experimental Social Psychology, 26*, 357–416.

Stangor, C., Lynch, L., Duan, C., & Glass, B. (1992). Categorization of individuals on the basis of multiple social features. *Journal of Personality and Social Psychology, 62*(2), 207–218.

Stangor, C., & McMillan, D. (1992). Memory for expectancy-congruent and expectancy-incongruent information: A review of the social and social developmental literatures. *Psychological Bulletin, 111*(1), 42–61.

Stangor, C., & Schaller, M. (1996). Stereotypes as individual and collective representations. In C. N. Macrae, C. Stangor, & M. Hewstone (Eds.), *Stereotypes and stereotyping* (pp. 3–40). New York: Guilford.

Stangor, C., & Thompson, E. (2000). Individual functions of prejudice: Group differentiation and self-enhancement. Manuscript under editorial review.

Stasser, G. (1992). Pooling of unshared information during group discussions. In S. Worchel, W. Wood, & J. Simpson (Eds.), *Group processes and productivity* (pp. 48–67). Newbury Park, CA: Sage.

Stasser, G., Kerr, N. L., & Bray, R. M. (1982). The social psychology of jury deliberations: Structure, process and product. In N. L. Kerr & R. M. Bray (Eds.), *The psychology of the courtroom* (pp. 221–256). New York: Academic Press.

Stasser, G., Kerr, N. L., & Davis, J. H. (1989). Influence processes and consensus models in decision-making groups. In P. B. Paulus (Ed.), *Psychology of group influence* (2nd ed., pp. 279–326). Hillsdale, NJ: Erlbaum.

Stasser, G., & Stewart, D. (1992). Discovery of hidden profiles by decision-making groups: Solving a problem versus making a judgment. *Journal of Personality and Social Psychology, 63*(3), 426–434.

Stasser, G., Stewart, D. D., & Wittenbaum, G. M. (1995). Expert roles and information exchange during discussion: The importance of knowing who knows what. *Journal of Experimental Social Psychology, 31*, 244–265.

Stasser, G., & Taylor, L. A. (1991). Speaking turns in face-to-face discussions. *Journal of Personality and Social Psychology, 60*, 675–684.

Stasser, G., Taylor, L. A., & Hanna, C. (1989). Information sampling in structured and unstructured discussions of three- and six-person groups. *Journal of Personality and Social Psychology, 57*, 67–78.

Stasser, G., & Titus, W. (1985). Pooling of unshared information in group decision making: Biased information sampling during discussion. *Journal of Personality and Social Psychology, 48*(6), 1467–1478.

Stasser, G., & Vaughan, S. (1996). Models of participation during face-to-face unstructured discussion. In E. Witte & J. Davis (Eds.), *Understanding group behavior: Consensual action by small groups* (Vol. 1, pp. 165–192). Mahwah, NJ: Erlbaum.

Stasson, M., Kameda, T., Parks, C., Zimmerman, S., & Davis, J. (1991). Effects of assigned group consensus requirement on group problem solving and group members' learning. *Social Psychology Quarterly, 54*(1), 25–35.

Staub, E. (1989). Individual and societal (group) values in a motivational perspective and their role in benevolence and harmdoing. In N. Eisenberg, & J. Reykowski (Eds.), *Social and moral values: Individual and societal perspectives* (pp. 45–61). Hillsdale, NJ: Erlbaum.

Staw, B. M., Sandelands, L. E., & Dutton, J. E. (1981). Threat-rigidity effects in organizational behavior: A multi-level analysis. *Administrative Science Quarterly, 26*, 501–524.

Stein, M. I. (1978). Methods to stimulate creative thinking. *Psychiatric Annals, 8*, 65–75.

Steiner, I. D. (1966). Models for inferring relationships between group size and potential group productivity. *Behavioral Science, 11*, 273–383.

Steiner, I. D. (1972). *Group process and productivity.* New York: Academic Press.

Steiner, I. D. (1974). Whatever happened to the group in social psychology? *Journal of Experimental Social Psychology, 10*, 94–108.

Stephan, W. G. (1999). *Reducing prejudice and stereotyping in schools.* New York: Teacher's College Press.

Stephan, W. G. (1986). Effects of school desegregation: An evaluation 30 years after *Brown.* In L. Saxe & M. Saks (Eds.), *Advances in applied social psychology* (Vol. 3, pp. 181–206). New York: Addison-Wesley.

Stephan, W. G., & Stephan, C. W. (1984). The role of ignorance in intergroup relations. In N. Miller & M. B. Brewer (Eds.), *Groups in contact: The psychology of desegration* (pp. 229–257). Orlando, FL: Academic Press.

Stewart, D. D., & Stasser, G. (1995). Expert role assignment and information sampling during collective recall and decision making. *Journal of Personality and Social Psychology, 69*(4), 619–628.

Stewart, G. L., & Manz, C. C. (1995). Leadership for self-managing work teams: A typology and integrative model. *Human Relations, 48*(7), 747–770.

Stiles, W. B. (1984). Role behaviors in routine medical interviews with hypertensive patients: A repertoire of verbal exchanges. *Social Psychology Quarterly, 47*(3), 244–254.

Stogdill, R. M. (1972). Group productivity, drive, and cohesiveness. *Organizational Behavior and Human Decision Processes, 1* , 26–43.

Stokols, D. (1978). Environmental psychology. *Annual Review of Psychology, 29*, 253–295.

Stoner, J. A. (1968). Risky and cautious shifts in group decisions: The influence of widely held values. *Journal of Experimental Social Psychology, 4*, 442–459.

Stotland, E., Cottrell, N. B., & Laing, G. (1960). Group interaction and perceived similarity of members. *Journal of Abnormal and Social Psychology, 61*, 335–340.

Stotland, E., Zander, A., & Natsoulas, T. (1961). Generalization of interpersonal similarity. *Journal of Abnormal and Social Psychology, 62*, 250–256.

Stouffer, S. A., Suchman, E. A., DeVinney, L. C., Star, S. A., & Williams, R. M. (1949). *The American soldier: Studies in social psychology in World War II.* Princeton, NJ: Princeton University Press.

Strange, J. M., & Mumford, M. O. (2002). The origins of vision: Charismatic versus ideological leadership. *Leadership Quarterly, 13*, 343–377.

Straus, S. G. (1996). Getting a clue: The effects of communication media and information distribution on participation and performance in computer-mediated and face-to-face groups. *Small Group Research, 27*(1), 115–142.

Straus, S. G., & McGrath, J. E. (1994). Does the medium matter? The interaction of task type and technology on group performance and member reactions. *Journal of Applied Psychology, 79*(1), 87–97.

Strayer, F. F. (1995). Child ethology and the study of preschool social relations. In H. C. Foot & A. J. Chapman (Eds.), *Friendship and social relations in children* (pp. 235–265). New Brunswick, NJ: Transaction.

Strodtbeck, F. L., & Lipinski, R. M. (1985). Becoming first among equals: Moral considerations in jury foreman selection. *Journal of Personality and Social Psychology, 49*(4), 927–936.

Stroebe, M. S. (1994). The broken-heart phenomenon: An examination of the mortality of bereavement. *Journal of Community and Applied Social Psychology, 4*, 47–61.

Stroebe, W., & Diehl, M. (1994). Why groups are less effective than their members: On productivity losses in idea-generating groups. *European Review of Social Psychology, 5*, 271–303.

Stroebe, W., Diehl, M., & Abakoumkin, G. (1992). The illusion of group effectivity. *Personality and Social Psychology Bulletin, 18*(5), 643–650.

Stroebe, W., & Stroebe, M. (1996). The social psychology of social support. In E. Higgins & A. Kruglanski (Eds.), *Social psychology: Handbook of basic principles* (pp. 597–621). New York: Guilford.

Stroebe, W., Stroebe, M., Abakoumkin, G., & Shut, H. (1996). The role of loneliness and social support in adjustment to loss: A test of attachment versus stress theory. *Journal of Personality and Social Psychology, 70*, 1241–1249.

Strube, M. J., & Garcia, J. E. (1981). A meta-analytic investigation of Fiedler's contingency model of leadership effectiveness. *Psychological Bulletin, 90*(2), 307–321.

Strube, M. J., Miles, M. E., & Finch, W. H. (1981). The social facilitation of a simple task: Field tests of alternative explanations. *Personality and Social Psychology Bulletin, 7*(4), 701–707.

Stryker, S. (1980). *Symbolic interaction.* Menlo Park, CA: Benjamin Cummings.

Stryker, S., & Serpe, R. T. (1994). Identity salience and psychological centrality: Equivalent, overlapping, or complementary concepts? *Social Psychology Quarterly, 57*, 16–35.

Sugisawa, H., Liang, J., & Liu, X. (1994). Social networks, social support, and mortality among older people in Japan. *Journals of Gerontology, 49*, 3–13.

Suls, J., & Miller, R. (Eds.). (1977). *Social comparison processes.* Washington, DC: Hemisphere.

Sundstrom, E., de Meuse, K. P., & Futrell, D. (1990). Work teams: Applications and effectiveness. *American Psychologist, 45*(2), 120–133.

Swets, J. A., & Bjork, R. A. (1990). Enhancing human performance: An evaluation of "New Age" techniques considered by the U.S. Army. *Psychological Science, 1*(2), 85–86.

Swezey, R., & Salas, E. (Eds.). (1992). *Teams: Their training and performance.* Norwood, NJ: Ablex Publishing Corporation.

Szymanski, K., & Harkins, S. G. (1987). Social loafing and self-evaluation with a social standard. *Journal of Personality and Social Psychology, 53*(5), 891–897.

Tajfel, H. (1978). *Differentiation between social groups: Studies in the social psychology of intergroup relations.* London: Academic Press.

Tajfel, H. (1981). *Human groups and social categories: Studies in social psychology.* Cambridge: Cambridge University Press.

Tajfel, H. (1982). Social psychology of intergroup relations. *Annual Review of Psychology, 33*, 1–39.

Tajfel, H., Billig, M., Bundy, R., & Flament, C. (1971). Social categorization and intergroup behavior. *European Journal of Social Psychology, 1*, 149–178.

Tajfel, H., & Forgas, J. P. (1981). Social categorization: Cognitions, values and groups. In J. P. Forgas (Ed.), *Social cognition* (pp. 113–140). New York: Academic.

Tajfel, H., & Turner, J. (1979). An integrative theory of intergroup conflict. In W. Austin & S. Worchel (Eds.), *The social psychology of intergroup relations.* Monterey, CA: Brooks-Cole.

Tajfel, H., & Wilkes, A. L. (1963). Classification and quantitative judgement. *British Journal of Psychology*, 101–114.

Tanford, S., & Penrod, S. (1984). Social influence model: A formal integration of research on majority and minority influence processes. *Psychological Bulletin, 95*(2), 189–225.

Tannen, D. (1995). *Talking 9 to 5: Women and men in the workplace.* Burnsville, MD: Charthouse International Learning Corporation.

Tarde, G. (1901/1969). *On communication and social influence: Selected papers* (T. N. Clark, Ed.), Chicago: University of Chicago Press.

Taylor, D. M., & McKirnan, D. J. (1984). A five-stage model of intergroup relations. *British Journal of Social Psychology, 23*, 291–300.

Taylor, D. M., & Moghaddam, F. M. (1994). *Theories of intergroup relations: International social psychological perspectives*. Westport, CT: Praeger.

Taylor, D. M., Moghaddam, F. M., Gamble, I., & Zellerer, E. (1987). Disadvantaged group responses to perceived inequality: From passive acceptance to collective action. *Journal of Social Psychology, 127*, 259–272.

Taylor, S. E. (1981). A categorization approach to stereotyping. In D. L. Hamilton (Ed.), *Cognitive processes in stereotyping and intergroup behavior*. Hillsdale, NJ: Erlbaum.

Taylor, S. E., & Crocker, J. (1981). Schematic bases of social information processing. In E. T. Higgins, C. P. Herman, & M. P. Zanna (Eds.), *Social cognition: The Ontario symposium* (Vol. 1, pp. 89–134). Hillsdale, NJ: Erlbaum.

Taylor, S. E., Fiske, S. T., Etcoff, N. L., & Ruderman, A. J. (1978). Categorical and contextual bases of person memory and stereotyping. *Journal of Personality and Social Psychology, 36*, 778–793.

Taylor, S. E., & Lobel, M. (1989). Social comparison activity under threat: Downward evaluation and upward contacts. *Psychological Review, 96*(4), 569–575.

Terry, D., & Hogg, M. (1996). Group norms and the attitude-behavior relationship: A role for group identification. *Personality and Social Psychology Bulletin, 22*, 776–793.

Tesser, A. (1988). Toward a self-evaluation maintenance model of social behavior. *Advances in Experimental Social Psychology, 21*, 181–227.

Tesser, A. (1991). Emotion in social comparison and reflection processes. In J. S. T. A. Willis (Ed.), *Social comparison: Contemporary theory and research* (pp. 117–148). Hillsdale, NJ: Erlbaum.

Tesser, A., & Campbell, J. (1983). Self-definition and self-evaluation maintenance. In J. Suls & A. Greenwald (Eds.), *Psychological perspectives on the self* (Vol. 2). Hillsdale, NJ: Erlbaum.

Tesser, A., Campbell, J., & Mickler, S. (1983). The role of social pressure, attention to the stimulus, and self-doubt in conformity. *European Journal of Social Psychology, 13*(3), 217–233.

Tesser, A., Campbell, J., & Smith, M. (1984). Friendship choice and performance: Self-evaluation maintenance in children. *Journal of Personality and Social Psychology, 46*, 561–574.

Tetlock, P. E. (1979). Identifying victims of groupthink from public statements of decision makers. *Journal of Personality and Social Psychology, 37*(8), 1314–1324.

Thibaut, J. W., & Kelley, H. H. (1959). *The social psychology of groups*. New York: Wiley.

Thoits, P. A. (1986). Social support as coping assistance. *Journal of Consulting and Clinical Psychology, 54*, 416–423.

Thoits, P. A. (1993). Multiple identities and psychological well-being: A reformulation and test of the social isolation hypothesis. *American Sociological Review, 48*(2), 174–187.

Thomas-Hunt, M. C., & Gruenfeld, D. H. (1998). A foot in two worlds: The participation of demographic boundary spanners in work groups. In D. H. Gruenfeld (Ed.), *Composition* (pp. 39–57). Stamford, CT: JAI Press.

Thompson, L. L. (1990). Negotation behavior and outcomes: Empirical evidence and theoretical issues. *Psychological Bulletin, 108*, 515–532.

Thompson, L. L. (1991). Information exchange in negotiation. *Journal of Experimental Social Psychology, 27*, 161–179.

Thompson, L. L., & Hrebec, D. (1996). Lose-lose agreements in interdependent decision making. *Psychological Bulletin, 120*, 396–409.

Tindale, R. S., Davis, J. H., Vollrath, D. A., & Nagao, D. H. (1990). Asymmetrical social influence in freely interacting groups: A test of three models. *Journal of Personality and Social Psychology, 58*(3), 438–449.

Tindale, R. S., & Larson, J. R. (1992a). Assembly bonus effect or typical group performance? A comment on Michaelsen, Watson, and Black (1989). *Journal of Applied Psychology, 77*(1), 102–105.

Tindale, R. S., & Larson, J. R. (1992b). It's not how you frame the question, it's how you interpret the results. *Journal of Applied Psychology, 77*(1), 109–110.

Tjosvold, D., & Deemer, D. K. (1980). Effects of controversy within a cooperative or competitive context on organizational decision making. *Journal of Applied Psychology, 65*(5), 590–595.

Tooby, J., & Cosmides, L. (1992). The psychological foundations of culture. In J. H. Barkow & L. Cosmides (Eds.), *The adapted mind: Evolutionary psychology and the generation of culture* (pp. 666). New York: Oxford University Press.

Trafimow, D., Triandis, H. C., & Goto, S. G. (1991). Some tests of the distinction between the private self and the collective self. *Journal of Personality and Social Psychology, 60*, 649–655.

Triandis, H. C. (1995). *Individualism and collectivism.* Boulder, CO: Westview.

Triandis, H. C., McCusker, C., & Hui, C. H. (1990). Multimethod probes of individualism and collectivism. *Journal of Personality and Social Psychology, 59*, 1006–1020.

Triplett, N. (1898). The dynamogenic factors in pacemaking and competition. *American Journal of Psychology, 9*, 507–533.

Trope, Y., & Thompson, E. (1997). Looking for truth in all the wrong places? Asymmetric search of individuating information about stereotyped group members. *Journal of Personality and Social Psychology, 73*, 229–241.

Trout, D. (1980). The role of social isolation in suicide. *Suicide and Life-Threatening Behavior, 10*(1), 10–23.

Tsui, A. S., Egan, T. D., & O'Reilly, C. A. (1992). Being different: Relational demography and organizational attachment. *Administrative Science Quarterly, 37*(4), 549–579.

Tuckman, B. W. (1965). Developmental sequences in small groups. *Psychological Bulletin, 63*, 384–399.

Turner, J. C. (1982). Towards a cognitive redefinition of the social group. In H. Tajfel (Ed.), *Social identity and intergroup relations.* Cambridge: Cambridge University Press.

Turner, J. C. (1987). *Rediscovering the social group: A self-categorization theory.* Oxford: Blackwell.

Turner, J. C. (1991). *Social influence.* Pacific Grove, CA: Brooks-Cole.

Turner, J. C., & Oakes, P. J. (Eds.). (1989). *Self-categorization theory and social influence* (2nd ed.). Hillsdale, NJ: Erlbaum.

Turner, J. C., Oakes, P. C., Haslam, S. A., & McGarty, C. (1994). Self and collective: Cognition and social context. *Personality and Social Psychology Bulletin, 20*, 454–463.

Turner, J. C., Wetherell, M. S., & Hogg, M. A. (1989). A referent informational influence explanation of group polarization. *British Journal of Social Psychology, 28*, 135–148.

Turner, M. E., & Pratkanis, A. R. (1998). Twenty-five years of groupthink theory and research: Lessons from the evaluation of a theory. *Organizational Behavior and Human Decision Processes, 73*(2-3), 105–115.

Turner, M. E., Pratkanis, A. R., Probasco, P., & Leve, C. (1992). Threat, cohesion, and group effectiveness: Testing a social identity maintenance perspective on groupthink. *Journal of Personality and Social Psychology, 63*, 781–796.

Turner, R. H. K., Lewis M. (1987). *Collective behavior* (3rd ed.). Englewood Cliffs, NJ: Prentice-Hall.

Tyerman, A., & Spencer, C. (1983). A critical test of the Sherifs' robber's cave experiments: Intergroup competition and cooperation between groups of well-acquainted individuals. *Small Group Behavior, 14*(4), 515–531.

Tyler, T. (1989). The psychology of procedural justice: A test of the group value model. *Journal of Personality and Social Psychology, 57*, 850–563.

Tyler, T., & Blader, S. L. (2000). *Cooperation in groups: Procedural justice, social identity, and behavioral engagement*. Philadelphia: Psychology Press/Taylor and Francis.

Tyler, T., & Lind, E. (1992). A relational model of authority in groups. *Advances in Experimental Social Psychology, 25*, 115–191.

Tyler, T., Degoey, P., & Smith, H. (1996). Understanding why the justice of group procedures matters: A test of the psychological dynamics of the group-value model. *Journal of Personality and Social Psychology, 70*(5), 913–930.

Uchino, B. N., Cacioppo, J., & Kiecolt-Glaser, J. (1996). The relationship between social support and physiological processes: A review with emphasis on underlying mechanisms and implications for health. *Psychological Bulletin, 119*, 488–531.

Uleman, J. S., & Bargh, J. A. (1989). *Unintended thought*. New York: Guilford.

Umberson, D., Chen, M. D., House, J. S., & Hopkins, K. (1996). The effect of social relationships on psychological well-being: Are men and women really so different? *American Sociological Review, 61*, 837–857.

Valacich, J. S., Dennis, A. R., & Nunamaker, J. F. (1991). Electronic meeting support: The Group Systems concept. *International Journal of Man-Machine Studies, 34*(2), 261–282.

Valacich, J. S., Jessup, L. M., Dennis, A. R., & Nunamaker, J. F. (1992). A conceptual framework of anonymity in group support systems. *Group Decision and Negotiation, 1*(3), 219–241.

van Dijk, E., & Wilke, H. (2000). Decision-induced focusing in social dilemmas: Give-some, keep-some, take-some, and leave-some dilemmas. *Journal of Personality and Social Psychology, 78*, 92–104.

Van Knippenberg, A. (1978). Status difference, comparative relevance, and intergroup differentiation. In H. Tajfel (Ed.), *Differentiation between social groups: Studies in the social psychology of intergroup relations* (pp. 179–199). London: Academic Press.

Van Knippenberg, A., & Dijksterhuis, A. (1996). A posteriori stereotype activation: The preservation of stereotypes through memory distortion. *Social Cognition, 14*, 21–54.

Van Knippenberg, A., Van Twuyver, M., & Pepels, J. (1994). Factors affecting social categorization processes in memory. *British Journal of Social Psychology, 33*(4), 419–431.

Van Knippenberg, D., & Van Knippenberg, A. (1994). Social categorization, focus of attention and judgements of group opinions. *British Journal of Social Psychology, 33*, 477–489.

Van Lange, P. A., & Kuhlman, D. M. (1994). Social value orientations and impressions of partner's honesty and intelligence: A test of the might versus morality effect. *Journal of Personality and Social Psychology, 67*(1), 126–141.

Van Lange, P. A., & Liebrand, W. B. (1991). Social value orientation and intelligence: A test of the Goal Prescribes Rationality Principle. *European Journal of Social Psychology, 21*(4), 273–292.

Van Sell, M., Brief, A. P., & Schuler, R. S. (1981). Role conflict and role ambiguity: Integration of the literature and directions for future research. *Human Relations, 34*(1), 43–71.

Van Zelst, R. H. (1952). Sociometrically selected work teams increase production. *Personnel Psychology, 5*, 175–185.

Vanbeselaere, N. (1987). The effects of dichotomous and crossed social categorization upon intergroup discrimination. *European Journal of Social Psychology, 17*, 143–156.

Vinokur, A., & Burnstein, E. (1978a). Depolarization of attitudes in groups. *Journal of Personality and Social Psychology, 36*(8), 872–885.

Vinokur, A., & Burnstein, E. (1978b). Novel argumentation and attitude change: The case of polarization following group discussion. *European Journal of Social Psychology, 8*(3), 335–348.

Vinokur, A., Burnstein, E., Sechrest, L., & Wortman, P. M. (1985). Group decision making by experts: Field study of panels evaluating medical technologies. *Journal of Personality and Social Psychology, 49*(1), 70–84.

Visser, P. S., & Krosnick, J. A. (1998). Development of attitude strength over the life cycle: Surge and decline. *Journal of Personality and Social Psychology, 75*(6), 1389–1410.

Vogt, J. F., & Griffith, S. J. (1988). Team development and proactive change: Theory and training implications. *Organizaion Development Journal, 6*, 81–87.

Von Hippel, W., Sekaquaptewa, D., & Vargas, P. (1997). The linguistic intergroup bias as an implicit indicator of prejudice. *Journal of Experimental Social Psychology, 33*(5), 490–509.

Vroom, V. H., & Yetton, P. W. (1973). *Leadership and decision making.* Pittsburgh, PA: University of Pittsburgh Press.

Vroom, V. H., & Jago, A. G. (1988). *The new leadership: Managing participation in organizations.* Englewood Cliffs, NJ: Prentice-Hall.

Wagner, D. G., & Berger, J. (1993). Status characteristics theory: The growth of a program. In J. Z. Berger, Morris, Jr. (Ed.), *Theoretical research programs: Studies in the growth of theory* (pp. 23–63). Stanford, CA: Stanford University Press.

Wagner, U., Lampen, L., & Syllwasschy, J. (1986). Ingroup inferiority, social identity, and outgroup devaluation in a modified minimal group study. *British Journal of Social Psychology, 25*, 15–23.

Wagner, W., Pfeffer, J., & O'Reilly, C. I. (1984). Organizational demography and turnover in top management groups. *Administrative Science Quarterly, 29*, 74–92.

Wall, J. A., & Lynn, A. (1993). Mediation: A current review. *Journal of Conflict Resolution, 37*(1), 160–194.

Walther, J. B. (1992). Interpersonal effects in computer-mediated interaction: A relational perspective. *Communication Research, 19*(1), 52–90.

Walther, J. B. (1993). Impression development in computer-mediated interaction. *Western Journal of Communication, 57*(4), 381–398.

Walther, J. B., Anderson, J. F., & Park, D. W. (1994). Interpersonal effects in computer-mediated interaction: A meta-analysis of social and antisocial communication. *Communication Research, 21*(4), 460–487.

Walton, R. E., & Hackman, J. R. (1986). Groups under contrasting management strategies. In P. S. Goodman (Ed.), *Designing effective work groups.* San Francisco: Jossey-Bass.

Watson, W., Michalsen, L., & Sharp, W. (1991). Member competence, group interaction, and group decision making: A longitudinal study. *Journal of Applied Psychology, 76*, 803–809.

Wayne, S. J., & Ferris, G. R. (1990). Influence tactics, affect, and exchange quality in supervisor-subordinate interactions: A laboratory experiment and field study. *Journal of Applied Psychology, 75*(5), 487–499.

Weber, R., & Crocker, J. (1983). Cognitive processes in the revision of stereotypic beliefs. *Journal of Personality and Social Psychology, 45*, 961–977.

Weber, Y. (2000). Measuring cultural fit in mergers and acquisitions. In N. M. Ashkanasy, C. P. M. Wilderom, & M. F. Peterson (Eds.), *Handbook of organizational culture and climate* (pp. 309–319). Thousand Oaks, CA: Sage.

Weingart, L. R. (1992). Impact of group goals, task component complexity, effort, and planning on group performance. *Journal of Applied Psychology, 77*, 682–693.

Weingart, L. R., Bennett, R. J., & Brett, J. M. (1993). The impact of consideration of issues and motivational orientation on group negotiation process and outcome. *Journal of Applied Psychology, 78*, 504–517.

Weisband, S. P. (1992). Group discussion and first advocacy effects in computer-mediated and face-to-face decision-making groups. *Organizational Behavior and Human Decision Processes, 53*(3), 352–380.

Weisband, S. P., Schneider, S. K., & Connolly, T. (1995). Computer-mediated communication and social information: Status salience and status differences. *Academy of Management Journal, 38*(4), 1124–1151.

Weiss, R. (1974). The provisions of social relationships. In Z. Rubin (Ed.), *Doing unto others* (pp. 17–26). Englewood Cliffs, NJ: Prentice-Hall.

Weiss, R., & Miller, F. (1971). The drive theory of social facilitation. *Psychological Review, 78*, 44–57.

Weldon, E., Jehn, K. A., & Pradhan, P. (1991). Processes that mediate the relationship between a group goal and improved group performance. *Journal of Personality and Social Psychology, 61*(4), 555–569.

Weldon, E., & Weingart, L. R. (1993). Group goals and group performance. *British Journal of Social Psychology, 32*, 307–334.

Wellman, B. (1992). Which types of ties and networks provide what kinds of social support? *Advances in Group Processes, 9*, 207–235.

Wellman, B., & Berkowitz, S. D. (1988). *Social structures: A network approach.* New York: Cambridge University Press.

Werthamer-Larsson, L., Kellam, S., & Wheeler, L. (1991). Effect of first-grade classroom on shy behavior, aggressive behavior, and concentration problems. *American Journal of Community Psychology, 19*, 585–602.

Wheeler, L. (1966). Toward a theory of behavioral contagion. *Psychological Review, 73*, 179–192.

Wheeler, L., Reis, H. T., & Nezlek, J. (1983). Loneliness, social interaction, and sex roles. *Journal of Personality and Social Psychology, 45*, 943–953.

White, M. I., & Levine, R. (1986). What is an "ii ko" (good child)? In H. W. Stevenson & H. Azuma (Eds.), *Child development and education in Japan* (pp. 55–62). New York: Freeman.

White, R. K., & Lippitt, R. (1968). Leader behavior and member reaction in three "social climates." In D. Cartwright & A. Zander (Eds.), *Group dynamics: Research and theory.* New York: Harper & Row.

Whyte, W. F. (1991). *Participatory action research.* Thousand Oaks, CA: Sage.

Widmeyer, W. N. (1990). Group composition in sport. *International Journal of Sport Psychology, 21*(4), 264–285.

Wiggins, J. A., Dill, F., & Schwartz, R. D. (1965). On "status-liability." *Sociometry, 28*, 197–209.

Wilder, D. A. (1977). Perception of groups, size of opposition, and social influence. *Journal of Experimental Social Psychology, 13*, 253–268.

Wilder, D. A. (1981). Perceiving persons as a group: Categorization and intergroup relations. In D. L. Hamilton (Ed.), *Cognitive processes in stereotyping and intergroup behavior.* Hillsdale, NJ: Erlbaum.

Wilder, D. A. (1984). Predictions of belief homogeneity and similarity following social categorization. *British Journal of Social Psychology, 23*, 323–333.

Wilder, D. A. (1986). Social categorization: Implications for creation and reduction of intergroup bias. In L. Berkowitz (Ed.), *Advances in experimental social psychology* (Vol. 19). New York: Academic Press.

Wilder, D. A., & Thompson, J. (1980). Intergroup contact with independent manipulation of in-group and out-group interaction. *Journal of Personality and Social Psychology, 38*, 589–603.

Wildschut, T., Lodewijkx, H. F. M., & Insko, C. A. (2001). Toward a reconciliation of diverging perspectives on interindividual-group discontinuity: The role of procedural interdependence. *Journal of Experimental Social Psychology, 37*, 273–285.

Willems, E. P., & Clark, R. D. (1971). Shift toward risk and heterogeneity of groups. *Journal of Experimental and Social Psychology, 7*, 304–312.

Williams, D. R., & Rucker, T. D. (2000). Understanding and addressing racial disparities in health care. *Health Care Financing Review, 21*(4), 75–91.

Williams, J. M., & Anderson, M. B. (1998). Psychosocial antecedents of sport injury: Review and critique of the stress and injury model. *Journal of Applied Sport Psychology, 10,* 5–25.

Williams, K. D. (1997). Social ostracism. In R. M. Kowalski (Ed.), *Aversive interpersonal behaviors* (pp. 133–170). New York: Plenum Press.

Williams, K. D., Cheung, C. K. T., & Choi, W. (2000). Cyberostracism: Effects of being ignored over the Internet. *Journal of Personality and Social Psychology, 79*(5), 748–762.

Williams, K. D., Harkins, S. G., & Latané, B. (1981). Identifiability as a deterrant to social loafing: Two cheering experiments. *Journal of Personality and Social Psychology, 40*(2), 303–311.

Williams, K. D., & Karau, S. J. (1991). Social loafing and social compensation: The effects of expectations of coworker performance. *Journal of Personality and Social Psychology, 61,* 570–581.

Williams, K. D., Nida, S. A., Baca, L. D., & Latané, B. (1989). Social loafing and swimming: Effects of identifiability on individual and relay performance of intercollegiate swimmers. *Basic and Applied Social Psychology, 10*(1), 73–81.

Williams, K. D., Shore, W. J., & Grahe, J. E. (1998). The silent treatment: Perceptions of its behaviors and associated feelings. *Group Processes and Intergroup Relations, 1*(2), 117–141.

Williams, K. D., & Sommer, K. L. (1997). Social ostracism by coworkers: Does rejection lead to loafing or compensation? *Personality and Social Psychology Bulletin, 23,* 693–706.

Wills, T., & Cleary, S. (1996). How are social support effects mediated? A test with parental support and adolescent substance use. *Journal of Personality and Social Psychology, 71,* 937–952.

Wilner, D. M., Walkley, R. P., & Cook, S. W. (1955). *Human relations in interracial housing: A study of the contact hypothesis.* Minneapolis: Univeristy of Minnesota Press.

Wilson, S. H., Greer, J. F., & Johnson, R. M. (1973). Synectics: A creative problem-solving technique for the gifted. *Gifted Child Quarterly, 17,* 260–267.

Wilson, W., & Miller, N. (1961). Shifts in evaluations of participants following intergroup competition. *Journal of Abnormal and Social Psychology, 63,* 428–431.

Witte, E. H., & Davis, J. H. (1996a). *Understanding group behavior, Vol. 1: Consensual action by small groups.* Mahwah, NJ: Erlbaum.

Witte, E. H., & Davis, J. H. (1996b). *Understanding group behavior, Vol. 2: Small group processes and interpersonal relations.* Mahwah, NJ: Erlbaum.

Wittenbaum, G. M. (1998). Information sampling in decision-making groups: The impact of members' task-relevant status. *Small Group Research, 29*(1), 57–84.

Wittenbaum, G. M., Vaughan, S., & Stasser, G. (1998). Coordination in task-performing groups. In S. R. Tindale & L. Heath (Eds.), *Theory and research on small groups.* New York: Plenum.

Wittenbrink, B., Judd, C., & Park, B. (1997). Evidence for racial prejudice at the implicit level and its relationship with questionnaire measures. *Journal of Personality and Social Psychology, 72,* 262-274.

Wofford, J. C., & Liska, L. Z. (1993). Path-goal theories of leadership: A meta-analysis. *Journal of Management, 19*(4), 857–876.

Wolf, S. (1987). Majority and minority influence: A social impact analysis. In M. P. O. Zanna, & M. James (Eds.), *Social influence: The Ontario symposium* (Vol. 5, pp. 207–235). Hillsdale, NJ: Erlbaum.

Wood, J. V. (1989). Theory and research concerning social comparisons of personal attributes. *Psychological Bulletin, 106*(2), 231–248.

Wood, J. V., Taylor, S. E., & Lichtman, R. R. (1985). Social comparison in adjustment to breast cancer. *Journal of Personality and Social Psychology, 49,* 1169–1183.

Wood, W. (1987). A meta-analytic review of sex differences in group performance. *Psychological Bulletin, 102,* 53–71.

Wood, W., & Karten, S. J. (1986). Sex differences in interaction style as a product of perceived sex differences in competence. *Journal of Personality and Social Psychology, 50*(2), 341–347.

Wood, W., Lundgren, S., Ouellette, J. A., & Busceme, S. (1994). Minority influence: A meta-analytic review of social influence processes. *Psychological Bulletin, 115*(3), 323–345.

Worchel, S., Coutant-Sassic, D., & Grossmann, M. (1992). A developmental approach to group dynamics: A model and illustrative research. In S. Worchel, W. Wood, & J. Simpson (Eds.), *Group processes and productivity* (pp. 181–202). Newbury Park, CA: Sage.

Worchel, S., Lind, E. A., & Kaufman, K. H. (1975). Evaluations of group products as a function of expectations of group longevity, outcome of competition, and publicity of evaluations. *Journal of Personality and Social Psychology, 31,* 1089–1097.

Worchel, S., Wood, W., & Simpson, J. A. (Eds.). (1992). *Group process and productivity.* Newbury Park, CA: Sage.

Word, C. O., Zanna, M. P., & Cooper, J. (1974). The nonverbal mediation of self-fulfilling prophecies in interracial interaction. *Journal of Experimental Social Psychology, 10,* 109–120.

Wosinska, W., Cialdini, R. B., Barrett, D. W., & Reykowski, J. (Eds.). (2001). *The practice of social influence in multiple cultures.* Mahwah, NJ: Erlbaum.

Wright, S. C., Aron, A., McLaughlin-Volpe, T., & Ropp, S. (1997). The extended contact effect: Knowledge of cross-group friendships and prejudice. *Journal of Personality and Social Psychology, 73,* 73–90.

Wright, S. C., Taylor, D. M., & Moghaddam, F. M. (1990). Responding to membership in a disadvantaged group: From acceptance to collective protest. *Journal of Personality and Social Psychology, 58*(6), 994–1003.

Wrightsman, L. S., O'Connor, J., & Baker, N. J. (Eds.). (1972). *Cooperation and competition: Readings on mixed-motive games.* Belmont, CA: Wadsworth.

Yetton, P., & Bottger, P. (1983). The relationships among group size, member ability, social decision schemes, and performance. *Organizational Behavior and Human Decision Processes, 32*(2), 145–159.

Yukl, G. A. (2002). *Leadership in organizations.* Upper Saddle River, NJ: Prentice-Hall.

Yzerbyt, V., Corneille, O., & Estrada, C. (2001). The interplay of subjective essentialism and entitativity in the formation of stereotypes. *Personality and Social Psychology Review, 5,* 141–155.

Zaccaro, S. J. (1984). Social loafing: The role of task attractiveness. *Personality and Social Psychology Bulletin, 10*(1), 99–106.

Zaccaro, S. J. (1995). Leader resources and the nature of organizational problems. *Applied Psychology, 44,* 32–36.

Zaccaro, S. J., Foti, R. J., & Kenny, D. A. (1991). Self-monitoring and trait-based variance in leadership: An investigation of leader flexibility across multiple group situaions. *Journal of Applied Psychology, 76,* 308–315.

Zaccaro, S. J., Gualtieri, J., & Minionis, D. (1995). Task cohesion as a facilitator of team decision making under temporal urgency. *Military Psychology, 7,* 77–93.

Zajonc, R. B. (1965). Social facilitation. *Science, 149,* 269–274.

Zajonc, R. B., Heingartner, A., & Herman, E. M. (1969). Social enhancement and impairment of performance in the cockroach. *Journal of Personality and Social Psychology, 12,* 83–92.

Zajonc, R. B., & Smoke, W. H. (1959). Redundancy in task assignments and group performance. *Psychometrika, 24,* 361–369.

Zander, A. (1971/1996). *Motives and goals in groups.* New Brunswick, NJ: Transaction.

Zander, A. (1985). *The purposes of groups and organizations.* San Francisco: Jossey-Bass.

Zander, A., Stotland, E., & Wolfe, D. (1960). Unity of group, identification with group, and self-esteem of members. *Journal of Personality, 28,* 463–478.

Zimbardo, P. (1969). The human choice: Individuation, reason and order versus deindividuation impulse and chaos. In W. J. Arnold & D. Levine (Eds.), *Nebraska symposium of motivation* (Vol. 17). Lincoln: University of Nebraska Press.

Name Index

Subject Index

Index note: page references in **bold** indicate a definition of the term.